THE EARLY HEIDEGGER &
MEDIEVAL PHILOSOPHY

THE EARLY HEIDEGGER & MEDIEVAL PHILOSOPHY

Phenomenology for the Godforsaken

S. J. MCGRATH

The Catholic University of America Press
Washington, D.C.

Much of chapter 6 appeared in "The Facticity of Being Forsaken: The Young Heidegger's Accommodation of Luther's Theology of the Cross," *American Catholic Philosophical Quarterly* (Spring 2005): 273–90. "Heidegger and Duns Scotus on Truth and Language" appeared in *Review of Metaphysics*, vol. 57 (2003): 323–43. Andrzej Wierciński, editor and president of the International Institute for Hermeneutics, Toronto, published my papers in *Between the Human and the Divine* (2002): 355–77; *Between Description and Interpretation* (2005): 265–73; and in *Studies in the Philosophy of Religion*, no. 3 (2005): 283–306.

Copyright © 2006
The Catholic University of America Press
All rights reserved
The paper used in this publication meets the minimum
requirements of American National Standards for Information
Science—Permanence of Paper for Printed Library Materials,
ANSI Z39.48-1984.
∞

Library of Congress Cataloging-in-Publication Data
McGrath, S. J., 1966–
The early Heidegger and medieval philosophy:
phenomenology for
the godforsaken / S.J. McGrath.
p. cm.
Includes bibliographical references and index.
ISBN-13: 978-0-8132-1471-9 (cloth : alk. paper)
ISBN-10: 0-8132-1471-8 (cloth : alk. paper)
ISBN-13: 978-0-8132-2187-8 (pbk.)
1. Heidegger, Martin, 1889–1976. 2. Philosophy, Medieval.
3. Phenomenology. I. Title.
B3279.H49M3755 2006
193—dc22
2006006391

For Sheilagh

Have I spoken of God, or uttered His praise, in any worthy way? Nay, I feel that I have done nothing more than desire to speak; and if I have said anything, it is not what I desired to say.

—AUGUSTINE

CONTENTS

Preface ix

1. Heidegger and the Medieval Theological Paradigm   1
2. Heidegger's Religious-Philosophical *Itinerarium*   25
3. The Phenomenology of the Early Heidegger   60
4. Duns Scotus   88
5. Mysticism   120
6. Luther   151
7. Primal Christianity   185
8. The Effort to Overcome Scholasticism   208
9. Being-Before-God in the Middle Ages   243

Selected Bibliography   257
Index   267

PREFACE

After Nietzsche, after the Holocaust, after modernity, can philosophy still ask about God? In the following work, I dare to suggest that not only *can* philosophy presume to ask about God, it *must* ask about God. Philosophy must lift the censure placed upon it by the main currents of twentieth-century thought. The two most influential thinkers of the twentieth century, Ludwig Wittgenstein and Martin Heidegger, both intensely preoccupied with religious questions, silenced any philosophy that presumed to speak of God. For Wittgenstein "God" belonged to the domain of that about which clear speech was not possible. "What we cannot speak about we must pass over in silence."[1] Heidegger makes an equally ambivalent gesture of reverence and censure toward the religious: "We honor theology by remaining silent about it."[2] I wish to bring these well-known acts of prohibition into question. Wittgenstein I do not discuss, although much of what I will say about Heidegger's silence has some application to Wittgenstein's "mysticism." The present work is an examination of the motives, justification, and tenability of Heidegger's theological silence.

As Jean Luc Marion points out, silence is an ambivalent thing. "Silence, precisely because it does not explain itself, exposes itself to an infinite equivocation of meaning."[3] Marion rightly questions whether the silence that Heidegger has enjoined upon us has any relation to the theological silence of a *via negativa* such as the one prescribed in the sixth century by Pseudo-Dionysius, who asked theologians to "honor the inef-

---

1. Ludwig Wittgenstein, *Tractatus Logico-Philosophicus,* trans. D. F. Pears and B. F. McGuinness (London: Routledge & Kegan Paul, 1972), prop. 7.

2. Martin Heidegger, quoted in Ebehard Jüngel, "Gottentsprechendes Schweigen? Theologie in der Nachbarschaft von Martin Heidegger," *Heidegger. Fragen an sein Werk. Ein Symposium* (Stuttgart: Philipp Reclam, 1977), 42.

3. Jean-Luc Marion, *God Without Being: Hors-Texte,* trans. Thomas A. Carlson (Chicago: University of Chicago Press, 1991), 54.

fable with a wise silence."⁴ "In order to keep silent with regard to God," Marion comments, "one must if not hold a discourse on God, at least hold a discourse worthy of God on our silence itself."⁵ As Merold Westphal puts it, "not all theological negation is negative theology."⁶ In medieval theology, mystical silence was not a general moratorium on theological speech, but an ascetical act appropriate to a certain stage of the *itinerarium mentis in Deum*. At the beginning of the spiritual life, silence was ill advised. The soul needed first to seek the path into the ineffable, a search that could only be accomplished by the patient exploration of belief.

Heidegger is just as frequently dismissed as a charlatan as he is celebrated as the end of metaphysics. He seems to have reveled in inscrutability. His writing gives such a shock of fathomless profundity, unsettling glimpses of ineffable depths, that it is often difficult, even for specialists, to explain his meaning. Somewhat self-consciously and not without affectation, he presents himself as a voice crying in the wilderness of twentieth-century philosophy, an emissary from the "unthought" beginnings of the Western tradition, commanding us to remember "Being." Yet in spite of his best efforts to emancipate himself, Heidegger belongs to a tradition. The subject of this book is the early Heidegger's relationship to the Scholastic tradition. I am interested not only in historical source work—although this occupies a great number of pages—but also in a philosophical evaluation of Scholasticism *after* Heidegger. Early on in my study of both Aquinas and Heidegger, I was puzzled by their apparent convergence on the topic of "being," and their radical divergence on its interpretation. I gradually came to understand that Aquinas's *analogia entis* is annulled by Heidegger's identification of temporality and being. "Time must be brought to light and genuinely grasped as the horizon of every understanding and interpretation of being."⁷ *Sein und Zeit* is an ef-

---

4. Dionysius the Areopogite, *Divine Names* I, 3, *Patrologiae Graecae*, vol. 3, 589b, cited in Marion, *God Without Being*, 54.

5. Marion, *God Without Being*, 54.

6. Merold Westphal, *Overcoming Onto-Theology: Toward a Postmodern Christian Faith* (New York: Fordham University Press, 2001), 234.

7. Martin Heidegger, *Sein und Zeit*, 17th ed. (Tübingen: Max Niemeyer, 1993), 17; English: *Being and Time*, trans. Joan Stambaugh (Albany: State University of New York Press, 1996), 15. Here-

fort to think being without God. Although this study is thesis-driven—I have an argument to make—I intend to open up a field of inquiry, not close one down. Heidegger's ontology is a crucial moment in twentieth-century philosophy. It has almost single-handedly revitalized metaphysics. Because of the intrinsic value of Heidegger's early work, I have gone into great detail on certain topics that have hitherto received scant attention in the literature—for example, Heidegger's first book, the *Habilitationsschrift* on Duns Scotus and Thomas of Erfurt. I intend the present study to serve as a source for further work.

It will be objected that because Heidegger does not intend a complete phenomenological anthropology in *Sein und Zeit*, he cannot be held accountable for failing to address religion. "The analytic of Dasein thus understood is wholly oriented toward the guiding task of working out the question of being. Its limits are thereby determined. It cannot hope to provide a complete ontology of Dasein, which of course must be supplied if something like a 'philosophical' anthropology is to rest on a philosophically adequate basis.... [T]he analysis of Dasein is not only incomplete but at first also *preliminary*. It only brings out the being of this being without interpreting its meaning. Its aim is rather to expose the horizon for the most primordial interpretation of being" (*SZ* 17/15). Has

---

after *SZ*. Quotations from Heidegger's works are hereafter cited in the text with the following abbreviations:

SZ: Sein und Zeit (above).

ID: Identity and Difference (*Identität und Differenz*, 1957), German-English ed., trans. Joan Stambaugh (New York: Harper & Row, 1969).

PIA: "Phänomenologische Interpretationen zu Aristoteles. Anzeige der hermeneutischen Situation" (1922), *Dilthey Jahrbuch für Philosophie und Geschichte der Geisteswissenschaften* 6 (1989): 228–69; English: "Phenomenological Interpretations in Connection with Aristotle. An Indication of the Hermeneutical Situation," trans. John van Buren, in *Supplements. From the Earliest Essays to Being and Time and Beyond*, ed. John van Buren (Albany: State University of New York Press, 2002), 111–45.

BZ: The Concept of Time (*Begriff der Zeit*, 1924), German-English ed., trans. William McNeill (Oxford: Blackwell, 1989).

VA: Vorträge und Aufsätze (1954) (Pfullingen: Günther Neske, 1978).

GA followed by a number refers to a specific volume of Heidegger's *Gesamtausgabe* (collected works), the published editions of which are listed at the beginning of the bibliography.

The second page reference following an abbreviated title refers to an English translation when one was available (for example, *SZ* 17/15, for the quotation above). When only one set of page references appears, the translation is my own.

Heidegger in fact elaborated the being of this being without interpreting its meaning? Is that even a possibility? Or has Heidegger allowed a theological decision to determine how "he brings out the being" of Dasein, what he brings out, and what he leaves concealed? I am arguing that Heidegger's ontology is not as formal as it presumes to be. It enables a certain ontic religiosity and precludes another. In broad terms, a certain version of Lutheranism is enabled and a certain kind of religiosity, characteristic of Roman Catholicism (but not exclusive to it) is precluded. That I take to be a violation of the ostensible neutrality of phenomenology (a point also made by Karl Löwith and Max Scheler), perhaps evidence that such neutrality is not even possible. Heidegger would argue that "religiousness" is in no way denied as a possibility for Dasein; rather, it does not enter into consideration because it is not germane to the topic of elaborating the horizon of the ontological question. Religiousness is not an ontological structure, not an existential, but, like aesthetic or ethical differentiations of Dasein, a concrete comportment to a particular domain of beings. It is an "ontic" matter, the subject of an "existentiell" interpretation. "At the beginning of the analysis, Dasein is precisely not to be interpreted in the differentiation of a particular existence; rather, it is to be uncovered in the indifferent way in which it is initially and for the most part" (SZ 43/41). Heidegger violates this rule himself with his presumption of a "definite ontic interpretation of authentic existence, a factical ideal of Dasein," which he reveals at a key moment in his analysis to have been determinative of the interpretation of "average everydayness" (SZ 310/286). *Pace* Heidegger, I hold that not only ontically, in certain forms of religious life, but ontologically, in our very *Existenz*, we live in the grip of the desire and fear of transcendence. We have a pre-understanding of our destiny in God. Hence religiousness is not inessential to "the interpretation of being." On the contrary, our average and everyday understanding is profoundly motivated by religious concerns.

Heidegger's voice does not speak to our age with quite the same force it had thirty years ago. His concerns no longer match our own. In the space of three decades, his generation saw Europe changed beyond recognition by two world wars, the collapse of the old empires, and the rise of technologized consumption. It seemed obvious to the German intellectuals writing between the wars that the old standards no longer applied. The former seminarian found theological solace in the Lutheran doctrine of *corruptio totalis*. Heidegger would prepare the ground for a new in-breaking of "the holy" by showing how human life concretely manifests itself *without* God. The ambiguity in this phrase is intentional: it would be a phenomenology in which God does not appear, not even as a term of a human desire, and it would be the phenomenology that ensues from the suspension of the theistic assumption, a formally atheistic hermeneutics. From the perspective of the rubble of ruined medieval towns in Germany and England, the millions of dead soldiers and civilians, the ghastly truth of the death camps, Europe did indeed appear to be Godforsaken.

Heidegger's idiosyncratic interpretation of human existence is not without its own religious motives, in particular, his Lutheran conviction that God is so far beyond our reach we are not even capable of adequately raising a question about Him. The Godless phenomenology of *Sein und Zeit* (in fact, a phenomenology *for* the Godforsaken) covers over an essential ontological structure: religiousness. This is to be carefully distinguished from *religio*, the virtue of adoring God. Religiousness is the condition of the possibility of being religious; as such, it is closely related to the Scholastic notion of *potentia obedientialis*, the natural capacity to receive an act of grace. *Religio*, by contrast, is an ontic structure, not *the* form of our being-in-the-world, but *a* form of being-in-the-world. I provisionally define religiousness as "being-before-God" (where the "before" is both temporal and spatial, thus both messianic and mystical), although other descriptions are possible, even necessary. In the Middle Ages, this ontological condition articulates itself in an ontic form of religiosity whose intentional structure I describe as "being-toward-accountability."

The topic of this book touches an area that has generated an unwieldy volume of print: Heidegger and theology.[8] My sole justification

---

8. An overview of Heidegger's relationship to Christian theology is found in John D. Caputo, "Heidegger and Theology," in *The Cambridge Companion to Heidegger*, ed. Charles B. Guignon (Cambridge: Cambridge University Press, 1993), 270–88. Annemarie Gethmann-Siefert's *Das Verhältnis von Philosophie und Theologie im Denken Martin Heideggers* (Munich: Karl Alber, 1974) contains a thorough bibliography of the literature of the '50s, '60s, and early '70s. Recent studies include Philippe Capelle, *Philosophie et théologie dans la pensée de Martin Heidegger* (Paris: Cerf,

for reopening this hornet's nest is the publication of Heidegger's *Frühe Freiburger Vorlesungen*, the lectures he gave at the University of Freiburg as Husserl's assistant (1919–23). We now possess a significantly fuller picture of Heidegger's work prior to *Sein und Zeit*, the pivotal years between the Scholastic *Habilitationsschrift* and the "hermeneutics of facticity," when Heidegger was explicitly concerned with theological issues. The archival work done by Theodore Kisiel and John van Buren has been crucial for drawing our attention to this undiscovered Heidegger.[9] While not as philosophically decisive as Kisiel or van Buren, the research of the Freiburg historian Hugo Ott has shown the extent of the young Heidegger's involvement with the Catholic intellectual community of Southern Germany.[10] "Martin Heidegger can, I dare say, be understood adequately only from out of his beginnings in which, I want to assert, he always remained and into which he was later to penetrate even further," Ott writes.[11] Although it would not have been possible without them, this book moves in a different direction from these groundbreaking studies. Using this historical research as data, the present study is determined by different questions: on what grounds has Heidegger silenced philosophical theology? What were the philosophical and theological motives for his dramatic defection from Scholasticism, and how do these motives impact his philosophical contribution?

On the train to Heidegger's hometown of Meßkirch, which passes through the Black Forest into the valley of the Upper Danube, I met a young German woman who engaged me in conversation. When I told her

---

1998); Jeff O. Prudhomme, *God and Being: Heidegger's Relation to Theology* (Loughton, England: Prometheus Books, 1997).

9. Theodore Kisiel, *The Genesis of Heidegger's* Being and Time (Berkeley: University of California Press, 1993); John van Buren, *The Young Heidegger: Rumor of the Hidden King*, Studies in Continental Thought, ed. John Sallis (Bloomington: Indiana University Press, 1994). See also *Reading Heidegger from the Start: Essays in His Earliest Thought*, ed. Theodore Kisiel and John van Buren (Albany: State University of New York Press, 1994).

10. Hugo Ott, *Martin Heidegger: Unterwegs zu seiner Biographie* (Frankfurt am Main: Campus, 1988); English: *Martin Heidegger: A Political Life*, trans. Allan Blunden (London: HarperCollins Publishers, 1993).

11. Hugo Ott, "Zu den katholischen Wurzeln im Denken Martin Heideggers. Der theologische Philosoph," in *Martin Heidegger. Kunst—Politik—Technik*, ed. Christoph Jamme and Karsten Harries (Munich: Wilhelm Fink, 1992), 230; English: "Martin Heidegger's Catholic Origins," *American Catholic Philosophical Quarterly* 69 (1995): 143.

I was going to Meßkirch because I was researching Heidegger, she said, *"also . . . auf dem spur Heideggers."* "Following the trace of Heidegger"—I can think of no better way of summing up the nature of this work. The trace of Heidegger leads me deep into his Catholic past. Through an examination of his biography and his earliest works, I show that his philosophy is essentially motivated by a direct confrontation with the medieval Christian theology in which he was steeped as a young man.

In the course of researching this work in Heidegger's medieval city of Freiburg, I came to a new appreciation of Heidegger, the man, the German nationalist, and the troubled Catholic. The fields and forests, the towns and churches of his beloved homeland, "staunchly Catholic" South Western Germany, are as essential to his thinking as Scotus, Kant, and Husserl. Catholicism pervades his philosophy as it pervaded his consciousness, like an atmosphere that colors everything that comes to light within it. "It has been said that my work is Catholic phenomenology—presumably because it is my conviction that thinkers like Thomas Aquinas and Duns Scotus also understood something of philosophy, perhaps more than the moderns," Heidegger said testily in 1927 (*GA24* 28/20). Even he would never deny that he could not help but see theological issues through Catholic eyes. "In its factual being Dasein always is as and 'what' it already was. Whether explicitly or not, it *is* its past" (*SZ* 20/17). Whether explicitly or not, Heidegger the great destroyer of metaphysics *is* the sexton's son, the former seminarian, the student apologist of the "Catholic world view," the newly minted *Privatdozent*, who pledged to dedicate his life's work to "harnessing the intellectual and spiritual potential of Scholasticism to the future struggle for the Christian-Catholic ideal."[12] Fritz Heidegger, who frequently read through his brother's writings at the latter's request, once remarked: "Whoever does not know Martin as the altar boy who grew up in the Meßkirch Sacristy has not understood his philosophy."[13] The present work cannot detach the question of Heidegger's critique of Scholasticism from Heidegger's biography because the two are indissolubly bound together.

---

12. Martin Heidegger, 1915 grant application to "The Constantin and Olga von Schaezler Foundation in Honour of St. Thomas Aquinas," quoted in Ott, *Biographie*, 91; Eng. trans., 90.

13. Undated letter from Fritz Heidegger to Franz Karl Huber, in Hans Dieter Zimmerman, *Martin und Fritz Heidegger. Philosophie und Fastnacht* (Munich: C. H. Beck, 2005), 163.

I started my tour of Heidegger's homeland at the Archabbey of Saint Martin, in Beuron on the upper Danube, a monastery founded by Augustinians in 1077, destroyed during the Thirty Years War, and rebuilt by Benedictines in the eighteenth century. As a young man, Heidegger often visited this large baroque complex on the banks of the Danube. His grandfather was born in a house a little ways downriver. The Abbey was once an oasis of peace for Heidegger; it always remained a symbol for him of the mystical depths of the Catholic tradition. In 1930, Heidegger, now a famous philosopher, returned to the cloister to deliver a lecture on Augustine to the monks in thanks "for years of hospitality." The Danube is narrow and tranquil here, a green-brown ribbon running through the Schwäbische Alb. The canyon carved by the river is over 100 meters deep in places, with steep white cliffs rising out from the green. A medieval fortress, Burg Wildenstein, clings to the rock opposite the monastery. The landscape images the steadfastness of South German Catholicism. Having withstood the Lutheran Reformation, it could withstand anything. Led by Heidegger, the Freiburg faculty of philosophy fled here in March 1945. Freiburg had been leveled by the Allies in an overnight air raid on November 27, 1944. (The cathedral had been miraculously spared. It greeted the survivors on the morning after, standing tall and defiantly erect amidst the ruin.) As the Americans, the French, the British, and the Russians poured over the borders of the Fatherland, Heidegger was holding seminars on Hölderlin in Burg Wildenstein.

In the late afternoon, I left the Danube and headed south toward Meßkirch. I had planned to catch a bus in Leibertingen, a small town just a couple of kilometers from the river. By the time I got there the last bus of the day had left, so I walked the twelve kilometers to Meßkirch. This was a trail that Heidegger had walked many times. It passes through forest into farmer's fields, which at this time of year, were blooming with poppies. A few hours after leaving Beuron, Meßkirch appeared in the golden rays of the setting sun, the square tower of Saint Martin's Church, where Heidegger's father had been sexton, lit up incandescently white. Saint Martin's was built in the Middle Ages. In the seventeenth century, it was transformed into a glittering, over-decorated baroque barn. Examining the dark paintings in their gilded frames, the white porcelain statues of saints, and the dizzying ceiling frescoes, I thought of the boy Heidegger looking in wonder at these images. The Heidegger family home stands a few feet opposite the church. The little square between the church and the sexton's house was Heidegger's playground.

Rüdiger Safranski tells us that Heidegger had fond memories of helping out with the church services, particularly ringing the bells:

> The most beautiful time was Christmas. Toward half past three in the morning, the boy ringers would come to the sexton's house, where mother Heidegger had laid the table with cakes and milky coffee. After this breakfast, lanterns were lit in the front-door passage, and everyone went out through the snow and the winter's night to the church opposite and up into the dark bell tower to the frozen ropes and ice-covered clapper. "The mysterious fugue," Martin Heidegger wrote, "in which the church feasts, the days of vigil, and the passage of seasons and the morning, midday, and evening hours of each day fitted into each other, so that a continual ringing went through the young hearts, dreams, prayers, and games—it is this, probably, that conceals one of the most magical, most complete, and most lasting secrets of the tower."[14]

The "Feldweg" (field-path) of Heidegger's famous essay by the same name is a trail that leads out of the town. Heidegger walked it regularly, meandering into the surrounding farmlands, the fields bordered by woods, and the farmhouses with red ceramic-tiled roofs. As I walked it myself, I found it is easier to understand Heidegger's passion for the "provinces." This love of his home, and not any particular anti-Semitic disposition, is the core of Heidegger's disastrous involvement with National Socialism. At a time when rural Germany was under attack by the forces of capitalism to the west and communism to the east, National Socialism alone seemed to put the interest of the farmers, the forest workers, the German *Volk*, first. National Socialism, alone, of all the powers competing for leadership of a Germany that was spiraling into chaos, spoke of preserving the land and its traditions. Heidegger never apologized for his collaboration, although he certainly regretted it. The suspension of his teaching license by the de-Nazification Committee—like

---

14. Rüdiger Safranski, *Ein Meister aus Deutschland. Heidegger und seine Zeit* (Munich: Carl Hanser, 1994); English: *Heidegger: Between Good and Evil*, trans. Ewald Osers (Cambridge: Harvard University Press, 1998), 7.

forbidding Einstein to do physics—precipitated a nervous breakdown. His obstinate refusal to apologize—that was his greatest sin. He can be forgiven for joining the party, for it was easy to be seduced by Nazi pageantry and patriotism in 1933. He can even be forgiven his opportunism, which caused him to turn his back on Husserl in his hour of need, when the Nazis banished the father of phenomenology from the University. But as a public figure, who enjoyed a postwar comeback and international recognition, Heidegger's refusal to acknowledge that the movement he had supported had perpetrated terrible crimes was a serious offence. Did he believe that such a statement was beneath him, a foray into the everyday, which would have distorted the ontological nature of his political involvement?

In any case, National Socialist ideology was never of serious interest to Heidegger. The talk of Aryan supremacy struck him as crude. Nor did he have any passion for world domination. Rather, he was drawn into politics by his commitment to the land from which he came, a home that appeared to be threatened and under attack from within and without. It was a matter of *Bodenständigkeit.* In the age of air travel and mass media, when everything and everyone can be everywhere in a matter of hours, *Bodenständigkeit* is the countercultural act of remaining rooted in one's homeland and safeguarding its traditions. Heidegger spoke of this crisis in 1955 in a public speech in Meßkirch:

> Many Germans have lost their homeland, have had to leave their villages and towns, have been driven from their native soil. Countless others whose homeland was saved, have yet wandered off. They have been caught up in the turmoil of the big cities, and have resettled in the wastelands of the industrial districts. They are strangers now to their former homeland. And those who *have* stayed on in their homeland? Often they are still more homeless than those who have been driven from their homeland. Hourly and daily they are chained to radio and television. Week after week the movies carry them off into uncommon, but often merely common, realms of the imagination, and give the illusion of a world that is no world. Picture magazines are everywhere available. All that with which modern techniques of communication stimulate, assail, and drive man—all that is already much closer to man today than his fields around his farmstead, closer than the sky over the earth, closer than the change from night to day, closer than the conventions and customs of his village, than the tradition of his native world. . . .

The *rootedness*, the *autochthony (Bodenständigkeit)*, of man is threatened today at its core. (*GA*16 521/48–49)[15]

Heidegger could diagnose the disease of rootlessness with such accuracy because he himself suffered from it. We know that his intellectual defection from the Catholic tradition troubled him to the end of his life. In a letter to Karl Jaspers, he described the unresolved issue of the religion of his upbringing as "a thorn" in his side.[16] To his fellow Meßkirchers, he was not the great critic of Catholicism, but one of them, a quiet kindly man, who walked the streets with cane and hat, silently watching whatever was going on. Meßkirch was a haven for him, a place where he was *known*, not as the famous philosopher, but as the sexton's son, Fritz's brother. He appeared regularly at the *Stammtische* at the Hotel Löwen to drink a *viertel* (a quarter liter of wine) with others of his generation. Fritz was usually there. A local card, Fritz would regularly send the company into peals of laughter, often at Martin's expense. Martin would smile, but say little.

Heidegger is buried between Fritz and their parents in the town cemetery. His tombstone bears the many-sided star that also stands above the well outside the hut in Todtnauberg in the Schwarzwald. Although he asked for a Christian (not a Catholic) burial, he did not want the Christian cross on his tombstone. What does the star mean? His single thought which, after a lifetime of thinking, still shone, cold, clear, and alone in the night sky? On this, as on most that concerned his spiritual life, he remained silent. Yet the strange star, so misplaced amidst the crucifixes in the Catholic cemetery, speaks volumes. It speaks of Heidegger's struggle to walk his own path while remaining true to his heritage, his ambivalent but enduring attachment to his Catholic roots. He wished to be buried there, in that most Catholic of cemeteries. Yet the star would indicate that, however much he belonged among the faithful of Meßkirch, his path of thinking was his own.

In the end, this book is a reverential *Auseinandersetzung* with Hei-

---

15. Martin Heidegger, "Gelassenheit," *GA*16 517–29, at 521; English: "Memorial Address," in Martin Heidegger, *Discourse on Thinking*, trans. John M. Anderson and E. Hans Freund (New York: Harper & Row, 1966), 43–57, at 48–49.

16. Martin Heidegger, letter to Jaspers, 1935, quoted in Ott, *Biographie*, 42; Eng. trans., 37.

degger on the question of the philosophical significance of Scholastic theology. Augustine writes: "If that is ineffable which cannot be spoken, then that is not ineffable which can be called ineffable. This contradiction is to be passed over in silence rather than resolved verbally. For God, although nothing worthy may be spoken of him, has accepted the tribute of human voice and wished us to take joy in praising him with our words."[17] Philosophy cannot unequivocally affirm anything of God, not even ineffability. Philosophy never gains the high ground in this discourse. It never has the privileged vantage point of being able to survey both sides of the limits of language and saying, here we can speak, there we cannot. *Not* to speak of God—this is an affront to Him, as much an affront as the presumption that we speak adequately of God. Philosophy can never properly speak of God, and yet it must speak of God. More than any other Christian author, Augustine exemplifies the virtue of bearing the poverty of religious language without giving into two perennial temptations: to presume to speak adequately of God, or to deny all possibility of speaking of God. The middle way, to stammer and speak inadequately but truly *of* God, is the most difficult.

Several people were involved in the writing of this book. I wish to name three: Professor Graeme Nicholson, Dr. Andrzej Wiercinski, and my beautiful wife, Esther. To each of them I offer my heartfelt thanks.

---

[17] "Quae pugna verborum silentio cavenda potius quam voce pacanda est. Et tamen Deus, cum de illo nihil digne dici possit, admisit humanae vocis obsequium, et verbis nostris in laude sua gaudere nos voluit." Augustine, *De doctrina Christiana* 1, 6, 3–13; English: *St. Augustine: On Christian Doctrine,* trans. Durant Waite Robertson, Jr., Library of Liberal Arts (Indianapolis: Bobbs-Merrill, 1958), 10–11.

CHAPTER ONE

HEIDEGGER AND THE MEDIEVAL THEOLOGICAL PARADIGM

Everything we think is the fruit of the Middle Ages and indeed of the Christian Middle Ages.

CARL GUSTAV JUNG

Like a great oak tree that has colonized a grove by driving roots deep into subterranean springs not reached by lesser trees, Heidegger's *Sein und Zeit* has dominated the twentieth century by feeding off traditions that lesser philosophical works cannot access. Not only a forgotten Aristotle, but also Martin Luther, Duns Scotus, medieval mysticism, and early Christianity are connected in numerous hidden ways to this massive monument to modern angst. These roots are buried deep beneath the surface of *Sein und Zeit*'s transcendental phenomenological discourse, but they are the source of the book's strength. A central root runs through Heidegger's biography: his defection from the reactionary Catholicism of his seminary days, a protest that required him to disentangle his spiritual and intellectual life, and then philosophy itself, from the neo-Scholasticism in which he had been schooled.[1] Another root stems from medieval Aristotelian ontology. The last philosophers prior to Heidegger to ask ques-

1. On Heidegger's Catholic roots, see Alfred Denker, "Heideggers Lebens- und Denkweg 1909–1919," in *Heidegger-Jahrbuch,* ed. Alfred Denker, Hans-Helmuth Gander, and Holger Zaborowski, vol. 1, *Heidegger und die Anfänge seines Denkens* (Freiburg and Munich: Verlag Karl Alber, 2004), 97–202; Holger Zaborowki, "'Herkunft aber bleibt stets Zukunft.' Anmerkungen zur religiösen und theologischen Dimension des Denkwegs Martin Heideggers bis 1919," in *Heidegger Jahrbuch,* 1:123–58; Ott, *Biographie;* Ott, "Zu den katholischen Wurzeln"/"Heidegger's Catholic Origins."

tions about the nature of being, the distinctions between different modes of being, and the difference between the being of beings and the being of being, were the "medieval schoolmen."[2] The largest root runs deep into the early Protestant objection to medieval theology, and, through Luther, into the faith of primal Christianity.[3] Heidegger was as intimate with this intellectual history as if it were his very own. His internalization of these ideas lends *Sein und Zeit* a historical *gravitas* lacking in other contemporary works.

And yet *Sein und Zeit* is a Godless eschatology. It is a phenomenological analysis of what Dilthey described as "historical consciousness," which Dilthey discovered, not in the Greeks, but in early Christiani-

---

2. On Heidegger and the Middle Ages, see *Quaestio. Annuario di storia della metafisica*, vol. 1, *Heidegger e i medievali. Attti del Colloquio Internazionale Cassino 10/13 maggio 2000*, ed. Costantino Esposito and Pasquale Porro (Turnhout, Belgium: Brepols, 2001). This volume contains an exhaustive bibliography of the literature on Heidegger's relationship to medieval philosophy. I have made use of *Heidegger und das Mittelalter*, ed. Helmuth Vetter (Frankfurt am Main: Peter Lang, 1999); Robert Bernasconi, "On Heidegger's Other Sins of Omission: His Exclusion of Asian Thought from the Origins of Occidental Metaphysics and His Denial of the Possibility of Christian Philosophy," *American Catholic Philosophical Quarterly* 69 (1995): 333–49; John Caputo, *Heidegger and Aquinas: An Essay on Overcoming Metaphysics* (New York: Fordham University Press, 1982); Johannes Baptist Lotz, *Martin Heidegger und Thomas von Aquin. Mensch—Zeit—Sein* (Pfullingen: Günther Neske, 1975); Thomas J. Sheehan, "Notes on a 'Lovers' Quarrel': Heidegger and Aquinas," *Listening* 9 (1974): 137–43; John M. Deely, *The Tradition via Heidegger: An Essay on the Meaning of Being in the Philosophy of Martin Heidegger* (The Hague: Nijhoff, 1971).

3. On Heidegger's early religion lectures, in addition to Kisiel's *Genesis of* Being and Time and van Buren's *Young Heidegger*, see *A Companion to Heidegger's Phenomenology of Religious Life*, ed. Sean J. McGrath and Andrzej Wiercinski (forthcoming); Jean Greisch, *L'Arbre de vie et l'arbre du savoir: Le chemin phénoménologique de l'herméneutique heideggérienne (1919–1923)* (Paris: Cerf, 2000); Gerhard Ruff, *Am Ursprung der Zeit. Studie zu Martin Heideggers phänomenologischen Zugang zur christlichen Religion in den ersten "Freiburger Vorlesungen"* (Berlin: Duncker & Humblot, 1997). For a more general treatment of Heidegger's appropriation of Christianity, see Hans-Georg Gadamer, *Heidegger's Ways*, trans. John W. Stanley (Albany: State University of New York Press, 1994). On Heidegger and Luther, see Otto Pöggeler, "Heidegger's Luther-Lektüre im Freiburg Theologenkonvikt," in Denker, Gander, and Zaborowski, *Heidegger-Jahrbuch*, 1:185–96; idem, *Martin Heidegger's Path of Thinking*, trans. David Magurshak and Sigmund Barber (Atlantic Highlands, N.J.: Humanities Press, 1987); Sean J. McGrath, "The Facticity of Being Godforsaken: The Young Heidegger's Accommodation of Luther's Theology of the Cross," *American Catholic Philosophical Quarterly* 79 (2005): 273–90; idem, "Das verborgene theologishe Anliegen von *Sein und Zeit*: Die Luther Lektüre des jungen Heideggers," in *Phänomenologie der Religion. Zugänge und Grundfragen*, ed. Markus Enders and Holger Zaborowski (Freiburg and Munich: Verlag Karl Alber, 2004), 271–78; John van Buren, "Martin Heidegger. Martin Luther," in Kisiel and van Buren, *Reading Heidegger from the Start*, 159–74; Richard Schaeffler, *Frömmigkeit des Denkens. Martin Heidegger und die katholische Theologie* (Darmstadt: Wissenschaftliche Buchgesellschaft, 1978), chap. 1.

ty—without God. Heidegger gives a formal interpretation of the apocalyptical sense, which he studied carefully in Paul and Luther. On the basis of this theological research, he constructs an apocalypse without end. The theological content of the New Testament is suspended, placed into phenomenological brackets. This becomes all the more clear when one compares the *Daseinanalytic* with Heidegger's 1920/21 lectures on Paul. For both Paul and Heidegger, the life that is self-understood as a "being-unto-an-end" is essentially historical. Paul's end is Christ, that for the sake of which the heavens and the earth have been created. Heidegger's end is death, Dasein's possibility of its own impossibility. What does it mean to be thrown toward an end that is not a *telos*? Robert Bernasconi also wonders about this. He asks: "The question is whether by confining the analysis of death to the 'this-worldly,' Heidegger had not implicitly made a decision against the 'other-worldly' and truncated the phenomenon at issue."[4]

At an early stage in his career, Heidegger appears to have allowed his enthusiasm for radical Protestantism to determine the phenomenological outcome of his questioning. To be sure, this argument, although not popular among Heideggerians, is not new. What is new is the full textual evidence necessary to confirm it. John Macquarrie once asked whether Heidegger's commitment to Barthian theology infected the purity of his phenomenology.[5] We can answer yes, with the proviso that it was not Barth as such, but Luther who won Heidegger's allegiance, perhaps as early as 1909, although it would not be until his Marburg years that he could set free the budding Protestant within him. Max Scheler was suspicious of the theological sources informing *Sein und Zeit* already in 1927, when he carefully worked his way through the copy Heidegger himself had sent him. "Thrownness," "fallenness," "being-unto-death," the futile call of "conscience," which only serves to remind Dasein of its finitude—these notions struck Scheler as neo-Calvinist tropes imported into phenomenology without phenomenological justification.[6] In paragraph 62

---

4. Robert Bernasconi, "Whose Death is it anyway? Philosophy and the Cultures of Death," in *Acta Institutionis Philosophiae et Aestheticae*, vol. 15, ed. Tomonou Imamichi (Tokyo, 1997), 13–25.
5. John Macquarrie, *Heidegger and Christianity* (New York: Continuum, 1994), 55.
6. Max Scheler, *Gesammelte Werke*, vol. 9, *Späte Schriften*, ed. Manfred Frings (Bern: Francke,

of *Sein und Zeit*, Heidegger admits that "a definite ontic interpretation of authentic existence, a factical ideal of Dasein," underlies his ontology (*SZ* 310/286). Scheler's suspicion is that this ontic conception is nothing other than radical-Protestant anthropology.

The thesis of this book is that Heidegger arrived at the Godless eschatology of *Sein und Zeit*, which will issue in the later critique of "ontotheology," through a systematic, if covert, overthrowing of the medieval theological paradigm, which has come to be known as "Scholasticism." Considering the great diversity of philosophical and theological positions in the Middle Ages, there is some question whether there is any sense in speaking of Scholasticism as a unity. Used as a derogatory category for dismissing the philosophy and theology of the Middle Ages (a period lasting a thousand years), the term "Scholasticism" covers a range of diverse philosophical positions that encompass the full spectrum of premodern Western philosophy: from strict rationalism, to direct realism, to proto-idealism and uncompromising nominalism. How can philosophers as polemically related as Anselm and Aquinas, Scotus and Ockham, be legitimately included in the same category? As Philipp Rosemann asks in his *Understanding Scholastic Thought with Foucault*, "What (if anything) characterizes and distinguishes medieval intellectual culture, beyond the mere historical fact that it took place during the period we call the 'Middle Ages'?"[7] A traditional answer to this question finds a unity in a "doctrinal body," the successful fusion of Christian and Greek thinking, which reaches its apogee in Thomas Aquinas.[8] However, as Rosemann notes, if the fusion of Christianity with Greek philosophy is the distinguishing feature of Scholastic philosophy then we would need to include Descartes and Hegel among the Scholastics. Rosemann finds the unity of Scholastic thought, not in any particular Scholastic doctrine, but in the form of Scholastic thinking, the way the Scholastics approach every subject matter. He describes the Scholastic way as a discursive and

---

1976), 295, 260. See Daniel Dahlstrom, "Scheler's Critique of Heidegger's Fundamental Ontology," in *Max Scheler's Acting Persons: New Perspectives*, ed. Stephen Schneck (Amsterdam: Rodopi, 2002), 67–92. A translation of some of Scheler's notes appeared as Max Scheler, "Reality and Resistance: On *Being and Time*, Section 43," trans. Thomas J. Sheehan, *Listening* 12 (1977): 61–73.

7. Philipp Rosemann, *Understanding Scholastic Thought with Foucault* (New York: St. Martin's Press, 1999), 45.

8. Ibid., 46.

dialectical balancing of authority *(auctoritas)*, principally the authority of theology with its roots in a divine revelation, and natural reason *(ratio)*.[9] Scholasticism never regards finite reason as a final court of appeal. "In the Scholastic *episteme*, the confidence in the powers of human reason to discover the texture of the real is counterbalanced by the insight that God, ultimately, transcends the text—every text."[10]

Rosemann's interpretation of Scholasticism closely parallels my own. It serves to highlight exactly what Heidegger objects to in medieval philosophy: not the notion of revelation as such, but the assumption that revelation and a philosophical approach to God could be complementary. Every philosophy that can be termed "Scholastic" ventures a precarious highwire act, balancing the primacy of a revealed theology and the freedom of philosophy. The Scholastics sought a theology that balanced the sovereignty of a supernatural revelation and the dignity of science; the finitude of reason—revealed in the revelation itself—and the possibility of a basic philosophical knowledge of God. The primacy of theology, the sovereignty of revelation, the finitude of reason—these are modifications of the Scholastic belief in the *fact* of a divine disclosure of supernatural truth. The freedom of philosophy, the dignity of science, the possibility of philosophical theology, all refer to the equally central Scholastic conviction that human reason is capable of a measure of truth. Revelation did not annul what reason had been able to establish "on its own," but confirmed, complemented, and empowered it. Even William of Ockham retains the Scholastic conviction that God can be grasped to some degree through a philosophical reflection of creation.[11] "Scholasticism," then, designates a spectrum of medieval philosophical and theological schools sharing a belief in revelation and simultaneously, a belief in the basic power of human reason to understand something of itself, its world, and God. It follows that Luther's declaration that reason is so disfigured by sin, it is incapable of seeking the truth without the guidance of revelation, was the ultimate anti-Scholastic bombast. As an unequivocal No to human philosophy and

---

9. Ibid., 47.
10. Ibid., 101.
11. Ockham holds that "adequate reasons" (but not *per se* demonstrations) can be found for God's existence. See Armand Maurer, *The Philosophy of William of Ockham in the Light of Its Principles* (Toronto: Pontifical Institute of Mediaeval Studies, 1999), 159–83.

religion, it has been revitalized by Barth's dialectical theology and its contemporary American version, "post-liberal theology" (the "theology of crisis" paradoxically reduced to a formula). The Reformation brought the age of Scholasticism to an end. After Luther, Scholasticism lived on within Catholic circles, but its preeminence in the secular university was greatly diminished if not obliterated.

Husserl required a suspension of any God-talk that could not be verified in phenomenological intuition.[12] Heidegger to some degree remains a Husserlian on this question; philosophy does not believe (*BZ* 1). However, Heidegger goes further than denying philosophy recourse to a revelation. Early on in his career, as Husserl's "phenomenologist of religion," he concluded that God is not *given* to philosophy in any way. Philosophy is factically Godless.[13] This is not to say that a discourse about God, drawing on supra-philosophical sources, and recognizing an alternative seat of authority, is not possible. A revealed theology has every right to contest philosophy's claim to ultimacy. It will, however, for this reason, remain philosophy's "mortal enemy" (*GA*9 66/53).

According to Merold Westphal, Heidegger is not interested in denying the existence of God, but rather in preserving the alterity of God.[14] Heidegger has left open a space for a certain kind of experience of God, to be sure, but this space has been cleared by closing down other philosophical ways of thinking about God, including the Thomistic way. There is no passage in Heidegger from a reflection on the being of the human being, or the being of creation, to the being of God. Heidegger abolishes the *analogia entis,* along with the doctrine of creation itself: "That beings must be understood as created by God is adhered to as an unshakeable conviction [in Scholasticism]. By this ontical declaration a putting of the ontological question is condemned from the start to impossibility" (*GA*24 140/100). These denials go beyond Westphal's minimalist reading

---

12. See Edmund Husserl, *Ideen zu einer reinen Phänomenologie und phänomenologischen Philosophie,* vol. 1, *Allgemeine Einführung in die reine Phänomenologie,* ed. Walter Biemel, *Husserliana,* vol. 3 (The Hague: Nijhoff, 1950, 1976), §58; English: *Ideas Pertaining to a Pure Phenomenology and to a Phenomenological Philosophy,* vol. 1, *General Introduction to a Pure Phenomenology,* trans. F. Kersten (The Hague: Nijhof, 1982).

13. *GA*61 196–97/147. See also *PIA* 246/193–94 n. 9; *BZ* 1.

14. Westphal, *Overcoming Onto-theology,* 243.

of the critique of onto-theology as an effort to preserve the alterity of God. The *analogia entis* does not lead to the onto-theology of Descartes and Hegel (Heidegger's real enemy). On the contrary, most Thomists will argue that it is precisely the forgetting of the *analogia entis* that has generated these onto-theologies.

The original motive of the early Heidegger's theological silence becomes clear through a close reading of Heidegger's earliest lectures and writings. He does not want to preserve a philosophy of religion but to show that none is possible. In 1922, Heidegger asks "Could it be that the very idea of a philosophy of religion, and especially if it does not take into account the facticity of human being, is pure nonsense?" (*PIA* 246/193–94 n. 9). Westphal convincingly argues that onto-theology concerns the *how*, not the *what*, of theology.[15] When the affirmation of God as First Cause is motivated by calculative thinking and advanced as the first step in a totalizing reduction of being to reason, it is clearly onto-theological. On the other hand, when the affirmation of God remains with the biblical revelation and does not endeavor to translate it into the language of metaphysics, it does not fall within the purview of the critique.[16] However, between the totalizing onto-theological thinking of the modern system builders and the theology of the Reformation there is the philosophical theology of much of Scholasticism. "The critique of onto-theology belongs to a tradition of dehellenizing repristination," Westphal writes.[17] Yes—and this is precisely what puts it into open conflict with Scholasticism.

What is the philosophical significance of the biographical root of *Sein und Zeit* for our question? The use of biography in philosophy tends to come under attack from students of Heidegger impressed by his *Sache*-driven methodology. Are biography and chronology not accidental to philosophy? Can we not say of Heidegger's life what Heidegger once said of Aristotle's—he lived, he worked, he died—and then move on to the issues at hand? I have not dealt with the *Sache*, it will be objected. Instead of thinking *what* Heidegger has said, I have busied myself with *why* Heidegger said it. This is biography, not philosophy. This is a serious

15. Ibid., 7.
16. Ibid.
17. Ibid., 18.

consideration. My answer: the *Sache* at issue here, Heidegger's objection to Scholastic ontology, essentially involves Heidegger's biography. Biographical contextualization, always to some degree helpful, is crucial to understanding Heidegger, with his concealed agendas and complex theological motivations. Without it, we cannot understand how Heidegger moved from being a self-appointed defender of "the spiritual potential of Scholasticism"[18] to being an advocate of formally atheistic hermeneutics in the space of six years. Nor can we fully understand how *Sein und Zeit* constitutes an alternative to Scholastic ontology.

Educated in the Scholastic way of thinking (particularly Franciscan Scholasticism),[19] Heidegger wrote his *Habilitationsschrift* on the problem of the categories in John Duns Scotus and moved more or less comfortably within neo-Scholastic circles.[20] In 1916, he saw himself as a Scholastic phenomenologist of some kind and anticipated making a major contribution to a renaissance of philosophical interest in the Middle Ages. Heidegger always admitted the importance of this medieval-theological provenance for his development, however tersely: "Without this theological start, I would never have come onto the path of thought. But our origins always lie before us *(Herkunft aber bleibt stets Zukunft)*" (*GA*12 96/10). As a newly minted *Privatdozent*, Heidegger argued that Scholasticism was ignored by contemporary thinkers at their own expense. The

---

18. Martin Heidegger, from his 1915 application for a grant from the Schaezler Foundation in honor of St. Thomas Aquinas. See Ott, *Biographie*, 75/74.

19. Martin Heidegger, "Mein Weg in die Phänomenologie," *Zur Sache des Denkens* (Tübingen: Niemeyer, 1969), 82; English: "My Way in Phenomenology," in *On Time and Being*, trans. Joan Stambaugh (New York: Harper & Row, 1972), 75.

20. Martin Heidegger, *Die Kategorien- und Bedeutungslehre des Duns Scotus, GA*1 189–401; English: *Duns Scotus' Theory of the Categories and of Meaning*, trans. Harold Robbins (Ph.D. diss., De Paul University, 1978). On Heidegger's study of Scotus, see Sean J. McGrath, "Die scotistische Phänomenologie des jungen Heideggers," in Denker, Gander, and Zaborowski, *Heidegger-Jahrbuch*, 1:243–58; idem, "Heidegger and Duns Scotus on Truth and Language," *Review of Metaphysics* 57 (2003): 323–43; W. Kölmel, *Heidegger und Duns Scoti*, in *Via Scoti: Methodologica ad mentem Joannis Duns Scoti*, ed. L. Sileo (Rome: Antonianum, 1995), vol. 2, 1145–55; M. Rampley, "Meaning and Language in Early Heidegger: From Duns Scotus to 'Being and Time,'" *Journal of the British Society for Phenomenology* 25 (1994): 209–28; Kisiel, *Genesis of* Being and Time, 21–68; Olivier Boulnois, *Entre logique et sémantique. Heidegger lecteur de Duns Scot*, in *Phénoménologique et logique*, ed. Jean-François Courtine (Paris: Presses de l'Ecole Normale Supérieure, 1996), 261–81; and John D. Caputo, "Phenomenology, Mysticism and the *'Grammatica Speculativa'*: A Study of Heidegger's Habilitationsschrift," *Journal of the British Society for Phenomenology* 5 (1974): 101–17.

cloister-bound history of *meditatio* and *disputatae* on the relationship between the Jewish-Christian scriptures and Greco-Roman *scientia* was the incubator of the Western genius.

Heidegger's approach to Scholasticism in the *Habilitationsschrift* stands in marked contrast to the polemical reading of Augustine in the 1921 lectures, "Augustinus und der Neuplatonismus" (GA60 157–299), or the 1927 reading of *essentia* and *existentia* (GA24 109–71/77–121), and its sequel in the 1941 Nietzsche lectures (GA6.2 363–416). During the years 1917 to 1919, Heidegger came to believe that the Scholastic assumption that we can understand *something* of the true God through a rational reflection on creation was an illusion. Not only was it deceptive of our theological predicament, it was also distortive of our philosophical situation. Philosophy must articulate the world as it is, not as it might appear to faith. In his notes and lectures from these years, Heidegger expressed an increasing suspicion that Scholastic philosophical theism obfuscates, if not precludes, the hermeneutics of facticity.

This "path of thinking" would lead Heidegger out of the Catholic Church into neo-orthodox Protestantism and finally to an a-theological stance that severed all philosophical ties to theism. Following Wilhelm Dilthey, the young Heidegger came to understand the life-consciousness of primal Christianity, the God-intensified "self-world" of Christian discipleship, which comes to acute expression in Augustine, as the birth of historical consciousness in the Western tradition. This pristine moment was betrayed by the Scholastic fusion of theology and ancient science. In the Reformation, particularly in the figure of the young Luther, the repressed self-world of primal Christianity rose up in rebellion, tearing down the suffocating constructs of Scholastic science and retrieving historically saturated, authentic Christian faith. Luther's *theologia crucis* became Heidegger's paradigm for separating theology, an ontic science of a putative historical revelation, from philosophy, the factical ontology of temporal life.[21] Heidegger took from Luther's *theologia crucis* an understanding of why philosophy must be "in principle atheistic" (PIA 246/121). He turned what Luther regarded as the theological limitations of philoso-

---

21. Van Buren, in his "Martin Heidegger. Martin Luther," and Greisch, in *L'Arbre de vie et l'arbre du savoir*, maintain similar positions.

phy into a strength: bereft of a natural consciousness of God, philosophy was in a privileged position to let the factic speak on its own terms. The 1921 Augustine lectures, the method and presuppositions of *Sein und Zeit*, the 1927 *Destruktion* of medieval ontology, and the later interpretations of onto-theology are fore-grounded in the prejudgment that the "object" of ontology is the temporal, finite, and Godforsaken being which we ourselves are. Interpreted by this presupposition, Scholasticism's role in the history of being becomes the inglorious one of precipitating the definitive forgetting of the ontological difference in the modern age. Scholasticism, like every philosophical theism, was not able to think the being of beings. The causal reduction of beings to an a-temporal principle, the first cause, the *actus purus*, eclipsed temporality. Not only was it a program for making historical life easier, a systematic flight from finitude, it created the conditions necessary for the modern hegemony of theory. When the paradigm for the real is God's judgment that grants existence to essences, the paradigm for truth becomes the *adaequatio* of judgment with things. Primordial truth, unconcealment *(aletheia)*, is forgotten, and the theoretical comportment is enshrined as the only way to access being.

In 1919, Heidegger expressed his interior (if not formal) break with "the system of Catholicism" to his priest friend Engelbert Krebs.[22] Although we have little textual record of Heidegger's study of Luther, which doubtless precipitated this break, he left traces of his interest in Luther in occasional remarks scattered throughout the early Freiburg and Marburg lectures. From these references, we can reconstruct Heidegger's early philosophy as a search for a hermeneutical phenomenological complement to Luther's *theologia crucis*. Already in the '50s, the Luther scholar Edmund Schlink described Heidegger's philosophy as "a radical secularization of Luther's anthropology."[23] Luther's objection to Scholasticism as the *theologia gloriae*, an intrusion of Greek metaphysics into Christianity, and a substitution of a philosophical principle for the crucified God, awakened Heidegger. In tandem with Luther's *theologia crucis*, Heidegger's hermeneutics of facticity exposes the derivative nature of Scho-

---

22. Martin Heidegger, letter to Engelbert Krebs, January 9, 1919, cited in full in Ott, *Biographie*, 106–7/106.

23. Edmund Schlink, "Weisheit und Torheit," *Kerygma und Dogma* 1 (1955): 6.

lastic philosophical theology and intensifies the uncertainty, difficulty, and Godforsakenness of human existence. Jean Greisch writes: "Without directly saying it, he [Heidegger] suggests that the hermeneutics of facticity can make a pact with the Theology of the Cross."[24]

The subtitle of this book, *Phenomenology for the Godforsaken*, requires some explanation. Strictly speaking, Godforsakenness is distinct from Godlessness. Only a believer can be Godforsaken. Jesus' cry from the Cross, "My God, my God, why have you forsaken me?" (Mk 15:33), is often misinterpreted as an expression of the Son's loss of faith at the moment of maximal suffering. Jesus is in fact quoting a psalm (Ps 22). While the cry expresses the distance from the Father suffered by the Son in effecting Redemption—the Son's participation in the experience of sin—this is still no "atheistic howl." Rather, it is the anguished cry of a believer who feels abandoned by God. It is the tormented faith of Job. Jesus does not cease to believe in the existence of God in his moment of Godforsakenness; on the contrary, the cry is an affirmation of the existence of God—in spite of everything. The cry is far from Godless; rather, it is the most extreme articulation of faith, a confession of belief when nothing confirms it. The Godless, on the other hand, has no God by whom he could be Godforsaken. He worships nothing and so does not complain either. When he suffers, he does not shout his indignation to the heavens. The Godless does not experience the *absence* of God, the *non-presence* of God; rather, he does not experience God at all.

What, then, does it mean to call *Sein und Zeit* a phenomenology *for* the Godforsaken? It means, first of all, that the *Daseinanalytic* is no neutral description of facticity, an experience of "average everydayness" which is available to all in the same way. It is a description of a historically and situationally determined existence, the experience of facticity that is the privilege and the curse of a certain kind of Christian faith. For only a Christian could describe facticity as Godforsaken. They would mean by this that human life is so disfigured by sin (the *aversio Dei*) as to be factically an experience of what ought not to be—createdness without an experience of the Creator, finitude without infinity. To claim, as I have, that Heidegger has deliberately overturned the neutrality central to Husserl's

---

24. Greisch, *L'Arbre de vie et l'arbre du savoir*, 247.

effort and written a phenomenology for the Godforsaken is to claim: (1) that Heidegger has situated himself within a certain form of Christian faith; (2) that what he describes in *Sein und Zeit* is only describable as it has been described from that faith-perspective; (3) that the question of Dasein's relation to God has not been left open; on the contrary, it has been decided in advance.

This is different from the tired accusation of secularization. *Sein und Zeit* is not a secularization of Luther but a hermeneutical complement to Luther, in a sense, a Lutheran phenomenology of Dasein. The Godless would perhaps find here much that illuminates their own experience. They may even be driven to seek further clues into the meaning of facticity in something like a radical theology of revelation, that is, a theology that denies a natural consciousness or experience of God. In this way, the early Heidegger understands himself to be serving the Lutheran cause, intensifying the Godforsakenness of life and thus preserving the integrity of a theology of revelation. This is the key to the dense 1921 claim that the formally atheistic hermeneutics of facticity is both a turn away from God and a remaining with God. "Philosophy is a departure from God, and, in its radical enactment of its 'way,' a singularly difficult remaining-near God" (*GA*61 197).[25] In the *Natorp Bericht*, Heidegger explains that philosophy must in some way turn away from God ("raise its hand against God") if it is to remain itself. Only thus can it realize an authentic relationship to God: "This throwing of life back upon itself which gets actualized in philosophy is something that in religious terms amounts to raising one's hand against God. But philosophy is thereby only being honest with itself and standing firm on this, that is, it is comporting itself in such a manner that is fitting to the only possibility of standing before God that is available to it as such" (*PIA* 246/193–94 n. 9). Heidegger has made a decision about what possible relation to God is available to philosophy. He has not denied the existence of God. Rather, he has denied philosophy the possibility of affirming this existence.

---

25. *GA*61 197: "Philosophie muss in ihrer radikalen, sich auf sich selbst stellenden Fraglichkeit prinzipiell a-theistisch sein. Sie darf sich gerade ob ihrer Grundtendenz nicht vermessen, Gott zu haben und zu bestimmen. Je radikaler sie ist, umso bestimmter ist sie ein weg von ihm, also gerade im radikalen Vollzug des 'weg' ein eigenes schwieriges 'bei' ihm."

There is, then, a fourth implication to the claim that *Sein und Zeit* is a phenomenology for the Godforsaken: (4) The human being is interpreted as having no phenomenological experience of God. Here Heidegger ventures a claim that is in principle phenomenologically falsifiable. The "disproof" would involve an elaboration of a factual experience of God "natural" to Dasein, that is, a religiosity independent of a biblical revelation. I have argued that phenomenology must take the possibility of such experience into account and endeavor to thematize it, however difficult that may be. But is this not simply a phenomenology that is theologically motivated in an alternative way? Is this not simply a Roman Catholic version of a *Daseinanalytic?* For the moment, I am committed to this: one need not be Roman Catholic to recognize Dasein's concern for what we call God. In the metaphysical tradition, the arguments for God's existence serve to bridge a theology of revelation and a philosophically independent investigation of nature. I wish to remain, at least in this discussion, within the phenomenological brackets. Even in suspension of metaphysics, being-before-God shows itself in human living. On these grounds, I believe that the *Daseinanalytic* fails to stay with the basic terms of factical life.

The context of the young Heidegger's turn to Luther was the reactionary neo-Scholasticism of early-twentieth-century Catholic theology. Leo XIII's 1870 encyclical *Aeterni Patris* declared Thomas Aquinas *the* philosopher for the Catholic Church. Pius X's 1907 encyclical *Pascendi* foreclosed as "modernism" most efforts to integrate the insights of modern philosophy, science, and historiography into Catholic theology. The 1914 encyclical *Motu Proprio* declared Aquinas necessary for priestly formation in the Church. It seemed to the young Heidegger that the Catholic hierarchy was dictating in advance what must be true and false for philosophy. Between the years 1909 and 1911, Heidegger came under the influence of Carl Braig, a theologian who sought to mediate medieval Scholasticism and German idealism. Braig was an outspoken critic of papally enforced neo-Scholasticism.[26] Some of Braig's rebelliousness

---

26. Bernhard Welte, "150 Jahre Theologische Fakultät Freiburg als Exempelfall theologischer Entwicklung," in *Zwischen Zeit und Ewigkeit. Abhandlungen und Versuche* (Freiburg im Breisgau: Herder, 1982), 135–57, at 150. Heidegger spoke of the importance of Braig for his development in

rubbed off on his student. In a 1914 letter to Krebs, Heidegger writes: "The *motu proprio* was all we needed. Perhaps you as an 'academic' could seek a better way, whereby those who have fallen away can correct their thinking by having their brains removed and replaced with 'Italian salad.' For our philosophical needs, we could line up at vending machines in the train station."[27] The neo-Scholasticism inspired by the Counter-Reformation, the political revolutions of the nineteenth century, and the papal pronouncements of the early twentieth century was rigid, formulaic, and usually ignorant of modern philosophy. Kant was generally regarded with suspicion, and therefore not read. Aquinas, Bonaventure, and Scotus were systematized into an alternative to the great modern systems, a Scholastic system which was then fed to seminarians in manuals as the only true philosophy.[28] This textbook Scholasticism is the same monster against which both Bernard Lonergan and Karl Rahner railed. The young Heidegger was suspicious of it from the beginning of his academic career. In a critical review, published in *Der Akademiker* in 1912, of one of the standard theological textbooks, Joseph Gredt's *Elementa Philosophiae Aristotelico-Thomisticae*, the student Heidegger argues that philosophy cannot be understood as "a settled summary of doctrinal theses," but only as "a continuous struggle for the truth." Scholastic logic should be "set free from its rigidity and supposed finality" (*GA16* 29).[29] The neo-Scholastics endeavored to develop a hermetically sealed philosophical system, which could serve as a secure foundation for the Church by excluding modern insights and questions, advancing itself as timeless truth, a *philosophia perennis*. Heidegger's *Habilitationsschrift*, a historical and hermeneutical investigation of Duns Scotus in the light of contemporary develop-

---

"Mein Weg," 81–82/74–75. On Braig, see Karl Leidlmair, "Carl Braig," in *Christliche Philosophie im katholischen Denken des 19. und 20. Jahrhunderts*, vol. 1, *Neue Ansätze im 19. Jahrhundert*, ed. Emerich Coreth, Walter M. Neidl, and Georg Pfligersdorffer (Graz: Styria, 1987), 409–19. On Braig's influence on Heidegger, see Caputo, *Heidegger and Aquinas*, 45–55; Schaeffler, *Frömmigkeit des Denkens*, 1–10.

27. Martin Heidegger, letter to Engelbert Krebs, July 19th, 1914, in Denker, Gander, and Zaborowski, *Heidegger-Jahrbuch*, 1:61–62.

28. Bernhard Casper, "Das theologisch-scholastische Umfeld," in Esposito and Porro, *Quaestio* 1:11–22, at 21.

29. Joseph Gredt, *Elementa Philosophiae Aristotelico-Thomisticae* (Rome, 1899–1901). Heidegger's review is published in *GA16* 29–30.

ments in phenomenology and neo-Kantianism, was an act of defiance.[30]

Heidegger's difficulties with neo-Scholasticism would quickly deepen into an objection to medieval philosophy itself. In his early lectures on phenomenology, Heidegger argues that the deduction of a first cause of being neuters ontology, de-temporalizes it, and makes a phenomenological investigation of historical life on its own terms impossible. When philosophy presumes access to an *ens infinitum*, the answer to the question of the meaning of being is given in advance: being means God; all other beings *are* insofar as they participate in the *actus purus*. Factical life is interpreted in terms of non-factical eternity. Temporality is excluded from the discussion, and theology is substituted for the understanding native to life. Against this trajectory, Heidegger maintains that philosophy is "the explicit and genuine actualization of the tendency towards interpretation that belongs to the basic movements of life in which what is at issue is this life itself and its being" (*PIA* 246/121). The phenomenological maxim, "back to the things themselves" is a call to hold thinking to life. Philosophy must resist the perennial temptation to take a balloon ride into the absolute; it must remain true to its theme, "conceptually grasping factical life in terms of the decisive possibilities of its being." Philosophy becomes, then, an existential act of bringing life to an authentic encounter with its own finitude. Heidegger enjoins philosophy "to throw factical life back on itself as this is possible in this factical life itself and to let it fend for itself in terms of its own factical possibilities" (*PIA* 246/121). Heidegger's notion of being as temporal horizon projected by Dasein, or later, as *Ereignis*, the occurrence of being, which sends Dasein into a particular dispensation of *Seinsverständnis*, is intended to break with every medieval ontology. Scholasticism defines potency in terms of act and identifies being with the *actus purus*, the infinite, divine act of existence. Heidegger elevates potency above act and identifies being with time. Medieval philosophy is *Seinsvergessenheit* to "the second power."[31] It compounds the distortion already at work in Plato, the identification of being with constant presence, with the causal derivation of all beings from the *actus purus*. As Thomas Sheehan puts it, "medieval philosophy articulat-

---

30. Casper, "Das theologisch-scholastische Umfeld," 21.
31. Sheehan, "Notes on a 'Lovers' Quarrel," 137.

ed being not as essentially temporal and finite but as eternally stable reality rooted in the actuality of the Supreme Act, and in so doing, delivered to modern philosophy all that it would need to transform being into the horizon of objectifiability posited by the transcendental subject."[32] The later Heidegger's etymological analyses derive the primordial Greek pre-ousiological notion of being, *physis*, from *phainesthai*, "to appear." Unlike *ousia*, *physis* denotes withdrawal and hiddenness as much as emergence and presence. This dynamic of "presencing," emerging from absence, can still be seen in Aristotle's notion of *energeia*. With the Scholastic translation of *energeia* into *actualitas*, that which is effected by a working activity, the temporal association in *physis* is forgotten. In the later Heidegger's view, this development was not a failure on the part of Scholasticism, but the fate of Western thinking. Heidegger writes in *Der Satz vom Grund*: "It would be foolish to say that the medieval theologians misunderstood Aristotle; rather, they understood him differently, corresponding to the different way in which being sent itself to them" (*GA*10 117–18/79).

Heidegger excludes from the outset of *Sein und Zeit* the possibility of a knowledge or experience of a nontemporal, immutable, and infinite being. *Sein und Zeit* is an ontology of the human being without reference to the possibility of God. To be sure, Heidegger acknowledges "being-toward-God" *(das Sein des Menschen zu Gott)*; it is summarily dismissed as a special mode of being-in-the-world, something for theology to work out (*SZ* 8/10). Thinking has no recourse to nontemporal being. "If being is to be conceived in terms of time and if the various modes and derivatives of being, in their modifications and derivations, are in fact to become intelligible through considerations of time, then being itself—and not only beings that are 'in time'—is made visible in its 'temporal' character. But then 'temporal' can no longer mean only 'being in time.' The 'a-temporal' and the 'supratemporal' are also 'temporal' with respect to their being; this not only by way of privation when compared to 'temporal' beings which are 'in time'. . . . Being is in each instance comprehensible only in regard to time"(*SZ* 18–19/16). It is crucial to see that the above passage hinges on a conditional: "*If being is to be conceived in terms of time. . .*" Why *should* being be conceived in terms of time? Heidegger

---

32. Ibid., 138.

is not recommending the substitution of one dogmatism for another. He believes that the assumption of the temporality of being, the reversal of the Scholastic thesis, to some degree decrypts the meaning of being. The assumption effects a reversal of the metaphysical tradition on multiple levels. The Scholastic thesis, the assumption of a first cause of being, forgets the ontological difference. Heidegger's antithesis accents the difference. The Scholastic thesis holds that changing beings participate in that which does not change and are real to that degree. Heidegger's antithesis holds that beings *are* to the degree that they are temporalized. The Scholastic thesis privileges act over potency, Heidegger's antithesis means that "higher than actuality stands possibility" (SZ 38/34). The Scholastic thesis makes God the starting point for philosophy. Heidegger's antithesis excludes God from ontology, for if being means time, God cannot be said to be.

With a philosophy of God removed from the scope of possibilities for thinking, the Scholastic bridge between a rational philosophy and a revealed theology is annihilated. Philosophy is freed from its tutelage to theology, and Christian theology is purified of Hellenistic philosophical infestation. Just as philosophy does not and cannot believe, theology, in Heidegger's view, does not philosophize. As "a thinking and questioning elaboration of the world of Christian experience, i.e., of faith" (GA40 9/8 August 16, 2005), theology's work has little or nothing to do with philosophy. "If I were to write a theology," Heidegger said in Zurich in 1951, "then the word *being* would not occur in it. Faith does not need the thought of being. When faith has recourse to this thought, it is no longer faith. This is what Luther understood" (GA15 436–37). Philosophy does not believe because it has no reason to believe. It is not *given* a God to think. The being of beings is not divine. It is not a cause, not an absolute, but an event, not something that subsists, but something that comes to pass, a process, the completion of which in some sense depends upon Dasein.

The early Heidegger's atheological position seems to be abrogated in his later writings. The celebrated theological neutrality of the *Humanismusbrief* and the *Beiträge*'s doctrine of "the last god" are apparent departures from the earlier talk of the necessary atheism of philosophy. By remaining silent about God, *Sein und Zeit* serves "the holy," we are told in the *Humanismusbrief*. It demolishes idols in order to clear a space for the truly divine God. *Sein und Zeit* is ostensibly a postmodern *via negativa* (*GA9* 350 ff./266 ff.). In the *Beiträge*, this *via negativa* becomes an explicit severing of ontology from divinity. Having destroyed onto-theology, Heidegger has cleared the space for the advent of the last god.[33] Should the unknown divinity reveal itself, it would not be the god of the philosophers, the *causa sui*, to whom "man can neither pray, nor sacrifice," before whom "he can neither fall to his knees in awe nor can he play music and dance" (*ID* 70/72). It is worth noting that many scholars see in these passages from the *Humanismusbrief* possibilities for a more positive relationship between Heideggerian thought and philosophical theology than the one I have presented in this book. Heidegger's *Wirkungsgeschichte* on philosophical theology may be loosely grouped under four headings: transcendental, metaphysical, deconstructive, and phenomenological. The post-Heideggerian transcendentalists seek a non-ontic foundation for theism in a transcendental analysis of subjectivity. The condition of the possibility of all our intellectual and volitional acts is held to be a pre-thematic experience of infinite being.[34] The post-Heideggerian metaphysicians, distancing themselves from the inchoate idealism of the former, retrieve from Aquinas a distinction between the being of being and the being of God, which allows for a temporalization of our finite understanding of being, without detracting from the infinity of God.[35] The de-

---

33. *GA65* 409–17/288–93.

34. See Karl Rahner, *Foundations of Christian Faith*, trans. William Dych (New York: Crossroads, 1978); Emerich Coreth, *Metaphysics*, trans. Joseph Donceel (New York: Herder and Herder, 1968). On the relationship of Rahner's theology to Heidegger's ontology, see Thomas Sheehan, *Karl Rahner: The Philosophical Foundations* (Athens: Ohio University Press, 1987).

35. See Gustav Siewerth, *Gesammelte Werke*, vols. 1–4, ed. Wolfgang Behler and Alma von Stockhausen (Düsseldorf: Patmos, 1971–87), especially "Das Sein als Gleichnis Gottes," in vol. 1. A translation of this seminal Siewerthian text is in preparation by Andrzej Wiercinski. On Siewerth, see Emmanuel Tourpe, *Siewerth 'après' Siewerth. Le lien idéal de l'amour dans le Thomisme spéculatif de Gustav Siewerth et la visée d'un réalisme transcendental*, Bibliothèque Philosophique de Louvain, vol. 49 (Louvain: Peeters, 1998); Andrzej Wiercinski, *Inspired Metaphysics? Gustav Siewerth's Hermeneutic Reading of the Onto-theological Tradition* (Toronto: Hermeneutic Press, 2003); idem, *Die scholastischen Vorbedingungen der Metaphysik Gustav Siewerths* (Frankfurt am Main: Peter Lang, 1991); idem, *Über die Differenz im Sein. Metaphysische Überlegungen zu Gustav Siewerths Werk* (Frankfurt am Main: Peter Lang, 1989). See also the work of Ferdinand Ulrich, especially *Homo Abyssus. Das Wagnis der Seins-frage (Sammlung Horizonte)* (Freiburg im Breisgau: Johannes Verlag, 1961, 2nd ed., 1998). See also Martin Bieler, "The Future of the Philosophy of Being," *Communio* 26 (1999): 455–85.

constructionist theologians (if they can still be called theologians) draw on Jacques Derrida to gesture rhetorically to a non-logocentric, non-ontological *via negativa*.[36] The post-Heideggerian phenomenologists of religion, deeply impressed by Emmanuel Levinas's ethical critique of Heidegger, advance a Husserlian phenomenological exploration of God, not as being, but as the possibility of absolute givenness.[37] An earlier school of post-Heideggerian phenomenology, founded by Bernhard Welte, interpreted Heidegger as an iconoclast, who liberates authentic theism from the conceptual idolatry of the onto-theological tradition.[38] Each of these deserves an extensive treatment of its own. Together, they are outlined here as markers of a field that is growing daily.

In a recent piece, the German philosopher of religion, Bernhard Casper, outlines an interpretation of Heidegger's relationship to Scholasticism informed by the basic positions of the Welte school.[39] Since it stands in tension with the interpretation advanced in this book, it deserves some attention here. Casper builds his argument on the undeniable fact that Heidegger's critique of onto-theology is rooted in his early theological objections to the formulaic rigidity of neo-Scholasticism. Casper argues that Heidegger's critique is not in itself opposed to phil-

36. See Harold Coward and Toby Foshay, eds., *Derrida and Negative Theology* (Albany: State University of New York Press, 1992); Gianni Vattimo, *After Christianity*, trans. Luca D'Isanto (New York: Columbia University Press, 2002); idem, *Belief* (Stanford, Calif.: Stanford University Press, 2000); John D. Caputo, *The Prayers and Tears of Jacques Derrida* (Bloomington: Indiana University Press, 1997).

37. See Jean Luc Marion, *Being Given: Toward a Phenomenology of Givenness*, trans. Jeffrey L. Kosky (Stanford, Calif.: Stanford University Press, 2002); idem, *God Without Being*. See also Emmanuel Levinas, *God, Death and Time*, trans. Bettina Bergo (Stanford, Calif.: Stanford University Press, 2000); idem, *Of God Who Comes to Mind*, trans. Bettina Bergo (Stanford, Calif.: Stanford University Press, 1998). Although his work maintains strict boundaries between philosophical and theological questions, Paul Ricoeur belongs to this post-Heideggerian phenomenological theology movement. See his *Figuring the Sacred: Religion, Narrative, and Imagination*, trans. David Pellauer, ed. Mark I. Wallace (Minneapolis: Fortress Press, 1995), 48–67. Richard Kearney has done much to develop the theological potential of Ricoeur's hermeneutics. See his *The God Who May Be: A Hermeneutics of Religion* (Bloomington: Indiana University Press, 2001).

38. Welte, *Zwischen Zeit und Ewigkeit*; idem, *Religionsphilosophie* (Freiburg im Breisgau: Herder, 1978); Klaus Hemmerle, *Auf den göttlichen Gott zudenken* (Freiburg im Breisgau: Herder, 1996); Bernhard Casper, Klaus Hemmerle, and Peter Hünerman, eds., *Besinnung auf das Heilige* (Freiburg im Breisgau: Herder, 1966). Although he seems to be unaware of the Welte school, Laurence P. Hemming's positions place him in a certain proximity to it. See his *Heidegger's Atheism: The Refusal of a Theological Voice* (Notre Dame: Indiana University Press, 2003).

39. Casper, "Das theologisch-scholastische Umfeld."

osophical theology but only to a certain variety of it, "the ecclesiastical neo-Scholasticism" which understands itself as "a closed system and a timeless and a-historical ground of all knowledge."[40] In Casper's view, Heidegger's 1919 "break with Catholicism" has more to do with the rejection of neo-Scholastic formulas than it does with Lutheranism. Casper sees a unity in Heidegger's path, from his student writings to the later work. Heidegger's lifework is a one-pointed search for "the ground," the foundation of thinking and being. Casper notes that already in the early student book reviews, Heidegger is articulating a notion of thinking as a will to the ground *(der Wille zum Grund)*, a directedness that "signifies [also] the desire for a knowledge of God."[41] The target of Heidegger's critique of onto-theology is, therefore, not Catholic theology as such, but any mitigation or foreclosure of questioning with a premature answer. Systematized neo-Scholasticism is not genuine theism. It is what Heidegger will call in 1928 the "ontic belief in God," which is basically "godless" (*GA*26 211 n. 3/165). Insofar as it closes down honest questioning with prescribed Church-approved answers, it is in fact idolatrous. Casper writes, "Every failure in the pursuit of this search must then be understood as a fall from the true relationship to God, as the worship of other gods."[42] The philosophy of the "causa sui," which Heidegger denounces as idolatry in *Identity and Difference,* is the textbook Scholastic theology, not the works of Aquinas or Scotus.[43] Hence Heidegger does not preclude but supports an authentic philosophical search for God and a genuine philosophical theism.

The present work argues otherwise. Heidegger's departure from the Catholic tradition, although precipitated by the modernist crisis, is shown to harden over time into a substantive divergence. Heidegger annuls the central Thomistic hermeneutical principle of the analogical unity of the being of God and the being of creation, the *analogia entis.* Scotus notwithstanding, this Thomistic principle grounds not only the sacramental life of the Church, but also the possibility of a philosophical knowledge of God. The interpretation of "being" as "time" is intended to make the *analogia entis* impossible. The assumption of time as the hori-

40. Ibid., 21.
42. Ibid.
41. Ibid., 13.
43. Ibid., 17.

zon of being is complexly related to Heidegger's appropriation of Luther. As such, it has a theological underside. It is not only a hermeneutical-phenomenological principle, it is also a declaration of what is and what is not theologically possible for the human being. The assumption of ontological Godlessness invites a radical theology of revelation to declare its No to philosophy. However—and this is my claim against Heidegger—it lacks full phenomenological confirmation in experience. Far from being Godless, the human being seems to be spontaneously religious. This ontological directedness toward the infinite must be distinguished from *religio*, the virtue of honoring and worshiping God. The former is an existential and thus an inalienable possession of every human being; the latter is a virtue practiced by some but not by others. But the virtue of *religio* would not be possible without ontological religiousness.[44] The central argument of this book is a hermeneutical objection to Heidegger's presupposition of formal atheism, on the ground that it conceals more than it reveals. The assumption of factical Godforsakenness is shown to be problematic insofar as it leaves an essential dimension of being-in-the-world in darkness.

The later Heidegger is on the track of something decisively non-Christian, a pre-Judaic experience of "the holy" free of theistic associations and interpretations. He has set up the conditions for the possibility of such a post-Christian religiosity by ransacking Jewish-Christian texts, formalizing their most characteristic features and declaring them the rightful property of philosophy. He frequently dismisses the very Christian sources upon which he himself so heavily relies. If occasionally the Christians hit upon something true, as for example, in the case of Augustine or Kierkegaard, they generally lack the power to follow the truth into its concealed ground. Jacques Derrida has remarked on the peculiar inauthenticity of Heidegger's treatment of his Christian sources. In *The Gift of Death*, he writes: "Heideggerian thought was not simply a constant

---

44. Markus Enders has called for the careful distinction of the ontological ground of religiosity from the practice of religion as such. See his "Ist der Mensch von Natur aus religiös? Zur Aktualität und Wiederkehr der Religion," in *Bildung. Identität. Religion. Fragen zum Wesen des Menschen*, ed. Hans Poser and Bruno B. Reuer (Berlin: Weidler Buchverlag, 2004), 221–39; "Ist 'Religion' wirklich undefinierbar? Überlegungen zu einem interreligiös verwendbaren Religionsbegriff," in Enders and Zaborowski, *Phänomenologie der Religion*, 49–87.

attempt to separate itself from Christianity.... The same Heideggerian thinking often consists, notably in *Sein und Zeit,* in repeating on an ontological level Christian themes and texts that have been 'de-Christianized.' Such themes and texts are then presented as ontic, anthropological, or contrived attempts that come to a sudden halt on the way to an ontological recovery of their own originary possibility."[45]

What are we to make of Heidegger's hermeneutical violence to the Christian tradition? What is Heidegger saying about the Christianity that he treats so badly? Can his position be made more explicit than he articulated, with his cryptic remarks about theological origins, and his gravid silence on religious matters? Can we find clues in a careful reconstruction of his research into medieval and early Christian texts? If we find that something is hermeneutically astray here, that in some way, the subject matter itself has been violated, does the exposure of a weakness in Heidegger's philosophy strengthen that which he sought to overturn? Could this rehabilitate medieval theism in some way? This is, admittedly, a circuitous way of showing the relevance of medieval philosophy. But perhaps, this indirect approach is exactly what is needed. There is no shortage of medieval enthusiasts who dream of a return to the thirteenth century. Scholasticism needs to be presented from a fresh perspective, in a more contemporary light, which could reveal its unexplored resources for addressing "postmodern" philosophical problems.

This book is about Heidegger's relationship with Scholasticism, it is not a retrieval of Scholasticism as such. Nonetheless, my reading of Heidegger is determined by a certain understanding of the subject matter. My approach to Scholasticism is fore-grounded in an appropriation of the following four, broadly "Thomistic," claims:

1. The distinction between the being of beings and the being of God is the true interpretation of the *analogia entis.* That we must affirm both a continuity and a discontinuity between the being of beings and the being of God precludes all one-sidedness in philosophical theology. Lutheran one-sidedness, with its modern representatives, Heidegger, Barth, perhaps even Derrida, exaggerates the discontinuity between the human

---

45. Jacques Derrida, *The Gift of Death,* trans. David Wills (Chicago and London: University of Chicago Press, 1995), 22–23.

and the divine and so compromises the integrity of the human being, who remains an *imago Dei*, even in his fallenness. The Scotist notion of *univocatio entis* encourages a one-sided exaggeration of the continuity between the human and divine. It finds many modern supporters, for example, Hegel, who so overemphasizes the human being as *capax Dei* as to compromise the transcendence of God.

2. The *analogia entis* makes possible a nonreductionistic philosophical theology, not a philosophy of "either/or" but of "both/and." It calls us to a delicate balance of tensions, a pardoxical affirmation/denial, a *via positiva* and a *via negativa*, a *theologia gloriae* and a *theologia crucis*, a God who is wholly with us and wholly other. This is not a Hegelian "both/and" but a Thomistic "both/and." The synthesis is not a possession of the human spirit, but a mystery hidden in God.

3. The Scholastic notion of a *desiderium naturale*, the human desire for the fullness of being, can be interpreted as the ground of human religiosity. We are not only redirected to God by grace, we are directed to God ontologically. Hence we need both a phenomenology of religiousness *and* a theology of revelation. The former would include a descriptive analytic of all forms of religiosity, not only the ways-of-being-in-the-world of the great religions, but also the faith of everyday life. This would elaborate the monotheism of human finality, showing how all human desires, although they emerge out of the polytheism of the human "unconscious," converge on a single transcendent point.

4. Ontological religiousness, the ground of human religiosity, is to be interpreted both eschatologically and mystically. It is both messianic and mystical. The being which we ourselves are is a being-before-God. The "before" has both a temporal and a spatial meaning: we await God and thus suffer the incompleteness that attends such awaiting, and, in rare moments of illumination, we experience the divine presence and awaken to our true position, before the Face.

My conclusion is a plea for a reappraisal of the factical ground of Scholastic philosophical theology. Factical religious experience is operative in Scholasticism. This leads to the question of the significance of factical religious experience in contemporary philosophy. Should this be only negatively and agnostically "formally indicated"? Or is something essentially human here, which was at the center of Scholastic investigations, calling for a more careful phenomenological exposition?

A methodological note: while this work primarily concerns the early Heidegger (the lectures and writings up to and including *Sein und Zeit*), I draw on the later writings when a parallel or echo of a point can be found. That this violates the traditional divide between Heidegger I and II does not disturb me, on the contrary. If I have raised questions about the legitimacy of this distinction, I will have achieved even more than I set out to do.

CHAPTER TWO

HEIDEGGER'S RELIGIOUS-PHILOSOPHICAL *ITINERARIUM*

> *A Jesuit by education, Heidegger became a Protestant through indignation; a Scholastic dogmatician by training, he became an existential pragmatist through experience; a theologian by tradition, he became an atheist in his research, a renegade to his tradition cloaked in the mantle of its historian.*
>
> KARL LÖWITH

Heidegger began his career at Freiburg University in 1915 as an interpreter of the Catholic Middle Ages and as, to all appearances, a devout Roman Catholic: former seminarian and son of the sexton in Meßkirch. As his views on facticity and historicity developed, he became increasingly critical of "the system of Catholicism." He came to believe that Catholicism inured itself from life through an architectonic of Scholastic concepts, a "pseudo-philosophy" with "police power" (*GA*60 313). Scholasticism (not identical to Catholicism in Heidegger's mind but nonetheless inseparable from it) distorted Aristotle and compounded the forgetfulness of being already underway in antiquity by inauthentically fusing Greek metaphysics with Christian theology. A religious journey lies behind this polemic: Heidegger's metamorphosis from Roman Catholic apologist to "non-dogmatic Christian" (i.e., Lutheran) and in his later period, neo-pagan prophet of "the fourfold of earth and sky, mortals and immortals."

Heidegger always admitted the importance of his theological education for his thinking. As an older man, he reflected on the personal difficulty of his critical relationship with his Catholic roots. Only a fellow Catholic could understand how, in spite of his break with Catholic theology, Catholicism could remain a decisive influence for his philosophy: "Who could deny that a hidden engagement with Christianity continued during the whole way [of thinking] until now, an engagement, which was and is no thematized 'problem,' but the preservation of personal origins—my parent's house, my native land, my youth—and the painful separation from them. Only he who is also rooted in a genuinely Catholic world, can suspect the necessity of my questionings that affect my path to this very day like subterranean earthquakes" (*GA66* 415). Heidegger's dialogue with Protestantism during the Marburg years was determined by questions that had emerged for him from his Catholic past. Protestantism had no lasting solutions for him: "The Marburg time brought a closer experience of a Protestant Christianity—however, already one that had to be overcome in its very foundations, but not abolished" (*GA66* 415). Eventually he would break with Christianity and theism altogether.

Brentano, Braig, and Roman Catholic Apologetics

Heidegger's family house lay in the shadow of the steeple of St. Martin's, the baroque church which his father looked after. Heidegger and his only brother grew up playing in the church courtyard, or helping their father in the church. The parish priest singled Heidegger out for the seminary at an early age. Whether or not Heidegger felt a vocation to the priesthood, his best chance at higher education was through the clergy; a sexton's salary was not enough to finance a university degree. In 1903, at the age of 14, Heidegger entered the seminary in Constance, 45 kilometers south of Meßkirch. The seminarians lived a semi-monastic life in the Konradihaus, but attended the local grammar school, where they were exposed to liberal anticlericalism. They were well prepared for it with studies of Aquinas and Bonaventure and were encouraged to write apologetical essays defending the faith.[1] Upon receiving a grant to study the-

---

1. For a colorful and detailed description of Heidegger's childhood and seminary years, see Rüdiger Safranski, *Ein Meister aus Deutschland* (Munich: Carl Hanser, 1994), 15–30; English:

ology in 1906, Heidegger moved to the St. Georg seminary in Freiburg. Recognizing the philosophical abilities of his young student, the headmaster of the Konradihaus and future archbishop of Freiburg, Konrad Gröber, made a present to Heidegger of Franz Brentano's dissertation, *Von der mannigfachen Bedeutung des Seienden nach Aristoteles*.[2]

Brentano, a former priest, was an expert in Scholasticism, and Husserl's teacher at Vienna. However it was not Husserl's Brentano who initially intrigued Heidegger—Brentano, the pioneer in phenomenology, who had famously retrieved the notion of intentionality from the tradition—[3] but Brentano, the Aristotelian ontologist. Brentano's approach to Aristotle differs significantly from the approach of his neo-Scholastic contemporaries. He had an encyclopedic knowledge of the Aristotelian corpus, with a particular strength in Aristotle's doctrine of categories—an interest Heidegger would share. His critique of the Scholastic interpretation of Aristotle first exposed Heidegger to cracks in the edifice of neo-Scholasticism. On many occasions, Heidegger referred to Brentano's *Von der mannigfachen Bedeutung des Seienden* as his initiation into metaphysics. In the preface to William Richardson's *Through Phenomenology to Thought*, Heidegger offers the following reflections on his connection with Brentano's book: "[The] first philosophical writing through which I worked again and again from 1907 on was Franz Brentano's dissertation: *Von der mannigfachen Bedeutung des Seienden nach Aristoteles*. On the title page of his work Brentano set down the sentence from Aristotle: *to on pollachos legetai*. I translate: 'Beings become manifest in many ways (i.e., with a view to their being).' Concealed in this sentence is the *question* that determined the way of my thought: what is the simple, unitary determination of being that permeates all its manifold meanings? . . . What then does being mean?"[4] Elsewhere, Heidegger

---

Heidegger: Between Good and Evil, trans. Ewald Osers (Cambridge: Harvard University Press, 1998), 1–15.

2. Franz Brentano, *Von der mannigfachen Bedeutung des Seienden nach Aristoteles* (Hildesheim: Olms, 1960); English: *On the Several Senses of Being*, trans. Rolf George (Berkeley: University of California Press, 1975).

3. See Franz Brentano, *Psychology from an Empirical Standpoint*, ed. Linda McAlister (New York: Humanities Press, 1973).

4. Heidegger, preface to *Heidegger: Through Phenomenology to Thought*, by William J. Richardson (The Hague: Nijhoff, 1963), x.

calls the book, "my first guide through Greek philosophy in my secondary school days" (GA12 88/7), "the 'rod and staff' of my first awkward attempts to penetrate into philosophy."[5]

Franco Volpi has pointed out that while Heidegger's ontological work was initiated by his perplexity with Brentano's study of Aristotle, Heidegger's thinking takes an opposite direction from Brentano's. Brentano identifies ontology with ousiology and underscores the centrality of the doctrine of substance. In Heidegger's eyes, this is a reduction of being to the ten categories. Heidegger's ontology problematizes the doctrine of the categories, exposing their limits and the need for further transcategorical distinctions to do justice to the experience of being.[6] But their question is the same: What does the word "being" signify, if it can be used in so many different ways? Brentano's dissertation examines Aristotle's thesis that the Greek participle *on*, "the little word that applies to everything,"[7] varies in meaning according to the way it is predicated, yielding a fourfold schema of analogies: being as accident ("Socrates is bald"); being as true ("It is the case that Socrates is bald"); being as potential or actual ("It is going to rain"; "It is raining"); and being according to the ten categories (e.g., substance: "Socrates is a man"; the accident of relation: "Socrates is shorter than Gorgias").[8] The being attributed to substances means something different from the being attributed to accidents; the being of potency is other than the being of actuality; how then can we meaningfully use the verb "being"? As Heidegger put it in 1927, If "the articulation of being varies each time with the way of being of a being," "the question of the possible multiplicity of being *(die Frage nach der möglichen Mannigfaltigkeit des Seins)* and therewith at the same time that of the unity of the concept of being in general becomes urgent" (GA24 170/120). For Aristotle, every object and attribute of objects presupposes being, yet being itself is neither an object nor an attribute of

---

5. Heidegger, "Mein Weg," 81/74.

6. Franco Volpi, "Brentanos Interpretation der aristotelischen Seinslehre und ihr Einfluss auf Heidegger," in Denker, Gander, and Zaborowski, *Heidegger-Jahrbuch*, 1:226–42. This article is a summary of Volpi's major work, *Heidegger e Brentano. L'aristotelismo e il problema dell'univocità dell'essere nella formazione filosofica del giovane Martin Heidegger* (Padua: Cedam, 1976).

7. Richardson, *Through Phenomenology to Thought*, 4.

8. Thomas Sheehan, "Heidegger's Early Years: Fragments for a Philosophical Biography," *Listening* 12 (1977): 4. See Aristotle, *Metaphysics* 6.2.1026a34 ff.; idem, *Categories* 1.1a.

objects. Being cannot be said to be in the way that substances, accidents, potencies, actualities, even truth itself, can be said to be. Being *qua* being is not the being of anything, neither a genus, nor an intelligibility: it names a group of equivocal natures, to which it is applied analogously, that is, as found in one instance in a primary sense, and in other instances insofar as they are related to it. As the notion of health refers primarily to a disposition of the body yet is analogously extended to all things that promote it, food, exercise, and so on, the notion of being refers primarily to divine being, the unmoved mover, yet is analogously applied to all that which partakes or is otherwise causally related to it.[9] The univocal notion of being is an abstraction from the rich multiplicity of ways to be. The multiple applications of the concept reflect the actual and concrete heterogeneity of the world of beings.

The high school student Heidegger was so captivated by Brentano's presentation of the problem that he began a program of self-directed, ontological research, checking out Aristotle's collected works from the library. Learning that Brentano had decisively influenced the burgeoning phenomenology movement, Heidegger turned to Husserl for answers to the ontological question: "Thus both volumes of Husserl's *Logische Untersuchungen* lay on my desk in the theological seminary ever since my first semester.... From Husserl's *Logische Untersuchungen* I expected decisive aid for the questioning stimulated by Brentano's dissertation.... I remained so fascinated by Husserl's work that I read it again and again in the following years without gaining sufficient insight into what captivated me."[10]

After graduating in 1909, Heidegger entered the novitiate of the Society of Jesus at Tisis near Feldkirch, Austria. His weak health did not permit him to stay beyond the two-week candidacy period. In the winter semester 1909, he transferred to the theological seminary in Freiburg, the Collegium Borromaeum, where he continued his theology studies until 1911. Here he came under the influence of Carl Braig, a member of the Faculty of Theology at the University of Freiburg. Braig introduced Hei-

---

9. See Joseph Owens, *The Doctrine of Being in the Aristotelian Metaphysics: A Study in the Greek Background of Mediaeval Thought*, 3rd rev. ed., with a preface by Etienne Gilson (Toronto: Pontifical Institute of Mediaeval Studies, 1978), 37, 456, 457.

10. Heidegger, "Mein Weg," 81–82/74–75.

degger to the basic principles of medieval metaphysics, the writings of Aquinas, Bonaventure, and Suárez, and the possibilities for theology in conversation with modern philosophy. He is best remembered as a representative of the Tübingen school of speculative theology, which integrated the insights of German idealism with Scholasticism. Later in life, Heidegger fondly remembered Braig as his first philosophical mentor: "It was from his lips, when he let me walk with him sometimes, that I first heard of the importance of Schelling and Hegel for speculative theology, as opposed to the doctrinal system of Scholasticism. In this way the tension between ontology and speculative theology as the developmental structure of metaphysics entered the horizon of my search."[11] The ambivalence of this reference must not be overlooked. Heidegger does not endorse Braig's fusion of theology and ontology. Indeed, the failure of Braig's attempt to negotiate "the tension between ontology and speculative theology" may have been Heidegger's first clue that something was askew in the crossbreeding of theology and ontology in the metaphysical tradition.

Braig is remembered as an important early opponent of both modernism and neo-Scholasticism.[12] In Braig's view, modernism is the rationalistically motivated effort to diminish the epistemic validity of revelation, either through Kant's reduction of religion to the symbolic articulation of universal human principles of knowledge and action, or romanticism's equally reductive view of religious doctrine as expressions of human feeling. Both contest the sovereignty of revelation by explaining religion as a human projection, the value of which rests solely in its reference to human truths. For Braig, revelation is super-rational, not sub-rational, ontological, not psychological, and truth-functional, not poetical or merely symbolic. Christendom and modernity are fundamentally opposed

---

11. Heidegger, "Mein Weg," 82/75. The passage begins: "The decisive, and therefore ineffable, influence on my own later academic career came from two men who should be expressly mentioned here in memory and gratitude: the one was Carl Braig, professor of systematic theology, and the last in the tradition of the speculative school of Tübingen which gave significance and scope to Catholic theology through its dialogue with Hegel and Schelling; the other was the art-historian Wilhem Vöge. The impact of each lecture by these two teachers lasted through the long semester breaks which I always spent at my parents' house in my hometown of Meßkirch, working uninterruptedly." Ibid., 81–82/74–75.

12. Leidlmair, "Carl Braig," 410.

conceptual constellations. The former recognizes the dignity of reason, but without denying the need for supernatural revelation; the latter exaggerates the self-sufficiency of human subjectivity.[13] In view of Heidegger's early apologetical essays in *Der Akademiker* and his later revelational positivism, it is undeniable that Braig's critique of modernism had a lasting influence on him. However, Braig's most decisive impact on Heidegger's development was not in theology but in ontology. Braig opposed neo-Scholastic textbook ontology and endeavored to present an overview of ontology in a new key, one critically informed by Kant, Hegel, and German idealism. If Brentano first drew Heidegger's attention to the ontological problem of the meaning of the word "being," Braig's *Vom Sein. Abriß der Ontologie* was Heidegger's first experience of a systematic answer to the question.[14] Braig's work is a synthesis of elements of Plato, Aristotle, Aquinas, Bonaventure, and Suárez into a fundamentally different view of the problem of being than that presented by any of these historical authors.

Braig regards Aristotelian Thomism as deficient on certain crucial questions. It is likely that Heidegger fist picked up a distaste for Thomism from Braig. Like Scotus, whose position he approximates in certain respects, Braig holds that Aquinas's *analogia entis* leaves theology vulnerable to philosophical agnosticism, for it fails to recognize the essential knowability of the first principle. Aquinas's real distinction between *essentia* and *existentia* leads to a problematic philosophical theology that affirms the existence of absolute being *(ipsum esse),* without being able to affirm anything else about the divine nature. Braig aligns himself with the Augustinian tradition, which develops a more substantial philosophical knowledge of God on the basis of a neo-Platonic theory of illumination.[15] For Augustine, our everyday understanding of being is made

---

13. Braig writes: "Christendom affirms the human spirit's need of faith and the human heart's need of salvation in opposition to a system of rational salvific truths.... Modernism tries to mediate 'the self-attestation' of religious truth through feeling, through the immediate interior intuition of religious conditions. Everything external and historical has meaning and value [for modernism] only as externalized symbols of a psychological inner state or inner experience." Carl Braig, introduction to *Apologie des Christentums*, by F. Duilhé de Saint-Projet, trans. Carl Braig (Freiburg: Herder, 1889), quoted in Schaeffler, *Frömmigkeit des Denkens*, 4.

14. Carl Braig, *Vom Sein. Abriß der Ontologie* (Freiburg: Herder, 1896).

15. Braig's ontology was criticized by his Thomist contemporaries on the grounds that, like

possible by a primal illumination, an innate understanding of absolute being. For Aquinas, on the other hand, we have no understanding of absolute being; our everyday understanding of being is made possible by an abstraction of the act common to all that we experience as existing, *ens commune*, the universal notion, richest in content and widest in extension, but nonetheless distinct from the notion of God.[16] Braig is partial to Augustine's notion that God's essence is "impressed" upon the intellect.[17] In our everyday acts of knowing, being "appears as something nonsensible, something supported by thinking and only determinable in thinking." Our ordinary patterns of thinking are only possible on the basis of an implicit knowledge of "the unconditioned being, which conditions particular forms of being."[18] Braig builds his ontology on the familiar Platonic argument that ethical, mathematical, and physical knowledge prove the existence of implicitly known standards of measurement. The essential forms of being for Braig—unity, otherness, self-identity—are neither "read off" of experience, nor deduced a priori from reason, but as in Plato, emerge from the encounter between the richly endowed intellect and the iconic beings of everyday experience. On the basis of these a priori principles, Braig establishes an objective metaphysical knowledge of God—not a substitute for revelation, but a self-evident and philosophically defensible theology that naturally supports revelation.

Braig's Augustinian lineage is illustrated in the long quotation from St. Bonaventure's *Itinerarium mentis in Deum*, which appears on the first page of his *Vom Sein*.[19] The ontological treatise that follows is in some re-

---

all efforts to found ontology on something other than the *analogia entis*, it collapses into pantheism. See M. Glossner, "Carl Braig. Vom Sein," *Jahrbuch für Philosophie und Spekulative Theologie* 13 (1899): 52–65.

16. Owens, *Doctrine of Being*, 1.

17. See Augustine, *De Trinitate*, 8, 3; English: *On the Holy Trinity*, trans. Arthur West Haddan, A Select Library of the Nicene and Post-Nicene Fathers of the Christian Church, ed. Philip Schaff, vol. 3 (Grand Rapids, Mich.: W. M. B. Eerdmans, 1956): "We would be unable to call one [good thing] better than the other... if the idea of the good itself [and by implication, being] had not been impressed upon us, according to which we approve something as good, and also prefer one good to another." For Aquinas, by contrast, we have no innate concept of *ipsum esse* (for none is possible). The two notions, *ens commune* and *ipsum esse*, are related but distinct: the first abstracts from all differences and in this respect, allows for the addition of generic and specific differences; the second is unlimited and perfect being to which nothing can be added.

18. Braig, *Vom Sein*, 5.

19. Bonaventure, *Itinerarium mentis in Deum* 5.4.334: "Being itself *(ipsum esse)* is so certain

spects an extended commentary on this quotation. In the passage cited by Braig, Bonaventure speaks of being/God as the vision-enabling light that is not itself visible, the first in the intellect, which cannot be known in the way individual beings are made known by it. Where the determinations of finite beings are always contingent upon evidence, infinite being requires no empirical evidence: it is self-evident and necessary. The first in the intellect is always already in the intellect; it is no abstraction or derivative construct, but an innate principle. The "most-certain" principle of thinking remains for the most part unthought. Being is concealed by particular beings, hidden behind that which it makes possible.

Bonaventure speaks of an inevitable blindness to being. The mind, preoccupied with the finite forms that it can define and understand, forgets that which makes them possible. Divine being, indicated in all that is thought, appears as nothing to the form-driven intellect. This "strange blindness of the intellect" is a function of its ontic orientation: for the most part we are occupied, not with the necessary ground of what we know, but rather, with the known. Braig does not suggest that, with proper effort, the intellect could intuit being itself; rather, the intellect always

---

and secure, that it cannot be thought not to be. For pure being itself occurs only in full flight from non-being *(non-esse)*. Therefore, just as absolute nothing shares no part of being or its attributes, so by contrast, being itself shares no part of non-being either in act or in potency, either in the truth of a thing or in our estimation. But if non-being is a privation of being, it does not enter the intellect except through being. However, being does not enter the intellect through anything other than itself because all that which is thought, is either potential being *(ens in potentia)* or being in act *(ens in actu)*. If therefore non-being *(non ens)* cannot be thought except through being *(ens)*, and potential being cannot be thought except through being in act, and being *(esse)* names the pure act of being itself *(ipsum purum actum entis)*, it follows that being is that which falls first into the intellect. Strange, then, is the blindness of the intellect, which does not consider that which it sees first and without which it could know nothing. The eye, concentrating on various differences of color, does not see the very light by which it sees other things; and if it does see this light, it does not advert to it. In the same way, the mind's eye, concentrating on particular and universal being, does not advert to being itself, which is beyond every genus, even though it comes to our mind first and through it we know other things. And it seems that 'as the eye is in the evening, so is the eye of our mind to self-evident natures' [Aristotle, *Metaphysics*, 2, 1]. Because it is accustomed to the darkness of beings and the images of sensible things, the intellect seems to see nothing when it intuits the light of the supreme being. It does not understand that this very obscurity is the supreme illumination of our mind, just as when the eye sees pure light, it seems to see nothing." Ott has discovered that during the war, Heidegger undertook an intensive study of Bonaventure's *Itinerarium* with Heinrich Ochsner. See Ott, "Heidegger's Catholic Origins," 137. On the relationship of Heidegger's thought to Bonaventure, see Sonya Sikka, *Forms of Transcendence: Heidegger and Medieval Mystical Theology* (Albany: State University of New York Press, 1997), 43–107.

intellects some being and cannot think without a determinate concept. In order for it to grasp being itself, it must think the conditions of being simultaneous with whatever it thinks. Braig's God is to be intuited, not by shutting out creatures, but rather by heeding that which shows itself in creatures, or rather, by heeding that which does not show itself in creatures, yet nonetheless belongs to them as ground and enabling condition.

"The ground of being is not found . . . in a sensible being," yet it shines through sensible beings, penetrating them, and making them possible.[20] To see being in a being, the intellect needs to practice dialectical discipline, neither ignoring the evidence of the senses, for the source of ontology is "the whole of the world of experience" *(die Gesamtheit der Erfahrungswelt)*,[21] nor losing itself in sensation, for being is "non-sensible . . . supported by thinking and only determinable in thinking."[22] Through reflection on the conditions of all that exists, the intellect proceeds from the uncertain knowledge of contingent beings to the innate, necessary, and self-evident knowledge of "the unconditioned being."[23] Braig functionally defines being as the dynamic self-positing act *(Tätigkeit)* by which every being differentiates itself from other beings and from non-being. Being is not a conceptual content that is projected onto things, an innate idea in a modern sense, not a "clear and distinct" idea, which could be defined or accessed through Cartesian introspection, but "the first determination which a being must have in order to be," the dynamic power manifest in everything.[24] Every attempt to define being inevitably fails, substituting some attribute of a particular being for being itself. "All the attempts to give Being conceptual determinations are defective and contradictory. Being is a 'position,' 'positing,' 'doing,' 'energy,' 'affirmation,' 'ground of possibility': these and similar definitions mix up the primary characteristic marks found in beings with the essential character of Being."[25] Reason finds itself in a Socratic *aporia*: it must affirm being, for it has always already assumed it, but it cannot define what it is that it affirms. Yet this inevitable assumption is neither "the name by which we indeterminately

20. Braig, *Vom Sein*, 5.
21. Ibid., 8.
22. Ibid., 5.
23. Ibid.
24. Ibid., 19.
25. Ibid., 22.

fuse all things," nor "the common source out of which things come"; but "the unnamed N which by itself signifies nothing, but which can take on all the values of the real predicates of an essential something and does indeed take them on insofar as the thing is."[26]

Braig's Augustinianism remained a decisive influence on Heidegger, positively and negatively. When Heidegger delivers a polemic against the Scholastics in the introduction to *Sein und Zeit*, attacking the Scholastic notion of being as the most universal and emptiest of concepts, it is the Scotist *univocatio entis* that he targets. With Scotus, Braig conceives being as empty universal, the univocal notion derived from timeless essence, which is applied in every act of thinking: self-evident, necessary, and all-applicable, but in itself content-free and undefinable.[27] Braig writes: "Being is that which is highest, most universal and simple, that which is abstracted *(abgezogen)* from beings, the distinctive feature in all concepts immediately imposed by thinking itself."[28] Positively, Heidegger may have been influenced by Braig's quasi-transcendental approach to ontology. By drawing on Bonaventure's fusion of the neo-Platonic light metaphor with the notion of being, Braig argues that the question of "the condition of the possibility of knowledge," if properly put, leads, not to Kant's transcendental subjective synthesis, but to *ipsum esse*.[29] Everything depends upon putting the question properly. Kant's problematic, which suspends all metaphysical and ontological judgments until first achieving a proper understanding of the rules by which reason operates, will never arrive at being in Braig's view, for being is not a "category," which could be deduced a priori. Being is hidden by beings, but it first shows its hiddenness in beings. Without an ontological datum, we would have no clue to being. Being is always the being of a being, *das Sein des Seienden*, an expression that occurs more than once in Braig's work, as John Caputo has pointed out.[30] Nevertheless, the nonempirical nature of being calls

---

26. Ibid.
27. Cf. Augustinus Karl Wucherer-Huldenfeld, "Zu Heideggers Verständnis des Seins bei Johannes Duns Scotus und im Skotismus sowie im Thomismus und bei Thomas von Aquin," in *Heidegger und das Mittelalter*, ed. Helmuth Vetter (Frankfurt am Main: Peter Lang, 1999), 41–59.
28. Braig, *Vom Sein*, 23.
29. Schaeffler, *Frömmigkeit des Denkens*, 7.
30. Caputo, *Heidegger and Aquinas*, 54. See Braig, *Vom Sein*, 8: "There is no speculative,

for a quasi-transcendental turn in ontology. Ontological knowledge is not a cognition of a being but the thematization of a presupposed immaterial intellectual principle. Braig speaks of "the law of thinking" which parallels "the law of being": the principles that determine the being of every being are not "positively" given in experience and passively received by the intellect; they are principles of thinking itself, the "crucial objective, logical and ontological concepts," which lie a priori in "the wealth of our self-knowledge."[31] The human being is turned toward being in its being and by this directedness makes possible an understanding of beings.[32] Hence a *transcendental-ontological* analysis of thinking—a transcendental analysis that does not abstract itself from the beings that it thinks and knows—is not only legitimate but necessary in ontology.

Without exaggerating the connection between Braig's and Heidegger's ontology, there is a relationship here that has yet to be explored in the literature. Heidegger retains Braig's model of being as non-ontic condition of the possibility of understanding beings, and the human being as the locus of this understanding of beings, while inverting Braig's theistic assumption that the being- and knowledge-enabling condition is eternal, simple, and divine. For Heidegger, rather, the condition is ecstatic horizonal temporality. The pattern of the early Heidegger's ontology, from the ontic to the ontological through transcendental analysis of the being that we are, is also prefigured in Braig's speculative Scholasticism.[33] The human intellect is the light of beings, not only in individual acts of knowing, but in its very being, for it makes possible every ontological determination. For both Heidegger and Braig, being must appear as nothing to the ontically oriented intellect. Yet being is not a privation or a negation, but the reverse. The "nothing" is the positive ground of every negation, the veil through which being simultaneously shows and conceals

---

absolute, intuitive, simply presuppositionless metaphysics, which could disregard experience and read philosophical knowledge off of 'empty' thinking, determining it out of 'pure' thinking, or producing it through 'creative' thinking—there is no scientific ground for such a metaphysics."

31. Leidlmair, "Braig," 412.

32. Carl Braig, *Vom Denken. Abriß der Logik* (Freiburg: Herder, 1896), 9; idem, *Vom Erkennen. Abriß der Noetic* (Freiburg: Herder, 1897), 156.

33. The following remark from Caputo seems doubtful in this light: "The idea of Being as a horizon of meaning projected by Dasein's understanding, within which beings are set free to appear as beings, is totally foreign to Braig." *Heidegger and Aquinas*, 50–51.

itself. Both Braig and Heidegger emphasize the importance of a contextual analysis of the ontic as the key to disengaging the meaning of being. More directly, Heidegger learned the hermeneutical approach to the history of philosophy from Braig. Braig's creative synthesis of Scholasticism emphasized accessing genuine problems through history and therefore studying history as a history of problems: "Let us not only study the philosophy *of* St. Thomas; let us also study philosophy *as* St. Thomas does," Braig wrote in reply to his neo-Scholastic critics.[34] Braig's daring example of Scholasticism fused with German idealism influenced Heidegger's method in the *Habilitationsschrift*: to foreground the reading of Scotus in the light of contemporary philosophical research (Rickert and Husserl).

During his formative years studying under Braig, Heidegger was busy writing. His early publications appeared in *Der Akademiker*, a right-wing, student-run journal, which advertised itself as "the voice that proclaims our high Christian ideals in all areas of student life."[35] *Der Akademiker* was opposed to early-twentieth-century efforts to introduce historical consciousness, historical-critical biblical scholarship, and theories of evolution into Catholic dogma. The student Heidegger showed himself to be a zealous proponent of this ultraconservative Catholicism. His first publication was a review of the autobiography of Danish writer Johannes Jörgensen, *Lebenslüge und Lebenswahrheit*, an account of a conversion from Darwinism to Catholicism. Heidegger lauds the author's personal triumph over modernity. By recovering a sense for the "transcendental value of life" *(Jenseitswert des Lebens)*, Jörgensen freed himself from what Heidegger describes as the illusion that self-will can bring "the 'I' to unlimited development."[36] In his second publication, a review of Friedrich Wilhelm Förster's *Autorität und Freiheit*, Heidegger defends the Church's "eternal store of truth" and "the ancient wisdom of the Christian tradition" against "the destructive forces of modernism."[37]

---

34. Carl Braig, "Eine Frage," *Philosophisches Jahrbuch des Görresgesellschaft* 12 (1899): 59–65; quoted in Caputo, *Heidegger and Aquinas*, 48.

35. From an editorial in *Der Akademiker*, quoted in Ott, *Biographie*, 63/59–60. The *Der Akademiker* writings have been republished in GA16.

36. Heidegger, "*Per mortem ad vitam* (Gedanken über Jörgensens Lebenslüge und Lebenswahrheit)," *Der Akademiker* 2 (March 1910), quoted in Safranski, *Meister aus Deutschland*, 36/20–21.

37. Heidegger, "Friedrich Willhelm Förster. *Autorität und Freiheit*," *Der Akademiker* 2 (May 1910), quoted in Ott, *Biographie*, 63/60.

"The false appearances of the modern spirit," seduce people into "paths of error." Heidegger attacks the narcissistic indulgence in "experiences" *(Erlebnisse)*, ideologies that reflect only "personal moods," and "the spirit of unlimited autonomism" that shirks the call of an infallible "religious-moral authority." He waxes eloquent about "the radiant light of truth," "the felicity that comes with the possession of the truth" *(Glück des Wahrheitsbesitzes)*, that is, the joy of being Catholic.[38] Heidegger's thinking at this time was unabashedly neo-Scholastic; the problems of modernity arose because modern philosophy had turned away from the sound principles of the "perennial philosophy" of the Middle Ages. Philosophy is not a subjective lens through which one views the world, a *Weltanschauung* freely chosen from among competing alternatives, but "a mirror of eternity." Modern "anti-intellectualism" has so overstressed "inner experience" *(Erlebnis)* that it forgets the ontological ground of thinking, turning philosophy into "impressionism." In "Zur philosophischen Orientierung für Akademiker," Heidegger offers guidance to philosophy students confused by "the maze of modern philosophies," recommending a book by the Aristotelian Scholastic Josef Geyser (the same Scholastic who will be chosen over Heidegger for the Freiburg Chair in Christian Philosophy in 1916), *Grundlegung der Logik und Erkenntnistheorie in positiver und kritischer Darstellung*.[39] To be a philosopher requires "ethical strength," "the art of self-composure and self-expression" *(Kunst der Selbsterfahrung und Selbstäußerung)*, to repudiate the relativism and individualism of the age.[40]

Some commentators see clear harbingers of Heidegger's path in these student writings. According to Casper, Heidegger was a practitioner of the piety of thinking already as a student: "As a relentless questioning of the ground, philosophical concern becomes [for the young Heidegger]

---

38. Heidegger, "Friedrich Willhelm Förster," quoted in Safranski, *Meister aus Deutschland*, 21/37.

39. Heidegger, "Zur philosophischen Orientierung für Akademiker," *Der Akademiker* 3 (March 1911), quoted in Ott, *Biographie*, 65/63. See Joseph Geyser, *Grundlegung der Logik und Erkenntnistheorie in positiver und kritischer Darstellung* (Münster: Schöningh, 1919); Ott, *Biographie*, 91–96/91–96.

40. Heidegger, "Orientierung," quoted in Safranski, *Meister aus Deutschland*, 66/48; Ott, *Biographie*, 65/62.

itself a religious act."⁴¹ Casper points to the 1910 Förster review where Heidegger speaks of a human "desire . . . for the end, a final answer to the question about Being" (*GA*16 11).⁴² It is unnecessary to overstate the importance of these early writings. Heidegger had not yet found his path of thinking. Nonetheless, two important Heideggerian themes emerge from the seminary days: the fallacy of subjectivism and the primacy of ontology. The student polemic with modern "individualism" and "relativism" foreshadows Heidegger's later polemic with Cartesian subjectivism. The young theology student was committed to "objectivity," a conviction that made Husserl's project of philosophy as *strenge Wissenschaft* instantly attractive to him. Secondly, the student writings show us how, already at this tender age, Heidegger, clearly under the influence of Braig, stresses the primacy of ontology. Rather than following the neo-Kantian trend toward epistemology, the student Heidegger argues that ontology precedes epistemology. However alluring modern subjectivism may be, it cannot satisfy the intellect, which yearns for being. "And as they flit to and fro, sampling different philosophies like so many delicacies, turning it into a kind of game, there wells up within them, for all their conscious awareness and self-satisfaction, an unconscious desire for clear-cut, definitive answers to the ultimate questions of Being, which flash upon them from time to time with such suddenness, only to lie unresolved for days on their tormented souls, which are without purpose or direction."⁴³ Philosophical problems could not be adequately addressed without first raising the most fundamental questions, and these, *pace* Descartes, Kant, and Husserl, were not the methodological and epistemological questions of modernity. They were metaphysical questions: What is the real? What is the un-real? How do we distinguish them? "Philosophy cannot avoid in the long run its proper optics, metaphysics," Heidegger writes in the 1916 *Schlusskapitel* to the *Habilitationsschrift* (*GA*1 406). When he burst on the phenomenological scene in 1919, Heidegger was coming from a different place than Rickert or Husserl, something that became rapidly appar-

---

41. Casper, "Das theologisch-scholastische Umfeld," 13.
42. Friedrich Willhelm Förster, *Autorität und Freiheit. Betrachtungen zum Kulturproblem der Kirche* (Kempten/Munich, 1910).
43. Heidegger, "Orientierung," quoted in Ott, *Biographie*, 65/62.

ent to his students. He was concerned, not with the problem of certainty, or the unity of knowledge, but more fundamentally, with the nature of reality, the foundations of existence, and the meaning of being and non-being. As Hanah Arendt put it, this "gale" blowing through philosophy was "not of our century," but "from the ancient."[44]

Scholastic Phenomenology

In February of 1911, Heidegger was forced to break off his seminary studies when a medical examination revealed heart trouble. Apparently he had overworked himself. He spent the summer semester of 1911 convalescing in Meßkirch. On the advice of his superiors, who believed he did not have a strong enough constitution for service in the Church, he abandoned the study of theology.[45] The years that followed brought an extreme change in Heidegger's religious convictions. Where the student writings reek of Catholic triumphalism, after 1916, Catholicism is the target of scathing critiques, even ridicule. Yet for a moment, in his 1915 *Habilitationsschrift*, Heidegger struck a precarious balance between appropriating his tradition and pioneering phenomenological research.

Heidegger's first two academic publications were "Das Realitätsproblem in der modernen Philosophie" and "Neuere Forschungen über Logik" (both published in 1912). They both appeared in Catholic journals, although they are strictly philosophical treatments of problems in epistemology and logic.[46] From Heidegger's correspondence, we know that he had hoped they would catch the attention of the Catholic philosophical community.[47] In 1913, Heidegger wrote his dissertation in philosophy, *Die Lehre vom Urteil im Psychologismus. Ein kritisch-positiver Beitrag zur Logik* (GA1 59–188), on a problem central to the early Husserl: psycholo-

---

44. Hannah Arendt, quoted in Safranski, *Meister aus Deutschland*, 11/xxi.
45. Ott holds this to be another reason for Heidegger's later grudge against the Church. The 1911 interruption of the seminary studies, the subsequent turn-down from the Jesuits, and the 1916 failure to get the chair of Christian Philosophy at Freiburg amount to three rejections Heidegger received from the Catholic Church. See Ott, *Biographie*, 67–72, 96/64–69, 95.
46. These appeared respectively in *Philosophisches Jahrbuch der Görresgesellschaft* 25 (1912): 3–53, 363, and *Literarische Rundschau für das katholische Deutschland* 38 (1912), no. 10: 465–72, no. 11: 517–24, and no. 12: 565–70. They are reprinted in GA1 17–43.
47. Ott, *Biographie*, 75/73.

gism. The reduction of logic to psychophysical events was a target common to neo-Scholastics and phenomenologists, for it amounted to a denial of the possibility of philosophical science. If the forms of meaning refer to nothing more than chemical interactions in the brain, philosophy, the systematic study of meaning, ought to be replaced by materialist psychology. Heidegger's dissertation reviewed the prevalent theories of psychologism and formulated a refutation based on the work of Emil Lask and Husserl. These early publications are marked by an inclination toward Aristotelian-Scholastic realism. In his 1915 grant application to "The Constantin and Olga von Schaezler Foundation in Honour of St. Thomas Aquinas," Heidegger made his Scholastic commitment explicit, dedicating himself to "the task of harnessing the intellectual and spiritual potential of Scholasticism to the future struggle for the Christian-Catholic ideal."[48] Although the statement must be read in context—the award was contingent upon the grantees' adherence to the principles of Thomistic philosophy—it does accurately summarize the professional thrust of Heidegger's graduate studies. Heidegger marketed himself as a Catholic philosopher.

The Catholic circles to which Heidegger sought entrance were conservative, yet his work on Scholasticism was unconventional. Heidegger sought to integrate neo-Kantianism and phenomenology into Scholasticism. He had learned much from Rickert, in particular, the understanding of philosophical problems *as* problems, not historical curiosities.[49] In his 1914 review of Charles Sentroul's *Kant und Aristoteles*, Heidegger argued that the transcendental attitude is lacking in Aristotelian-Scholastic philosophy, which has much to learn in this regard from Kant (*GA*1 49–54).[50] Heidegger was looking for an account of the being of subjectivity to supplement Aristotelian-Scholastic substance metaphysics.[51] The opening chapter of the *Habilitationsschrift* contains several interesting methodological remarks that foreshadow Heidegger's later "destroy and retrieve" approach to traditional texts. Even at this early stage, Heidegger's interpre-

---

48. Heidegger, quoted in Ott, *Biographie*, 91/90.
49. Van Buren, *Young Heidegger*, 59.
50. Originally published in *Literarische Rundschau für das katholische Deutschland* 40, no. 7 (1914): 330–32.
51. Caputo, *Heidegger and Aquinas*, 30.

tative methods were so *Sache* oriented, so overtly occupied by the problems themselves and oblivious to text critical issues, that the achievement of the *Habilitationsschrift* is in no way undermined by Martin Grabmann's later discovery that Thomas of Erfurt authored the *Grammatica speculativa*, a work which Heidegger attributed to Duns Scotus and on which he commented extensively. Although many years will pass before Heidegger formulates his principles of "violent" interpretation, his first major work in philosophy is spontaneously, one might even say intuitively, governed by a hermeneutics that cuts itself loose from the author and the historical situation and heeds only the subject matter. Heidegger's reading is not restricted by historical context or historical-critical problems, but neither is it free-floating or willful. He painstakingly examines certain moments of phenomenological insight intrinsic to the Scholastic mind (GA1 202). The medieval attempt to discern the roots of metaphysics in the grammatical structures of ordinary language is interpreted as a prototype of Husserl's search for an "a priori pure grammar," a transcendental logic of intentions (GA1 328). Scotus—and Thomas of Erfurt—disclose semantic layers not accessed through Aristotle's ten categories, indications of what Heidegger will later call the "fore-theoretical," or "primordial understanding." The subject matter of Scholastic speculative grammar and early phenomenology is assumed to be the same phenomenon showing itself differently in history.

Ott has unearthed Heidegger's 1915 résumé, a requirement of the habilitation procedure. Heidegger intended the *Habilitationsschrift* as a first step in an ambitious rehabilitation of the Middle Ages. It was to be an exposure of the phenomenological significance of Scotus's metaphysics and what we now know to be Thomas of Erfurt's speculative grammar. The *Habilitationsschrift* was the first step in the young Heidegger's plan for a "synthesis of Scholasticism," his "life's work," an "interpretive" overview of "medieval logic and psychology in the light of modern phenomenology."[52] Through analysis of the historical significance of individual Scholastics, Heidegger intended to lead the way to a contemporary appraisal of medieval philosophy, proving its enduring value and relevance. The young Heidegger set out upon this ambitious course with characteris-

---

52. See Heidegger's 1915 curriculum vitae, reprinted in Ott, *Biographie*, 86–87/85–86.

tic daring in 1915–16, only to abandon Scholasticism in 1919 for seemingly more promising phenomenological sources. In the year following the *Habilitationsschrift*, Heidegger began teaching at the University of Freiburg as a *Privatdozent* with his first university lecture course, "Die Grundlinien der antiken und scholastischen Philosophie."[53] Regardless of his growing closeness with Edmund Husserl, others still saw him, positively or negatively, as primarily a Catholic philosopher.[54]

Heidegger's first mature philosophical work *Die Kategorien- und Bedeutungslehre des Duns Scotus* (1915–16) is an oddity: a seldom read, meticulous exegesis of a text in Scholastic logic, the *Grammatica speculativa* (of Thomas of Erfurt). Most scholars see an unbridgeable chasm separating the neo-Scholastic phenomenology of the *Habilitationsschrift* from the hermeneutics of facticity of *Sein und Zeit*. As Kisiel put it, "The gap between 1915–1916 and 1927 has always been too broad for interpreters to leap, itself indicative of how much and how rapidly Heidegger modified and deepened his orientation over the intervening years."[55] The *Habilitationsschrift* introduces us to a Heidegger at home in the Middle Ages, discovering in its labyrinthine metaphysics rich disclosures of historical life and prefigurations of phenomenological concepts. To the text submitted for habilitation to the Department of Philosophy at the University of Freiburg in 1915, Heidegger added a crucial concluding chapter when he published it in 1916, supplementing the drier exegetical treatment of Thomas of Erfurt's work with a fascinating speculative synthesis, which I will examine in some detail in the following chapter.

In a solid piece of interpretation, Philippe Capelle draws attention to the heterogeneity of Heidegger's theological sources, a heterogeneity often overlooked by commentators who characterize Heidegger's origins as "staunchly Catholic."[56] Between the years 1910 and 1914, when he was a student at Freiburg university, Heidegger tells us he read Nietzsche, Dos-

---

53. All that survives of this course is a few notes at the Deutsches Literaturarchiv in Marbach. See Kisiel, *Genesis of Being and Time*, 552 n. 3.

54. Ott recounts how in 1917, Paul Natorp rejected Heidegger's application for a full-time position because of Heidegger's "confessional allegiances." Ott, *Biographie*, 97–98/96–97.

55. Kisiel, *Genesis of Being and Time*, 25.

56. Philippe Capelle, "'Katholizismus,' 'Protestantismus,' 'Christentum' und 'Religion' im Denken Martin Heideggers. Tragweite und Abgrenzungen," in Denker, Gander, and Zaborowski, *Heidegger Jahrbuch*, 1:346–70, at 347.

toevsky, Kierkegaard, Rilke, Trakl, and Dilthey (*GA1* 406). Capelle sees this eclectic reading list—hardly devotional reading for a seminarian—as a first indication of Heidegger's coming religious difficulties.[57] This may be true. Such a reading list, however, would not have been so unusual for a student of Carl Braig, a theologian who regarded the encounter with modernity as the most important task for contemporary Christian philosophy. In any case, the reading list certainly indicates Heidegger's early interest in what would come to be known as "existentialism" and, along with the friendship with Karl Jaspers, the proximate sources for the existential thrust of *Sein und Zeit*. Capelle also sees Hegel as a major dialogue partner for the young Heidegger.[58] This claim has some textual evidence in its support, particularly the *Schlusskapitel* of the *Habilitationsschrift* (discussed at length in chapter 5 below). It is certainly the case that the problem of history, the question of historical knowledge—not only how we come to know history, but also how we come to know anything in history—was at the center of Heidegger's philosophical preoccupations in the years leading up to the *Habilitationsschrift*. His break with Catholicism in 1919 was precipitated by issues in the philosophy of history. Early-twentieth-century neo-Scholasticism, with which Heidegger was entangled for academic, cultural, and not the least, financial reasons, resisted the modern turn to "historicism" and advanced, as an alternative, an ecclesiastically approved a-historical system of philosophy, a *philosophia perennis*.[59] This theological system reinscribed the Platonic exclusion of the historical from the realm of the intelligible. In this light, Heidegger's decision to examine Scotus's notion of *haecceitas*, the "formality" of historical being, in his *Habilitationsschrift* lends credence to Capelle's view that already in this ostensibly Catholic work, Heidegger is thrashing against the bars of the cage.

Radical Protestantism

Heidegger's relationship to "organized religion" came to an end in 1919 when he unofficially broke with the Catholic Church in a now famous

---

57. Ibid., 351.
58. Ibid., 352–53.
59. See Casper, "Das theologisch-scholastische Umfeld," 17.

letter to his close friend, the priest and Freiburg theologian Engelbert Krebs.[60] He had spent the previous two years seeking a "fundamental clarification of his philosophical position," and for that reason, had laid aside "all other scientific projects." These were Heidegger's lost years, the period Kisiel calls "the interregnum," 1917–19, years in which Heidegger divided his time between army service and teaching at the University of Freiburg. The result of Heidegger's soul-searching made it impossible for him to maintain any "extra-philosophical allegiances"—his previous religious beliefs infringed on the "freedom of his inquiry." His research had annulled his faith in Roman Catholicism: "Epistemological insights reaching to the theory of historical knowledge have made the system of Catholicism problematic and unacceptable to me." The "Catholic system" was incompatible with Heidegger's philosophical position, but he did not reject "Christianity or metaphysics," the value of "the Catholic Middle Ages," or the "Catholic life-world." Rather, he understands these "in a new sense." We can fill in the gaps in this letter through reference to Heidegger's thinking at this time on the nature of theology. The Church's sense of a secure possession of the unchanging truth obstructs a historically minded theory of knowledge. Heidegger now regards Christianity from a radically Protestant perspective (*GA60* 312–13). Metaphysics is to be interpreted through "the hermeneutics of facticity," "the genuine, explicit actualization of the tendency toward interpretation that belongs to life's own basic movements (movements within which life is concerned about itself and its own Being)" (*PIA* 246). Theology may contain formal indications of life, but it tends toward concealing the factic by interpreting it through revelation.

The young Heidegger's characterization of Catholicism as an a-historical, pseudo-philosophical system must be situated: Heidegger is reacting to the anti-hermeneutical Catholicism of the Modernist crisis, a regimented, propositional Catholicism, which declared anything that appeared to contradict the dogmatic tradition "anathema." Pope Pius X's 1907 "Oath Against Modernism," which required Catholic professors to repudiate mediations of theology with modernity, was particularly dif-

---

60. The text of this letter of January 9, 1919, is reprinted in Denker, Gander, and Zaborowski, *Heidegger Jahrbuch*, 1:67–68. An English version can be found in Ott, *Biographie*, 106–7/106.

ficult for a young philosopher on the verge of "discovering" the historicity of being. Inspired by Dilthey's analysis of the historical consciousness of primal Christianity, Heidegger undertook investigations in Protestant theology, notably, Luther, Kierkegaard, and Schleiermacher, which bore fruit in his explicitly anti-Scholastic lectures on Paul and Augustine of 1920/21. He interpreted the Reformation as an effort to retrieve the facticity of early Christianity through a dismantling of the theoretical system of medieval Catholicism. Scholasticism smothered the historical self that comes to acute expression in the New Testament and the early Fathers with an illegitimate synthesis of Greek science and Christianity. In his 1920 lecture "Phänomenologie der Anschauung und des Ausdrucks," Heidegger called for "a fundamental analysis of Greek philosophy and the disfigurement of Christian existence through it" in order to secure "the true idea of Christian philosophy," which he characterizes as "primordially Christian" and "un-Greek" (*GA*59 91).

Ott's archival work proves that Heidegger's change of view, though not without philosophical motives, was accompanied by a personal religious crisis.[61] On the 23rd of December 1918, Elfride Heidegger, expecting her firstborn, told Krebs that they would not baptize the child, as promised at their Catholic wedding (over which Krebs had presided), because Heidegger had "lost his institutional faith" *(kirchlichen Glauben).*[62] Although she and her husband remained "Christian," they could no longer keep their commitment to raise the child Catholic: "We have both ended up thinking along Protestant lines, i.e., with no fixed dogmatic ties, believing in a personal God, praying to him in the spirit of Christ, but outside any Protestant or Catholic orthodoxy."[63] In 1921, the new religious outlook manifested itself in Heidegger's notion of the atheism of philosophy. That same year he described himself to Karl Löwith as "a Christian theologian." Heidegger believed himself to be "thrown" into a theological context, just as metaphysics was historically entwined with theology. The

---

61. Kisiel also believes that Heidegger's turn to Protestant sources was precipitated by a personal religious struggle. See *Genesis of Being and Time*, 15. Husserl says that Heidegger had undergone a religious conversion in a letter to Rudolf Otto of 5 March 1919, quoted in Ott, *Biographie*, 116/118.
62. The children were eventually baptized.
63. Entry in Krebs's diary, 1918, quoted in Ott, *Biographie*, 108/109.

task of extricating himself and philosophy from Christian theology was his destiny.

Heidegger was given a job at Marburg University in 1923. It came as no surprise to those who knew him that the former seminarian would fit in well in this stronghold of Protestantism. Here at last, no longer under the scrutiny of a close-knit Catholic community, Heidegger could give free reign to his theological interests, going so far as to participate in Rudolph Bultmann's New Testament seminars.[64] In his discussions with the Marburg theologians, he repeatedly refers to Franz Overbeck's notion of *Christianness,* especially Overbeck's argument that the Christian notion of *eschaton* breaks with the Greek understanding of time. The Christian Last Judgment is not an event toward which we move, but something that breaks into our present at every point. As such, it is a formal indication of primal temporality. Overbeck holds that early Christianity neither formulated a theology nor required one; Christianity announced the immanent end of the world. The construction of a theology was a sign of Christianity's decay, a compromise with a world in which it did not believe. As Christianity lost its apocalyptic edge and sought to accommodate itself to the world in the first century, Christian theology emerged, a process of decay already at work in Paul. "Christianity equipped itself with a theology only when it wanted to make itself possible in a world which it, as a matter of fact, rejected."[65] In its essence,

---

64. Heidegger's contributions to Bultmann's seminar can be seen at the Bultmann Archiv in Tübingen. Hermann Mörchen summarizes their contents in *Adorno und Heidegger* (Stuttgart, Klett-Cotta: 1981). See Kisiel, *Genesis of* Being and Time, 557. The mutual exchange between Bultmann and Heidegger is well documented. Distinguishing the early Christian sense of moral impotence from the self-sufficiency idealized in Greek philosophy *(volle Selbstverfügung),* Bultmann brings Heidegger's authentic/inauthentic dialectic into conversation with the New Testament. See Eberhard M. Pausch, *Wahrheit zwischen Erschlossenheit und Verantwortung. Die Rezeption und Transformation der Wahrheitskonzeption Martin Heideggers in der Theologie Rudolf Bultmanns* (Berlin: Walter de Gruyter, 1995); Michael E. Zimmerman, "Heidegger and Bultmann: Egoism, Sinfulness, and Inauthenticity," *Modern Schoolman* 58 (1980): 1–20; Hans Georg Gadamer, "Die Marburger Theologie," in Gadamer, *Gesammelte Werke,* vol. 3 (Tübingen: Mohr, 1987), 197–212; English: *Heidegger's Ways,* trans. John W. Stanley (Albany: State University of New York Press, 1994), 29–43; John Macquarrie, *An Existentialist Theology: A Comparison of Heidegger and Bultmann* (London: SCM Press, 1955).

65. Franz Overbeck, *Über die Christlichkeit unserer heutigen Theologie* (Darmstadt: Wissenschaftliche Buchgesellschaft, 1989), 33. See István M. Fehér, "Heidegger's Understanding of the Atheism of Philosophy: Philosophy, Theology, and Religion in His Early Lecture Courses up to *Being and Time,*" *American Catholic Philosophical Quarterly* 69 (1995): 204.

Christianity is untheological, nonscientific, and the enemy of culture.[66]

From scattered notes, we know that Heidegger was immersed in the study of Luther in 1919.[67] While Kisiel dates Heidegger's Luther reading to this date, Otto Pöggeler recalls a conversation with Heidegger in which Heidegger spoke of reading Luther as early as 1909, as a Catholic theology student.[68] Heidegger was attracted by two Lutheran doctrines: the theology of the Cross, and the Lutheran notion of faith as trusting in a promise. Both drive Christianity away from the timeless metaphysics of Scholasticism back to historical life. The theology of the Cross spurns philosophical speculation in theology as a strategy for avoiding the uncertainty and insecurity of discipleship to the crucified God. Faith as trust in a promise rejects the Scholastic formula of "holding for true" and anchors discipleship in the day-to-day struggle with despair and unbelief. On the basis of a close reading of Heidegger's scattered references to Luther, van Buren concludes that "Heidegger's very term *Destruktion* and its sense came not only from Kant's notion of 'critique,' but more so from Luther's 1518 *Heidelberg Disputation*."[69]

In 1923, Heidegger referred to Luther as "a companion in searching" (*GA63* 4/4). The word "companion" is well chosen. Heidegger never critically engages Luther's theology but finds in it a model for his own reformation of metaphysics. Just as Christian faith eludes canonical control, life eludes speculative philosophy. The only way to understand Lutheran faith is to live it; the only way to understand Heidegger's phenomenology is to enact it. By illegitimately fusing faith and knowledge, Catholicism speculatively appropriates and so neutralizes Christianity. Trusting in a promise calls for no metaphysical support structure; rather, it challenges the unbelief implicit in philosophy's presumption of access to eternal knowledge. Heidegger admires the way Luther stays with the factic. His reading of Luther precipitated a revolution in his thinking. From specu-

---

66. Overbeck, *Christlichkeit*, 33: "In the oldest Christian Alexandrianism we see as clearly as possible that theology directed its look absolutely somewhere else—that Christianity, with its own theology, wanted to offer itself also to the wise men of the world and wanted to be noticed by them. Looked at in such a way, theology is nothing else than part of the secularization of Christianity—some luxury which Christianity could afford, but which, as all luxury, is not indispensable."

67. See *GA60* 308, 309, 310.

68. See Pöggeler, "Heidegger's Luther-Lektüre," 185.

69. Van Buren, *Young Heidegger*, 167.

lation about "the true worldview" in the *Habilitationsschrift*, we are suddenly thrust into "primal science," which has no recourse to eternal truth. From the philosophical theology of the neo-Scholastics, we are plunged into a hermeneutics of facticity, which cannot speak of God—neither in denial nor in affirmation.

In the 1917 note, "Das religiöse Apriori," Heidegger takes up Luther's cause and lambastes Catholicism as a "dogmatic and casuistic pseudo-philosophy, which poses as a particular system of religion," a system that "totally excludes an original and genuine religious experience of value" (*GA*60 313). In the 1919 letter to Krebs, Heidegger is restrained and deferential to his former spiritual mentor. In his notes on medieval mysticism, he holds no punches, letting fly the fullness of his objection to the religion of his youth: "[Catholicism is] a tangled, non-organic, dogmatic hedgerow of propositions and proofs that are theoretically wholly unclarified; as canonical statutes with police power, they overwhelm and oppress the subject and encumber it in darkness." No longer a source for phenomenology, Scholasticism is now regarded as a principal player in the forgetting of the factic. "Within the totality of the medieval Christian life-world Scholasticism severely jeopardized the immediacy of religious life and forgot religion for theology and dogma" (*GA*60 314/238).

Luther was not the first Protestant theologian to win Heidegger's serious scholarly attention. Heidegger read Friedrich Schleiermacher, the father of modern Protestantism, between 1917 and 1918.[70] Schleiermacher's emphasis on "life" and "feeling," which can never be theoretically conceptualized, resonated with Heidegger's interest in facticity and the foretheoretical. On August 2, 1917, he gave a talk to a group of friends on Schleiermacher's *Über die Religion: Reden an die Gebildeten unter ihren Verächtern*. One of the attendees, Heinrich Ochsner, wrote: "the impression it made on me still lingers through the whole week."[71] In 1919, Heidegger argued that Schleiermacher "discovered primal Christianity" (*GA*56/57 134). Heidegger was drawn by Schleiermacher's distinction between religion and speculative thought. Religion is not a body of meta-

---

70. *GA*60 319–22; 330–32. On Heidegger's early reading of Schleiermacher, see Kisiel, *Genesis of Being and Time*, 89–93.

71. Quoted in van Buren, *Young Heidegger*, 147.

physical truths, nor a system of ethical principles, but unobjectifiable feeling: intuition *(Anschauung)* in the early Schleiermacher, feeling *(Gefühl)* in the later.[72] With an opposition to the speculative appropriation of Christianity equal to Luther's, Schleiermacher calls for a return to foretheoretical religious experience, "the taste and feeling for the infinite." Christianity is not a thought-system but a way of being; it becomes a parody of itself when it presumes to be science. In a 1917 note, Heidegger cites with approval Schleiermacher's call to purify Christianity of alien conceptual structures in order to free up its "primordial" and "proper content." He adds the comment: "God in the world of theory [*Sphäre des Wissens*], posited as the ground of knowledge and the knower, is not the same as the God known and accessed in piety" (GA60 320/243). The essence of religion according to Schleiermacher, Heidegger cites, is located in the "inmost sanctuary [*Heiligtum*] of life" (GA60 321). Heidegger returned to this theme in a 1919 note bearing the title "Glauben und Wissen," drawing a Schleiermacherian distinction between theology and religiosity. The former is a theoretical construct; the latter is the foretheoretical life of faith (GA60 310).

Schleiermacher's effort to defend religion from its "cultured despisers" by demarcating the sphere of experience proper to it highlights a foretheoretical intelligibility intrinsic to historical life. Schleiermacher's phenomenology of primal feeling aims at an interpretation of life without distortion or objectification. Heidegger cites the following passage from *Über die Religion:* "But I must direct you to your own selves. You must apprehend a living movement. You must know how to listen to yourselves in advance of your own consciousness or at least reproduce this state for yourselves from it. What you are to notice is the very becoming of your consciousness and not to reflect on a consciousness which has already become."[73] The romantic agenda of "listening in on life" has more than a family resemblance to Heidegger's phenomenological "actualization of the tendency toward interpretation that belongs to life's own basic move-

---

72. Friedrich Schleiermacher, *Kritische Gesamtausgabe,* ed. Günter Meckenstock, vol. 12, part 1, *Über die Religion: Reden an die Gebildeten unter ihren Verächtern,* 3rd and 4th ed. (Berlin: Walter de Gruyter, 1995), 51; English: *On Religion: Speeches to its Cultured Despisers,* trans. John Oman, 3rd ed. (London: Routledge & Kegan Paul, 1958), 35.

73. Schleiermacher, *Über die Religion,* 59/41. Cited by Heidegger, GA60 321.

ments" (*PIA* 246). The notes Heidegger took on Schleiermacher give us important clues to what he was looking for in Protestantism: not a new religious outlook for himself, but indications of facticity.

Schleiermacher's notion that religion is manifest in an infinite variety of historical religions reverses the Platonic privileging of the timeless over the historical: history discloses truths that cannot be accessed in any other way. Heidegger paraphrases Schleiermacher: "The highest object of religion is history in the authentic sense: religion begins and ends in history" (*GA*60 322).[74] *Pace* Hegel, religion cannot be understood as a speculative content. It can only be grasped by being lived. Religious life revolves around concrete enactments of meaning in history, the symbols and myths by which a religious community articulates for itself a particular and unrepeatable experience of the infinite. With its concern for expressing lived experience, Schleiermacher's romantic notion of religion presented Heidegger with a theological analogy for the hermeneutics of facticity.

While we have ample textual evidence to corroborate the influence of Schleiermacher and Luther on the young Heidegger, the influence of Kierkegaard is less textually evident. There are the three footnotes in *Sein und Zeit* referencing Kierkegaard. Heidegger acknowledges Kierkegaard's analysis of angst (*SZ* 190 n. 4/405) and his grasp of the problems of existence (*SZ* 235 n. 6/407) and of the moment (*SZ* 338 n. 3/412–13). For all that, however, Kierkegaard ostensibly remains on the level of the ontic and the existentiell (no doubt because of his religious concerns). His thinking on the moment is stuck in the vulgar concept of time, defining the moment in reference to eternity. There exists an analogy between Heidegger's method of formal indication and Kierkegaard's notion of indirect communication, something Heidegger acknowledges in

---

74. The reference is to Schleiermacher's *Über die Religion*. The full passage reads: "But there is not merely the swinging of feeling between the world and the individual in the present moment. Except as something going on, we cannot comprehend what affects us, and we cannot comprehend ourselves, except as thus progressively affected. Wherefore, as feeling persons, we are ever driven back into the past. The spirit furnishes the chief nourishment for our piety, and history immediately and especially is the richest source for religion. History is not of value for religion because it hastens or controls in any way the progress of humanity in its development, but because it is the greatest and most general revelation of the deepest and holiest. In this sense, however, religion begins and ends with history. Prophecy and history are for religion the same and indistinguishable, and all true history has at first had a religious purpose and has taken its departure from religious ideas." Schleiermacher, *Über die Religion*, 103/79–80.

his 1919 review of Jasper's *Psychologie der Weltanschauungen*.[75] Here Heidegger sees Kierkegaard's major contribution as one of methodology: "It must indeed be pointed out that it is not often in philosophy or theology... [that] such a height of rigorous consciousness of method has been achieved" (*GA9* 36).[76] These few references conceal a greater debt to Kierkegaard than Heidegger was willing to acknowledge. The convergence of themes in Kierkegaard and Heidegger is too striking to be coincidental. Not only angst, the moment, and *Existenz*, but the crucial distinction between content and relational sense, the notion of an oblique approach to life, and the effort to think time in an existential sense have clear prefigurations in Kierkegaard.[77]

In *The Philosophical Fragments*, under the pseudonym Johannes Climacus, Kierkegaard explores how history cannot exist for the Greek because no moment has decisive significance within a paradigm of recollection. The experience of truth is a return to what we always already knew; thus the moment of its discovery disappears in eternity. For the Christian, by contrast, the experience of truth is an experience of conversion, a discovery that we are in untruth, and a rebirth into a new relationship to truth. In the discovery, the paradoxical reality of time comes into view: "A moment such as this is unique. To be sure, it is short and temporal, as the moment is; it is passing, as the moment is, past, as the moment is in the next moment, and yet it is decisive, and yet it is filled with the eternal. A moment such as this must have a special name. Let us call it: *the fullness of time*."[78] In the *Concluding Unscientific Postscript*, what Heidegger calls the distinction between content sense and relational sense emerges under the rubric "objective truth" and "subjective truth." These terms do not refer to different content—they do not name *whatness*—but to different ways of being related to truth. The accent falls on the *how*. Objective truth is the truth in which I have no existential interest, the

---

75. *GA9* 1–38.

76. Other references to Kierkegaard: *GA1* 56; *GA63* 5.

77. According to Michael Theunissen, Heidegger misrepresents Kierkegaard when he regards him as not being capable of moving beyond an ontic/existentiell analysis of time. In his *Sickness unto Death*, Kierkegaard breaks through to an ontology of time. But for Kierkegaard, being a whole, authenticity, and resoluteness are only possible in faith. See Michael Theunissen, *Negative Theologie der Zeit* (Frankfurt am Main: Suhrkamp, 1991), 345–55.

78. Søren Kierkegaard, *Philosophical Fragments: Johannes Climacus*, trans. Howard V. Hong and Edna H. Hong (Princeton, N.J.: Princeton University Press, 1985), 18.

truth that shows itself to me in what Heidegger calls the theoretical comportment. Subjective truth is the truth in which I am infinitely interested because it concerns my existence. The Diltheyan thesis that Christianity thinks historical existence is also originally Kierkegaardian. "Christianity... attaches an enormous importance to the individual subject; it wants to be involved with him alone, and thus with each one individually."[79] Kierkegaard regarded these moves as distinctively Christian. It is not hard to guess what he would have thought of Heidegger's effort to appropriate them into a nonreligious philosophy. It would have struck him as funny, more Hegelian acrobatics, but now in a reverse mode. Instead of speculating himself out of existence with Hegel, Heidegger speculates himself into existence, which is equally impossible.

Atheology

As Heidegger said himself, his Catholic origins always remained before him *(Herkunft aber bleibt stets Zukunft)*. He never resolved the issue of his relationship to the Church. In a 1935 letter to Karl Jaspers, he spoke of "two great thorns in my flesh—the struggle with the faith of my birth, and the failure of the rectorship."[80] It is impossible to know exactly what Heidegger meant by this, but we can surmise that for a philosopher whose central thesis was the historicity of thinking, emancipation from the religion of his *Volk*, his fellow Meßkirchers, was not something to be taken lightly. Late in life, he would tell a confidant, almost defensively, that he had never left the Catholic Church: *Ich bin niemals aus der Kirche getreten.*[81] On 14 January 1976, a few months before he died, Heidegger had "a long conversation" with Bernhard Welte. We do not know what they talked about, but we can assume that it was at that time that Heidegger asked for a Christian (not a Catholic) burial.[82]

---

79. Søren Kierkegaard, *Concluding Unscientific Postscript to Philosophical Fragments*, trans. Howard V. Hong and Edna H. Hong (Princeton, N.J.: Princeton University Press, 1992), 49.

80. Ott, *Biographie*, 42/37.

81. Heidegger, quoted in Thomas J. Sheehan, "Reading a Life: Heidegger and Hard Times," in Guignon, *Cambridge Companion to Heidegger*, 72.

82. Bernhard Welte, "Suchen und Finden," in *Gedenkschrift der Stadt Meßkirch an ihren Sohn und Ehrenbürger Professor Martin Heidegger* (Meßkirch: H. Schönebeck, 1976), 6; English: "Seeking and Finding: The Speech at Heidegger's Burial," *Listening* 12 (1977): 106. Heidegger was not given an official Catholic funeral.

After his 1918 "break" with "the system of Catholicism," Heidegger refused to be aligned with any religious camp. He began to argue for the formal atheism of philosophy in the winter semester 1921/22. Unlike religion, philosophy lives by questioning, and the spirit of questioning demands a radical detachment from already formulated answers, be they philosophical or theological. "The philosopher does not believe," he wrote in 1924 (*BZ* 1). Such a stance is neither irreligious nor atheistic, but atheological. It may be perfectly compatible with religious faith; indeed, in its uncompromising honesty, Heidegger holds that it is closer to the truth of religion than a safe and unthinking piety.[83] The argument against Christian philosophy was put in its harshest terms in the 1930s. In the 1935 lecture course "Einführung in die Metaphysik," we are told that a Christian cannot genuinely philosophize. The biblical story about the divine origin of beings has no relation to the philosophical question, why is there something rather than nothing? The horizon of the question, radical wonderment that anything should be, is banished by the creation myth. Faith in the createdness of beings mitigates the angst natural to our being-held-out-into-the-nothing, our wonder that something should be rather than nothing:

> Anyone for whom the Bible is divine revelation and truth has the answer to the question "Why is there anything rather than nothing?" even before it is asked: everything that is, except God himself, has been created by Him. God himself, the uncreated Creator, "is." One who holds to such faith can in a way participate in the asking of our question, but he cannot really question without ceasing to be a believer and taking all the consequences of such a step. He will only be able to act "as if".... On the other hand a faith that does not perpetually expose itself to the possibility of unbelief is not faith but mere convenience: the believer simply makes up his mind to adhere to the traditional doctrine. This is neither faith nor questioning, but the indifference of those who can busy themselves with everything, sometimes even displaying a keen interest in faith as well as questioning. What we have said about security in faith as one position in regard to the truth does not imply that the statement "In the beginning God created heaven and earth" is an answer to our question. Quite aside from whether these words from the Bible are true or false for faith, they can supply no answer to our question because they are in no way related to it. Indeed, they cannot even be brought into relation with our

---

83. Cf. *GA*61 197.

question. From the standpoint of faith our question is "foolishness." Philosophy is this very foolishness. A "Christian philosophy" is a round square and a misunderstanding. (GA40 8–9/6)

The polemic with Scholasticism could not be more extreme: the biblical notion of creation has no relationship to the question of the meaning of being. The critique of Christianity became a political agenda during Heidegger's infamous rectorship of 1933. One of Heidegger's projects as Rector was the establishment of an academic summer camp at Todtnauberg. In the pure environment of the *Hochschwarzwald*, students would be trained in the three disciplines outlined in the Rectorship Address, the three "bonds" that would bind German students to the "ethnic and national community" [*Volksgemeinschaft*] and "the spiritual mission of the German *Volk*," namely, "labor service," "military service," and "the service of knowledge."[84] A participant in the camp, Heinrich Buhr, who went on to become a Protestant pastor, remembers being subjected to a passionate anti-Christian indoctrination by Heidegger outside the philosopher's cottage.

I think it was in the autumn of 1933, in Todtnauberg (I was a young student of Protestant theology at the time) that I heard Martin Heidegger speak for the first time, when he addressed student representatives from the universities of Heidelberg, Freiburg and Tübingen. I was the only theologian in the group—and one who was fully committed to theology. Martin Heidegger made a speech against Christianity (that much I could just about understand at the time)—against Christian theology, against this whole interpretation of existence and reality. If one wanted to attack Christianity, he said, it was not enough to confine oneself to the second article of this doctrine (that Jesus was the true Christ). One must start by rejecting the first article, that the world was created and sustained by God, that what exists is merely an artifact, something that has been made by a divine craftsman. This was the origin of the false devaluation of the world, that contempt for the world and denial of the world—and the source of that false feeling of comfort and security, founded on subjective ideas about the world that are untrue compared with the great noble awareness of the insecurity of "existence."[85]

84. Martin Heidegger, *Die Selbstbehauptung der deutschen Universität* (Breslau: Korn, 1933); English: "The Self-Assertion of the German University," trans. William S. Lewis, in *The Heidegger Controversy: A Critical Reader*, ed. Richard Wolin, (Cambridge, Mass.: MIT Press, 1993), 35.

85. "Heinrich Buhr," in *Erinnerung an Martin Heidegger*, ed. Günther Neske (Pfullingen: Günther Neske, 1977), 53, quoted in Ott, *Biographie*, 216/227.

The new Rector expressed his support for the Nazi policy against Christianity by attacking what he regarded as the root of the problem. Christianity precludes philosophy by substituting belief for philosophical questioning. This was not only an affront to philosophy; it was a betrayal of being itself. To trace being back to the causal agency of God diminishes it, devalues it, and reduces it to a product.[86] This open hostility to Christianity also manifested itself in Heidegger's professional duties. During the 1930s, Heidegger had the unwanted task of being a second examiner for Martin Honecker, the Chair of Christian Philosophy at Freiburg, reviewing dissertations and *Habilitationsschriften* of theologically inclined philosophy students, some of whom later became disseminators of Heidegger's philosophy: Johannes Lotz, Gustav Siewerth, and Max Müller. Heidegger's reviews returned repeatedly to one damning critique: by operating within a belief system, the author in question had forsaken genuine philosophizing. Lotz's project, Heidegger wrote, stays within a "prescribed framework, which decides the outcome in advance";[87] Siewerth's book did not pursue science "without presuppositions," but "as a means of defending and developing the Catholic faith."[88] Müller's work was Thomism, "dressed up in contemporary patterns of thought," and as such, it failed to break free of "dogmatic theology"—it was a pseudo-philosophy, "in which the crucial philosophical questions are not asked because they cannot be asked."[89] This hostility was not limited to Heidegger's rectorship year. In 1938, he wrote a report to the head of the Freiburg office of the League of University Lecturers to block Müller's promotion to a lectureship on the grounds that a genuine philosopher could not be a Christian. In the interest of the "radical new order," Heidegger proclaimed that Christians of all denominations should be banned from University appointments.[90]

---

86. Against Heidegger, Gadamer holds that the Judaeo-Christian theological tradition was much more open to "the great challenge of the Da" than the Greeks. "One gets a hint of this from the Judaeo-Christian theological doctrine of creation, for this thinking that had been molded by the Old Testament, that had heard God's voice or experienced his mute refusal, had developed much more of a receptivity to the 'Da' (and its obfuscation) than to the organized forms and the 'what-content' of *Da*-beings [*Was-Gehalt von Da-Seiendem*]." Gadamer, "Sein Geist Gott," in *Werke*, vol. 3, 320–32, at 327; English, *Heidegger's Ways*, 181–95, at 189.

87. Heidegger's review of Lotz's dissertation in Ott, *Biographie*, 261/276.
88. Heidegger's review of Siewerth's dissertation in Ott, *Biographie*, 261/276.
89. Heidegger's review of Müller's *Habilitationsschrift* in Ott, *Biographie*, 264/280.
90. Ibid.

These were dark times for Germany and dark times for Heidegger. His hostility to Christianity waned with his enthusiasm for National Socialism. In his later return to religious questions, one can see that Christian notions, especially medieval mystical approaches to God, reasserted their grip on him. The later Heidegger avoids the word "God," yet speaks with reverence about "the holy." In the 1946 "Brief über den Humanismus," Heidegger writes that philosophy can prepare the ground for a genuinely philosophical reflection on the essence of the holy. The contemporary triumph of calculative thinking had closed the dimension of the holy; nothing meaningful could be said about God until "the clearing of Being" was cleared once again. "Perhaps what is distinctive about this world-epoch consists in the closure of the dimension of the sacred *(Heilen).* Perhaps that is the only sin *(Unheil)*" (*GA*9 352/267). To call this a retraction of his earlier views would be going too far. Nonetheless, it cannot be denied that the later Heidegger opens up a possibility that he explicitly rejected in the 1920s and 1930s, the possibility of philosophy of religion, a phenomenological interpretation of the factical roots of Dasein's religiosity. "With the existential determination of the essence of man, therefore, nothing is decided about 'the existence of God' or his 'nonbeing,' no more than about the possibility or impossibility of gods. Thus it is not only rash but also an error in procedure to maintain that the interpretation of the essence of man from the relation of his essence to the truth of Being is atheism" (*GA*9 350–51/266). Philosophy keeps open the possibility of a relationship to the divine *(das Gottesverhältnis des Daseins),* while reserving for ontology the task of providing the terms through which this relationship is to be understood. By clarifying the truth of being, we make it possible to think the essence of the holy and therefore, for the first time, understand the meaning of the word "God." "Only from the truth of Being can the essence of the holy be thought. Only from the essence of the holy is the essence of the divinity to be thought. Only in the light of the essence of the divinity can it be thought or said what the word 'God' is to signify" (*GA*9 350–51/267).

"Questioning is the piety of thought" (*VA* 43/341)—Heidegger's "piety" stands in marked contrast to the *fides quaerens intellectum* of medieval philosophy. For Heidegger, doubt is a quasi-religious stance. Much like the early Wittgenstein, Heidegger delimits theology from within language, by uncovering "the boundaries that have been set for thinking," that is, by showing, as much by silence as by any statement, what cannot be said (*GA*9 352/267). Unconcealment *(aletheia)* is always also concealment; in every disclosure of being, the ground withdraws and conceals itself. All ways of thinking are incomplete ways *(Abwege, Irrgänge)*, paths that disappear after a time like trails in the forest *(Holzwege)*. The hidden ground of unconcealment is "the mystery," the source of being, which cannot be penetrated and mapped by human thinking. "All unconcealing [*Entbergen*] belongs in a sheltering [*Bergen*] and a concealing [*Verbergen*]. But that which frees—the mystery—is concealed and always concealing itself" (*VA* 33/330).[91] Thinking is essentially related to a ground that remains un-comprehended by it. This is not the incomprehensibility of the irrational or the intrinsically unintelligible. Rather, the ground of thinking necessarily remains un-thought in every act of thinking. When I think, I bring what is thought into the light of understanding. What is thought is taken from the darkness of the not-thought. Thinking is an *Ereignis* whose origins are always hidden. According to Heidegger, we never master thinking. We respond to that which calls to thinking and heed its appeal and, with reverent silence, acknowledge its withdrawal into the un-thought ground.

Heidegger's theological silence does not deny a legitimate task for theology within the Church. In a throwback to the Scholastic notion of *praeambula fidei*, Heidegger suggests the possibility of philosophy providing theology with basic concepts necessary to understanding Dasein's relation to the divine. In the early Heidegger, this was expressed in terms of an ontological clarification of concepts presupposed by theology but not originating there. The later task is one of uncovering the divine absence, Dasein's largely unfulfilled expectation of the holy. The human being has a natural openness to the divine, an unsatisfied expectation of divinity.[92] The later Heidegger's thinking on religion was deeply influenced

91. Cf. van Buren, *Young Heidegger*, 40; Gadamer, "Sein Geist Gott," 328/191.
92. Gadamer, "Sein Geist Gott," 325/187: "For Heidegger, the issue had always been one dealing with the 'Da' in the Dasein of human beings; it has to do with this characterization of existence, this being outside of itself and exposed like no other living being. But this exposedness meant, as displayed by the 'Letter on Humanism' written to Jean Beaufret that humans, as humans, stand out in the open, that they are in the end more proximate to the furthermost, to the divine, than they are to their own: 'nature.'"

by Hölderlin. Gadamer writes that Hölderlin freed Heidegger's tongue for speaking about the divine.[93] For Hölderlin, the last god of the old world was Christ; after his departure, we await a new god whose identity is obscure. The religiosity of our age is marked by a romantic longing for the departed divinity, a feeling of having lost that which is most precious. Heidegger transposes Hölderlin's romantic theology into a post-Christian context. We are bereft of the religion of the ancients and the moderns and await the arrival of a new divinity, the "last god" (*GA65* 409–17/288–93).

Heidegger's religious-philosophical itinerarium was marked by a progressive defection from Roman Catholicism. He dismantled his own faith as he deconstructed the Western synthesis of philosophy and theology. Like the *Destruktion* of the history of ontology, the dismantling had a positive intent. In Heidegger's eulogy, Bernhard Welte made the point that Heidegger's devotion to thinking was a grateful response to an appeal from a hidden divinity: for Heidegger "to think was to thank." An anecdote I heard in Freiburg tells of how Heidegger, an enthusiastic walker, always venerated the covered crucifixes that one sees on trails in the Schwarzwald. Asked by a companion why he did so since he was not a practicing Catholic, Heidegger answered, "Where so many have prayed, the holy is most present." With the oracular solemnity of Nietzsche's Zarathustra, Heidegger commissions us with a philosophico-religious task: "to dwell" *(wohnen)* on the earth in such a way that we "preserve" *(schonen)* and "shepherd" *(hüten)* the unconcealment of "the holy." Heidegger became an "un-believer" in order to retrieve a religiosity that preceded and had been largely concealed by Judaeo-Christian religion. The epithet, "neo-pagan," is in this sense justified: Heidegger wishes to think being without a Creator God in order to restore a sense of reverence to the earth.

93. Ibid., 328/190.

CHAPTER THREE

THE PHENOMENOLOGY OF THE EARLY HEIDEGGER

... the name traveled all over Germany like the rumor of a hidden king.

HANNAH ARENDT

The early Heidegger's circuitous path, from the *Habilitationsschrift* to *Sein und Zeit* ultimately moves in a single direction. The question that drives the *Daseinanalytic* of *Sein und Zeit*—the question of the being of time—first surfaces in Heidegger's 1915 Scotus research. It reappears in the 1917–19 mysticism research, the remarks on Luther, the 1920–21 religion lectures, and the 1921–26 Aristotle research. The early Freiburg lectures document the variety of approaches Heidegger took to this problem, tentative solutions, experiments with language, and forays into the tradition, some that became lifelong projects, like the retrieval of non-Platonic Greek thinking, others that were stillborn, such as the retrieval of primordial Christianity and medieval mysticism. The question arose out of Heidegger's interest in the medieval *quaestio disputata* about the status of the singular. The Scotist doctrine of *haecceitas* led Heidegger into an investigation of intentional being *(ens logicum)* and the intentional structure of temporality. In his Scotist research, Heidegger discovered that the historical is singularized in a specific intentional mode, a directedness toward the here and now *(hic et nunc),* which is entirely ineffable. How could something as close to us and everyday as *haecceitas* be so hidden? Heidegger was struck by Augustine's observation that although we always already understand the meaning of time, we are not able to express its meaning. With Scotus and Augustine pointing the way, Heidegger undertook in *Sein und Zeit* a phenomenological demonstration of how time functions as a pre-understood fore-theoretical horizon of everyday experience, a structure which, if never objectifiable, makes historical experience possible. He came to believe that the concealment of time in the history of philosophy was not coincidental. Our existential anxiety in the face of the finitude of time has in a hidden way guided the metaphysical tradition. If phenomenology was to see through this fog of existentially motivated deception, it would have to destroy the ontological tradition (trace it back to its original factical sources) and bring about something like a transvaluation of values. The onto-theological interpretation of being as changelessness, self-identity, actuality, and infinity would have to be overturned; being must be thought as change, difference, possibility, emergence into presence, and withdrawal into absence, in a word, facticity.

In this chapter, I give an overview of the early Heidegger's approach to phenomenology with a particular focus on its relationship to Aristotelian Scholasticism. Heidegger's sources, Scotus, medieval mysticism, Luther, and early Christianity will be discussed in detail in the chapters that follow.

Phenomenological Ontology and Aristotelian Scholasticism

It is widely know that intentionality, the founding concept of phenomenology, is originally an Aristotelian-Scholastic concept.[1] What is not so widely known is how the concept functions in Scholastic philosophy. For the Scholastics, intentionality is not the essence of consciousness, as it is for Franz Brentano and his student, Husserl; it is an indication of the immateriality of the intellect. In his largely unrecognized early study of Hei-

---

1. Jacques Maritain has gathered together texts of Aquinas on intentionality in the appendix to his *Distinguer pour unir ou les degrés du savoir*, 7th ed. (Paris: Desclée de Brouwer, 1963), 769–919; English: *The Degrees of Knowledge*, trans. Gerald B. Phelan, from the 4th ed. (New York: Charles Scribner's Sons, 1959), 387–417.

degger and Scholasticism, *The Tradition via Heidegger*, John Deely argues that the notion of intentional being *(esse intentionale)* is crucial to understanding the non-Cartesian nature of Aristotelian-Scholastic psychology. The Scholastics distinguish the being of that which exists for the soul in its cognitive and volitional acts, *esse intentionale*, from the being of things, *esse entitativum*. The soul exhibits a feature found in no physical thing, the capacity to appropriate an object into its own mode of existing. This is a function of its immateriality. Because the soul is a form that is not fastened to any particular matter, it remains free to take on the forms of other things. The soul is a pure openness to beings. *Esse intentionale*, the being of knowledge (forms in the soul), is distinct from both the being of an extra-mental entity and the being of the soul. It is neither a substance nor an accident—evidence that the Aristotelian categories were always inadequate to the phenomenon of mind *(psyche)*. What is known has a mode of existence in the soul distinct from its mode of existence outside the soul. The intelligible form is dematerialized and universalized. The known form is not a representation, whose truth consists in its adequation with an extra-mental thing. Rather, in the soul, the thing comes into a mode of existence not otherwise possible for it. Deely describes *esse intentionale* as that order of reality "wherein subject and object are united in a single suprasubjective mode of existing, in an *actus perfecti* which is precisely other than the actuality either of the subject known or the subject knowing—other even from the mind *(anima)* of the subject (actually or possibly) knowing."[2]

Jacques Maritain draws out the anti-Cartesian and phenomenological significance of *esse intentionale*. Intentional being makes possible the identity of the knower and the known in the act of knowledge. "It [*esse intentionale*] is something that makes known before itself be-

2. Deely, *Tradition via Heidegger*, 67. See Maritain, *Distinguer pour unir*, 200/103: "[*Esse intentionale*] is not only that property of my consciousness of being a transparent directedness, of aiming at objects in the depths of itself. Above all intentionality is a property of thought, a prerogative of its immateriality, whereby being in itself, posited 'outside it,' being which is fully independent of the act of thought, becomes a thing existing within it, set up for it and integrated into its own act through which, from that moment, they both exist in thought with a single self-same suprasubjective existence . . . an existence according to which the known will be in the knower and the knower will be the known, an entirely tendential and immaterial existence, whose office is not to posit a thing outside nothingness for itself and as a subject, but on the contrary, for another thing [a subject] and as a relation."

ing known as object by a reflective act, [it] is known only by the very knowledge that brings the mind to the object through its mediation. In other words, it is not known by 'appearing' as object but by 'disappearing' in the face of the object, for its very essence is to bear the mind to something other than itself."[3] Maritain points out that with the notion of intentional being, the Cartesian critical problem ("How can the mind get outside itself to reach being?") is precluded. "Cognition [*la connaissance*] has no need to get outside of itself to attain the thing that exists or can exist beyond it . . . because the very glory of the immateriality of thought is not to be a thing in space exterior to another extended thing, but rather a life which is superior to the whole order of space . . . a higher life which perfects itself by that which is not it, even without going outside itself."[4]

Franz Brentano (1838–1917), a specialist on Aristotle and a former Catholic priest, retrieved the Aristotelian-Scholastic notion of intentionality in an effort to provide philosophical foundations for the new science of psychology.[5] Crucial to Brentano's reading of Aristotle's psychology is the structure of intentional directedness (which is not identical to *esse intentionale*, but is one of its properties). A thought or an act of will is directed to its object in such a way that the object is immanent to it. To differentiate the act properly, one must describe how it intends its object. This immanence is the distinguishing feature of the psychological. Whereas intentional objects are immanent to their correlative acts, a thing cannot indwell a non-psychological being. As Husserl puts it, "Each *cogito*, each conscious process . . . 'means' something or other, and bears in itself, in this manner peculiar to the meant, its particular *cogitatum*."[6]

---

3. Maritain, *Distinguer pour unir*, 232/119–20.

4. Ibid., 201–2/104. See Aquinas, *Quodlibet* VII, q. 1, a. 4: "Considered in what is proper to it, thought is not in the soul as in a subject; in this context it exceeds the mental insofar as something other than the mind is apprehended in the medium (the 'in-between') of thought . . . And in this respect there is a certain equality of thought to the mind inasmuch as it embraces everything to which the mind is able to extend itself." See Deely, *Tradition via Heidegger*, 74. See also Aquinas, *Summa theologiae* 1a, q. 93 (hereafter *ST*); *Quaestiones disputatae De veritate*, q. 10 (hereafter *De ver.*).

5. On Brentano's contribution to phenomenology, see Dermot Moran, *Introduction to Phenomenology* (New York: Routledge, 2000), 23–59.

6. Edmund Husserl, *Cartesian Meditations: An Introduction to Phenomenology*, trans. Dorian Cairns (The Hague: Nijhoff, 1960), 33.

All consciousness is "consciousness of." The known is a *cogitatum* of a *cogito*, the *intentum* of an *intentio*, the object pole of an indissoluble relation to a subject. Brentano combines intentionality analysis with Descartes's notion of consciousness as a domain of apodictic self-evidence in order to found a descriptive psychology. Mental states, according to Brentano, exhibit a unique kind of self-evidence. Properly described, they could serve as a bedrock of self-evident truths upon which to erect a science of the mental life of the human being.

Husserl picks up Brentano's notion of intentionality (he seems to have had little knowledge of either the Scholastics or Aristotle) and makes it the founding concept of his new science of phenomenology. To understand the given, it is not enough to look at its objective features; we must examine the way consciousness is directed to it. Perception of objects is piecemeal, but meaning is holistic and contextual; every *noema* has a noetic "horizon" constitutive of its meaning.[7] For example, we synthesize one-sided views of spatial objects into anticipated wholes. Intentional analysis explicates these implicitly given "wholes," generating an a priori system of categories which encompasses the formal structure of anything that can be thought. Husserl first conceives phenomenology along Brentanian lines, as the science of psychic life. "For psychology, the universal task presents itself: to investigate systematically the elementary intentionalities and from out of these unfold the typical forms of intentional processes, their possible variants, their syntheses to new forms, their structural composition, and from this advance towards a descriptive knowledge of the totality of mental processes, towards a comprehensive type of the life of the psychic."[8] In the later Husserl, the source of all intentional structures is thematized as "the transcendental ego," the a priori field of pure experience that not only grounds the object, but the psychological subject as well. All intentional acts are traced back to an absolute horizon of transcendental subjectivity, a field of transcendental

---

7. Edmund Husserl, *Ideas Pertaining to a Pure Phenomenology and to a Phenomenological Philosophy* (Ideen zu einer reinen Phänomenologie und phänomenologischen Philosophie), vol. 1, *General Introduction to a Pure Phenomenology*, trans. Fred Kersten (The Hague: Nijhoff, 1982), 199–216.

8. Edmund Husserl, "Phenomenology," trans. Richard Palmer, *Journal of the British Society for Phenomenology* 2 (1971): 87.

experience within which subject and object, self and other, are originally constituted.

Heidegger's transposition of phenomenology from a Cartesian-style introspective analysis of the structure of conscious acts into a hermeneutical analysis of the ontological conditions of the possibility of intentionality is to some degree a return to the Aristotelian-Scholastic notion of *esse intentionale*. Heidegger admits that his notion of Dasein as transcendence or disclosedness, the site of the unveiling of beings, has a relationship to the Aristotelian-Scholastic notion of intentional being. In the first chapter of *Sein und Zeit*, Heidegger references Aristotle and Aquinas on the immateriality of the intellect. For Aristotle, the soul is "in a manner all things."[9] In Aquinas's words, it is "the being whose nature it is to gather together all other beings" *(ens quod natum est convenire cum omni ente)*.[10] While these formulations remain "ontologically unclarified," they are nonetheless indications of "the ontic-ontological priority of Dasein," and far removed from any "vapid subjectivizing."

> The ontic-ontological priority of Dasein was already seen early on, without Dasein itself being grasped in its genuine ontological structure or even becoming a problem with such an aim. Aristotle says, *he psyche ta onta pos estin*. The soul (of the human being) is in a certain way beings. The "soul" which constitutes the being of the human being discovers its way to be—*aisthesis* and *noesis*—all beings with regard to their thatness and whatness, that is to say, always also in their being. Thomas Aquinas discussed this statement ... appealing to a being which in conformity with its kind of being is suited to "come together" with any being whatsoever. This distinctive being, the *ens quod natum est convenire cum omni ente*, is the soul *(anima)*. The priority of Dasein which emerges here without being ontologically clarified obviously has nothing in common with a vapid subjectivizing of the totality of beings. (SZ 14/12)

Later on, the Scholastic metaphor of the intellect as "a natural light" *(lumen naturale)* is even more strongly identified with Dasein.

> When we talk in an ontically figurative way about the *lumen naturale* in human being, we mean nothing other than the existential-ontological structure of this being, the fact that it *is* in the mode of being its there. To say that it is "illumi-

---

9. Aristotle, *De anima* 3.8.431b21.
10. Aquinas, *De ver.*, q. 1, a. 1.

nated" means that it is cleared (*Aletheia*—openness—clearing, light, shining) in itself *as* being-in-the-world, not by another being, but in such a way that it *is* itself the clearing. Only for a being thus cleared existentially do objectively present things become accessible in the light or concealed in darkness. (SZ 133/125)

These passages show Heidegger's positive appropriation of the Aristotelian-Scholastic psychology on which he cut his teeth. Deely persuasively argues that the Aristotelian notion of the immaterial intellect structurally coincides with Heidegger's notion of Dasein. To make the case, he distinguishes the Brentanian-Husserlian understanding of intentionality as "consciousness of," or directedness, from the richer Aristotelian-Scholastic notion of *esse intentionale*. Dasein is not intentionality but the condition of its possibility. Intentionality as a relation between two beings, the subject and its objects, is made possible by the ontological dimension of Dasein, but cannot be identified with it. Dasein is the condition of the possibility of intentional directedness. Without its openness to beings, there could be no "consciousness of." But this pre-understanding is not consciousness. Deely notes that *esse intentionale* is also a condition of the possibility of cognition. It is the immateriality without which nothing could be cognized, but it is not itself cognition. *Esse intentionale* is "a state according to which a being is open to the presence of other entities and consequently to a communication with and certain ... sharing in their being."[11]

Deely maintains that from an Aristotelian-Scholastic perspective, the thematization of the *ontological* structure of intentional being is Heidegger's decisive contribution to the tradition. While recognizing that an ontology of purely intentional structures, such as history and culture, is wanting in Scholasticism, he interprets Dasein as "the intentional life of man."[12] The phenomenological reduction brackets the extra-experiential metaphysical thrust of Aristotelian-Scholasticism and brings the order of the meaningful to light. But this order is already implicit in Aristotle's psychology. From an Aristotelian-Scholastic perspective, the intentional order is the field of basic human experience. This is the whole of our liv-

11. Deely, *Tradition via Heidegger*, 84. See Aquinas, In II *De anima*, lect. 5, nn. 282–84.
12. Deely, *Tradition via Heidegger*, 78.

ing, where things are suffused with significance. It precedes abstraction and is in that sense "fore-theoretical." It is not an aggregate of mute sense data; it has structure, a first grade of intelligibility. Distinct from the order of "things," *esse intentionale* is the mode of being proper to meaning, possibility, and history. Deely comments, "Heidegger opens the way for a properly philosophical, that is, ontological, consideration of the decisive formalities of historical, cultural, social, and personal data which are primarily intentional, that is, inter-subjective, and only derivatively or secondarily 'subjective,' that is entitative."[13] Had Deely been more familiar with Heidegger's *Habilitationsschrift* (he clearly had not read it when he wrote *The Tradition via Heidegger* in 1971), he would have seen that his speculative thesis has far more solidly historical grounds than he suspected. As we will see in the next chapter, Heidegger's *Habilitationsschrift* revolves around a discussion of Scotus's notion of *ens logicum*, logical being, the being of anything that can be conceived, and the Scholastic prototype for what phenomenology will call "the given."

Heidegger's most serious departure from the Aristotelian-Scholastic tradition concerns the conception of the immaterial intellect as a variety of substance (a point which Deely overlooks). Immateriality in Aristotelian Scholasticism is an attribute, not an ontological difference. The soul is categorized under the class of things having properties, a species of *substantia*.[14] According to Aristotle, we are the *zoon logon echon*, the rational animal, the class of living things possessing the power to speak. But Dasein is not a substance; it cannot be characterized as subsisting. It is not an in-itself but a for-itself, not *a being* in the sense of a thing, but a *to be*. "The kind of being of the *zoon*," Heidegger writes, "is understood here in the sense of occurring and being objectively present. The *logos* is a higher endowment whose kind of being remains just as obscure as that of the being so pieced together" (SZ 48/45). "The sources which are relevant for traditional anthropology—the Greek definition and the theological guideline—indicate that, over and above the attempt to determine the essence of 'human being' as a being, the question of its being has remained forgotten; rather, this being is understood as something 'self-

13. Ibid., 183.
14. See, for example, Aquinas, *ST* 1a, q. 75, a. 2.

evident' in the sense of the *objective* presence of other created things" (*SZ* 49/46). Aristotle and the Scholastics define the being of the human being in categories applicable to things: as animal or substance.

Lurking behind the reification of Dasein is a deeper problem: the reduction of being to *substantia*, which Heidegger holds to be the heart of the forgetfulness of temporality in Western philosophy. *Substantia* is that which subsists and supports changes, that which can stand alone and bear properties, that which can be named. Yet "being" is a verb before it is a noun. The Greek infinitive *einai*, "to be," originally meant *parousia*, "to be present." In the Greek New Testament, which Heidegger lectured on in 1921, *parousia* connotes modulation in time. *Parousia* means *coming into* presence, arrival, advent. The Christ who has come will return or re-presence. In this primordial word, *parousia*, "there prevails, in an unthought and concealed manner presence and duration—there prevails time" (*GA9* 376/285–86). The temporal connotation is to some degree retained in the technical Aristotelian term *ousia*, which, in everyday ancient Greek, meant household goods, property, that which one has at one's disposal. With the reification of being-present in the Latinization *substantia*, the dynamism inherent in the infinitive *einai* is ostensibly lost. The notion of that which appears in time is eclipsed by the concept of that which lies always present-at-hand, that which has no time because it does not change.

Finding a Way into the Fore-theoretical

Notwithstanding Heidegger's sometimes savage criticism of Husserl, Heidegger dedicated *Sein und Zeit* to Husserl "in friendship and admiration" and generously acknowledged Husserl's positive influence on his work.[15] Heidegger and Husserl basically agree that the proper theme of

---

15. Heidegger's uncharacteristically generous tribute to Husserl in *Sein und Zeit* (*SZ* 38 n. 1/400 n. 5) must be read in context. *Sein und Zeit* was originally published in Husserl's *Jahrbuch für Philosophie und phänomenologische Forschung*. That Heidegger is to some degree playing a political game here is clear from scathing remarks about Husserl that appear in his correspondence at the time. See for example, Martin Heidegger to Karl Jaspers, December 26, 1926, in Martin Heidegger/Karl Jaspers, *Briefwechsel 1920–1963*, ed. Walter Biemel and Hans Saner (Frankfurt am Main: Vittorio Klostermann, 1990), 71. Recent studies of Heidegger's relationship to Husserl include Stephen Galt Crowell, "Heidegger and Husserl: The Matter and Method of Philosophy," in *A Companion to*

phenomenology is the meaningful as such. Heidegger departs from Husserl on the structure and mode of access to the meaningful. Neither Heidegger nor Husserl is a system builder, so a facile reduction of either to a set of theses is not helpful. Moreover, Husserl's view changes over his long career, undoubtedly under the influence of the work of Heidegger, Scheler, and his other students. Much of what the early Heidegger advances finds some correlate in the later Husserl. The traditional contrast between Husserl as a *reflective* phenomenologist and Heidegger as a *hermeneutical* phenomenologist is not without its problems. Nevertheless, it succeeds in underscoring Heidegger and Husserl's divergence on the question of the structure and access to the meaningful. More importantly for the purposes of the present book, the distinction highlights Heidegger's central critique of Western philosophy (which is also his critique of Scholastic thinking): by absolutizing the theoretical comportment to beings, Husserl's phenomenology compounds Western philosophy's forgetfulness of the fore-theoretical ("factical") sources of thinking. Husserl reinscribes the prejudice in his contention that directedness to an object is the essence of thinking. According to Heidegger, the subject-object relationship is only one of many ways in which Dasein is comported to being. Moreover, it is a "founded" relationship. The most basic relationship of Dasein to being cannot be articulated in the language of subject/object or noesis/noema. Prior to the project of knowledge, Dasein is immersed in everydayness, lost in practical concerns, which are determined by its unthematized preoccupation with its own death. In everydayness, Dasein is disclosed, not as a subject/ego/soul, but rather, as being that is always outside itself in the temporalizing practical, social, and existential preoccupations, which Heidegger formalizes as "care" *(Sorge)*, "being-ahead-of-itself-in-already-being-in-a-world" (*SZ* 179/192).

Where phenomenology for Husserl is a nondistortive elaboration of

---

Heidegger, ed. Hubert L. Dreyfus and Mark A. Wrathall (Malden, Mass.: Blackwell, 2005), 49–64; idem, *Husserl, Heidegger, and the Space of Meaning: Paths Toward Transcendental Phenomenology* (Evanston, Ill.: Northwestern University Press, 2001). My reading of the Heidegger-Husserl dispute is indebted to Kisiel's superb studies. See, in particular, Theodore Kisiel, "From Intuition to Understanding: On Heidegger's Transposition of Husserl's Phenomenology," in Kisiel, *Heidegger's Way of Thought*, ed. Alfred Denker and Marion Heinz (New York: Continuum, 2002), 174–86; idem, "Heidegger (1907–1927): The Transformation of the Categorial," in ibid., 84–100.

subjectivity, a transcendental reflection on conscious acts, phenomenology under Heidegger becomes hermeneutical, the provisional thematization of that which is hidden, that which cannot be directly accessed through reflection but must be "formally indicated."[16] Kisiel characterizes this as a move from "intuition" to "understanding." For Husserl, intentions are fulfilled in intuitions, where the paradigm for an intuition is a sense experience, the immediate grasp of content. The intention heads for the intuition. If it is not fulfilled, it is an "empty" intention. Heidegger finds this view artificial, struggling under the baggage of the epistemological construct of experience as a subject/object confrontation. Intentionality analysis, however sensitive to the concrete unity of subject and object in an intellectual act of knowing or perceiving, remains inadequate to phenomenology reconceived as "the hermeneutics of facticity." Heidegger's phenomenology would dig beneath intentionality, and the cognitive paradigm implied by it, into the fore-theoretical foundations of all human experience. The difference in the being of the intentional, a difference indicated by the phenomenon of directedness, goes unrecognized by Aristotle and the Scholastics, as much as by Husserl.[17] For Heidegger, experience is always already structured before it becomes the term of an intentional act. Consciousness does not "intuit" things, but "understands" them, that is, it *finds* them understandable, laden with meaning, and appearing within the horizon of Dasein's practical involvement with them. A thing is not first "given" to us as an intentional object; it is first revealed to us as a historically charged nexus of meaning. What is understood is not an object for a subject but a lived experience for a living human being. According to Heidegger, Husserl's intentionality analysis (and by implication intentionality analysis in Aristotelian Scho-

---

16. The key discussion on formal indication occurs in *GA60* 58–64. For other references, see *GA9* 9; *GA56/57* 100–101; *GA58* 85. On formal indication, see James Risser, "Truth in Time and History: Hermeneutics and the Truth that Strikes Back," in *Between the Human and the Divine: Philosophical and Theological Hermeneutics*, ed. Andrzej Wiercinski (Toronto: Hermeneutic Press, 2002), 428–33; Ryan Streeter, "Heidegger's Formal Indication: A Question of Method in *Being and Time*," *Man and World* 30 (1997): 413–30; John van Buren, "The Ethics of *Formale Anzeige* in Heidegger," *American Catholic Philosophical Quarterly* 69 (1995): 157–70; Daniel Dahlstrom, "Heidegger's Method: Philosophical Concepts as Formal Indications," *Review of Metaphysics* 47 (1994): 775–95; Kisiel, *Genesis of* Being and Time, 50–56, 160–70.

17. On this point, see Heidegger's critique of Husserl's approach to the notion of intentionality in *GA20* 140/104 ff.

lasticism) never accesses the most basic level of lived experience, because it remains stuck in a theoretical paradigm, where Dasein is interpreted as primarily a knower/perceiver. For Heidegger, the practical concerns of life precede knowing and perceiving. Knowing is an act characteristic of a special kind of activity, the theoretical project of science. But Dasein is more than a knower. Care *(Sorge)* is possible because the world is not a mute aggregate of uninterpreted sense data, awaiting the naming activity of intentional consciousness. The world is pervaded by understandability.[18] Husserl touches upon the fore-theoretical in his doctrine of "categorial intuition," the notion that categories are not imposed on raw data, but received into an experiential order, which is already precategorially structured.[19] However, his phenomenology of essences abstracted from existence remains bound to the modern notion of consciousness and its objects. Heidegger speaks, not of consciousness, but of *Existenz*, thrownness into a world. Whatever intentions may emerge in the "subject" are always already preceded by nonintentional horizons of meaning, what Kisiel describes as "the ecstatic structures of worldly existence."[20]

Through a series of historical investigations into the limits of theory in Scotus, early Christianity, and Aristotle's ethics, Heidegger came to see that the fore-theoretical is not a prehuman world or a prelingual world. It is not the "created order," "nature," or "noumena." Rather, it is world in its primordial sense. Hermeneutical phenomenology does not presume to access meaning in transcendental reflection directly. Rather, it begins with historically situated existential *understanding*, the familiarity with factical life that textures being-in-the-world. Dasein's directedness is not originally the intention of objects of cognition or volition, but the ecstatic overpassing of self in our everyday life-tendencies, being-in-the-world. There is no "transcendental subject." Dasein does not reflectively possess itself but enacts itself in living. Every life-tendency is directed to-

---

18. Kisiel precisely formulates the difference between Husserl and Heidegger on this point: "The Heideggerian retrieve opposes Husserl in situating the understanding and exposition of meaning not in acts of consciousness but first of all in a pre-conscious realm of being-in-the-world, which is already pervaded by 'expressivity.'" Kisiel, "The Transformation of the Categorial," 98.

19. On categorial intuition, see Edmund Husserl, *Logische Untersuchungen*, vol. 2, Investigation VI, §§40–48; English: *Logical Investigations*, trans. J. N. Findlay (London: Routledge & Kegan Paul, 1970). For Heidegger's interpretation of categorial intuition, see GA20 63–99/47–72.

20. Kisiel, "The Transformation of the Categorial," 100.

ward a certain content, but this is not originally an object or a thing with a distinct essence. Rather, the term of a tendency is a concretely determined, historically singularized, meaningful whole. By 1921, Heidegger had introduced the notion of "comportment" *(Verhalten)* into his lectures as a term for fore-theoretical directedness, underscoring the factical involvement of the self with its world. The situational connotation of the German word *Verhalten* corrects the worldlessness of Husserl's intentionality. *Verhalten* is an attitude, a behavior adopted under particular circumstances. A comportment occurs in a determinate life context. It is inextricably en-worlded.

The distinction between the theoretical and the fore-theoretical in the early Freiburg lectures develops into *Sein und Zeit*'s distinction between the "present-at-hand" *(Vorhandenheit)*, and the "ready-to-hand" *(Zuhandenheit)*. *Vorhandenheit*, from the common German word for availability (literally, "being-before-the-hand"), means objectified being, the theoretical determination of a thing as an object, a thing with a distinct essence. Things can only be so defined by being "de-worlded," abstracted from the nest of relations in which they originally show themselves. The form of the present-at-hand bears traces of the deeper fore-theoretical ground, the thing as "ready-to-hand" *(Zuhandenheit)*, nested in the contextual whole of my living. The hammer, which weighs such and such, has a certain shape, and belongs to a class of artifacts, represents the tool swinging in my hand as I build my house, and the referential whole within which such activity is possible, the world of human construction, planning, and sheltering. A tool is fore-theoretically determined by what it serves to do. As such, it cannot be understood apart from those whom it serves, their purposes, and the other things to which it is related. By contrast to *Vorhandenheit*, *Zuhandenheit* cannot be thought without the relational whole of factical life *(die Bewandtnisganzheit)*. To define a thing, I first lift it out of the world and place it before myself as an instance of a class. Without the fore-theoretical context, I would have no acquaintance with the thing whatsoever.

Heidegger wishes to break the theoretical glass that encases the philosophical thinker, the wall that renders him personally invulnerable to the matter in question. The questioner must experience a redirection of inquiry if the hermeneutics of facticity is to succeed. We, the questioners, are the ones who are put into question. The safe impartiality of a theoretical inspection is no longer possible. To make facticity questionable is to resist the subtle substitution of general ideas for concrete experience. We are called to think our own existence. In the interest of staying as close to life as possible, Heidegger works with historically situated and provisional expressions (formal indications). The goal is to establish an oblique access to the everyday, to light up the factic from within. This requires Heidegger to abandon Husserl's Cartesian ideal of apodicticity. If phenomenology is to thematize life as it is lived by us, it must share in the being of the historical. Heidegger's phenomenology is therefore inescapably provisional. Hermeneutical phenomenology's "results" are directives for thinking, which must remain open to diverse historical applications. Formal indications are never set in stone; rather, they are subject to continual revision. The point is not to freeze life before the theoretical gaze, but to jump into life, midstream as it were, to *live* phenomenologically. This is not something the phenomenologist can do for anyone. Phenomenology is an invitation to apply a way of thinking, *to think,* on the assumption that every application will yield a different result. Phenomenology's task is to work with this ambiguity, to push back the darkness, without assuming that a final illumination is possible.

The provisionality of formally indicative phenomenology does not undermine its rigor. Rather, it makes the analysis ever more demanding, an act that must be perpetually reenacted. In this difficulty, this "staying with," phenomenology finds its only possible justification: to let life show itself by allowing it to live in our speaking and thinking. The hermeneutics of facticity cannot be completed, for to speak of completion makes no sense here.

The hermeneutics of facticity is an oblique approach to life, a showing of "something" which always accompanies us, yet which eludes direct scrutiny. While formal indication, so essential to the early Freiburg lectures, all but disappears from *Sein und Zeit* as an explicit methodological technique, the reasons that led Heidegger to articulate the notion remain central to his phenomenology.[21] The idea was to find a noninvasive way

---

21. Heidegger uses the term *formale Anzeige* in *Sein und Zeit* without methodological elaboration when an articulation of an *existential* structure of being-in-the-world is needed without

into the fore-theoretical, to philosophize without disturbing "the stream of life." This would be more akin to medieval mysticism than to Scholasticism. A formal indication does not dictate the theme in advance (it does not define content), but it invites the thinker to discover the theme for himself. Read as formally indicative, *Sein und Zeit* is a practical manual of exhortations that call us to a hermeneutical performance of thinking. It has more in common with *The Cloud of Unknowing* than with Aquinas's *De ente et essentia*. It is "an empty book," as Ryan Streeter puts it.[22]

Heidegger's development of the method of formal indication is rooted in his *Habilitationsschrift* and its examination of the problem of the ineffability of the singular. According to Aristotle, intellection is universal, while sensation is singular. Yet intellection depends upon sensation. While we cannot think without the singular, we never cognize it as such. Individual things are cognized only insofar as they are instances of a universal. Scotus's work on this problem generated the doctrine of *haecceitas*, the notion of the concrete intelligibility of the singular. For Scotus, Aristotle's doctrine of the ineffability of the singular exposes the limits of the mode of thinking constituted by defining and judging universals. Ineffability does not signify unintelligibility but the limitations of theoretical cognition. If the singular exhibits an intelligibility that eludes abstract intellection, we can speak of a fore-theoretical stratum of intelligibility, which is in fact the ground of theory. When we look at how we use language, Heidegger says, we see that defining content and judging are not the only ways of expressing intelligibility.[23] Where definitions are not possible, language can performatively and exhortatively point to that which cannot be named. The exhortation calls the recipient, not to think certain thoughts, but to perform a *way* of thinking.

Formally indicative language is a spur to existential self-engagement. To understand a formal indication, I must break out of the self-forgetfulness of theoretical speculation and apply it; I must enact it. Formal indication highlights historically differentiated semantic structure by

---

committing to any particular *existentiell* (ontic) interpretation of its meaning. See *SZ* 109/116; 213/231; 289–90/313.

22. Streeter, "Formal Indication," 426.

23. On this point, see my "Heidegger and Duns Scotus on Truth and Language."

suspending the relational sense, the *how* of the phenomenon.[24] We are not told how to interpret the matter. Rather, we are invited to interpret the matter ourselves. Formal indication is an exhortation to apply a way of thinking, without being given any clear directives as to what way of thinking must be applied. Thus, the formal indication puts the recipient into crisis. It is an intentional and strategic ambiguity.[25] Determinate meaning is in some way withheld and application (the enactment sense or *Vollzugssinn*) is highlighted as the locus of significance. The formal indication is therefore semantically unsatisfying yet formally charged with suggested and possible meaning.

The formal indication is analogous to the ironic speech act. The semantic gap in the formal indication, like the ambiguity in the ironic statement, startles us into interpretation. The contradiction between the form and content of the ironic speech act emphasizes a contextual significance that exceeds the content of the individual words. In order to understand the expression, I must enact it. I have to put myself into the situation of the speaker and see what it could mean for him. The understanding of irony is only possible through self-transposition: we see the expression through the eyes of the one who uses it and only then grasp its meaning. But to "see something through the eyes of another" is to see it through our own eyes, that is, to apply the meaning in a certain way.

Formal indication is necessary because of the singularity *(Jemeinigkeit)* of Dasein. The being of this being is absolutely historical. It is there-

---

24. "The formal indication is intended primarily as an advance indication of the relational sense of the phenomenon, in a negative sense at the same time as a warning! A phenomenon must be pre-given in such a way that its relational sense is held in suspense. One must guard against assuming that its relational sense is originally theoretical. This is a position that opposes the sciences in the extreme. There is no insertion into a content-domain, rather the opposite: the formal indication is a warding off, a preliminary protection, so that the enactment character remains free. The necessity of this precaution lies in the decadent tendency of factical life experience, which forces us into the objective, from which we must nevertheless draw the phenomena" (*GA*60 64/44).
25. "The formal indicator, although it guides the consideration, brings no predetermined opinion into the problem.... The formal predication is not bound to any content, however it must be motivated somehow. How is it motivated? It arises from the *meaning of the attitudinal relation* itself. I do not look from the *what* determination to the object, rather I view the object in a manner of speaking in its determinateness. I must look away from the given what-content, and instead see *that* the given content is given, attitudinally determined" (*GA*60 55; 58–59).

fore never theoretically thematized. Like the Scholastic God, *ipsum esse*, no names apply here. The medieval mystics taught that the task was not to define God but to love Him. The heart sees where the mind cannot. Heidegger says something similar. The only way to thematize a being that cannot be named is to indicate it formally, to point to it exhortatively in such a way that we are drawn to perform the act of thinking that will light up the being for ourselves.

The Return to Aristotle

Heidegger's fascination with the elusiveness of the factic determined his research trajectory from the *Habilitationsschrift* to *Sein und Zeit*. Directly after his Scotus work, he embarked upon a study of the problem of ineffable experience in religion (Schleiermacher and medieval mysticism). From there, he turned to Paul and Augustine via Dilthey's argument that early Christianity discovers historical consciousness. After the religion lectures of 1921, Heidegger immersed himself in the study of Aristotle. He interprets Aristotle's objection to Plato's essentialism as a Greek breakthrough to facticity. The concepts of matter *(hule)*, privation *(steresis)*, nature *(physis)*, and above all, concretely grounded intelligence *(phronesis)* indicate Aristotle's factic orientation. Heidegger lectured on Aristotle in 1921,[26] 1922,[27] 1924,[28] 1926,[29] and 1931.[30] Under job pressure to publish in 1922, Heidegger prepared an introduction to a book on Aristotle, "Phänomenologische Interpretationen zu Aristoteles. Anzeige der hermeneutischen Situation." The Aristotle book was abandoned in favor of *Sein und Zeit*, but some commentators still regard the latter as a commentary on Aristotle because it is so closely intertwined with Aristotle's

---

26. *GA*61, *Phänomenologische Interpretationen zu Aristoteles: Einführung in die phänomenologische Forschung*.

27. *GA*62 (forthcoming), *Phänomenologische Interpretationen ausgewählter Abhandlungen des Aristoteles zur Ontologie und Logik*.

28. *GA*18 (forthcoming), *Grundbegriffe der aristotelischen Philosophie*. See also the first hundred pages of *GA*19, *Platon: Sophistes*. That same year (1924), Heidegger delivered a lecture entitled "Dasein und Wahrsein nach Aristoteles, Ethica Nicomachea 7" to the Kant-Gesellschaft in Cologne (unpublished, planned for *GA*80).

29. *GA*22, *Grundbegriffe der antiken Philosophie*.

30. *GA*33, *Aristoteles: Metaphysik IX*.

project of grounding philosophy in life.³¹ In his autobiographical reflections, the later Heidegger remarks that his reading of Aristotle was a crucial stage in the development of his phenomenology.³²

Yet Heidegger's phenomenology is typically represented as a decisive break with Aristotle's "realist metaphysics." For example, in a recent article, Thomas Sheehan writes, "Aristotle's material object was the real *(to on)*, and his formal focus was on the realness of the real, *ousia* understood as independent of the human subject. By contrast, Heidegger's material object is the meaningful *(to alethes* or *to par-on)*, and his formal focus is on the meaningfulness of human interests and purposes."³³ Sheehan's dichotomy creates the false impression of Heidegger's phenomenology as a strict antithesis to Aristotle. The characterization of Aristotle as focusing on "the realness of the real," understood as mind-independence, is perhaps applicable to Aristotle's metaphysics (although a much more precise formulation of Aristotle's understanding of *ousia* is called for). But it falls wide of the mark with respect to Aristotle's psychology or ethics. In the *De anima* and the *Nicomachean Ethics,* Aristotle is concerned with the questions of possibility and historical meaning. His model of knowledge as an identity of knower and known, subject and object, proves that he is no naive realist, positing already-now-real things "outside" the subject. And Heidegger can only be characterized as an antirealist with qualification. It depends on whose realism is at issue. Realism in Aristotelian-Scholastic philosophy is to be distinguished from realism in the positivistic and empiricist sense. The real for Aristotle is not that which is already-out-there and independent of thinking, an order of pregiven objects against which the soul measures its concepts. The real includes the soul and the being of things that only have existence in the soul: universals, possibilities, and so forth. Knowledge for Aristotle is not *confrontation* with the already-out-there-now-real, but *identity.* The soul becomes what it knows. Phenomenology's break is not with Aristotle, but with what Husserl called "the natural attitude," the assumption

---

31. See Franco Volpi, *"Being and Time:* A 'Translation' of the *Nicomachean Ethics?"* in Kisiel and van Buren, *Reading Heidegger from the Start,* 195–211.
32. Heidegger, "Mein Weg," 81–90/74–82.
33. Thomas Sheehan, "Dasein," in Dreyfus and Wrathall, *A Companion to Heidegger,* 196.

that the structures given to consciousness are independent of the mind. On the naive realist view, knowledge is a representation of mind-independent things in the intellect. On the phenomenological view, which Aristotle anticipates, knowledge is a synthesis of conscious acts and intuited contents.

Heidegger's phenomenology repudiates a deductive approach to that which transcends experience. To this degree, it breaks with the Aristotelian idea of demonstrative knowledge, *episteme,* which becomes in Scholasticism the ideal of *scientia* (and in modernity, the search for apodictic foundations). Heidegger's ontology of things as relational matrices also clearly breaks with the Aristotelian idea of substance. Even as early as the *Habilitationsschrift,* Heidegger was critical of Aristotle's limitation of the categories to substance and its nine attributes. However, Heidegger is directly influenced by Aristotle's anti-Platonic attempt to remain faithful to this world.

Aristotle inherited the Greek prejudice against history but fought against it and eventually showed its limits by elaborating an experience of cognition that is concrete, singular, and bound to the play of unconcealment and hiddenness in historical life. In the lengthy introduction to the 1924 lecture course, "Interpretation platonischer Dialog: Sophistes" (*GA*19), Heidegger examines the Platonic consolidation of the theoretical comportment in Socrates' ocular metaphor for knowledge. To know is to "see" the form of a thing *(eidos),* to have an immediate intellectual grasp of the permanent idea showing itself in the shadowy sense data. Why, Heidegger asks, this fixation on vision as the best metaphor for cognition? Why not speak of hearing or touching? William McNeill summarizes Heidegger's answer: the ocular metaphor is motivated in an original aversion to time, for vision gives us the thing in its greatest degree of changelessness: "For only sight grants the simultaneity of what is present and what has been ... holds them together in one vision, as opposed to the mere sequential apprehending that occurs through the other senses."[34] The identification of being with *eidos* is a substitution of changelessness, constant presence, for the flux of the concrete.

---

34. William McNeill, *The Glance of the Eye: Heidegger, Aristotle, and the Ends of Theory* (Albany: State University of New York Press, 1999), 8.

Through a close reading of Aristotle's *Metaphysics,* book 1, and the *Nicomachean Ethics,* books 6 and 10, Heidegger outlines the degrees of theoretical cognition in Aristotle as a progressive de-worlding of the thing, from *aisthesis* (sensation) and *empeiria* (experience), through *techne* and *episteme,* to *sophia.* The movement represents a progressive abstraction from history. *Episteme,* the transition from the implicit universality of *techne* to the fullness of the whole in *sophia,* has as its object the necessary and eternal. It seizes on the *eidos* implicit in *techne* and drags it into perpetual unconcealment. *Episteme* contests the self-concealment of beings, resists history and sets up an alternative order of changeless essences. McNeill comments: "The *eidos* in this proto-independence is initially 'simply there,' implicit within *techne* itself. Its increasing separation—precisely via the Platonic-Aristotelian determination of being—is nevertheless indicative, as Heidegger points out, of an increasing independence of the Greek *logos* itself. Within the process of dealing with things, of doing and making, '*legein* becomes more and more independent'" (GA19 91).

In the practical domain, Aristotle discovers an opposite movement, away from the a-historical *eidos* back to the concrete ambiguities of daily life, from the universal to the singular. Ethics cannot be taught theoretically, Aristotle says, because it is not a matter of information. The practice of living well is inextricably historical, bound up with unique historical situations, "things that can be otherwise." The only way to learn virtue is by watching the virtuous man in action, seeing how he responds appropriately to every situation, giving in neither to excessive self-love, nor to excessive self-abnegation. The theoretical mind cannot abstract a universal principle that might supervene over all acts of ethical judgment. One must habituate oneself to choosing rightly, acquiring the virtue of *phronesis,* and this can only be done by moral practice. The theoretician can do little more than give a rough outline of the subject matter.[35]

Phronesis turns from the abstract back to the concrete, from worldless *theoria* to the en-worlded moment, where principles must be applied. We need to understand *how* the ethical principle applies in the given situation. Such understanding is never theoretical; it is only given with the

---

35. See Aristotle, *Nicomachean Ethics,* 1.3.

application of the principle. *Phronesis* is not a seeing that precedes practice, it is understanding through enactment. *Phronesis* is thinking in the situation, the historical moment, which cannot be apprehended by *logos*. Heidegger writes: "*Phronesis* is thus itself *indeed an aletheuein, but not an independent one, rather it is an aletheuein in the service of praxis; it is an aletheuein that makes an action transparent to itself*" (*GA*19 53). *Phronesis* apprehends an order of being that "exceeds the *logos*" (*GA*19 139). Guided by a "circumspect looking" (*umsichtiges Hinsehen*) (*GA*19 163), *phronesis* stays with the en-worlded thing, for it seeks a way of proceeding in the world. The practical syllogism projects an anticipated end, grasps the situation in the light of the end, and judges the situation in accordance with that end. The grasp of the situation, the minor premise, is a function of *nous*, and thus an intellectual act. It is not however the worldless seeing of *eidos*. Rather, it is insight into the concrete intelligibility of the historical. Aristotle writes "In demonstrations, *nous* apprehends the immutable and primary delimitations, in practical inferences it apprehends the ultimate fact *(eschaton)* that can be otherwise."[36] Heidegger finds in Aristotle's ethics the same phenomenon that attracted him in Scotus: the intellection of the intelligibility of the temporalized singular. Practical wisdom is insight into *kairos*, the concrete moment of actuation, "the most extreme limit," at which "an action engages" (*GA*19 157–58). "*Phronesis* is a *catching sight of the here-and-now* [*Erblicken des Diesmaligen*], of the concrete here-and-now character [*Diemaligkeit*] of the momentary situation. *As aisthesis, it is the glance of the eye, the momentary glance at what is concrete in each specific case and as such can always be otherwise*" (*GA*19 163–64).

Heidegger's reading of Aristotle is certainly selective. It could be said that he inflates Aristotle's sense for history into his own thesis concerning the finitude of being. Aristotle never elevates practical wisdom above theoretical wisdom *(sophia)*, quite the reverse. In a telling statement that foreshadows and passes judgment on Heidegger's elevation of praxis above theory, Aristotle says that to subordinate *sophia* to *phronesis* is to forget the divine. "It would be strange if someone thought that politics or practical wisdom was the most excellent kind of knowledge, unless man

---

36. Aristotle, *Nicomachean Ethics*, 6.11.1143a35.

is the best thing in the cosmos."³⁷ Practical wisdom is concerned with human living; theoretical wisdom raises its sights to the absolute, thought thinking itself. McNeill notes that Heidegger deliberately ignores Aristotle's theology because it does not serve the purposes of the hermeneutics of facticity. "Commensurate with the emphasis on the tendency of *theoria* to become an independent *praxis* is Heidegger's choosing largely to circumvent . . . the divine aspect of *theorein*."³⁸

Heidegger's Aristotle interpretation culminates in his appropriation of the primordial Greek notion of truth, *aletheia* or unconcealment, in *Sein und Zeit* (SZ 32–34/28–30). The truth of judgment, propositional truth, is derivative, or *founded*, secondary to the unconcealment without which it cannot occur. The correspondence theory of truth, *adaequatio*, suggests that truth is the match of a mental representation with a given thing, a relation between two present-at-hand beings, idea and object. *Aletheia*, by contrast, has no reference to correspondence. To be true is to be unconcealed, to emerge from a state of hiddenness into presence. The hegemony of theory is effected through the substitution of *adaequatio* for *aletheia*. Heidegger points out that Aristotle is often mistakenly cited as justifying this move. According to Heidegger, truth in Aristotle is not originally judgmental. The expressed *logos* is *apophainesthai*, an act of "letting be seen."³⁹ *Logos* points to something, letting the unconcealed be manifest to the speaker and those addressed. Because it can point out in such a way that it allows the thing to show itself or covers it over once again, *logos* can be true or false. *Logos* removes or creates obstacles to seeing, indicating something that has already shown itself or covering it over once again.⁴⁰

Aletheia is not wordless intuition. "The idea of an 'originary' and 'intuitive' grasp and explication of phenomena must be opposed to the naive-

---

37. Ibid., 6.5.1141a20–22.
38. McNeill, *Glance of the Eye*, 53.
39. Heidegger references Aristotle, *De interpretatione*, chaps. 1–6; *Metaphysics* 8.4; *Nicomachean Ethics* 7.
40. "The 'being true' of logos as *aletheuein* means: to take beings that are being talked about in *legein* as *apophainesthai* out of their concealment; to let them be seen as something unconcealed (*alethes*); to discover them. Similarly 'being false,' *pseudesthai*, is tantamount to deceiving in the sense of covering up: putting something in front of something else (by way of letting it be seen) and thereby passing it off as something it is not" (SZ 33/29).

té of an accidental, 'immediate,' and unreflective 'beholding'" (*SZ* 37/32). The fore-theoretical is lingually mediated. It shows itself as always already interpreted. What is seen is seen *as* something. The fore-theoretical foundation of language is not intuition but "discourse" *(Rede)*. As Kisiel puts it, "In being already intentionally structured, immediate experience is itself not mute, but 'meaningful,' which now means that it is already contextualized like a language."[41] The world into which we are thrown is already lit up by meaning; it is a domain of previously interpreted beings, to which, however inexplicably, we find we belong. Fore-theoretical experience is constitutively shaped by primal meanings coincident with the self-showing of the things. The primal sense of the thing is understood without judgmental mediation. Its opposite is not falsehood but nonapprehension, ignorance: *agnoein*. When things make themselves manifest, they "speak" their names to us. The task for a formally indicative phenomenology is to loosen up the primordial sense of experience, to go along with life in the way it is always already "worded" for us. *Aletheia* is not a vision of "things-in-themselves," rather, it is the unveiling of things as they are always already understood and interpreted by us. The condition of the possibility of *aletheia* is Dasein and its "worlding" activity.

With the distinction between judgmental truth and primordial truth, Heidegger breaks the bond between truth and knowledge.[42] In the view of some commentators, Heidegger thereby becomes vulnerable to the charge of relativism. Ernst Tugendhat, for example, holds that Heidegger's notion of truth annuls the possibility of verifiable philosophical knowledge. That which cannot be false cannot be verifiably true either.[43]

---

41. Kisiel, *Genesis of* Being and Time, 49. In 1925, Heidegger wrote: "It is also a matter of fact that our simplest perceptions and constitutive states are already *expressed*, even more, are *interpreted* in a certain way. What is primary and original here? It is not so much that we see the objects and things but rather that we first talk about them. To put it more precisely we do not say what we see, but rather the reverse, we see what *one says* about the matter" (*GA*20 75/56).

42. John Sallis, "The Truth that is not Knowledge," in Kisiel and van Buren, *Reading Heidegger from the Start*, 390.

43. "If truth means un-concealment, in the Heideggerian sense, then it follows that an understanding of world in general is opened up but not that it is put to the test. What must have seemed so liberating about this conception is that, without denying the relativity and opaqueness of our historical world, it made possible an immediate and positive truth-relation, an explicit truth-relation which no longer made any claim to certainty and so could not be disturbed by uncertainty either. . . . That he already calls disclosure in and of itself truth leads to the result that it is precisely

Tugendhat's objection would be shared by most Scholastic critics of Heidegger. An Aristotelian-Scholastic doctrine of truth includes both an aletheic and an apodictic or judgmental moment. The aletheic moment in Aquinas is *illuminatio;* in Scotus, it is *simplex apprehensio,* the first moment in thinking, the indubitable showing of the given. The essence of Heidegger's doctrine of *aletheia* is the claim, with which neither Aquinas nor Scotus would disagree, that prior to judgment, the soul experiences a world. Yet Heidegger's suspension of Aristotle's doctrine of judgment no Scholastic could support. Phenomenology could only be appropriated into a Scholastic ontology by being subordinated to metaphysics. Understanding is not knowledge. That which shows itself, the Scholastics would say, must ultimately be submitted to the tribunal of judgment before its ontological weight can be decided.

Dasein/Care/Being-Unto-Death

Heidegger's most radical departure from Aristotelian ontology revolves around his claim that beings *are* only *for* Dasein. This is not so much an endorsement of idealism as a reconceiving of being in the light of the phenomenon of intentionality. Being is no longer thought as *subsistence* but as *appearance.* To be means to be determinable within Dasein's comprehension of being. That *is* which can appear to Dasein. The Aristotelian-Scholastic notion of the immaterial intellect is replaced by Dasein as the site of the appearing of beings. "With the *Existenz* of humankind an irruption in the whole of being occurs such that, by this event, the particular being becomes revealed in itself, i.e., revealed as a being" (*GA*3 228/235). Beings depend on Dasein for their being. Without the fissure in the night of being, or in Heidegger's preferred metaphor, the clearing *(Lichtung)* of being, which is Dasein, beings could not appear as beings. This is not idealism. The early Heidegger is concerned to end the idealism-realism dispute by making both positions impossible. Things are not independent of Dasein, but neither are they projections of Dasein. They *are* only for

---

not related to the truth but is protected from the question of truth." Ernst Tugendhat, "Heidegger's Idea of Truth," trans. Christopher Macann, in *Critical Heidegger,* ed. Christopher Macann (London: Routledge, 1996), 238.

Dasein, but they *are as* non-Dasein. "Only as long as Dasein *is*, that is, as long as there is the ontic possibility of an understanding of being, 'is there' being. If Dasein does not exist, then there 'is' no 'independence' either, nor 'is' there an 'in itself.' Such matters are then neither comprehensible nor incomprehensible. Innerworldly beings, too, can neither be discovered, nor can they lie in concealment. *Then* [if Dasein does not exist] it can neither be said that beings are, nor that they are not. *Now,* [as long as Dasein exists] as long as there is an understanding of being and thus an understanding of objective presence, we can say that *then* [when Dasein no longer exists] beings will still continue to be" (*SZ* 212/196). This puzzling passage shows the nonsensicality of asking about the existence of beings independent of the being that *alone* understands being. In effect, the question means, do things conditioned in a certain way exist as so conditioned when the conditioning conditions no longer obtain? The beings that are at issue are always beings *for* Dasein. Things-in-themselves could not exist "outside" Dasein, for all possible ways of being are encompassed by Dasein's pre-understanding of being. No conditions for being can be posited where and when Dasein does not exist. What we mean by the "independence" of the "in-itself" is in fact a way of being related to Dasein.

The preeminence of Dasein in Heidegger's ontology represents a decisive overturning of the Scholastic notion of the hierarchy of being. If Dasein is the condition of the possibility of beings appearing as beings, then it cannot be fit into an ordered hierarchy. It is not a step in a system of being but the source of all hierarchies, the orderer. We are struck by the exalted place of the human being in Heidegger's thinking and at the same time, by his fragility. Dasein is godlike, letting beings be by liberating them from concealment. Yet it does not posit itself, nor unconceal itself. It is not the source of its own being, but finds itself thrown into the world. It is usually and for the most part lost in the things of the world and oblivious to its difference from all other beings. It cannot always and everywhere hold itself before being; forgetting is as constitutive of its being as understanding.

Heidegger's focus on what a Scholastic would regard as the psychological and spiritual life of the soul leads him away from the theoretical ontological discussions of the Scholastics toward the ascetical and mystical literature of the Middle Ages. It is not in the metaphysical treatises of the Middle Ages that the *Daseinanalytic* finds its clearest medieval resonance but in the pious writings of Bonaventure, in the sermons of Bernard of Clairvaux, in Augustine's *Confessions* and Teresa of Avila's *Interior Castle*. The challenge faced by the soul finding its way back into God as it struggles with sin and distraction highlights features of our being-in-the-world essential to Heidegger's ontology. Formalizing a structure that he discovered in early Christian eschatology, Heidegger traces our ability to disperse ourselves on the world—to pour ourselves out onto the things and people that preoccupy us—to the essential futurity of Dasein. Care shows us that we are *ahead* of ourselves, projected a priori toward an end. The end, which draws us ineluctably toward itself, or comes to meet us, or pushes us from behind (each metaphor is in some way applicable and in some way inadequate), is our ownmost extreme possibility for being, which is also our possibility not to be, our imminent impossibility: death. These three phenomena, Dasein, care, and being-unto-death, are intimately related—Scotus would say the distinctions between them are formal. They are in fact three "formalities" of one being. Dasein can reveal itself as a being-in-the-world because its being is structured by care. Care, in turn, is an indication of being-unto-death.

Dasein, unthinkable without its world—the "subject" and its situation unified in a single concept—is above all historical. It is a product of its past; it is what it has become (the *Gewordensein* of Heidegger's Paul lectures). Dasein is thrown into the world, finding itself in moods, in its preoccupation with other Dasein and with everyday things, none of which it creates or ultimately controls. Out of this thrownness, Dasein projects itself upon its possibilities. It plans and designs and schematizes a path ahead for itself. Its past is the ground of its essentially futural existence. In Heidegger's peculiar language, Dasein is a thrown-projection (*ein geworfener Entwurf*). Both thrownness and projection (primordial pastness and futurity) are indications of the care structure that founds being-in-the-world. In its care, Dasein is always outside itself. For the most part, care shows how Dasein is never *in itself* but always dispersed in its world. At its root, care is determined by Dasein's fore-theoretical flight from itself, its *angst* in the face of its own nothingness and finitude.

Angst is not just one of many moods from which Dasein suffers; rather, it is *the* being-disclosing mood, for it reveals that which we essentially are: being-unto-death. Death does for Heidegger's phenomenological anthropology what Christ does for Christian mysticism. It is at once the source of everything that we are and the destiny of our ever-unfolding being. It is that from which we run in our worldly dispersions, and that toward which we run when we recollect ourselves. It is the judgment hanging over us and our only salvation. Dasein has no peace while it fails to appropriate death into its life. To live authentically is to *be* resolutely unto-death, to be transparent to our being-toward-death (this is not resignation, but self-appropriation), to recover ourselves from our worldly dispersion, our flight from death, and to achieve a moment of what can only be described as Godless equanimity.

The nonrelationality of death is crucial to Heidegger's anthropology. When I resolutely appropriate my death (this is not suicide, but living fully out of what I am), I throw myself back onto the irreducible singularity of my being. The first two "existentials" or ontological structures of Dasein that Heidegger disengages in *Sein und Zeit* are "Existenz" and "ever-mineness" *(Jemeinigkeit)*. To ex-ist (to be outside oneself or ex-stasis) means to have an ontological relationship to possibility, that is, to be grounded in a basic futurity. Dasein is never simply identical with itself, like an animal or a thing. Its being lies ever before it as a task to be undertaken. It is always a "to be." For this reason, it is a being that is always concerned about its being. In other words, Dasein is always answerable to itself for itself. It is thrown into this task of being itself, and the throw releases it into possibilities. Ever-mineness indicates the singularity and unrepeatability of that into which Dasein is thrown. In its solitary call to be, Dasein awaits its being. Its being is never finished. Something essential is always outstanding. The unfinishedness of its being is the source of its restlessness and anxiety. Death brings me back to myself, for no one can take it from me or die in my place. In resoluteness unto death, I am fully myself, ex-isting in the fullness of my irreducible singularity. I am *eigentlich*—the German is badly translated as "authentic." What the word means literally is "own-ly." To be resolute is to own myself, to grasp myself as a singular and solitary call to a task that is never accomplished, which, in a sense, can only finish in failure, and yet, *not* to fly from this, not to mitigate the experience with distractions and further self-dispersions.

The *Daseinanalytic* is not intended as an exhaustive account of the human being, but as a prolegomena to an investigation into the being of time. Only that dimension of human living is examined which Heidegger deems necessary to the ontological analysis that is to follow. This is his principle justification for suspending ethical and religious phenomena, a suspension that will be questioned later in this work.

CHAPTER FOUR

DUNS SCOTUS

That I was constantly concerned with Duns Scotus and the Middle Ages and then back to Aristotle was by no means an accident.

HEIDEGGER

The influence of Scotus on Heidegger, while long a subject of general speculation, has not yet received a careful study. Heidegger's debt to Scotus manifests itself on the opening page of *Sein und Zeit*. Heidegger asks about the *meaning* of being, that is, to what essence *(logos)* does the word "being" refer (SZ 2/1). He assumes a single meaning of being, a *univocatio entis,* which determines and makes possible all thinking and discourse. And he assumes that this notion of being is the a priori possession of Dasein; it is pre-understood in all that Dasein thinks and says. Further on, Heidegger writes: "higher than actuality stands possibility" (SZ 38/34). With Scotus, the factuality of the existing thing, what Aquinas describes as the pure positivity of *esse,* is displaced and subordinated to the intelligible conditions of the thing's possibility. Even Etienne Gilson, the great enemy of "essentialism," and Gustav Siewerth, his German counterpart, failed to recognize the Heidegger-Scotus connection. Gilson used to recommend Heidegger's 1935 *Einführung in die Metaphysik* to his undergraduates. This suggests that he completely misjudged the polemical relationship of Heidegger's ontology to Aquinas's. Siewerth passionately believed that Heidegger was one with him in his project of ridding metaphysics of the influence of Scotism! He assumed that Heidegger's forgetfulness of being was the forgetfulness of the act of being, *esse*. Gilson and Siewerth failed to see that being for Heidegger is not Aquinas's *esse*, the pure positivity of that which is; it is, rather, historical *understandability*.

This oversight is due to the widespread neglect of the *Habilitationsschrift*. We have too long assumed (on the later Heidegger's suggestion) that this is a youthful work lacking direction, with no intrinsic connection to *Sein und Zeit*. On the contrary, the text is shot through with a concern for what Heidegger will later call facticity.[1] Medievalists for their part ignore the work because one of Heidegger's principle source texts, *De modis significandi sive Grammatica speculativa*, long attributed to Duns Scotus, was discovered by Martin Grabmann in 1922 to be a work of Thomas of Erfurt.[2] The text-critical problem is compounded by Heidegger's hermeneutical approach, which typically annoys medievalists. Heidegger is explicitly suspending historical questions in the interest of a *Sache*-oriented discussion, which will allow him to expose the resonance between the philosophy of language of Scotus/Erfurt and the phenomenology of Edmund Husserl. The *Habilitationsshcrift* is not a historical study of medieval texts but a phenomenological treatise, which draws on medieval sources. It is in fact the first of Heidegger's many "violent" interpretations. Heidegger assumes historical access to the matter at issue in the text. He is not interested in determining precisely what the author said on an issue, or what he intended in a particular text. He is not all that interested in who said it, either. He is, rather, zeroing in on the issue itself, on the assumption that it shows itself in our historical epoch dif-

---

1. While earlier commentators had difficulty drawing connections between the *Habilitationsschrift* and *Sein und Zeit*, Kisiel writes that Heidegger's first book "is totally governed by the tendency toward facticity." Kisiel, *Genesis of Being and Time*, 20.

2. Martin Grabmann, "De Thoma Erfordiensi auctore Grammaticae quae Ioanni Duns Scoto adscribitur speculativae," *Archivum Franciscanum Historicum* 15 (1922): 273–77. Grabmann later showed that the misidentification occurred as early as the first half of the fifteenth century. Martin Grabmann, "Die Entwicklung der mittelalterlichen Sprachlogik," in *Mittelalterliches Geistesleben. Abhandlung zur Geschichte der Scholastik und Mystic*, ed. Ludwig Ott, vol. 1 (Munich: Max Heuber, 1926), 116–25. Erfurt's treatise was printed along with authentic works by Scotus in volume 1 of Luke Wadding's seventeenth-century edition of the *Opera omnia* of Duns Scotus (Lyons, 1639), reprinted in the nineteenth century by Juan-Luis Vivès (Paris, 1891). On the mistaken authorship and Heidegger, see Jack Zupko, "Thomas of Erfurt," *The Stanford Encyclopedia of Philosophy* (Spring 2003 edition), ed. Edward N. Zalta, URL = <<http://plato.stanford.edu/archives/spr2003/entries/erfurt/>>.

ferently than it did in the fourteenth century. Grabmann appears to have understood this subtle point, while noting how Heidegger's fast and free handling of medieval texts is problematic to medievalists. "Martin Heidegger has demonstrated the continuity of the *Grammatica speculativa* hitherto attributed to Duns Scotus with the terminology and overall intellectual outlook of Husserl, so that the structure and distinctiveness of the medieval original is somewhat obscured."[3]

It would be going too far, however, to dismiss the *Habilitationsschrift* as a work that is not about Duns Scotus at all, for in addition to the *Grammatica speculativa*, Heidegger makes use of authentic texts of Scotus. The *Habilitationsschrift* is divided into two parts: (1) "Die Kategorienlehre" ("The Doctrine of Categories"), and (2) "Die Bedeutungslehre" ("The Doctrine of Meaning"). The first half deals with the transcendentals in Duns Scotus, drawing on Scotus's *Opus oxoniense* and the authentically Scotist commentaries on Porphyry's *Isagoge*, Aristotle's *Categories*, and Aristotle's *De sophisticis elenchis*. The second half, "die Bedeutungslehre," is based on Thomas of Erfurt's *Grammatica speculativa*. There is an intrinsic affinity between Erfurt's speculative grammar and Scotus's metaphysics, which doubtlessly contributed to the mistaken authorship. Scotus and Erfurt share a proto-idealist assumption that identifies being *(ens)* with intelligibility *(essentia)*, and knowing *(scientia)* with understanding *(intellectus)*. The being of the thing is wholly intelligible—no act of existence remains outside of the light of *essentia*. Consequently, ontology is fully reflected in language. Thus, in a quasi-transcendental move, Erfurt endeavors to prove how a complete account of modes of meaning coincides with a complete set of ontological categories.[4]

The following chapter does not presume to sort out this hermeneutical mess. It is not a study of Erfurt or Scotus, nor a comparison of Scotus, Erfurt, and Heidegger. It is an examination of *what Heidegger finds in Scotus and Erfurt*. I alternate as freely as Heidegger himself between

---

3. Grabmann, "Die Entwicklung," 118.

4. In fact, Scotus was influenced by Modism, if not by Erfurt, by other Modist authors such as Simon of Faversham and Andrew of Cornwall. See the editors' introduction to B. Ioannis Duns Scoti, *Quaestiones in Librum Porphyrii Isagoge et Quaestiones super Praedicamenta Aristotelis*, ed. R. Andrews et al., *Opera Philosophica* I (St. Bonaventure, N.Y.: The Franciscan Institute, 1999): xxxi–xxxiv.

passages where Heidegger is commenting on Erfurt's text and passages where he comments on Scotus. I am trying to expose the medieval roots of Heidegger's thinking, without presuming to disentangle those roots historically-critically. That work I leave to other scholars. For the sake of clarity, I refer to "Erfurt" when the point concerns Heidegger's reading of the *Grammatica speculativa* and "Scotus," when treating Heidegger's reading of texts of Scotus.

Heidegger's Neo-Kantian Approach to Speculative Grammar

The *Habilitationsschrift* belongs to the early Heidegger's twilight years. He was growing out of his "theological beginnings" but had not yet developed into the hermeneutician of factical life he would become in 1919. The text lies on the border of these two clearly distinguishable phases of Heidegger's development, blending characteristics of both without the distinctness of either. Yet in the light of the early Freiburg lectures, in particular the morphology of the *Seinsfrage* from the 1919 search for a non-distortive thematization of factical life, we can conclude that this seldom read text is the beginning of Heidegger's way. The roots of Heidegger's early thinking about being, time, and historical *Existenz* reach into the issues that motivated this intensive study of Scotus and speculative grammar. Duns Scotus's notion of the intuition of singulars *(simplex apprehensio)* and Thomas of Erfurt's grammatical modes *(modi significandi)* have an essential relationship to Heidegger's 1919 concept of "hermeneutical intuition" of the fore-theoretical forms of meaning that "live in life itself" (*GA*56/57 117), and through that, to the existential of *Verstehen* in *Sein und Zeit*. More importantly, the central impulse of Scotus's metaphysics, the search for a unifying concept of being, which makes all univocal, anological, and metaphorical predications possible, is transposed by Heidegger into a transcendental phenomenological key, while remaining basically intact. Heidegger has no sympathy for the Thomist *analogia entis*. His decisive departure from Scotus, the rejection of an infinite mode of being, does not break with the Scotist project of maintaining a univocal notion of being. On the contrary, Heidegger's refusal to entertain infinite ontological predicates might be read as an intensification of the Scotist project.

Widely reproduced and commented upon in the Middle Ages, Thomas of Erfurt's *De modis significandi sive Grammatica speculativa* is the most complete "speculative grammar" extant.[5] Against nominalism, Erfurt affirms a metaphysical foundation to language, which could be disengaged through grammatical analysis.[6] He transforms metaphysics into ordinary-language philosophy on the assumption that grammatical forms, the *modi significandi* of common verbs, nouns, and adjectives, indicate deep, unobjectifiable, but no less intelligible ontological structures embedded in historical life. Roger Bacon inspired the speculative grammar movement with his observation that all languages are built upon a common grammar, a shared foundation of ontically anchored linguistic structures: "Grammar is substantially the same in all languages, even though it may undergo in them accidental variations."[7]

We have it on Heidegger's own word that the *Habilitationsschrift* was pivotal to his development.[8] Heidegger understood his Scotus study to be a first step in a lifelong retrieval of Scholasticism and medieval mysticism, a retrieval that would avoid both the archaicism of neo-Scholasticism and the antimedieval prejudices of modernity. Officially, he was working with Heinrich Rickert, the neo-Kantian, to whom the text is dedicated. The immediate concerns driving the *Habilitationsschrift* are neo-Kantian: the problem of knowledge, the idealism/realism debate, and the search for an exhaustive deduction of a priori categories. Heidegger learned at least two important philosophical lessons from Rickert: first, the power of transcendental critique; second, the historical nature of philosophical problems.[9] Transcendental philosophy need not hover in the view from

---

5. G. L. Bursill-Hall, introduction to Thomas of Erfurt, *Grammatica speculativa*, trans. G. L. Bursill-Hall (London: Longman, 1972), 27.

6. On speculative grammar, see Martin Grabmann, *Thomas von Erfurt und die Sprachlogik des mittelalterlichen Aristotelismus* (Munich: Verlag der Bayerischen Akademie der Wissenschaften, 1943); Etienne Gilson, *History of Christian Philosophy in the Middle Ages* (New York: Random House, 1955), 312–13, 781.

7. Roger Bacon, quoted in Gilson, *History of Christian Philosophy*, 19 n. 1.

8. See Heidegger's letter to Karl Löwith, in *Zur philosophischen Aktualität Heideggers*, ed. Dietrich Papenfuss and Otto Pöggeler, vol. 2: *Im Gespräch der Zeit* (Frankfurt am Main: Vittorio Klostermann, 1990), 37.

9. In his *curriculum vitae* written for the 1915 habilitation procedure, Heidegger has the

nowhere of idealism; properly applied, it could engage the temporality of thinking. The guiding problematic of the *Habilitationsschrift* is the question concerning categories or the theory of meaning, *die Kategorien- und Bedeutungslehre*. The problem was central to neo-Kantianism, which sought to supplement Kant's table of categories with a further elaboration of the a priori forms of meaning intrinsic to different patterns of living, aesthetic, ethical, religious, and so forth. Heidegger takes it upon himself to inform his neo-Kantian colleagues about the wealth of material relevant to the question of the categories buried in the Scholastic tradition. In a 1917 letter to Grabmann, Heidegger writes that in one respect Scholasticism has an advantage over Kantianism: its doctrine of categories is not confined by the limited theoretical purview of natural science. "The value of the Scholastic theory of knowledge is grounded directly in the fact that it is worked out not according to natural science but according to the theory of meaning." He boasts of the accomplishment of his *Habilitationsschrift*: "Rickert now sees the Scholastics with different eyes."[10]

To be sure, the interest in fore-theoretical patterns of thinking was not foreign to the neo-Kantians. In Rickert's seminars, Heidegger learned of Rickert's star student who had recently been killed on the battlefield, Emil Lask. Lask's mediation of Rickert, Husserl, and Aristotle, coupled with an analysis of the fore-theoretical ground of the categories in everyday life, inspired Heidegger to do something similar in his *Habilitationsschrift*: bring neo-Kantian concerns to bear on a seminal text in the history of philosophy.[11] Against a psychologistic reading of Kant, Lask ar-

---

following to say about Rickert: "In this new school [Rickert's neo-Kantianism] I learned first of all to recognize philosophical problems as problems, and gained an insight into the nature of logic, the philosophical discipline that still continues to interest me the most. At the same time I acquired a proper understanding of modern philosophy since Kant, which I found was covered only very sketchily and inadequately in the Scholastic literature. My basic philosophical convictions remained those of Aristotelian-Scholastic philosophy. In time I came to see that the ideas contained in it must permit of—and indeed demanded—a much more fruitful interpretation and application.... My reading of Hegel and Fichte, my close study of Rickert's *Limits of Conceptualization in the Natural Sciences* and the investigations of Dilthey, and not least the lectures and seminars given by Professor Finke, all combined to destroy completely the antipathy for history that my taste for mathematics had previously fostered in me." Heidegger quoted in Ott, *Biographie*, 86/85–86.

10. Martin Heidegger to Martin Grabmann, January 7, 1917, in Denker, Gander, and Zaborowski, *Heidegger Jahrbuch*, 1:73–74.

11. In his review of Heidegger's *Habilitationsschrift*, Rickert wrote that Heidegger "is in

gued that we do not impose a priori form on the raw "matter" of sense; we live in form, as in a context or an environment *(Umgebung),* which embraces that which it "in-forms."[12] Categories accommodate themselves to matter, which they "surround" *(umschließen)* and contextually "validate" *(umgelten).* Lask argues that the immediate is formed at its most basic level. A category is "nothing other than a particular objective context [*Bewandtnis*] pertaining to . . . the material," a "moment of clarity" in which the matter is "lit up."[13] For Lask, the Kantians miss an important phenomenological point when they overemphasize theoretical categories: the preformal intelligibility of the given. The categories light up *something* that is already showing itself. Matter is not passive and without structure. It determines form by receiving it according to preformal intelligible structures embedded in concrete historical life.[14] Lask speaks of a "preformal something" *(das vorformale Etwas)* or "fore-predicative something" *(das vorprädikative Etwas),* which underlies categorial and judgmental knowledge.[15] Fore-theoretical structure is grasped in the first act of the intellect, what Lask (borrowing from Husserl) calls "categorial intuition."[16] The preformal is the primordially given patterns of expe-

---

particular very much obligated to Lask's writings for his philosophical orientation as well as his terminology, perhaps more than he himself is conscious of." Rickert's report on Heidegger's *Habilitationsschrift,* in *Martin Heidegger/Heinrich Rickert. Briefe 1912 bis 1933,* ed. Alfred Denker (Frankfurt am Main: Vittorio Klostermann, 2002), 96. Heidegger's letters to Rickert during the years he was writing the *Habilitationsschrift,* 1914 to 1916, are full of references to Lask. See ibid., 18, 19, 23. Upon finishing the *Habilitationsschrift,* Heidegger began to write on Lask, apparently not finishing the work. See ibid., 32–33. On Lask, see Steven Galt Crowell, "Making Logic Philosophical Again (1912–1916)," in Kisiel and van Buren, *Reading Heidegger from the Start,* 62–65; Kisiel, *Genesis of Being and Time,* 25–38; idem, "Why Students of Heidegger Will Have to Read Emil Lask," in *Emil Lask and the Search for Concreteness,* ed. Deborah G. Chaffin (Athens: Ohio University Press, 1993).

12. See Emil Lask, *Die Logik der Philosophie und die Kategorienlehre,* vol. 2 of *Gesammelte Schriften,* ed. Eugen Herrigel (Tübingen: J. C. B. Mohr, 1923), 75. See ibid., p. 69: "Was ist Gegenständlichkeit, Sein, objektiver Bestand, Wirklichkeit, Realität, Existenz anderes als jene besondere objektive Bewandtnis, die es mit der sinnlich alogischen Inhaltsmasse hat? Nichts anderes als eine schützende, verfestigende Hülle, wovon das Alogische wie von einer logischen Kruste umfangen ist. Nicht etwa vom Erkennen geformt und hineingestellt wird jedoch das Material, sondern an sich ist es betroffen von logischer Form, so wahr logischer Gehalt an sich Hingeltungsgehalt ist." See Kisiel, *Genesis of Being and Time,* 33.

13. Lask, *Logik,* 1:69, 75.   14. Ibid., 2:59–61.

15. Ibid., 1:174, 281, 367, 378.

16. See Husserl, *Logical Investigations,* vol. 2, Investigation VI, §45: "If we are asked what it means to say that *categorially structured meanings* find fulfilment, confirm themselves in perception, we can but reply: it means only that they relate to the object itself *in its original structure.* The

rience presupposed in every act of thinking. Hence Lask describes his work as "transcendental empiricism," the transcendental analysis of the primordially given forms of all possible forms of meaning, the "categories of categories." Heidegger discovered in Lask the insight that the factic is charged with prereflective understandability, structure that is never theoretically grasped but is nonetheless experienced. As Kisiel puts it, "this immediate experience of living through the forms in order to mediately know the cognitive object, the matter, is the moment of categorial intuition in every cognition. Thus the non-sensory form is at first not known but only experienced or lived. This constitutes the immediacy of human life fraught with meaning and value."[17] Judgment is a second level of truth, an affirmation that is either "in accord with truth" or "contrary to truth." The primordial truth against which judgments are measured first shows itself in categorial intuition. One lives in the preformally intelligible without "knowing" it as such.[18] We are at first "lost" in meaning, given over in "pure absorption."[19]

The horizons of Lask's neo-Kantianism, Duns Scotus's metaphysics, and Thomas of Erfurt's speculative grammar fuse in the assumption that ontology could be a priori or transcendental. In his 1912 essay "Neuere Forschungen über Logik" (*GA*1), Heidegger, working against the neo-Kantian trend that reads Kant as an epistemological skeptic, explores the possibility of a unity of logic with ontology. "Kant has created the logic of the categories of being. To understand this, it must be observed that being has forfeited its translogical independence, that being has been reworked into a concept in transcendental logic. This does not mean that objects should be stamped as 'pure logical content,' but only that objectivity, thingness as opposed to things, being as opposed to beings, is a logical value, a form" (*GA*1 24). Heidegger here touches upon a first figure for ontological difference: being, as formal, "a logical value," is distinct from beings. Heidegger develops the distinction by drawing on Lask's concept of validity. By distinguishing the domain of logical meaning (validity)

---

object with these categorial forms is not merely referred to as in the case where meanings function purely symbolically, but it is set before our very eyes in just these forms. In other words: it is not merely thought of, but intuited or perceived."

17. Kisiel, *Genesis of Being and Time*, 27.   18. Lask, *Logik,* 1:191 f.
19. Ibid., 1:190–91, 56, 85, 103, 129, 132.

from the domain of spatio-temporal things (existence), Lask intended to resolve the dispute between Aristotelians and Kantians on the nature of categories. Unlike existing things, categories are nonspatial and timeless. The Scotist direction of Heidegger's thinking at this time could not be plainer: being is not act of existence but meaning, validity, *essentia*. Being as a "logical value," a "form," is the essence of essence, that which is common to everything that has an essence. As purely ideal, being is transparent to understanding, a logical structure with which the intellect is always already conversant. On this premise, transcendental logic becomes ontology, a theme Heidegger will take up again years later in his 1929 *Kant und das Problem der Metaphysik*.

Heidegger's 1913 dissertation *Die Lehre vom Urteil im Psychologismus* is a study of Lask's critique of psychologism. The attempt to reduce the validity of judgments to psycho-physical phenomena, either biochemical or emotional responses (the "physics of thinking," as Theodor Lipps puts it), violates empirical fact (*GA1* 158). Validity makes a claim on subjectivity. "The true sentence—according to its content—does not exist like a house, but validates itself" (*GA56/57* 50).[20] And yet the validity of the sentence is something other than its ontic reference. In his 1913 dissertation, Heidegger insists that the grammar of existence and the grammar of validity are distinct: we cannot say that the valid *is*—this would be the category mistake of subsuming validity under existence—but only that it validates, "es gilt" (*GA1* 170, the first example of a German "impersonal" grammatical structure explored by Heidegger).[21] What is judged as valid

20. Van Buren, *Young Heidegger,* 61; Caputo, *Heidegger and Aquinas,* 32. By the early 1920s, Heidegger had become critical of the notion of validity as an "unstable concept." See *SZ* 156/146.

21. Kisiel has thoroughly studied Heidegger's lifelong interest in this grammatical structure, which first appears in Heidegger's dissertation, becomes the central theme of the 1919 lecture course, "Die idee der Philosophie und das Weltanschauungsproblem" (*GA56/57*), and resurfaces in the late discussions of *Ereignis*, the *es gibt* that sends being. See Kisiel, *Genesis of* Being and Time, 23–25: "Out of ordinary German and its vast pool of impersonals, Heidegger has found his very first and most perduring formally indicative grammatical form. Like 'It's raining!' in English, 'It' points to a most singular, unique, and comprehensive Event happening now. What is this mysterious It, no longer a substantifying It but a sheer Event, when it is directed to the sheer fact of life, of being, of being here and now? . . . Throughout his long career, Heidegger will never seek to surpass this central insight which gives priority to the impersonal event enveloping the I *which* 'takes place' in that Event. He will never in any way moderate or mitigate this lifelong fascination with the impersonal sentence which proliferates in the German language, this German infection which he

validates itself; it shows itself as valid independent of psychological comportment. Psychology heeds validity, not vice versa. The judgment, 7 + 5 = 12, remains valid regardless of whether I have a neurological synapsis that occasions a feeling for its validity. Existence is the domain of changing material conditions; validity is the domain of meaning *(Sinn)*, independent of the physical conditions that accompany judgment. Every being has valid sense, yet validity is not identical to "real" or "actual" being. Rather, validity is the horizon of meaningfulness presupposed in every ontological determination, the ground of the possibility of anything's being thought. Heidegger concludes his dissertation with the highest praise for Lask's accomplishment: "Lask aspires after nothing less than a doctrine of categories that encompasses the totality of what can be thought with both its two hemispheres of beings, existence and validity, and his attempt can be placed among the ranks of great thinkers" (*GA1* 24).

In Erfurt's speculative grammar, Heidegger discovers a medieval prototype for transcendental logic. Husserl's phenomenology, which characterized itself as "a priori grammar," recapitulates Erfurt's deduction of categories from the varieties of ways we use words (*GA1* 327–28).[22] The existence of this medieval precedent for phenomenological logic is an indicator of the philosophical depths hidden in the Scholastic tradition. Heidegger reads Erfurt's contribution as indicative of the Scholastics' "absolute devotion *(Hingabe)* to the knowledge transmitted by tradition" (*GA1* 198), a moment of "phenomenological observation," "an objective-noematic orientation," which "favors the prospective of intentional phenomena" (*GA1* 202, 205). "The value of the matter to be thought *(der Sachwert)* takes precedence over the value of the I ... the individuality of the single thinker disappears in the fullness of the matter to be dealt with" (*GA1* 198). But Erfurt does not simply anticipate modern logic. He remains free of certain modern prejudices that hinder phenomenology.

---

picked up in his early neo-Kantian years. The original something is an original motion, the facticity of our being is an event or happening, the facticity of Time itself. And the most direct, indicative, way which Heidegger finds to simply name this It which happens to us, to point to its sheer action, to attempt to describe its character and basic tenor, is the German impersonal sentence."

22. "The existence of a doctrine of meaning within medieval Scholasticism reveals a sensitive disposition and attunement to the immediate life of subjectivity and its immanent contexts of meaning, without having achieved a more precise concept of the subject" (*GA1* 401).

He does not need to disentangle logic from subjectivism. The categories embedded in the intentional structures of ordinary language are not merely psychological; they are ontological.

Intentional Being

Heidegger's task in the *Habilitationsschrift* is to show how Scotus and Erfurt offer contemporary philosophy resources for overcoming the idealist-realist impasse. At the center of the *Habilitationsschrift* is the Scholastic notion of intentional being, *ens logicum*. The being of the *intentum* is both a being for consciousness and a being-in-itself. It is what it is by virtue of the *intentio*, yet it remains *objectum*, a thing in its own right, irreducible to subjectivity. Subjectivity goes out to the object; objectivity is that toward which subjectivity is directed. The intentional "form" is not a subjective imposition on matter; the intention is as much determined by the matter as it is determinative of it.[23] Philosophy must be liberated from both naive realism and subjective idealism, which are equally guilty of dichotomizing subject and object. The move will involve a retrieval of the intentional structure of being. Intentions are neither within me, nor do they stand over and against me. They belong to a domain *between* subject and object, self and world.[24] The object does

---

23. In 1914, Heidegger wrote to Rickert: "Your valuable input with respect to Duns Scotus, to understand and evaluate him through the medium of modern logic, has encouraged me to make a first, and in any case, preliminary attempt to retrieve his 'language logic.' In the meantime, I have learned to see that a real doctrine of meaning lies at its basis, which can be illuminated by the doctrine of meaning and categories in 'transcendental empiricism.' I soon saw that restricting myself to this great tractate will not lead me to full understanding, and therefore, I started to study the great commentaries on Aristotle's logic and metaphysics. I was able to distinguish the levels of the domains of being, meaning, and knowledge, which I believe were not maintained before transcendental philosophy, the point where, as far as I can see, 'realism' must be essentially transformed. First of all, the needy fear of 'subjectivism'—which has become the etiquette of every non-extreme Thomistic 'standpoint'—must be eliminated. It depends primarily on an explicit understanding of Duns Scotus. According to him, the forms of meaning receive determination by matter. What you call 'empirical (objective) reality' is natural to him, first and last. However, if he allows his forms of meaning *(modi significandi)* to be determined by this [empirical reality], the question becomes whether something can be retrieved from Scotus for the doctrine of the forms of fore-scientific reality." Heidegger, letter to Rickert, 24 April 1914, in Denker, *Heidegger/Rickert Briefe*, 17–18.

24. "This expression [*ens in anima*] can only stand for what today is called 'noematic sense': as a correlate of consciousness, intentionality is inseparable from consciousness and yet not really

not subsist outside the subject, nor is it a mere projection of the subject. The intentional form is "in" the matter; in another respect, the intended matter is in the form. The object is "in" the subject just as the subject is "in" the object. The "in" of intentionality cannot be interpreted in spatial terms. Consciousness is not a part of a whole designated by the term *ens,* nor is *ens* a part of consciousness; the model of part and whole does not apply to the relationship of being and thinking. Without this isomorphism of thinking and being, intentional analysis would not be possible.

The *Habilitationsschrift* begins with a study of Scotus on *ens logicum,* logical or ideal being, the being common to all that is or can be. Scotus argues that being is the first intentional object, the objectivity in which all subsequent objects participate: *Primum objectum intellectus est ens, ut commune omnibus.*[25] Being is the first of all things known, thus the most knowable and certain concept *(maxime scibile).* Everything thinkable is encompassed by it, privations and perfections, ideas and sense impressions, feeling and thought—the whole of our psychic life. *Ens* is a *transcendens,* a trans-categorial concept. In Heidegger's neo-Kantian reading of the notion, *ens logicum* is "the world of sense" in which we live move and have our being (GA1 280). It is transcendental, that is transcategorical, not a category distinct from substance and the nine accidents, for every substance and accident presupposes it. The other transcendental notions, unity, truth, goodness, are convertible with *ens.* Everything that is, is also in some sense one (undivided and unique), true (identical to itself), and good (desirable in itself).

Scotus's metaphysics is typically regarded by Thomists as a species of *essentialism,* and a precursor of modern idealism.[26] For Scotus, meta-

---

contained in it. The 'in' designates the relationship wholly proper to consciousness, the interconnectedness of all meanings and values with spiritual life and not some kind of inherence of an element as a part in a whole" (GA1 277).

25. Duns Scotus, *Quaestiones subtilissimae super Metaphysicam Aristotelis* bk. 4, q. 1, 148a (hereafter *Quaest. sup. Met.*). The first chapter of the *Habilitationsschrift* is replete with citations from this authentic text of Duns Scotus's.

26. The critique of Scotus as a proto-idealist and essentialist is found in both Lonergan and Siewerth, but the sharpest articulation is perhaps Etienne Gilson's. See his *Being and Some Philosophers* (Toronto: Pontifical Institute of Mediaeval Studies, 1952), 86: "[For Scotus] being *(esse)* is nothing else than the intrinsic reality of essence itself, in each one of the various conditions in which it is to be found. This is why, wherever there is essence there is being, and what we call

physics is not a science of the existent, for a science of the contingent is not possible; science is by definition of the necessary. Metaphysics is the study of essence: possibility, meaning, form. Against Aquinas's *analogia entis*, which Scotus believes opens theology to the threat of philosophical agnosticism, Scotus makes being into a univocal concept *(univocatio entis)*: it has the same meaning in every instance. Being is distinguished into two modes, infinite and finite, the first referring to the being of God, the second, to the being of creatures. On the basis of our knowledge of finite beings (Scotus remains an Aristotelian), Scotus argues that we abstract a notion of being equally applicable to the infinite, or, in his language, indifferent to the modes of finitude and infinity. *Ens logicum* applies to both infinite and finite being, indeed it applies to every possibility for being, everything thinkable. Without a real distinction between essence and existence, possibility and actuality become different degrees of being. Possibility is higher than actuality, for it embraces more of *essentia*. Existence is not really distinct from essence, nor is it accidental to essence; rather, it is a mode of essence, the fullest determination of intelligible form. This essentialist metaphysics is tempered by a certain degree of skepticism, for *ens logicum* in its fullness always eludes comprehension. We have no intuitive knowledge of being, but only an approximate knowledge, based on flawed sense experience, which attains a lower mode of being. Our common notion of being, *ens commune*, is not adequate to infinite being. It is a functional definition, which does not define the essence and fails to encompass both the highest and the lowest mode of being. As the most determinate manifestation of being, Scotus's form of individuality, *haecceitas*, is at the furthest extreme from *ens infinitum*. These two extreme poles of the universe of being define being as essence. Both are in different ways singularities: *ens infinitum* because God is one and unique (He has no other); *haecceitas* because a concrete *thisness* is incommunicable, it cannot be shared among a plurality of individuals.

What catches Heidegger's attention is Scotus's contention that we possess a horizonal and foundational understanding of being. As the ground of every predication, *ens logicum* is not subject to further predication. Of

---

existence is simply the definitive mode of being which is that of an essence when it has received the complete series of its determinations."

it one can only say "it is." *Ens logicum* is the primordial *that*. On it all further determinations rest. It is neither formless matter, raw sense data, nor a schema of a priori categories; it is, rather, the whole of understandable life. Before a being belongs to any category—before it is determined as substance or accident, real or merely possible—it shows itself as unthematized logical being. Interpreting Scotus through Lask, Heidegger describes *ens logicum* as "a moment of clarity" *(Klarheitsmoment),* which makes everything initially visible. Being is the luminous field within which essences can appear. "Without this first moment of clearness, I could not experience darkness, for darkness itself only exists in clearness. Rather, it should be stated, I would have no object at all; I would live blindly in absolute darkness. I could not get myself mentally and intellectually in motion; thinking would stand still" (GA1 224). Being is not something we bump up against in experience but a light-filled space of *possibilitas.*

Ens logicum, perhaps best defined as the form of being, is the overarching ontological determination, the *univocatio entis,* which encompasses all other senses of being. The being of physical entities *(ens reale)* is a subdivision of *ens logicum* and thus presupposes it. The proof is that *ens reale* can be subsumed under *ens logicum*, but not vice versa (GA1 252, 276–77). Heidegger takes pains to stress the nontheoretical nature of *ens logicum*. It includes the fullness of our intellectual and emotional life. "Psychic reality certainly is not an *'ens diminutum.'* On the contrary, it is the *essential form* of the human being" (GA1 277).[27]

In chapter 2 of the *Habilitationsschrift,* Heidegger explores the phenomenological significance of the Scotist doctrine of the convertibility of being and truth *(verum).*[28] That a being is true by virtue of its being means that being has an essential relationship to intellect, for truth is relation to intellect. Scotus ultimately relates being to the divine intellect. God grounds the truth of things by willing them to be. Through an immanent reading of the convertibility of being and truth, that is, without reference to God, Heidegger interprets the Scotist convertibility of being and truth as an indication of the primordial givenness-for-a-subject of all

---

27. Heidegger takes this citation from Hermann Siebeck, "Die Anfänge der neuen Psychologie in der Scholastik," *Zeitschrift für Philosophie und philosophische Kritik* 94 (1888): 167, 178 ff.

28. In this chapter, Heidegger references a wide variety of Scotus's texts, including *De sophisticis elenchis* and the *Ordinatio.*

that is or can be.²⁹ The truth that corresponds to judgments is a limited mode of truth, an island of actuality within the sea of possibility. Transcendental truth is the pre-judgmental form of that which is immediately apprehended, "trueness," which consists in the simple and undeniable self-showing of an "object." It has as its opposite, not falsehood, but noncognizance. More than the totality of existing things, it includes everything that has an essence, all that is known and knowable. Everything that can be an object, either mental or physical, is transcendentally true. By interpreting *verum transcendentale* as the givenness of the given, the objectivity of the object, the self-showing of being, rather than as Scotus (and every other Scholastic) understood it, the createdness of the creature, Heidegger reorients the whole of Scotus's metaphysics away from infinite being toward finite being.

This is not, however, subjectivism. Heidegger argues that subjectivism, the view that certainty is not possible because we can never guarantee that our judgments correspond to real things, is founded on an inadequate phenomenology. When I judge something to be the case, I respond to a posited possibility, a transcendentally true object, which makes a claim on me. I do not need an extra-judgmental verification to guarantee my judgment. In an argument that hearkens back to Newman's "illative sense" and foreshadows Lonergan's refutation of transcendental skepticism, Heidegger holds that truth is immanent in thinking, yet sovereign and independent of my will (*GA1* 278). The modern notion that certainty is conditional on a verification of a thing-in-itself, the correspondence of a judgment with an object—a third eye view of—is a groundless assumption. The thing receives the form of objectivity in judgment. The object *known* is the fullness of objectivity; nothing remains beyond it that could limit it or render it *merely* phenomenal.³⁰

---

29. "Just as *unum* turns out to be the primordial form of the object in general, so too *verum* must be apprehended as a *formal relation*. The object is true object in regard to cognition. Insofar as the object is *object of cognition, it can be called true object*. The object shows the *fundamentum veritatis*. Transcendental philosophy has found the most precise expression for this relation: the object is only object as object of cognition: cognition is only cognition as cognition of the object. There is no object without a subject and *vice versa*" (*GA1* 267–68).

30. "For it is simply impossible to compare the sense of judgment to real objects since I only know of real objects through cognition—judgment. An object that is not cognized is no object for me. We do not need to transcend judgmental content in order to reach real objects. The copy theo-

Heidegger's analysis of *ens logicum* without a divine referent is an early sign of the this-worldly, anti-Scholastic emphasis of his thinking. When he interprets *verum transcendens* as indicative of a primary relation of being to the human intellect, Heidegger shows that as early as 1915, he was a violent interpreter of the tradition, drawing out of it, not whatever historical authors might have had in mind, but that which he thought was struggling to come to light through it. Intentional being is unthinkable apart from relation to intellect; it is by definition *ens in anima*. In Heidegger's view, the intellect in question here is ours. *Ens* is correlative to Dasein. But must we not posit being outside the soul *(ens extra anima)* to secure "objective" truth? The Scholastics answer yes: non-intentional being is the efficient cause of sense experience. However, when Heidegger reduces the notion of being to intentional being, it becomes difficult to say what *ens extra anima* could mean. If *ens* is always permeated by meaning, it is purely intentional. Heidegger's point is sharpened in *Sein und Zeit*, where intentional being is replaced by the notion of the *Bewandtnisganzheit*, the meaningful whole of relations within which beings are always already understood. Suffused as it is by meaning, the world is not "independent of consciousness." Meaningfulness is not an objective property of things; it is a formal indicator of the being which we are. Things are only meaningful for a being with a project to be, that is, for a human being. Because the world *is* a meaningful whole, it cannot be thought without Dasein. To ask about the extra-mental reality of the world makes no more sense than asking about the extra-mental reality of thinking. The "proof of the reality of the external world" presupposes a worldless subject and a subject-free world, constructs annulled by the concept of Dasein.[31]

---

ry *(Abbildtheorie)* presents an insurmountable difficulty in this respect. Duns Scotus gives the theory up and decides for immanent thought. The reality of the external world will not be 'argued away.' Scotus does not side with 'subjectivism,' 'idealism,' or any other epistemological specter. A properly understood idea of immanence does not abolish reality, or dissolve the external world into a dream. On the contrary, *it is precisely because of the absolute primacy of valid sense (geltender Sinn) that the measuring rod of all physiological, psychological, and economic-pragmatic theories of cognition is broken, and the absolute validity of truth, genuine objectivity, is inviolably grounded.* . . . The meaning content of the data, the thing *(Sachverhalt)* as such, is the measure of the sense of judgment: from out of it the sense of judgment draws its objective validity. In other words, the sense of judgment is the logical form of reality" (GA1 273).

31. "The question of whether there is a world at all and whether its being can be demonstrated,

The immanent reading of *verum transcendens* allows Heidegger to bring out the analogy beween Scotus's metaphysics and Husserl's phenomenology. Husserl's *epoché* is a reduction from the order of facts to the order of essences. The reduction brings thinking back to the intentional field prior to the distinction between extra-mental and psychic being. Husserl made the mistake of assuming this to be a fundamentally new effort in philosophy. With his broader understanding of the history of philosophy, Heidegger saw the situation differently: Husserl was inadvertently reviving Scotist metaphysics.[32] The late thirteenth and the early twentieth centuries converge in a startling fashion. For both Scotus and Husserl, fundamental philosophy suspends questions of fact and gives an account of meaning, the "basic field of experience." Scotus also anticipates Husserl's distinction between the real and the ideal. What makes being "outside the intellect" different from ideal being is temporality. The essence is timeless, the existent is here and now, or there and then.[33] Scotus's notion of *haecceitas* is also a temporal notion. The intelligible structure of being is determined to concrete *haecceity* by its presence "here and now."

---

makes no sense at all if it is raised by Dasein as being-in-the-world—and who else should ask it? Moreover it is encumbered with an ambiguity. World as the wherein of being-in, and 'world' as inner-worldly beings, that in which one is absorbed in taking care of things, are confused or else not distinguished at all. But world is essentially disclosed with the being of Dasein" (*SZ* 202–3/188).

32. Husserl's description of the task of phenomenology recapitulates Scotus's notion of metaphysics. Compare Husserl, *Ideas*, vol. 1, 44 with Allan B. Wolter, *The Transcendentals and their Function in the Metaphysics of Duns Scotus* (St. Bonaventure, N.Y.: The Franciscan Institute, 1946), 29.

33. In his *Logische Untersuchungen,* Husserl writes: "How can we talk about something if it does not at least exist *in our thought?* The being of the ideal is therefore obviously a being in consciousness; the name 'content of consciousness' rightly applies to it. As opposed to this, real being is no mere being in consciousness, or being-a-content: it is self-existence, transcendent being, being outside of consciousness. We do not wish to lose ourselves in the erring paths of such a metaphysics. For us what is 'in' consciousness counts as real just as much as what is 'outside' of it. What is real is the individual with all its constituents: it is something here and now. For us temporality is a sufficient mark of reality. Real being and temporal being may not be identical notions, but they coincide in extension. We do not, of course, suppose that psychical experiences are in a metaphysical sense 'things.' But even they belong to a thing-like unity, if the traditional metaphysical conviction is right in holding that all temporal existents must be things, or must help to constitute things. Should we wish, however, to keep all metaphysics out, we may simply define 'reality' in terms of temporality. For us the only point of importance is to oppose it to the timeless 'being' of the ideal." Husserl, *Logical Investigations,* vol. 1, Investigation II, §8.

Grammatical Forms

Part Two of the *Habilitationsschrift* contains Heidegger's study of Erfurt's *De modis significandi sive Grammatica speculativa*. Heidegger is particularly interested in Erfurt's assumption that deep levels of meaning are hidden under more obvious and theoretically accessible linguistic structures. The medieval enterprise of speculative grammar shows how concealed ontological form can be decrypted by a careful analysis of semantic structure. For the Modists, the modes of signifying indicate intentional forms; intentional forms in turn indicate ontological structure. The key term here is "indicate"—as in Aristotle's ethics, the indication is rough and in outline. For the most basic level of structure cannot be exhaustively defined in the terms of founded levels of meaning. The mode of being *(modus essendi)* is never defined but only formally indicated in grammatical form *(modus significandi)*. At a certain point of analysis, definition and deduction break down and the factical ground must be *shown* through the said, pointed to, not named.

Erfurt's speculative grammar promises an exhaustive theory of meaning, a table of categories of categories, "a definite division of the whole of that which can be known, that is, that which can be determined theoretically" (*GA1* 207). Three modes of increasingly primordial meaning are nestled within one another like Russian dolls. Every grammatical form *(modus significandi)* is reducible to a mode of understanding *(modus intelligendi)*, which can in turn be reduced to the mode of being *(modus essendi)*. Grammatical form is grounded in concepts; modes of expression formally indicate modes of understanding. Modes of understanding in turn refer to modes of being. To use another figure, the outer word proceeds from an inner word, a concept, which proceeds from an ontological "word," the *essentia* of the thing. The universal grammatical structures common to different languages—nouns, verbs, adjectives, and so forth—reflect primordial ways of intending being: "[Grammatical] forms are nothing but the objective expressions of the various ways in which consciousness is intentionally related to the objective" (*GA1* 319).

According to Erfurt, every mode has a passive and an active modality, a material and a formal moment. The active modes alone are distinguishable, for the passive modes converge.³⁴ In other words, the *modus activus* and *modus passivus* of every stratum of intentionality are materially identical and formally distinct. Materially, a mode refers to the term of an intention, a content; formally, a mode refers to a way of intending, a relation. The active mode of expression *(modus significandi activus)* is the *intention* of an object as a bearer of a particular name. The passive mode of expression *(modus significandi passivus)* is the *intended* object as the bearer of the name. The active mode of understanding *(modus intelligendi activus)* is the *intention* of an object as an instance of a concept. The passive mode of understanding *(modus intelligendi passivus)* is the *intended* object as an instance of a class (*GA1* 317–18). The bearer of a name and the term of a concept can be materially identical, referring to the same *what*; nonetheless naming and conceptualizing remain distinct intentional acts.

Heidegger, assuming that Erfurt is Scotus, reads Erfurt's assumption that distinct grammatical forms refer, not always to distinct things, but sometimes to distinctions within the thing, as a consequence of Scotus's *distinctio formalis*. Notwithstanding the mistaken authorship, there is an analogy. According to Scotus, ontological forms may be distinct without being materially separable from each other. Scotus's *distinctio formalis* has two principle features: (1) different "aspects" or relational senses of a single phenomenon, which although never found apart, are not reducible to each other; (2) these different formalities are to be interpreted ontologically; they are not only different ways of *thinking* about the same being, they are also distinct *ontological* modes of a thing's being.³⁵ In other words, ways of thinking are sometimes grounded in ways of being. The distinction is best grasped in contrast to two other Scholastic distinctions: the *distinctio realis* and the *distinctio rationis*. A *distinctio realis* exists between forms that can exist apart from one another. Rationality

---

34. See Thomas of Erfurt, *Grammatica speculativa*, 5, 9, p. 147: "The passive mode of signifying is in the thing materially, as it is in the subject; because from the material point of view it is the property of the thing; moreover, the property of the thing exists in that of which it is the property just as it is in the subject. However, from a formal point of view it is in the subject as the active mode of signifying, because formally it does not differ from the active mode of signifying."

35. On Scotus's *distinctio formalis*, see Allan B. Wolter, *The Philosophical Theology of John Duns Scotus*, ed. Marilyn McCord Adams (Ithaca, N.Y.: Cornell University Press, 1990), 43–49.

is really distinct from animality, for nonrational animals exist, as do nonanimal rationalities (angels). A *distinctio rationis* distinguishes ways of thinking about the same form, which are not grounded in being but in intellect. "Human being" and "rational animal" are not different beings but different ways of thinking the same being. Scotus argues that a mediation of these two positions is possible: ontologically distinct forms exist, which are never found apart from certain other forms. This means that the criterion of ontological distinction is not separate existence.[36] There is a link between Scotus's *distinctio formalis* and Husserl's categorial intuition: distinct formal aspects of a phenomenon are not necessarily ideal. But neither are they ontically distinct things. Formal aspects may indicate distinct formal structures inherent in a single being. A being is a multidimensional reality, which can exist in a variety of distinct modes, for example, as possible or actual. One hundred dollars in my pocket is formally distinct from one hundred dollars in my imagination, but it is not a different "thing" altogether. The *what* is identical, but the *how* (relational sense) is formally distinct. More generally, the *distinctio formalis* is only possible on the assumption of a correlativity of subject and object, an assumption that is a mainstay of phenomenology.

For Erfurt, grammatical forms, however intentionally structured, have ontological foundations: "It should be noted immediately that since forms of this kind or active modes of signifying are not fictions, it follows necessarily that every active mode of signifying must originate basically from some property of the thing."[37] An analysis of the forms of speech acts is also an analysis of the properties of things. Erfurt continues: "The

---

36. A word is formally distinct from the idea that it names—word and idea are not identical—although the meaningful word does not exist apart from the idea. When I say the word, I say the idea also, and vice versa. In 1927, Heidegger pointed out that the *distinctio formalis* also goes under the name *distinctio rationis ratiocinata* (as distinct from the *distinctio rationis pura* or *ratiocinantis*). He has the following to say about it: "[The *distinctio rationis ratiocinata*] refers not simply to the mode of apprehension and the degree of clarity but is present *quandocumque et quocumque modo ratio diversae considerationis ad rem relatam oritur,* when the distinction arises as not in some sort motivated by the apprehending in its active operation but *ratiocinata,* by that which is *objicitur,* cast over against, in the *ratiocinari* itself, hence *ratiocinata.* The essential point is that for the second *distinctio rationis* [the *distinctio rationis ratiocinata*] there is a motive having to do with the thing-content in the distinguished thing itself. . . . [It is] motivated not only by the apprehending intellect but by the apprehended thing itself" (GA24 134–35/96).

37. Erfurt, *Grammatica speculativa,* 137.

active mode of signifying is the mode or property of the expression produced by the intellect by means of which the expression signifies the property of the thing."[38] The *modi significandi* are indications of ontological structure, which can only be accessed through intentionality analysis.

The *modus essendi* is the mode of primordially given *ens*, the undetermined whole of the *prima intentio*. Heidegger describes it as "that which generally can be experienced *(das Erlebbare überhaupt)* ... that which stands over and against consciousness in the absolute sense, 'robust' reality which irresistibly obtrudes in consciousness and can never be eliminated" (*GA1* 318). All intentions are founded upon this original givenness, the sheer, fore-theoretical and unfathomable *thisness* of being. "Whatever is signified in the mode of being," Erfurt argues, "expresses the property of the thing absolutely or under the formality of being *(sub ratione essentiae).*"[39] In a 1915 prefiguration of the 1919 notion of the "primordial something," Heidegger describes the *modus essendi* as the universal domain of "the something in general" *(der universale Bereich des "Etwas überhaupt")* (*GA1* 314). The *modus essendi* is never directly grasped, for being is always mediated by the *modus intelligendi*, the mode of understanding. The *modus intelligendi* is the objectifying intention, the cognizing of a being as an instance of a class. Only at this stage is the object known in the full sense of the word. On the basis of the intellection of the *modus essendi*, the intellect names the object, attaches a distinct word or expression to it, and intends it under the form of the *modus significandi*.

Heidegger notices that Erfurt does not elaborate an active mode of being *(modus essendi activus)*, although a distinction between an active and passive *modus essendi* is implied by the distinction of every intention into an active and passive mode. Erfurt tends to refer to the *modus essendi* only in its passive sense, as that which receives intentional determinations. Yet we must assume a *modus essendi activus* if we are to distinguish it from the other intentional modes, for the passive modes are identical. The young Heidegger discovers that speculative grammar is subject to a further reduction: from the passive givenness of being to the active comportment of being. The active mode of being would be the

38. Ibid., 1, 2, p. 135.
39. Ibid., 4, 8, p. 143.

most primordial intentional act, the *prima intentio*, the intention of being as being, that is, without further determination, the fundamental directedness of *intellectus* toward the unthematized already meaningful whole of life. The existence of a *modus essendi activus* means that the given is the term of a primordial orientation of the intellect; it shows itself as given according to a basic intentional comportment. This comporting is not something that I deliberately do but a structure within which I habitually dwell. It is not an attitude that I can suspend or change but the basic way in which I exist in the world. It is not theoretical but average and everyday. Heidegger writes: "It should be noted that Duns Scotus [in fact Thomas of Erfurt] characterizes empirical reality as subject to a *ratio*, that is, a point of view, a form, a contextual structure *(Bewandtnis)*. This is nothing less than what is nowadays expressed in the following terms: even 'givenness' exhibits a categorial determination" (*GA*1 318/143). Rickert is cited in this context with approval: "'Pre-scientific' knowing must also be brought into the sphere of our [logical] investigations" (*GA*1 318). The breakthrough to the topic of the fore-theoretical, so central to the early Freiburg lectures, occurs here, in 1915.

It is interesting to note how Heidegger's reading of Erfurt brings Dasein into question: the being who intends being as being. The ambiguity in the notion of the *modus essendi activus*, the intention of being, leads naturally to questions concerning the nature of the being who is capable of intentional relations. The key to more precise understanding of *ens* will not be found by interrogating things, but rather by interrogating the "soul." As Heidegger put it in 1927, "It is to the human Dasein that there belongs the understanding of being which first makes possible every comportment toward being. The understanding of being itself has the mode of being of the human Dasein. The more originally and appropriately we define this being in regard to the structure of its being, that is to say, ontologically, the more securely we are placed in a position to comprehend in its structure the understanding of being that belongs to the Dasein, and the more clearly and unequivocally the question can then be posed, What is it that makes this understanding of being possible at all?" (*GA*24 21/16).

Haecceitas

Hovering over the whole of the *Habilitationsschrift* is Heidegger's interest in Scotus's notion of *haecceitas*. For Scotus, the individual is essentially, not accidentally, individuated. The individual exhibits a "sense species," a materially embedded determination that makes it a *distinct* this.[40] Scotus's concrete and unnameable *haecceitas* is the final determination of *essentia*, thoroughly intelligible yet undefinable. It is never known in abstraction from matter but is only grasped in a simple intuition of existence, *simplex apprehensio*.[41] Heidegger discerns in this central Scotist concept a figure for Lask's preformal intelligibility and Husserl's categorial intuition. Lask showed how categorial predication (abstraction) hides primordial structure, an *Etwas*, which makes it possible.[42] Husserl's notion of categorial intuition also points to a level of intelligibility prior to abstraction. For Scotus, the universal definition proceeds from a simple apprehension of preexisting intelligibility, the prepredicative intelligibility of *haecceitas*. The thing known in a universal definition is an *actually* intelligible singular that is never fully comprehended by the concept. The historically singularized thing speaks a primordial word to us, and this original *verbum*, which we might call the *verbum entis*, the word of being, makes possible the inner word of understanding, the *verbum interius*. The young Heidegger discovers that Husserl and Scotus converge on this point, although neither recognized the ramifications of the notion of precategorial intelligibility for the understanding of historical life. It was for Heidegger, Husserl's young assistant, to point out that if the singular is actually intelligible in its singularity, history cannot be disregard-

---

40. On Scotus's notion of *haecceitas*, see Wolter, *Philosophical Theology of Scotus*, 48–53, 68–97. On the development of Scotus's notion of intuitive cognition of singularity, see ibid., 98–122.

41. Allan Wolter comments, "Just because our intellect cannot apprehend haecceity intellectually does not mean it is per se unintelligible. God and the angel can know it directly and per se. The reason we cannot grasp it intellectually is due not to any lack of intelligibility on the part of the individuating entity but to the imperfection of our intellect and the way it functions in our present life." Wolter, *Philosophical Theology*, 96. See also p. 48.

42. See Lask, *Logik*, 1:129: "Ein Etwas, dessen Unzugänglichkeit für kategoriale Betroffenheit behauptet wird, das steht bei jegleichem, auch bei solchem leugnenden Nachdenken darüber bereits in kategorialer Umgriffenheit. Nur vor der 'unmittelbaren,' unreflektierten, theoretisch unberührten Hingabe steht ein Etwas als logisch nackt und vorgegenständlich. Der Reflexion dagegen tritt es immer schon als Gegenstand entgegen."

ed as ineffable. History becomes a domain of fore-theoretical experience, which exhibits its own proper understandability.

While counting himself an Aristotelian, Scotus did not accept the Aristotelian disjunction between the universality of the idea and the singularity of the thing. The universal idea is born of an intuition of the concrete, actual intelligibility of the singular.[43] The gap between a singular thing, held to be at first only potentially intelligible, and a universal essence struck Scotus as too wide to be bridged by the agent intellect. How could the phantasm be universalized if the singular in its singularity were not actually intelligible? How could the agent intellect "illuminate" an unintelligible singular?[44] Our inability to define the singular is not due to any unintelligibility in the singular. Scotus writes: "The singular thing is intelligible in itself, as far as the thing itself is concerned; but if it is not intelligible to some intellect, to ours, for example, this is not due to unintelligibility on the part of the singular thing."[45] The full haecceity of the singular escapes our powers of comprehension. Yet a modicum of knowledge of the singular, grasped in simple apprehension *(simplex apprehensio)* or simple intellection *(simplex intelligentia)*, is the foundation of abstract knowledge.[46] Abstraction is not original knowledge; it presupposes a more basic experience of intelligibility.[47] Consequently, abstraction has a negative connotation for Scotus: it is derivative, incomplete, and imperfect knowledge. The transposition of essence into universals

---

43. See Scotus, *Opera omnia*, vol. 9, d. 3, q. 6, 10–12. For a Thomist, Scotus's position amounts to "conceptualism," the view that the intellect is primarily conversant with essences, not with existing things. See Lonergan, *Verbum: Word and Idea in Aquinas* (Toronto: University of Toronto Press, 1997), 38–39, especially 39 n. 126: "The Scotist rejection of insight into phantasm necessarily reduced the act of understanding to seeing a nexus between concepts; hence, while for Aquinas understanding precedes conceptualization which is rational, for Scotus understanding is preceded by conceptualization which is a matter of metaphysical mechanics."

44. See Scotus, *De Anima* 23, 3: "It is impossible to abstract universals from the singular without previous knowledge of the singular; for in this case the intellect would abstract without knowing from what it was abstracting." Translated in Frederick Copleston, *A History of Philosophy*, vol. 2: *Medieval Philosophy* (New York: Image Books, 1962), part 2:217.

45. Scotus, *Opus oxoniense* 2, d. 3, q. 3, no. 16; translated in Copleston, *History*, 2:2:215.

46. See Scotus, *Opus oxoniense* 4, d. 45, q. 3, no. 17; see Copleston, *History*, 2:2:210–22.

47. Scotus, *Opus oxoniense* 1, d. 3, q. 4: "A being can be grasped by an act of simple understanding, and in such a case the thing which is true is known. But the truth-value itself is known only by an act of judgment. Simple understanding, however, precedes an act of judgment." Translated in Allan Wolter, *Duns Scotus: Philosophical Writings* (New York: Bobbs-Merrill, 1964), 99.

is not a perfection but a modification of essence. Abstraction brings out certain dimensions of the essence that are hidden in the singular thing, for example, commonality with other things of the same species. Yet it forgets *haecceitas*. Speculative grammar is possible in a Scotist context because the pre-judgmental act of understanding for Scotus, the act that precedes the procession of the inner word, is not a wordless insight into a sense image, but an intuitive grasp of a pretheoretical mode of essence, a hearkening to the word of the thing itself.[48]

Haecceitas de-limits the applicability of a certain type of Scholastic scientific knowledge, that which proceeds via deduction on the basis of universal definitions. *Haecceitas* can only be known by "acquaintance," that is, it can only be experienced or "simply apprehended." Nothing is more understandable than *essentia,* and *haecceitas* is its most concrete manifestation. For Scotus, essence is neither universal nor singular. It is universalized by the intellect that thinks it and singularized by the singular that embodies it in a particular space and time. The singularization is effected through *haecceitas*—neither a form in itself, nor the matter of a form. *Haecceitas* is the perfection of essence. As Armand Maurer puts it, *haecceitas* "is added to form from within" "the ultimate act which restricts the form of a species to the singularity of its individuals."[49] It is the most extreme manifestation of difference: "The *haecceity* . . . of the individual and that of another individual are so radically and absolutely diverse that neither the one nor the other can be grasped in itself or as such by a concept that is universal."[50]

The universality of language means that *haecceitas* is always in danger of being forgotten. For Scotus, "something inexpressible remains" in every expression, "which is at best only approximated, without ever being exhausted by language" (*GA1* 352–53). Heidegger cites Scotus on this

---

48. See Armand Maurer's interpretation of Scotist abstraction in his *Medieval Philosophy,* rev. ed. (Toronto: Pontifical Institute of Mediaeval Studies, 1962, 1982), 237: "Because [for Scotus] natures are common in reality and are represented as such by the senses, all the agent intellect has to do is to make them completely universal by abstracting them from sense data. In order to do this, the agent intellect does not have to act upon images in the sense powers and prepare them for the abstraction of universals, as St. Thomas taught. *It can read as in an open book the intelligible message presented by the senses and directly form its universal concept from it* [italics mine]."

49. Maurer, *Philosophy of Ockham,* 462.

50. Ibid., 48.

point: *Totia entitas singularis non continetur sub universale*, the full being of the singular is not contained by the universal (*GA*1 351).⁵¹ *Haecceitas* is never subsumed under a general concept, yet it remains intrinsically understandable. Before we conceptualize, we intuit the already meaningful "heterogenous, unobjectifiable manifold content of reality" (*GA*1 352–53). Heidegger relates *haecceitas* to Lask's notion that form does not first differentiate undetermined matter; rather, matter differentiates form.⁵² The precategorial is structured and already intelligible prior to objectification. It is that which is nearest to us, the meaning-suffused worlds in which we live and think, "a certain referential whole" *(Beziehungsganzes)*, out of which domains of being and category distinctions first arise (*GA*1 212). Heidegger sees that Scotus and Lask both point to the necessity of an expansion of ontology beyond Aristotle's ten categories: "A doctrine of categories confined to the ten Aristotelian categories is not only incomplete, but unstable and inaccurate in its determination, because it lacks consciousness of the differences of its domains, and thus consciousness of the difference that arises from the nature of domains that are determined by the meaning-differentiations of categorial forms. It was known to Scotus too that the ten traditional categories are valid only for actual reality. Doubtless, the domain of the intentional calls for other structures" (*GA*1 287–88). Even at this early stage of his career, Heidegger was captivated by the idea that being cannot be exhausted by the distinction of substance and accident, genus and species. "That there is [*es gibt*] a domain of reality, still more, that there are diverse domains of reality, cannot be deductively demonstrated a priori. Facticity can only be pointed to *(Tatsächlichkeiten lassen sich nur aufweisen)*. What is the sense of the *showing?* What is shown stands before us as itself. Figuratively speaking, it is immediately grasped: no detour through something else is neces-

---

51. Scotus, *Opus oxoniense* 2, dist. 3, q. 11, no. 9.

52. See Heidegger's citation from Hermann Lotze's *Logik* at *GA*1 324: "A pile can easily be made with balls alone when it isn't important how they lie. But a building of regular proportions is only possible with blocks, each one of which has already been made into forms, which can be used in ascending layers that join securely and stay in place. Something similar must be the case here [in thinking]. As mere excitations of our inner being, the states that follow on outer stimuli can exist together in us without further preliminaries and can so affect one another just as the most general laws of the life of our soul allow or order it. But in order to be able to be unified in the determinate form of a *thought, each one of them needs a prior structuring.*"

sary; the *showable* one fixes our gaze. In the practice of knowing, we need only look and grasp all there is to grasp, and to exhaust the pure selfhood of what shows itself. There can be no doubt, no probabilities, no illusions about what is immediate. For the immediate does not allow of anything between itself and its grasp *(simplex apprehensio)*" (GA1 213).

Heidegger holds that *haecceitas* must have a transcendental ground: difference must be included among the transcendental attributes of being. His argument is simple and compelling. *Haecceitas* is the difference that rules throughout being, making possible the distinctions between singulars, categories, and domains of meaning. There is no unity without difference, no one without the other; everything is one in juxtaposition to another that it is not. Difference is a primordial determination of the object (GA1 217–24; 229–32). Multiplicity is a privation of unity: things are many by lack of unity. Yet unity itself is the privation of multiplicity: things are united by lack of difference. Transcendental unity is thus a negation of the negation of difference. "Relative to its content, *unum* designates something positive: in view of the mode of meaning in which it is signified *(modus significandi)*, it means a privation. *Unum* is a *privation* of the *privation* that is in the *multum*—this, for its part, is the privation of *unum*. So *unum* is defined by *multum* and conversely. Hence it is evident how *unum* is joined to the object: *Unum* bestows a determination on the object through the privative mode of meaning. An object is one object and not any other object" (GA1 381). It is not enough that a being is identical to itself, it must also be differentiable from others. It must be both transcendentally one and transcendentally different. Transcendental difference underscores the contextual nature of ontological concepts. The object cannot be defined in isolation from other objects. "Equally primordial as the object in general is the object's state of affairs *(Sachverhalt)*; with every object there is a contextual structure *(Bewandtnis)*, even if it be merely *that it is identical with itself and different from another*" (GA1 226).

Scotus's notion of *haecceitas* went against the tide and prepared the way for nominalism. The Thomistic tendency was to interpret history as a theater of unintelligible singularity. Contradicting the mantra-like old formula, *singularitas repugnat intellectioni*, Scotus argued that the singular has its proper mode of intelligibility. This most basic level of structure is ineradicably temporal. *Haecceitas* is grasped in a preconceptual intuition of historical presence. In the 1915 *Habilitation* lecture "Der Zeitbegriff in der Geschichtswissenschaft," Heidegger called *haecceitas* the "understandable oneness and onceness" of historical life (*GA1* 427).[53] The *how* of *haecceitas* is time. "*Individuum* implies determinateness as this unique one, which can be encountered at no other time or place.... The individual is an *irreducible ultimate*. It intends the real object *kat exochen prout includit existentiam et tempus*. Two apples on the same tree don't have the same 'view' to the heavens. Each one is already different from the other in its spatial determination, even though they may be completely the same. Everything that really exists is a such-here-now. The form of singularity *(haecceitas)* provides a primordial determination of the really actual. This reality constitutes an 'unsurveyable multiplicity,' and a 'heterogenous continuum'" (*GA1* 253).

Anticipating his later critique of the technological reduction of being to a quantifiable *Bestand*, Heidegger argues that *haecceitas* shows "the preeminent impossibility of comprehending empirical reality through pure number" (*GA1* 262). The generic unity of number must be distinguished from the heterogeneity of transcendental unity.[54] The latter expresses unity in multiplicity; the former excises haecceity and flattens the real into a uniform continuum. The countable is "a homogenous medium," projected onto things, an abstraction, which reduces being to unmediated identity by cancelling difference. The singular thing in its uniqueness must be left out of the count. Counted beings are diminished essences, *rebus secundum rationem mensurae et mensurabilis*, things under the formal aspect of measure and measurability (*GA1* 236).[55] Because *haecceitas* must be cancelled in the count, "mathematic-scientific knowledge is simply not knowledge as such" (*GA1* 263). Modern science cannot deal directly with the haecceity of life; it must reconstruct reality in terms of uniform quantities. "A comparison with the modern scientific treatment of natural reality shows that it has to redo thoroughly the un-

---

53. A translation of this text, "The Concept of Time in the Science of History," by Harry S. Taylor, Hans W. Uffelmann, and John van Buren, has been published in *Supplements. From the Earliest Essays to* Being and Time *and Beyond*, ed. John van Buren (Albany: State University of New York Press, 2002), 49–60.

54. Heidegger cites Scotus on this point: "Unum est aequivocum ad unum, quod est convertibile cum ente et unum, quod est principium numerorum" (*GA1* 222).

55. See Scotus, *Quaest. sup. Met.* bk. 2, q. 6, 539a.

surveyable multiplicity of empirical reality into a homogenous domain if theoretical physics is to come into use as a method of investigation" (GA1 263).[56]

On the level of everyday speech, the heterogeneity of reality is preserved through the use of analogous concepts. Analogous terms mean the same thing in different ways: a healthy meal and a healthy body are united in the common meaning, health, which is indicated differently in the two expressions. "The identity in the difference in the analogical expression [is] like a bundle of rays flowing together in a single point" (GA1 334). Not only is health signified differently in different *modi significandi*, it is never instantiated in the same way, even when it is signified in the same way. Everything is at once one and many, identical and different, even with itself. In such a universe, language must be analogical.

The Influence of Scotus on Heidegger

Long ignored by commentators, Heidegger's *Habilitationsschrift* is nonetheless philosophically significant for his later development. The *Habilitationsschrift* proves that as early as 1915, Heidegger was on the track of a factical ontology. The hermeneutics of facticity began as an exploration of an ontology grounded in a *univocatio entis* but restricted to the finite. In those areas where Scotus's theology incurs into his chosen theme, Heidegger appears deliberately to ignore it. In the many pages in which he discusses the transcendentals, for example, Heidegger never mentions that being, truth, and goodness are names of God for Scotus.[57]

---

56. This critique of the derivative nature of mathematical unity also appears in Heidegger's habilitation lecture, "Der Zeitbegriff in der Geschichtswissenschaft." Heidegger distinguishes "historical time," from "physical time." The former is "authentic time," the object of historical science: time specified by nonquantifiable evaluations. The latter is the flattened and generic quantifiable time of natural science, the "condition of the possibility of mathematical determinability." Physical time is a homogenization of historical time for the sake of measurability: "The stream is frozen, becomes a level plane, and only as such is it measurable; time becomes a homogenous frame of reference" (GA1 424).

57. The one reference to God in the body of the *Habilitationsschrift* (excluding the *Schlusskapitel*, which is best treated as a separate text, it is so different in tone and in approach) is at GA1 260. "In the strictest, absolute sense, only God is real. He is the absolute that is *existence, which exists in essence and 'essences' in existence* [*im Wesen existiert und in der Existenz 'west'*]. Natural reality, the *sensibly real*, exists only as created; it is not existence, like the Absolute, but *has* existence through

Heidegger wants a Scotus whose *univocatio entis* has no infinite mode. In some ways, he becomes that kind of Scotist.

Beyond Scotus's ontological thrust, Heidegger drew two basic hermeneutical principles from Scotus, which determined all his subsequent philosophical work: (1) the conceptual and objectifiable is not coextensive with the understandable; the latter exceeds and de-limits the former; (2) the horizon of the primordially understandable is time. It is tempting to draw a further connection between Scotus's *distinctio formalis* and Heidegger's formal indication *(formale Anzeige)*. Kisiel writes that Scotus's "feel for formality and concreteness at once" led to Heidegger's breakthrough to a formally indicative approach to facticity.[58] Thomas of Erfurt finds concealed and indefinable ontological structure in the forms of ordinary language. *Formale Anzeige* is a method for phenomenologically thematizing that which cannot be directly expressed but which nonetheless formally determines the expressible. Dasein's *Existenzialien*, for example, are not universals. They are enmeshed in the singularized experience of being-in-the-world. They can never be isolated from one another but are intertwined in the web of relations that constitutes "my" world. The *Existenzialien* must be teased out of the phenomenological description of everydayness, approached obliquely, or formally indicated. The frequently repeated term *gleichursprünglich* in *Sein und Zeit* highlights this inextricable coentwinement of *Existenzialien*. In Scotus's language, the distinctions between these phenomena are formal. Heidegger takes pains to show that certain phenomena "imply" or disclose each other without being causally related to each other—one is not the ground of the other. Rather, the phenomena are "equiprimordial," that is, always co-given.

Perhaps the strongest resonance between Heidegger and Scotus concerns the derivative nature of abstract and theoretical language. Abstraction according to Scotus is a limiting of essence and to that degree a distortion. The product of abstraction, the definition, names a dimin-

---

'*communicabilitas.*' Although both Creator and creation are real, they are so, however, in *different* ways. Here we meet the heterogenous moment in analogy. *The difference lies in the degree of reality.* The *unum infinitum*, as absolute reality centered in itself, is the *highest value*, the absolute measure of all reality" (GA1 260). The phrase *"Gott west"* originates in Eckhart.

58. Kisiel, *Genesis of Being and Time*, 20.

ished modality of the essence, an intuitively grasped common nature that shows itself in the thing, but which is not identical to the thing. The truth of judgment, propositional truth, is derivative, or *founded*, secondary to the direct apprehension of being without which it cannot occur. Scotus's simple apprehension is thus a figure for *aletheia*.

Aletheia is more complex than an immediate apprehension of presence. Heidegger dissembles the traditionally identified notions of intuition and preverbal immediacy. Like all Dasein's experience, unconcealment is fundamentally and ineradicably mediated by language. Truth only occurs within language. In one sense, truth generates language, for the *logos apophainesthai* is an expressed interpretation of *aletheia*. In another sense, truth is generated by language. We live in language and have no access to experience that is not permeated by language. The task of hermeneutical phenomenology is to loosen up the primordial words through which life first expresses itself. Phenomenology does not attach words to preverbal intuitions; it goes along with the way historical life is already "worded" for us. Heidegger's notion of understanding makes expression equiprimordial with intuition.[59] In other words, Heidegger destroys the traditional dichotomy between intuition and expression. The intuited is always already expressed. With Scotus, Heidegger argues that theoretical concepts and definitions fail to give full expression to the concrete intelligibility with which we deal in everyday life. Scotus's view that the singular thing is intelligible in itself, yet never fully grasped in abstract cognition, confirmed Heidegger's conviction that something of the thing is always left out of categorial or theoretical knowing. Theoretical knowledge, *scientia*, is a partial and limited view of a thing, an interpretation.

Heidegger zeroes in on Husserl's notion of categorial intuition as a figure of Scotus's *simplex apprehensio*. Against neo-Kantianism, Husserl argues that the categorial structure of an essence is intuited not constructed; the ground of the categorial is *given* to subjectivity. Intuition is not restricted to sense data. It was the genius of the young Heidegger to relate this Scotist/Husserlian breakthrough to primordial structure to the problem of the forgetting of history. The historical is the arena of concrete singularity prior to universalization by the intellect. To deny actual intel-

---

59. See GA20 65/48.

ligibility of the singular is to deny an intelligibility proper to history. Fusing the notions of *haecceitas* and categorial intuition, Heidegger turned Husserl's reflective phenomenology into the "hermeneutics of facticity," a phenomenological investigation of the precategorial manifestations of historical being. We are in a certain way always already aware of the meaning of historical singularities. *Knowledge* is categorial and universal, but *understanding* is pre-categorial and historical, inextricably bound up with life as we live it. From Scotus, Heidegger learned that the "logos of the phenomenon" must be liberated from thinking that arrogates to itself the production of meaning; it must be permitted to show itself, or better, to speak itself. We are enjoined to *let language speak*. Language is not a human construct, something we do. Being is permeated by language, the primordial words coincident with the self-showing of things. This Scotist position, which captivated Heidegger in 1915, resurfaces in his later writings. "Mortals live in the speaking of language," Heidegger writes in 1950. "Language speaks. Man speaks in that he responds to language."[60] A cryptic saying, but one that Duns Scotus would have understood.

Nevertheless it would be taking this analysis too far to call Heidegger a Scotist. Between the *Habilitationsschrift* and *Sein und Zeit* lies a fundamental change in direction, away from traditional metaphysics toward phenomenological ontology. Yet the relationship to Scotus remains close. Had Heidegger remained an Aristotelian-Scholastic thinker, as he once described himself, he would have been a Scotist. When Heidegger broke with the Scholastic project of a philosophy that inescapably issues in a theology, he broke with Scotus as well. For Scotus, the transcendental notion of truth indicates a primordial relation of being to the divine intellect, not to a human subject. The tension between the Scotist notion of divine being, *ens infinitum*, being-in-itself, and intentional being, being-for-us, remains unresolved in the *Habilitationsschrift*. The resolution would come later, when Heidegger would surgically remove the notion of *ens infinitum* from ontology.

---

60. Martin Heidegger, "Language," in idem, *Poetry, Language, Thought*, trans. Albert Hofstadter (New York: Harper & Row, 1971), 210. The German is much more graceful, if not more comprehensible. See Martin Heidegger, "Die Sprache," in *Unterwegs zur Sprache* (Pfullingen: Günther Neske, 1975), 32–33: "Die Sprache spricht. Der Mensch spricht, insofern er der Sprache entspricht."

CHAPTER FIVE

MYSTICISM

There is an analogy of ineffabilities here: As the mystic is immediately related to the influx of the Divine Life, so am I immediately related to my own life.

THEODORE KISIEL

"*The most extreme sharpness and depth* of thought belong to genuine and great mysticism," Heidegger wrote in 1955.[1] The insight came to him far earlier. Joseph Sauer's course in the history of medieval mysticism, which Heidegger took in 1910–11, was the beginning of a lifelong interest in Meister Eckhart.[2] In the *Habilitationsschrift*, Heidegger spoke of mysticism as the other side of the Middle Ages, "the living heart of medieval Scholasticism" (*GA*1 205–6). The fragments published in *GA*60 under the erroneous title "The Philosophical Foundations of Medieval Mysticism [Outlines and Sketches for a Lecture, Not Held, 1918–1919]" actually date back as early as 1917 to the young Heidegger's first researches in the phenomenology of religion. Phenomenological research into religious consciousness discloses mysticism as a particularly intensive experience of facticity, "the fulfilment of a totally original 'I can'" (*GA*60 306). Mysticism remained Heidegger's lifelong interest. In the 1955/56 lecture course "Der Satz vom Grund," Heidegger returns to Eckhartian tropes. The course is a concentrated critique of metaphysical traditions that presume a self-suf-

---

1. Martin Heidegger, *Der Satz vom Grund*, 3rd ed. (Pfullingen: Günther Neske, 1965; reprinted in 1997 as *Gesamtausgabe*, vol. 10), 71; English: *The Principle of Reason*, trans. Reginald Lilly, Studies in Continental Thought, ed. John Sallis (Bloomington: Indiana University Press, 1991), 38.
2. Van Buren, *Young Heidegger*, 62–63.

ficient explanatory ground of beings, the *causa sui*. Heidegger juxtaposes the principle of sufficient reason, the law formulated by Leibniz as "nothing is without ground," with a text from the seventeenth-century Eckhartian mystic Angelus Silesius. "The rose is without why," Silesius writes, "it blooms because it blooms. It pays no attention to itself, asks not whether it is seen."[3] Just so, we only enter into our essence when we are content to exist without explanation, *ohne warum*.[4] At this stage in Heidegger's thinking, metaphysics and mysticism are polarized as paradigms of calculative and meditative thinking respectively. In the *Habilitationsschrift*, however, Heidegger saw medieval mysticism as the complement to Scholastic metaphysics. In 1916, the retrieval of the mystical tradition would not run counter to the rehabilitation of Aristotelian-Scholasticism; on the contrary, it would support it: "For the decisive insight into the basic character of Scholastic psychology, I regard a philosophical, more exactly, phenomenological elaboration of the mystical, moral-theological, and ascetical writings of medieval Scholasticism to be crucial. By pressing forward on such paths, one first penetrates to the living heart of medieval Scholasticism, as that which decisively grounded, enlivened, and strengthened a cultural epoch" (*GA1* 205–6).

The mysticism notes in *GA60* show that as early as 1917, Heidegger had reversed his 1916 position on the symbiosis of Scholasticism and mysticism. Scholasticism is presented as part of Catholicism's emphatically unmystical effort to freeze life, translate it into theory in order to control it.[5] Only one year after publishing the *Habilitationsschrift*, his thinking on the philosophical value of Scholasticism had undergone an extreme transfor-

---

3. Heidegger, *Satz vom Grund*, 72/39.
4. Caputo has shown that Silesius's poem popularizes a doctrine of Meister Eckhart's, the notion of the groundlessness of the self that is grounded in the self-grounded. Eckhart writes: "God's ground is my ground and my ground is God's ground. Here I live on my own as God lives on His own.... You should work all your works out of this innermost ground without why. Indeed I say, so long as you work for the kingdom of heaven, or for God, or for your internal happiness and thus for something outward, all is not well with you." Meister Eckhart, *Deutsche Predigten und Traktate*, ed. Josef Quint (Munich: Carl Hanser, 1965), 180, 5–13; English: *Meister Eckhart: A Modern Translation*, trans. Raymond B. Blakney (New York: Harper & Row, 1941), 126–27. See John D. Caputo, *The Mystical Element in Heidegger's Thought* (Athens: Ohio University Press, 1978), 100.
5. In the 1917 note "Das religiöse Apriori," Heidegger wrote: "medieval Scholasticism renewed... Aristotle's natural-scientific and naturalistic theoretical metaphysics of being with its radical exclusion and eclipse of Plato's problem of value" (*GA60* 313).

mation. We know from biographical sources that Heidegger's about-face was bound up with his loss of faith in the Church of his upbringing. Scholasticism is bound up with "dogmatic and casuistic pseudo-philosophies, which pose as philosophies of a particular system of religion (for example, Catholicism)" (*GA*60 314). Mysticism is no longer a complement but a corrective, an "elementary countermovement" to Scholastic metaphysics. The mystics rebelled against the theoretical turn of Scholasticism by initiating a retrieval of nonspeculative faith in the hidden God.

Heidegger's 1916 Program for a Factical Philosophical Theology

Heidegger's initial endeavor in the phenomenology of religion is the *Schlusskapitel* of his *Habilitationsschrift*, published one year after the dissertation was finished.[6] Drawing more on romanticism than Scholasticism, Heidegger plays with the possibility that a phenomenological anthropology carried far enough could issue in evidence of a factical experience of God. As van Buren says, this text represents the young Heidegger's effort at "philosophical mysticism."[7] Heidegger argues that Scholasticism and mysticism must not be sundered through the imposition of an artificial rationality/irrationality dichotomy. The two constitute an indissoluble unity. The false dichotomy of mysticism and Scholasticism is symptomatic of a general reduction of the variety of human experience, "the multiple domains of meaning," to one, the theoretical. The complementarity of Scholasticism and mysticism in the Middle Ages demonstrates the medieval sensitivity to the varieties of modes of meaning. "The two 'antithetical pairs': rationalism and irrationalism, Scholasticism and mysticism do not coincide. The attempt to put them on the same plane rests on an extreme rationalization of philosophy. As a rationalistic construct detached from life, philosophy is powerless; as an irrationalistic experience, mysticism is aimless" (*GA*1 410). Mysticism was the spontaneous expression of the life-world of the Middle Ages; Scholasticism was

---

6. A translation of this text by Roderick M. Stewart and John van Buren has been published in Heidegger, *Supplements*, 62–70.

7. Van Buren, *Young Heidegger*, 122.

its science. Without mysticism, Scholasticism would have been empty and lifeless. Without Scholasticism, mysticism would have been blind.[8]

Strikingly different in tone, the *Schlusskapitel* develops a theme barely touched upon elsewhere in the *Habilitationsschrift*: the relationship of transcendental logic to historicity. The Scotist doctrine of *haecceitas* shows how the irreducible manifold of reality is composed of individuals, each of which is essentially determined by time. But what is the relationship of time itself to being? The conflict between timeless validity, *essentia*, and history, the *hic et nunc* of *haecceitas*, remains unresolved in the text. As van Buren puts it, "The philosophical tension between timelessly valid sense and spatio-temporal reality was at this time also a tension within Heidegger's own philosophical personality—and it would soon snap."[9] According to Heidegger, judgment is not the act of a worldless ego but the expression of a being who experiences the occurrence of meaning in time. The inquiry into the relationship of temporal life to the timelessly valid becomes an urgent task in the light of a doctrine of the categories expanded to include *haecceitas*. The results of such an inquiry would supplement Scotus with a concretely grounded account of the historical epochs that differentiate meaning. Meaning is not a-historical and free floating. It is primarily disclosed in concrete, historical application. "History and its cultural-philosophical-teleological sense must become a

---

8. Even apparent defenders of the mystical dimension of religion fall into the trap of regarding mysticism as something nonrational. In the 1917 notes on Rudolf Otto's *Das Heilige*, Heidegger appreciates Otto's effort to give a phenomenological account of religion (*GA*60 332–34). However, Otto's assumption that the religious belongs to the "numinous," and as such, falls outside the domain of the thinkable, reinscribes a detrimental homogenizing of meaning, the presumption that the theoretical alone is intelligible. A construct of rationality is permitted to tyrannize the original manifestation of "living consciousness" and its "primordial world." Rationality in the limited sense of the term, that which can be expressed through generic concepts, is not the original and primary manifestation of life, but a founded phenomenon. When Otto characterizes the holy as "irrational," he tacitly accepts the reduction of experience to two antithetical modes. The "irrational" is as much a theoretical construct as the "rational." See Rudolf Otto, *Das Heilige: Über das Irrationale in der Idee des Göttlichen und sein Verhältnis zum Rationalen* (Stuttgart: Gotha, 1917). In a note from 1919 entitled *"Glauben und Wissen,"* Heidegger touches on the faith/reason problematic as symptomatic of the basic failure to appreciate the variety of modes of human meaning. A one-sided orientation to the epistemological scientific domain denigrates the meanings arising within faith. When scientific understanding is relativized as only one possible mode of meaning, the critique of faith as "irrational" collapses (*GA*60 310).

9. Van Buren, *Young Heidegger*, 88.

meaning-determinative element for the problem of categories" (*GA1* 408). As primordially determined by the "matter" that they illuminate, the categories are determined and differentiated by history. In the corpus of the *Habilitationsschrift*, Heidegger had repeatedly returned to the point that the Aristotelian categories are only "the ordinal forms for a determinately bounded area." As such, the life-world eludes them (*GA1* 263; 211). In the *Schlusskapitel*, he envisions a philosophy that breaks free of the homogenized theoretical world of substance and accidents and breaks through to the living ground of the categories, life in its primordial temporality. As a necessary compliment to transcendental logic, Heidegger calls for a hermeneutical elaboration of historical horizons, "the individual epochs of the history of spirit" (*GA1* 408). The full understanding of the doctrine of the categories in the Middle Ages would have to take into account "the qualitatively imbued, value-laden, and transcendentally-related world of experience of the medieval man" (*GA1* 409). It is in this context that Heidegger draws on the German romantic Friedrich von Schlegel and introduces a new term for historical consciousness, a first figure for what will become Dasein: "the living spirit" *(der lebendige Geist)*. This is "the historical spirit," the being that realizes itself and its meanings through time. "The theoretical-epistemological subject fails to indicate the metaphysically most meaningful sense of spirit, and says nothing of its full content. The problem of the categories first gets its proper depth-dimension and richness by incorporating this content. The living spirit is essentially the historical spirit. . . . The spirit is only to be comprehended when the whole fullness of its performances *(Leistungen)*, i.e., its history, is sublated [*aufgehoben*]" (*GA1* 406–8).

The resolution of the tension between history and spirit will involve a return to concrete life before it is flattened into numerically ordered forms by natural science, or universal genera and species, by traditional Aristotelian metaphysics. Validity is no longer understood apart from history; rather, different regions of validity are disclosed in history. The living spirit evaluates, takes stock of what has been, and projects values, which determine the forms of meaning available to it in the present. The valid prevails over the historical as the wellspring of meaning. "In the concept of living spirit and its relation to the metaphysical 'origin,' we get an insight into its metaphysical foundation, in which singularity, the individuality of acts, is joined in living unity with universal validity, the independence of meaning. Put objectively, the problem of the relationship between time and eternity, change and absolute validity, world and God, presents itself, which is scientifically and theoretically reflected upon in the study of history (forms of value) and philosophy (the validity of values)" (GA1 410). History studies the genesis of forms of value from historical life; philosophy tests these forms for validity.

At this point, the text takes a surprising turn. In the concluding five pages of the *Schlusskapitel*, Heidegger transposes the discussion of logic and ontology into a theological key. A transcendental logic grounded in historical life would be a disclosure of the divine. The grasp of the morphology of meaning from historical life generates the "means" for a developing comprehension of the spirit of God. "The [lively] spirit is only graspable in the sublation of the fullness of its accomplishments, that is, in its history. With the philosophical conceptualization of this constantly growing fullness, we are given an increasingly secure means for the living grasp of the Absolute Spirit of God" (GA1 408).[10] Unlike other difficult passages of the *Habilitationsschrift*, which become clear in the light of later developments of Heidegger's thought, this peculiar passage resists interpretation. On a neo-Kantian interpretation, "the Absolute Spirit" is a euphemism for the timelessly valid, the domain of logical sense, which transcends time, even while arising in time. The securing of an exhaustive account of the forms of meaning lifts us out of time.[11] Although textually justified, this is too prosaic an interpretation; the passage stands out as the early Heidegger's only reference to the possibility of a factically founded philosophical theology. By contrast with his later statements concerning the necessity of a formal atheism if the factic is to be allowed to show itself in itself, here Heidegger suggests the possibility of thinking the divine without distorting the human. The phenomenology of the historical self could be an unveiling of the divine mind.

The discussion of a historical unfolding of absolute spirit in conjunc-

10. "Der Geist ist nur zu begreifen, wenn die ganze Fülle seiner Leistungen, d.h. seine Geschichte, in ihm aufgehoben wird, mit welcher stets wachsenden Fülle in ihrer philosophischen Begriffenheit ein sich fortwährend steigerndes Mittel der lebendigen Begreifung des absoluten Geistes Gottes gegeben ist."

11. This is Pöggeler's interpretation of the passage. See Otto Pöggeler, *Der Denkweg Martin Heideggers*, 2nd ed. (Pfullingen: Günther Neske, 1990), 22.

tion with the use of the verb *aufheben* invokes Hegel. On a Hegelian view, the accomplishments of historically revealed rationality would be dialectically identified with the self-knowledge of the absolute. The eternally realized self-knowing of absolute spirit is carried out in history through the dialectic of human reason coming to an ever more secure grasp of itself. However, it is clear from Heidegger's anti-Hegelian introduction to the *Habilitationsschrift*, as well as the crucial sentence that finishes the book, that Heidegger intends a polemic with Hegel. "The philosophy of living Spirit, of fruitful love, of reverent intimacy with God *(verehrende Gottinnigkeit)*," Heidegger writes, "stands before the great task of a fundamental opposition to the fullness and depths, wealth of experience and conceptualizations of the powerful systematic historical world-view, which has taken up into itself all previous fundamental philosophical problems, that is, with Hegel" (*GA1* 410). The task for philosophy is not to enact a mediated return to the origins, but to undo mediation and return to the unthought beginning.

This anti-Hegelian thrust of Heidegger's hermeneutics is at work in the introductory methodological remarks of the *Habilitationsschrift*. Heidegger argues that the study of the history of philosophy is unlike any other historical study, for in philosophy we are not primarily concerned with past events, but with recurring philosophical phenomena, which need to be re-thought in different epochs of history. "Progress," understood as the linear development of solutions and new questions that determines the growth of the natural sciences, is impossible in philosophy. Philosophers circle around the same questions without appearing to make any progress at all. Yet this is not a scientific deficiency, but the way of thinking: it is the essence of philosophy to return to recurring themes because philosophy engages meaning, which shows itself differently in different historical horizons. The development *(Entwicklung)* of philosophy is an unwrapping or uncoiling *(Auswicklung)* of perennial problems, which must be undertaken anew in every generation. Philosophy never returns to the same place, nor does it simply progress: if it is successful, something new is uncovered, even as older insights recede into forgetfulness.[12] In the *Schlusskapitel*, Heidegger returns to his theological ori-

12. "In view of the constancy of human nature, it becomes understandable that philosophical problems repeat themselves in history. There is no development [*Entwicklung*] here in the sense of

gins and suggests that this endless circling around recurring primordial problems can be a knowing of God. The Scotist notion of God is transposed into a historical-hermeneutical key: *ens infinitum* contains all possible forms of meaning, revealing itself in the kaleidoscope of historical epochs. In the 1915 qualifying lecture, Heidegger argues against Hegel that "there is no law determining how periods of history follow and succeed one another" (*GA*1 431). Nonetheless, the disclosure of meaning in history is not arbitrary. When we grasp that the human being only understands by drawing upon *essentia,* and *essentia* in its ground is identical with the divine mind, we see the theo-ontological direction of the young Heidegger's thinking. Although subjectively projected, meaning is not subjectively created. Human history is a drama of divine ideas: God creates the historical subject and the historical subject projects different worlds—semantic wholes, not spun out of nothing, but sent to us by the divine, which "worlds" itself through us. History is not linear; time is as much a progress in forgetting as it is a progress in understanding. Yet in its primordial ground, every disclosure of meaning is a disclosure of the divine, an outflow of divine simplicity into difference. The infinite reveals itself in an infinity of horizons of understanding. History is the outflow of divine simplicity into difference, the *Ereignis* of the infinite revealing itself in successive epochs of human understanding.[13]

The term *der lebendige Geist* is Schlegel's.[14] Heidegger would have first

---

a progress toward new questions on the basis of already found solutions of the past. Rather, one finds an always fruitful attempt to uncoil [*Auswicklung*] and exhaust [*Ausschöpfung*] a limited domain of problems. This ever-renewed struggle with more or less the same group of problems, this pervading sameness of the philosophical mind [*durchhaltende Identität des philosophischen Geistes*] not only makes possible but demands a corresponding comprehension of the 'history' of philosophy.... In accord with the character of the development [*Entwicklung*] of all philosophy as an uncoiling [*Auswicklung*] of specific problems, progress lies for the most part in the deepening and the restatement of the questions to be formulated" (*GA*1 196–97).

13. Heidegger's thinking at this stage has an unmistakable Schleiermacherian echo. Spearheading the nineteenth-century remembering of history that sparked the development of the human sciences, Schleiermacher wrote in 1799: "This multiplicity [of historical religions] is necessary for the complete manifestation of religion. It [religion] must seek for a definite character, not only in the individual, but also in the society. Did the society not contain a principle to individualize itself, it could have no existence. Hence we must assume and we must search for an endless mass of distinct forms.... [Religion] is an endless progressive work of the Spirit that reveals himself in all human history." Schleiermacher, *Über die Religion,* 213–14.

14. *Kritische Friedrich Schlegel Ausgabe,* ed. Ernst Behler (Munich: Schöning, 1958–), vol. 10, 81. On the influence of Schlegel on Heidegger, see Wolf-Dieter Gudopp, *Der junge Heidegger:*

heard through Braig of Schlegel's middle way "between the opposed fallacies of idealism and realism," a philosophy that sought to preserve both the empirical foundations of the natural sciences and the revealed foundations of religion. With his "Philosophie des Lebens," which influenced Dilthey, Schlegel was a founding father of life philosophy. Life is an infinite, uncreated "organic" context in which subject and object, self and world, are primordially one. "Everything is ensouled and penetrated by the same living spirit *(der lebendige Geist),*" Schlegel writes, "the infinite power and activity that binds everything into a great system, which is as effective in the individual as in the whole, and reveals itself everywhere."[15] The living spirit transforms the heterogeneous manifold of being into an organic unity in which the purpose of the whole is manifest in every part. Philosophy is the living spirit's reflection upon itself, "life's consciousness of itself."[16] In 1922, Heidegger defined philosophy in similar terms, "as the genuine, explicit actualization of the tendency toward interpretation that belongs to life's own basic movements (movements within which life is concerned about itself and its own Being)" (*PIA* 246). For both Schlegel and Heidegger, the philosophical self-interpretation of life must be historical, but a history that unfolds cyclically, not dialectically, returning again and again to inexhaustibly rich origins. In Schlegel's words, "the whole of the development constitutes a circle, which returns to its beginning."[17] The origin is not primitive, but pure and primordially charged with divinity.

This romantic reading of the young Heidegger is supported by clues in Heidegger's 1915 lecture "Der Zeitbegriff in der Geschichtswissenschaft." Heidegger took the motto for the lecture from Eckhart: "Time is that which changes and diversifies; eternity simply endures" (*GA*1 415). In a note in the *Habilitationsschrift*, Heidegger says that the lecture was intended to show "that time has a decisive function as the determinant

---

Realität und Wahrheit in der Vorgeschichte von "Sein und Zeit," Zur Kritik der Bürgerlichen Ideologie, ed. Manfred Buhr, vol. 102 (Frankfurt am Main: Marxistische Blätter, 1983), 80 ff.

15. Friedrich Schlegel, "Propädeutik und Logik," in *Kritische Ausgabe,* vol. 13, 263, quoted in Gudopp, *Junge Heidegger,* 90.

16. Friedrich Schlegel, "Die Entwicklung der Philosophie," in *Kritische Ausgabe,* vol. 12, 366, quoted in Gudopp, *Junge Heidegger,* 90.

17. Schlegel, "Die Entwicklung der Philosophie," 27, quoted in Gudopp, *Junge Heidegger,* 91.

characteristic of the individual" (*GA1* 253 n. 53). The Eckhart motto gives the lecture an unlikely theological overtone. Eckhart held that the self-generativity of life, which "lives out of its own ground and wells forth out of what is its own," originates in the overabundance of being in the *Gottheit*. The divine is life in the absolute sense, infinite fecundity, overflowing and spilling forth into creation "without why."[18] Eckhart expresses the super-fecundity of the divine with the metaphor of the maternity of God. "What does God do all day long? God gives birth. From all eternity God lies on a maternity bed giving birth."[19] A God who diversifies and multiplies the divine essence in the heterogeneity of history is at once self-revealing and self-concealing. The motto of the *Schlusskapitel*, taken from the romantic poet Novalis, expresses the problem presented by such a *Deus absconditus:* "We seek the unconditioned everywhere and always find only things" (*GA1* 341).

The fragmented ideas of the *Schlusskapitel* are rich with suggestions for a factical and hermeneutical philosophy of religion, which could circle from the human to the divine, and from the divine to the human, without distortion of either. As a phenomenological reduction, Heidegger's 1916 theo-ontological movement from history back to the divine is not equiprimordial with the previous reductions in the *Habilitationsschrift*, but in a decisive sense plunges beneath all other reductions into a moment of primordial understanding that is somehow identical with God. Whatever else this means, it shows that the young Heidegger had not yet come to the view that the divine and the human are mutually exclusive conceptual structures. Facticity would later be presented as only accessible in an atheistic context, because the idea of God draws us away from the factic. The *Schlusskapitel* contains no such opposition. Transcendental logic, phenomenology of history, and theology converge in a confused and disjointed way indicative of the young Heidegger's conflicting philosophical interests.

---

18. Eckhart, *Deutsche Predigten*, 180, 23–31/114–17, Blakney trans.
19. Eckhart, quoted in Matthew Fox, *Original Blessing: A Primer in Creation Spirituality* (Santa Fe, N.Mex.: Bear & Company, 1983), 220.

Toward a Phenomenology of Medieval Mysticism: The 1917–1919 Notes

By 1919, Heidegger had abandoned the project of relating a phenomenology of historical life to philosophical theology. The task for philosophy is to thematize existence, not eternity; human life, not God. The atheological turn in Heidegger's thought, which occurred sometime between 1917 and 1919, did not make him indifferent to theology. Rather, he discovered a new approach to theological texts. While philosophy could not presume to access religious phenomena the way they are experienced by the religious, it could nonetheless make use of certain formal moves made in religious texts for its own purposes. In a 1919 note speculating on Husserl's assigned project—to become the phenomenologist of religion in the collaborative enterprise of Husserlian phenomenology—Heidegger writes that a philosophical analysis of mysticism would not derive a substantive philosophical content from mystical texts (GA60 304). It would not speculate on the validity or invalidity of purported mystical experiences of God. Phenomenological understanding does not rise to the absolute, but descends into time, following language back to the meanings immanent in finite existence. The mystic's articulation of a factical experience of God demands an extreme fidelity to historical life, a non-objectifying language analogous to phenomenology. Hence mystical literature has a formal phenomenological significance independent of its theological content.

The coeditor of *GA60*, Claudius Strube, explains that the title of the volume, "Phenomenology of Religious Life," was taken from the cover sheet of a bundle of notes, which appear in the volume under the title, "Die philosophischen Grundlagen der mittelalterlichen Mystik" (1918–19) (*GA60* 346–48). This title refers to a cancelled lecture course Heidegger announced at Freiburg in 1919. The title is misleading, for it suggests that the notes were gathered for the sake of the cancelled 1919 course, when in fact, the notes were scattered reflections on mysticism, the earliest of which predates the cancelled course by three years.[20] Heidegger dropped

---

20. Theodore Kisiel has remarked that there is more to this bundle of notes, which he has himself examined, than appeared in print. The editor of *GA60* fails to inform us that he is making a

the 1919 course in mysticism in favor of an introductory course to phenomenology and never developed a coherent presentation of the topic. The notes are a random compilation of fragmented themes sketched as directions for further thinking, some of which, such as the relation of the soul to the nothing, or letting be *(Gelassenheit)*, Heidegger took up again, others, to which he never returned. The topics include the following: irrationality in Meister Eckhart; historical consciousness in Bernard of Clairvaux; Schleiermacher's notion of religion; and Rudolf Otto's "noumenal experience."

The medieval mystic's experiential imperative led to the thematization of a different dimension of *ipsum esse subsistens*. For Eckhart, actuality in the finite and familiar sense is always in part a negation of possibility: to be *this* means not to be *that*. Every finite being, everything that can be the subject of predication contains a 'not.' God, on the other hand, is the negation of all negation. Consequently God is free of actuality. Hence the only proper name for God is "the One," or *"esse indistinctum."* Eckhart writes: "Everything that is less than God, since it is less than existence, is [both] being and non-being, and some kind of existence is denied to it since it is below and less than existence. And so negation is a part of it. But to existence itself no existence is denied. . . . Therefore, no negation, nothing negative belongs to God, except for the negation of negation, which is what the One signifies when expressed negatively, 'God is one' (Pt 4; Ga 3:20). The negation of negation is the purest and fullest affirmation—'I am who am.' It returns upon itself 'with a full return'; it rests upon itself, and through itself, it is Existence itself."[21] Eckhart elevates the divine essence to a level that absorbs the whole of being, actuality and possibility. The divine is perfect simplicity of form, in a sense, formless, for transcending all difference, God cannot be differentiated from other forms. But the "formlessness" of God is not a limitation, not a lack; rather, it is freedom from limitation and determination.[22] As Heidegger

---

selection. We are thus denied a complete record of the full range of the literature Heidegger was considering in preparation for a treatise on the phenomenology of religion. For Heidegger's reading list at the time of mysticism notes, see Kisiel, *Genesis of* Being and Time, 525–27.

21. Eckhart, *Commentary on Exodus*, chap. 15, para. 74, in *Meister Eckhart: Teacher and Preacher*, trans. Bernard McGinn (New York: Paulist Press, 1986), 68.

22. See ibid., 15, 40/55.

puts it in an early note, God is "neither not-yet-determined nor not-yet-determinable, but determinate-free *(Bestimmungslose)*" (GA60 316).

Eckhart's radical reading of the traditional Scholastic identification of God and being leads to his heterodox denial of the possibility of metaphysical theological language. The essence of God, *Gottheit*, is sharply distinguished from the God spoken of in theology. The latter can be said to have distinct attributes, goodness, justice, and so forth; the former has no qualities. Beyond all determination, nothing can be affirmed of the *Gottheit*. "God is a being beyond being and a nothingness beyond being. God is nothing. No thing. God is nothingness. And yet God is something."[23] Infinite being contains within itself all possible determinations of beings. No particular determination can be attributed to it without falsification—not because God is unreal, but because determinate being is unreal. If God alone *is* in the strict sense, creatures are not. "Every created being taken or conceived apart as distinct from God is not a being, but nothing. What is separate and distinct from God is separate and distinct from existence, because whatever exists is from God himself, through him and in him."[24] In an important aside in the 1927 lecture course, *Die Grundprobleme der Phänomenologie*, Heidegger elaborates "peculiar" ontological consequences of Eckhart's understanding of God. "It is the characteristic quality of medieval mysticism that it tries to lay hold of the being ontologically rated as the properly essential being, God, in His very essence. In this attempt mysticism arrives at a peculiar speculation, peculiar because it transforms the idea of essence in general, which is an ontological determination of a being, the *essentia entis,* into a being and makes the ontological ground of a being, its possibility, its essence, into what is properly actual. This remarkable alteration of essence into a being is the presupposition for what is called mystical speculation" (GA24 127/90). Because essence is what the thing is, Heidegger calls it "the on-

---

23. Eckhart, quoted in Fox, *Original Blessing,* 149.

24. Eckhart, *Exodus,* 15, 40/55. Although he comes at the problem of religious language from a direction opposite to Scotus, Eckhart can be read as propagating a doctrine of *univocatio entis*. For both Scotus and Eckhart, Aquinas's analogous religious language does not work. However, where Scotus holds that the univocity of our notion of being preserves the possibility of speaking of both God and finite things, Eckhart holds the opposite. Precisely because our language of being is univocal, we have no words that could be meaningfully applied to God.

tological ground." Considered apart from existence, it is possibility. *Gottheit* is free of the actualizations that localize essences in space and time.

> Therefore, Meister Eckhart speaks mostly of the "superessential essence"; that is to say, what interests him is not strictly speaking, God—God is still a provisional object for him—but Godhead. When Meister Eckhart says "God" he means Godhead, not *deus* but *deitas,* not *ens* but *essentia,* not nature but what is above nature, the essence—the essence to which, as it were, every existential determination must still be refused, from which every *additio existentiae* must be kept at a distance. Hence he also says *"Spräche man von Gott er ist, das wäre hinzugelegt."* "If it were said of God that he is, that would be added on." Meister Eckhart's expression *"das wäre hinzugelegt"* is the German translation, using Thomas' phrase, of "it would be an *additio entis."* *"So ist Gott im selben Sinne nicht und ist nicht dem Begriffe aller Kreaturen."* Thus God is for himself his "not"; that is to say, he is the most universal being, the purest indeterminate possibility of everything possible, pure nothing. He is the nothing over against the concept of every creature, over against every determinate possible and actualized being. Here, too, we find a remarkable parallel to the Hegelian determination of being and its identification with nothing. The mysticism of the Middle Ages or, more precisely, its mystical theology, is not mystical in our sense and in the bad sense; rather it can be conceived in a completely immanent sense. (GA24 127–28/90–91)[25]

As superessential essence, God is not a being, *ens,* but absolute *essentia,* not *actus* but *possibilitas.* This resonates powerfully with the principle of Heidegger's mature ontology: "Higher than actuality is possibility" (*SZ* 38/34). Eckhart's *Gottheit* is not the nothingness of non-being but the nothingness of possibility. Heidegger recommends that we understand this "in an immanent sense"; that is, as formally indicative of the primacy of nothingness. To be given over to the *Gottheit* is to be released from objectification, the confines of theoretical categories. This release is not a new mode of being but a return to our most primordial mode of being. "Dasein means: being-held-out-into-the-nothing" (*"Dasein ist Hineingehaltenheit in das Nichts"*) (*GA*9 115/91). *Das Nichts* is not the absurd but the negation of all determination. In a horizon cluttered by things, Dasein loses sight of the nothing that enables it to be and to understand. Yet

---

25. Heidegger cites Meister Eckhart, *Predigten, Traktate,* ed. Franz Pfeiffer (Leipzig, 1857), 659, lines 17–18; 506, lines 30–31.

the nothing is always there, or rather, never there, and makes itself felt in moods, in boredom, angst, and joy. In these everyday experiences, a fore-theoretical grasp of the whole of beings profiled against the nothing breaks through the trance of our day-to-day concerns. We stand before the nothing and recognize that we are not at home in the world. Van Buren has identified an earlier version of the notion of the nothing in Heidegger's 1919 "primordial something" *(Ur-etwas)*. The primordial *Etwas* is experienced as an "indeterminate, vague, undefined" horizon within which all experience occurs. It is a region where we are simultaneously at home and homeless. Heidegger writes, "The fore-theoretical *Etwas* bears the highest, potential, and utterly uncanny not-being-at-home of life." It grips us in moods, presses against us, without ever becoming an object for us: "The *Etwas* is fulfilled as the indeterminate in a context of significance, is charged with life, such that it can take on an impending character that engenders anxiety" (*GA*58 107, 125, 217).[26]

In the early notes, as in his lectures on religion in the '20s, Heidegger is not particularly interested in the question of the existence of God. What intrigues him are the methodological moves to which the mystic is driven in the effort to articulate an experience that is entirely concrete, singular, and nonobjective. Heidegger seems to have been clear from early on that the task for the philosophy of religion is not an evaluation of the truth value of the mystic claim but rather a formalization of the relational senses disclosed in mystical discourse. Mysticism intrigues him, not as an indication of ultimate reality, but as various indices of ways of being-in-the-world. The mystic's relationship to *Gottheit* encompasses a variety of intentional acts, which recur at various stages in Heidegger's philosophy: letting be *(Gelassenheit)*, detachment *(Abgeschiedenheit)*, and devotion *(Hingabe)*. For the mystic, these are the acts by which the soul rises to a special mode of being-in-the-world correlative to *Gottheit*. In Heidegger's formalized reading, they become life-tendencies of average and everyday historical existence. Heidegger never fully clarifies the nature of the analogies between the mystical and phenomenological meanings of these words. He does not deny that they might mean something different in mysticism than they do in phenomenology. Where he develops their

---

26. See van Buren, *Young Heidegger,* 297.

phenomenological meanings at some length, both in the early lectures and notes and in the later works, the theological meanings of the terms remain in darkness.

The young Heidegger notes that the *unio mystica* is accomplished through "letting be," *demütige Gelassenheit* (GA60 309). *Gelassenheit* comes from the German verb *lassen,* "to let." It has been translated as "acquiescence" (incorrectly), or "releasement." It means literally "letting-be." For Eckhart, it means letting go of self-will and letting God irrupt from within. Eckhart writes: "Where the creature ends, there God begins to be. Now God desires nothing more of you than that you go out of yourself according to your creaturely mode of being and let God be God in you."[27] We do not have to clear a space for God to enter the soul; God is already within us. We have only to let go of a false notion of ourselves, the belief that the self is the master of itself and its world. *Gelassenheit* means that the *unio mystica* is not something we do, but something we let be done. Kisiel describes this as "the reversal of initiative from the human agency to the divine agency." Heidegger's formalization of *Gelassenheit* begins in 1917 but only comes to fruition in the 1944 *Feldweg—Gespräch.* He refers to *Gelassenheit* again in the 1949 Memorial Address commemorating the 175th anniversary of the birth of the Meßkirch composer Conradin Kreutzer.[28] The distinction at the heart of these texts is the essence of Heidegger's critique of technology. Calculative thinking *(rechnendes Denken)* must be distinguished from meditative thinking *(besinnliches Denken).* The former plans, researches, organizes, takes account of given conditions, and anticipates definite results; the latter waits for beings to show themselves, and contemplates "the meaning which reigns in everything that is." Thinking waits patiently, like the farmer "for the seed to come up and ripen." It is relaxed and open and lets beings show themselves as they are. As the breakthrough to the *Gottheit* is achieved in Eckhart by not-doing, so the breakthrough to "the fore-theoretical" is a letting go of the grasping and control of the theoretical attitude. Eckhart's *Gelassenheit* allows the soul's original being-given-over-to-God to show

---

27. Eckhart, *Deutsche Predigten,* 180, 32–34/127, Blakney trans.

28. Martin Heidegger, *Gelassenheit* (Pfullingen: Günther Neske, 1959), 25–28; reprinted in GA16. English: *Discourse on Thinking,* trans. John M. Anderson and E. Hans Freund (New York: Harper & Row, 1965), 54–57.

itself. Heidegger's *Gelassenheit* allows Dasein's original being-given-over-to-life to show itself. Heidegger is not interested in the moral and religious connotations of Eckhart's *Gelassenheit* but in the formal structure of overcoming willing and allowing being to show itself.[29]

In an early reference to Eckhart's notion of detachment, Heidegger writes that the object of mystical devotion shows itself more and more free of limitation as the mystic becomes more and more free of attachment and desire; the less self-will, the purer and simpler the form becomes (*GA*60 308, 318). Since like is only known by like, the soul that would draw near to the nothingness of God, must be denuded of multiplicity, attachment to concepts, images, and conflicting desires. A God who is free of all determination can only be approached by a being that is also free from determination. *Abgeschiedenheit* is not so much a transformation as a return to the essence of the soul, the imperturbable solitude of the divine unity within us. Knowing the absolute is a progressive simplification, the repelling of all that limits, and the return to the divine origin and root of the self. "God is not found in the soul by adding anything," Eckhart writes, "but by a process of subtraction." Detachment is not something we add to our lives, like an exercise program or a diet. It is, rather, our original way of being.

In a 1917 note bearing the title "Religiöse Phänomene," Heidegger touches upon another side of detachment in brief remarks on the subject of silence *(Schweigen)*. Heidegger notes that silence is intrinsic to the religious life. The German verb *schweigen* has a positive connotation that is lost in English. More than just falling silent or not speaking, *schweigen* is an act with its own positive intentional structure. "The mystic silences in effusive astonishment" *("Der Mystiker schweigt in überschwenglicher Verwunderung")* (*GA*60 312). According to Eckhart, "nothing in all creation is so like God as stillness."[30] In mystical silence, Heidegger's note contin-

---

29. In *Gelassenheit*, Heidegger criticizes Eckhart for remaining on the level of *willing* not to will. This is a problematic interpretation of Eckhart. The one who has reached mystical union in Eckhart does not will to do God's will, or even will to have no will, but is rather will-less. Eckhart writes, "So long as a man has it in himself that it is his will to fulfill the most beloved will of God, then such a man does not have the poverty of which I speak; for this man still has a will, with which he wishes to satisfy God's will." Eckhart, *Deutsche Predigten*, 304, 22–27/208, Blakney trans. Heidegger recapitulates precisely this Eckhartian argument as a position that purports to go beyond Eckhart. Caputo correctly questions Heidegger on this point. Caputo, *Mystical Element*, 174 ff.

30. Eckhart, quoted in Fox, *Original Blessing*, 133.

ues, the whole of beings emerges profiled against "the primary brightness *(Helle)*." We ourselves are revealed as a place of light in which things can appear: "Each Dasein is a brightness, which develops through particular illuminations" (*GA*60 312). This cryptic fragment is a glimmer of a theme that emerges fully developed in "Was ist Metaphysik?" Dasein is the clearing within which things can be unconcealed. Silence enables the unconcealment, opening up a "brightness" *(Helligkeit)* in which "all things and values become distinguished from the nothing." "In the clear *(hellen)* night of the nothing of anxiety the original openness of beings as such arises: that they are beings—and not nothing" (*GA*9 114/90). This experience is never put into words; on the contrary, it emerges from silence and returns us to silence. In mystical *Schweigen,* phenomena themselves are permitted to speak, and in their speaking, that which is not said shows itself.[31]

Abgeschiedenheit turns away from the world and no longer sees it in a certain sense. It is not a "theoretical not-seeing" but an "emotional not-seeing," detachment from desire (*GA*60 308). Eckhart assumes that regardless of how dispersed in the cares of life we may be on other levels, at the innermost core of the soul, we are alone before God. Knowing the absolute is a progressive simplification *(Entmannigfaltigung),* the repelling of all that limits, and the return to the divine origin and root of the self. In Heidegger, certain moods liberate us from everydayness. In anxiety, "The being no longer speaks to us" *(Das Seiende spricht uns nicht mehr an)* (*GA*9 111/88). We descend into the groundless ground of our beings, what Eckhart regards as the place of primordial *Abgeschiedenheit.* The task for the mystic (like that of the phenomenologist) is not to create the self anew but rather, to resist the fall into self-alienation. The young Heidegger comments, "The process of the progressive emancipation from contents, differences, dualities, has an essential relationship to an ethical *telos.* Multiplicity disperses, brings the subject into disquiet" (*GA*60 317). The *telos* of *Abgeschiedenheit* is freedom from difference, conflict, and multiplicity. "Absolute value is absolute freedom from opposition *(Gegensatzlosigkeit),* that is, freedom from determination *(Bestimmungslosigkeit)*" (*GA*60 318).

---

31. In 1919, Heidegger wrote: "a great reserve allows the religious person to keep silent *(schweigen)* before his ultimate mystery" (*GA*56/57 5). Cf. *SZ* 165/154.

For Eckhart, *Abgeschiedenheit* is the *noesis* of the *unio mystica*. In Heidegger's immanent reading, *Abgeschiedenheit* is a non-theistic human comportment, nothing supernatural, but on the contrary, average and everyday. In boredom, for example, beings lose their hold on us. Dasein is freed from all emotional involvement with the world, or better, from all emotional involvement with anything in the world, even if it finds this freedom burdensome. Dasein is not bored about anything in the world but about being-in-the-world as such. Lifted above its average and everyday cares, Dasein is free to feel the world as a whole. In these moments of being-held-above-all-that-is, we understand that we are always outside ourselves; we are temporality, transcendence. Nothingness-disclosive moods liberate us from a certain kind of thing-oriented care. We can heed being precisely because "beings no longer speak to us" (*GA*9 111/88).

The recovery of simplicity through *Gelassenheit* and *Abgeschiedenheit* is not ultimately an accomplishment but a surrender *(Hingabe)* to that which gives itself. *Gelassenheit* and *Abgeschiedenheit* are essentially modes of *Hingabe*. On first glance, *Gelassenheit* and *Abgeschiedenheit* seem to describe passivities, modes of nonaction, while *Hingabe* is an act. This tension between action and passion in the mystical life is vital. By maintaining that *Gelassenheit* and *Abgeschiedenheit* are *hingegeben*, and *Hingabe* is always *gelassen* and *abgeschieden*, Heidegger shows us that *Gelassenheit* and *Abgeschiedenheit* are not passive but active in a higher way.[32]

---

32. The theme of the nonactive act, the effortless effort to mystical breakthrough, which Heidegger touches on in these notes, and again in *Gelassenheit*, has a long history in mystical literature. Indeed, the Christian monastic life consists in suffering the tension between an active ascetic program and receptivity to grace. The monk exacerbates the tension until all vestiges of self-will break down and the soul lets God be God. Grace would not be grace if it were earned. Yet paradoxically the monastic life is intended to be a training in sanctity. The monk must take his asceticism with complete seriousness and yet never forget for a moment that the whole outcome of his ascetical-mystical life depends entirely on the grace of God. If God wills, He can sanctify him "without why." This monastic paradox between effort and effortlessness lies at the core of the Christian mystical tradition and the Christian ethical life. Thomas Merton writes: "Monastic solitude, poverty, obedience, silence and prayer dispose the soul for this mysterious destiny in God. Asceticism itself does not produce divine union as its direct result. It only disposes the soul for union. The various practices of monastic asceticism are more or less valuable to the monk in proportion as they help him to accomplish the inner and spiritual work that needs to be done to make his soul poor, and

In the 1917 note "Irrationalität bei Meister Eckhart," Heidegger describes Eckhart's mysticism as an "an extreme realism" (*GA*60 317).[33] Eckhart's realism consists in the attitude of devotion *(Hingabe)*, which is a self-diremptive being given over *(hingegeben)* to God. Heidegger had touched on *Hingabe* in the *Habilitationsschrift*: In "the primordial relation of the soul to God," the self is "given over" *(hingegeben)* to its world (*GA*1 198–200, 406, 408–10). He admires the Scholastic's phenomenologically sensitive surrender to the things themselves (*GA*1 198). The medieval mystic is so *hingegeben* that he is no longer capable of distinguishing self and God: the beloved fills the whole horizon of possible experience. Heidegger transposes this mystical-Scholastic understanding of *Hingabe* into his early hermeneutics of facticity. Meaning is not something I deliberately choose; it is rather that to which I am always already given. Lask used the term *Hingabe* to describe our categorial immersion in the world of meaning: we are given over to the fore-theoretical, surrendered to it, already committed to it, as in aesthetic, ethic, or religious dedication *(Hingabe)*.[34] In 1919, Heidegger elaborated Husserl's "principle of all principles," the turn back to the things themselves, as a dedicated submission *(Hingabe)* to the subject matter. This dedication does not isolate an essence and theorize; rather it descends into the fore-theoretical ground of life and illuminates the primordial understanding of historical existence.[35] *Hingabe* characterizes "phenomenological life in its growing intensification of itself" (*GA*56/57 110). Heidegger finds a similar use of the term *Hingabe* in Schleiermacher (*GA*60 319). For Schleiermacher, theology is primar-

---

humble, and empty, in the mystery of the presence of God. . . . The victory of monastic humility is the full acceptance of God's hidden action in the weakness and ordinariness and unsatisfactoriness of our own everyday lives. It is the acceptance of our own incompleteness, in order that He may make us complete in His own way." Thomas Merton, *The Silent Life* (New York: Farrar, Straus & Giroux, 1957), 4, 6.

33. The note was based on Heidegger's study of two texts by Eckhart: "Diu zeichen eines wârhaften Grundes," and "Von der Geburt des êwigen wortes," in *Deutsche Mystiker des vierzehnten Jahrhunderts*, ed. Franz Pfeiffer, vol. 2, *Meister Eckhart* (Göttingen: Vandenhoeck und Ruprecht, 1906), 475–83. See Kisiel, *Genesis of* Being and Time, 522 n. 25.

34. Lask, *Logik,* 190–91.

35. See van Buren, *Young Heidegger,* 295: "The medieval mystic's *unio mystica* and abandonment *(Hingabe)* in the *mysterium tremendum* of the analogical efflux of the Divine Life also tells us something about the way that all experience is abandoned in the mysterious depth-dimension of the differentiating *Ereignis* of being."

ily a rhetorical and poetic discourse, which intensifies a primordial self-surrender to the Universe, a *Hingegebenheit* that we do not need to perform but have always already enacted. Because his subject matter, the feeling for the infinite, cannot be theoretically thematized, Schleiermacher practices the phenomenological attitude. For Heidegger, this being-given to life is the essence of phenomenology. Before we intend "objects," before subject is distinguished from object and object is differentiated into substance and accident, we find ourselves given over to the undifferentiated whole of life. That to which we are given over is not other than us. It is our life, the self in its original appearance, self and world as one, self as not yet distinguished from its life and all that constitutes it.

In a footnote in the *Schlusskapitel,* Heidegger refers to a future study of the relationship of Eckhart's mysticism to the Scholastic notion of truth. "I hope to show on some other occasion how the mysticism of Eckhart first gets its philosophical significance and value for the metaphysics of the problem of truth that is to be touched on in the context of what is below" (*GA1* 402 n. 2). The context of the footnote is a reference to Lask's principle of the material determination of form:

Because of its return to a fundamental problematic sphere of subjectivity (the level of acts), the theory of meaning in conjunction with the problem of categories—despite its immediate schematized character—has especial import for a philosophical interpretation of medieval Scholasticism. The investigation of the relation between the *modus essendi* and the "subjective" *modus significandi* and *modus intelligendi* leads to the principle of the material determination of each form. For its part this principle includes the fundamental correlation of object and subject in itself [Eckhart note]. This essential connectedness of the object of cognition and the cognition of the object receives its clearest expression in the concept of the *verum* as one of the transcendentals, a determination of objects in general. (*GA1* 402)

The material determination of form indicates the moment prior to conceptualization when the historically given determines the categories. The Scholastic doctrine of *verum transcendens* expresses the intentionally structured interdependence of *intellectus* and *ens*. By virtue of its being, every object is true, that is, primordially related to intellect. Both Lask's principle of material determination of form and the Scholastic doctrine of transcendental truth point to a precategorial mutual conditioning of intellect and being. Heidegger's cryptic footnote suggests that the doctrine of *verum transcendens* can illuminate the philosophical relevance of Eckhart's mysticism. Caputo interprets Heidegger as assuming a relationship between Eckhart's notion of *Abgeschiedenheit* and Aristotle's notion of the soul as "in a manner all things." As the soul that would draw near to God must divest itself of desires and attachments for created things, the knowing intellect cannot cling to any particular form, but must be free of all forms. Caputo then relates *Abgeschiedenheit* to the later Heidegger's understanding of Dasein as a "clearing" in which beings can be.[36]

This interpretation, plausible though it appears, has broken the cardinal rule of hermeneutics: it has left the text out. If we look carefully at the presentation of the problem of truth in the *Habilitationsschrift* to which Eckhart's mysticism is purported to give an alternative expression, we see that the issue under discussion is subject/object dualism, more specifically, the way in which the Scholastic notion of transcendental truth precludes such a dualism. That truth is a transcendental convertible with being means that it is not a subjective phenomenon—a reflection of a being in an intellect. The primordial relation to intellect manifest in *verum transcendens* is ontological, a formal structure of the objective itself. Like *unum* and *bonum* with which it is convertible, *verum* is not something the subject adds to the given by thinking it, but an ontological determination of the object. The Scholastics never think being without a relation to intellect (even if ultimately a divine intellect). The coincidence of subject and object is summed up in the Aristotelian dictum *intellectus in actu est intellectum in actu*. Eckhart spoke in an analogous way about the unity of the soul with God: "The eye with which I see God is the same eye with which God sees me. My eye and God's eye are one eye, and one vision or seeing, and one knowing and one loving."[37] We are not distin-

---

36. See Caputo, *Mystical Element*, 152: "For Dasein, like the soul, must make a clearing in itself by detaching itself from beings *(Abschied vom Seienden)*, in order to 'let' Being itself come to pass 'unrefracted' and undistorted by human subjectivity. Dasein must prepare an open 'place,' not for God, but for Being. 'Being' 'needs' the 'clearing' Dasein provides, even as Meister Eckhart will say that God needs the detached heart. The most extensive and even startling analogy can thus be built up between the 'birth of God' in the 'ground of the soul' in Meister Eckhart and the primal event *(Ereignis)* of Truth in Heidegger's later thought."

37. Eckhart, *Deutsche Predigten*, 216, 24–27/288, Blakney trans.

guished from God by some positive, ontological determination, for God lacks no ontological determination; rather, the distinction is based on a privation, a "not," the absence of the fullness of being in the creature. At a certain level of mystical experience, the distinction disappears.

Eckhart's Platonism tends to conceal his own profound grasp of the historicity of mystical life. *Gelassenheit, Abgeschiedenheit,* and *Hingabe* are not suspensions of the historical but intensifications of it. They represent, not freedom from time, but freedom from attachment to that which occurs in time. As such, they are ways of being historical. In a 1917 note, Heidegger remarks on this often-overlooked feature of mystical consciousness: "The historical is one of the most important and foundational elements of meaning in religious experience. The specific disclosure of meaning in religion is experiential. The primordial religious world of experience is not centered upon theoretical or theological abstraction, but in a great and singular historical form, a personally transformative feeling for life. This constitutes the nature of revelation and the concept of tradition in the essence of religion" (*GA*60 323). The primordial understanding disclosed in mystical life is nested in historical existence. The connection between history and mysticism is brought out by Schleiermacher. In his 1917 note "Zu Schleiermachers zweiter Rede 'Über das Wesen der Religion,'" Heidegger refers to the following passage from Schleiermacher:

But there is not merely the swinging of feeling between the world and the individual in the present moment. Except as something going on, we cannot comprehend what affects us, and we cannot comprehend ourselves, except as thus progressively affected. Wherefore, as feeling persons, we are ever driven back into the past. The spirit furnishes the chief nourishment for our piety, and history immediately and especially is the richest source for religion. History is not of value for religion because it hastens or controls in any way the progress of humanity in its development, but because it is the greatest and most general revelation of the deepest and holiest. In this sense, however, religion begins and ends with history. Prophecy and history are for religion the same and indistinguishable, and all true history has at first had a religious purpose and has taken its departure from religious ideas.[38]

---

38. Schleiermacher, *Über die Religion,* 103/79–80. See *GA*60 322.

For Schleiermacher, the infinite is refracted through an infinity of historical disclosures. No historical disclosure of religion is equal to the infinite, yet each is valid for a particular time and place. Individual "religious geniuses" give expression to their particular "intuitions of the infinite" and draw to themselves a circle or church of like-minded disciples. Thus a religious tradition is always only an approximation of the infinite. It calls for development and supplementation by other traditions. Religious life directs us to history because religion is essential feeling, not theory, and feeling is always something "going on," never a static and abstract idea. In the living context of religious feeling, history becomes a theater of revelation. The religious person is thrust away from a-temporal speculation back to the concrete and never-complete processes of temporal life. He lives out of his memory of past intuitions of the infinite, lives in attentiveness to the ongoing aesthetical and emotional revelations of the infinite, and stands in expectation of future revelations.

In 1918, Heidegger took a few pages of notes on the eleventh-century mystic Bernard of Clairvaux's *Sermones super Cantica canticorum*. The notes consist in little more than a few cited passages, with hints at a commentary. Yet the citations are charged with this Schleiermacherian sense for the intimate relationship of mystical life to historicity. *"Hodie legimus in libro experientiae,"* Heidegger cites from Clairvaux, "Today we read from the book of experience."[39] In mysticism, experience is given primacy over everything else, for book knowledge counts for little. Experience is the mystic's source text. The mystic turns away from the public and universal, the timeless and generic, to the most personal sphere of historical experience. Heidegger describes the mystical turn as a proto-phenomenological moment, the individuals' "turn back to their own sphere of experience and attention to that which is given in their own consciousness" (GA60 334). The citation continues: *"Est fons signatus cui non communicat alienus"*: "It is a sealed fountain which does not communicate to a stranger." The mystical font of experience is not publicly available. Like the notion of *Ereignis* in the later Heidegger, the notion that being sends itself in different ways in different epochs, the mystical

---

39. See Bernard of Clairvaux, *Sermones super Cantica canticorum* 3, 1; *Patrologia Latina* 183: 794.

"font" of divine life chooses its communicant. Among the initiated, each "book" of experience has only one reader, the one whose experience it is. Obedience to external authorities, to "foreign" interpretations, obfuscates. Heidegger comments: "Such experiences are not accessed through obedience to canonical prescriptions" (GA60 334). For Clairvaux, nothing can be gleaned about the mystical life from secondhand sources: the springs of mystical life are hidden in the *haecceity* of individual life. "*Qui bibit, adhunc sitiat*": "He who drinks thirsts for more." God as a metaphysical notion may direct the Scholastic's thinking to the eternal, but God as an experience sends the mystic back to temporal life. Indeed, the temporal is felt more intensely by the mystic who has tasted the eternal spring. The mystic embraces an infinite thirst—nothing in this life can satisfy the soul's hunger for God. The hunger becomes the foundation of life, an existence of ever-increasing desire, always *in via*, intensifying desire through ascetical practice. The ascetical path sensitizes the mystic to historical existence. Heidegger notes how for Clairvaux, religious experience grows and develops in time, like a living thing. The mystic receives the finitude of temporal existence, the call to continual conversion, to always becoming a Christian, as a gift. "*Nolo repente fieri summus; paulatim proficere volo. . . . Citius placas eum, si mensuram tuam servaveris, et alteriora te non quaesieris*": "I do not wish to be suddenly at the heights, my desire is to advance by degrees. . . . You will please God more readily if you lie within the limits proper to you and do not set your sights on things beyond you" (GA60 335–36).

The historicity implicit in the enactment sense of the mystical life comes to acute and hyperbolic expression in Eckhart's doctrine of *Gottesgeburt*, the birth of God in the soul. Heidegger makes a passing reference to Eckhart's *Gottesgeburt* in an early note (GA60 309). Eckhart writes: "What good is it to me if Mary gave birth to the son of God fourteen hundred years ago and I do not also give birth to the son of God in my time and in my culture." Even more strongly: "We are all meant to be mothers of God. For God is always needing to be born."[40] These statements develop directly out of Eckhart's Trinitarian theology. The essence

---

40. Eckhart quoted in Fox, *Original Blessing*, 221, 22. See Eckhart, *Deutsche Predigten*, 415, 6–8/95, Blakney trans.

of the Father is to beget the Son. The essence of the Son is to be begotten. The distinctions of persons in God are eternal distinctions: thus God is always and everywhere begetting and being begotten. The *Gottesgeburt* in the soul of the mystic is not different from the *Gottesgeburt* in Bethlehem. The Son begotten in the act of the mystical birth of God is not different from the Son begotten in Bethlehem.

> The Father bears His Son in eternity like to Himself. "The Word was with God and the Word was God." He was the same as God and of the same nature. Yet beyond this I say: He has begotten Him in my soul.... The Father bears His Son in the soul in the same way that He bears Him in eternity, not in any other way. He must do it, whether He wishes or not. The Father bears His Son incessantly, and I say still more: He bears me as His Son, and as the same Son.[41]

For Eckhart, God is, on the one hand, *esse indistinctum*, the absolutely simple being, the one of whom nothing can be affirmed. As absolutely simple, God is a-temporal and unrelated to that which occurs in time. But God is also a dynamic efflux, an emanation into progressively greater differentiation. The first differentiation occurs in the procession of the divine simplicity into the three divine persons. The second differentiation is the emanation of eternity into time and multiplicity with the creation of the universe. The third differentiation is the Incarnation. The self-differentiation of the undifferentiated *Gottheit* continues in the mystical life of the individual. In the mystic's breakthrough to the ground of the soul, God is born into history once again. Eckhart describes concentric spheres of emanation, God becoming progressively more temporalized and differentiated, until He reaches the utmost particularization in the soul of the mystic. The divinized soul then mirrors the efflux of God by radiating divinity into the world. For Eckhart, the *unio mystica* does not result in monastic isolation. As inevitably as the divine life overflows its simplicity and begets the Son, the divinized soul brings God into the marketplace by going about day-to-day life in the presence of the Father. Eckhart says, "Not that one should give up, neglect or forget his inner life for a moment, but he must learn to work in it, with it, and out of it,

---

41. Eckhart, *Deutsche Predigten*, 185, 12–13; English: *Meister Eckhart: An Introduction to the Study of his Works with an Anthology of his Sermons,* trans. James M. Clark (London: Nelson & Sons, 1957), 188.

so that the unity of the soul may break out into his activities and activities may bring him back to that unity."[42] Eckhart holds that in the Gospel story of Mary and Martha, it is in fact Martha, the one busy about many things, who displays the more advanced mystical life. While Mary has distinguished her contemplative and her active life, and chooses "the better part," to sit at the feet of the master, Martha does not distinguish contemplation and action. She is with the master in the housework and the serving.[43] Notwithstanding the strong neo-Platonic strain in his thinking, Eckhart conceives the divine life as a progressive temporalization, an emanation into history and the quotidian cares that constitute it.

Caputo sees a close analogy between the event of truth in Heidegger and Eckhart's *Gottesgeburt:* "The great being of the soul is to be the 'birth place' of the Son, the 'clearing' in which the 'event of appropriation' *(Ereignis)*, the event of truth, comes to pass. In both cases, the true dignity of man lies in his poverty, i.e., in the humble way in which he provides a shelter and a preserve for a transcendent event. Man can in no way effect this event of himself; he can only make a 'clearing' in which it might take place."[44] This undeniable parallel points to the later Heidegger's ambiguous appropriation of Christian mystical theology. In the light of the early Freiburg lectures, especially the 1917–19 notes on mysticism, we see how Heidegger finds in Eckhart an often-overlooked connection between historical consciousness and mystical life. Eckhart's mysticism represents a descent from the rarified a-historical speculative Scholastic theology into the life-world of the historical self. The mystic is the medium through which God effects the perpetual *Gottesgeburt.* Around the time of the 1917–19 notes, Heidegger was reading Dilthey on the shattering of Greek metaphysics by the Christian doctrine of Incarnation. The first principle, which had hitherto been conceived as necessarily outside of time, enters into history in the person of Christ and by doing so, validates the historical. In Greek neo-Platonism, time is a shadow realm; in Christianity, time is ontologically validated by the Incarnation. Among Heidegger's unpublished notes is the following citation from Dilthey's *Einleitung in*

42. *Eckhart,* Blakney trans., 37.
43. Lk 10:41–42. Meister Eckhart, "Intravit Jesus in quoddam castellum," in *Deutsche Predigten,* 280 ff.
44. Caputo, *Mystical Element,* 162.

die Geisteswissenschaften: "God's essence, instead of being grasped in the self-enclosed concept of substance of antiquity, was now [with the Incarnation] caught up in historical vitality. And so historical consciousness, taking the expression in its highest sense first came into being."[45] In Eckhart's mysticism, the validation of history effected by the Incarnation is carried yet further. Through the rebirth of God in the soul of the mystic, God becomes further incarnated in the minute details of daily historical life. The eternal God is now not only born in the epochal events of the Incarnation, Crucifixion, and Resurrection, He is also born in the forgettable events of the divinized man or woman serving the community—or, even more quotidian—cleaning the floor of his or her monastic cell. The distinction between the divine and the temporal, so decisive for Western metaphysics, breaks down. The moment in all its *haecceity* is now charged with divinity.

The analogies between mysticism and phenomenology unfold one upon the other. The mystic's directedness toward the *Gottheit* images Dasein's directedness toward the nothing. Being is to Dasein as Eckhart's *Gottheit* is to the soul.[46] As the mystic is in immediate and prereflective relationship to divine life, so are we in immediate, "fore-theoretical" relationship to our own facticity. The nature of these analogies is ambiguous. From the perspective of its content-sense, mysticism may be bound to a dimension of religious life about which philosophy can have little to say. Formally, however, certain patterns found in mysticism disclose phenomenological structures that Heidegger assumes can be found apart from religious life. Heidegger studies Paul, Augustine, Bernard of Clairvaux, Meister Eckhart, and Teresa of Avila to see how their struggle to articulate their experience of union with God formally indicates something far more average and everyday: historical being-in-the-world. If the claim that the historical self is given over to life as the mystic is given over to the divine is what the Scholastics called an analogy of metaphoric (or improper) proportionality, it says nothing about the being of mysticism. Mysticism is simply a metaphor for life: the self is immersed in life

---

45. Wilhelm Dilthey, *Einleitung in die Geisteswissenschaften,* Gesammelte Schriften, vol. 1 (Stuttgart: Teubner, 1973), 253 ff.; English: *Introduction to the Human Sciences,* trans. Ramon J. Betanzos (Detroit: Wayne State University Press, 1988), 230.

46. See Caputo, *Mystical Element,* 183.

as the mystic is devoted to God. Heidegger could have made his point drawing on some other body of literature, for example, aesthetics: the self lives its life as the artist creates his art. More negatively, one could argue that the analogy exists because mysticism is a mythologized expression of a common human experience—and it is not clear that Heidegger would disagree.[47] If, however, the analogy is more than a metaphor, if mysticism has an *intrinsic* relationship to historical life, if the analogy between phenomenology and mysticism is one of proper proportionality, that is, based on the being of mysticism and the being of historical life, the question arises, by virtue of what is mysticism analogous to phenomenology? What is the "analogated perfection" common to mysticism and phenomenology? Is there something essential to the mystic's being-toward-God that discloses historical life in a unique way? Is there a mystical dimension to historical life?

Mysticism and Scholasticism

At a certain point in his development, Heidegger seems to have succumbed to the dichotomy between medieval mysticism and Scholasticism, a view which he repudiated in his *Habilitationsschrift*. He chose to forget what he once explicitly acknowledged, that medieval Scholasticism was at its root mystical, as is illustrated by a brief review of the biographies of the great Scholastics, Aquinas and Bonaventure (the former

---

47. Philippe Capelle argues that in the notes on medieval mysticism, Heidegger interprets the mystic's God, not theologically, but as a symbol for a fundamentally human experience of transcendence. See Capelle, *Philosophie et théologie*, 168. Kisiel makes a similar point about Heidegger's formalization of religious texts: "Is the phenomenological life therefore the religious life? The course of KNS 1919 [GA56/57] seeks to set forth phenomenological philosophy as a fore-theoretical primordial science outside of any connection with the ultimate human questions, which would turn it into a worldview. To make this step in the present context, a kind of 'religious reduction' is called for. For all that Eckhart, Schleiermacher, Dilthey contributed to shaping the phenomenological topic for the young Heidegger, there is a qualification to such assertions as 'the stream of consciousness is already religious' which must be kept in mind. The 'is' here is not an expression of identity between religion and life but of the identification of the motivating ground of philosophy, art, morality, science, in short, of all human culture. The conditions that make the soul receptive to religion thus also make it receptive to philosophy.... The fore-theoretical and pre-worldly primal something which is the topic of phenomenology, life in and for itself, gives rise to and so lies on this side of the scientific, ethical, aesthetic, and religious life worlds." Kisiel, *Genesis of* Being and Time, 113.

of whom wrote hymns when he was not writing theological treatises).[48] Medieval mysticism in turn received profound impulses from Scholastic speculation. The mystical dimension of Scholasticism is not something tangential to Scholastic theology. It does not represent a suspension of Scholastic "theory." Rather, it is built into the conceptual structure of Scholastic theo-ontology. Thomas Aquinas writes: "the essences of things are unknown to us."[49] They are unknown because as pure expressions of the divine intellect they are identical with the divine, and we do not know and cannot know the essence of God in this life. "All creatures are images of the first agent, namely God, since the agent produces its like."[50] The thing does not explain itself and points toward the mystery from which it emerges and toward which it is destined. Intelligible form reflects the absolute intelligibility of God in ways that we cannot comprehend without the beatific vision. As a twentieth-century interpreter of Aquinas puts it, "The world of sense is, more than all else, a mystery that signifies God as we know Him and symbolizes the further depths that lie beyond our comprehension."[51] The theo-ontological depth dimension of creation means that our explanatory concepts never succeed in fathoming the infinite intelligibility indicated by things; on the contrary, they highlight their incomprehensibility. "The range of possible questions is

---

48. A powerful example of the Scholastic mysticism is found in the first chapter of Anselm's *Proslogion*. Anselm begins this seminal treatise on metaphysical theology with an impassioned and personal entreaty to the Creator. The text is drenched in a sense of creatureliness: Anselm is reminding himself that everything depends upon God; he can do nothing on his own. In the light of this prayer, the famous ontological argument is not a rationalistic reduction. Anselm thinks of "that than which no greater can be conceived" in wholly relational terms. He is the One whose ubiquity is felt primarily as an absence, the term of the unsatisfiable desire for being. Anselm theorizes the One whom he first and finally approaches on the level of symbol. The First Cause is also the God before whom he bows down in prayer. This God is indicated by everything, since all things came from Him, yet He Himself is nowhere. As infinite, He is necessarily absent from the finite order.

49. Aquinas, *De.ver.*, q. 10, a. 1 See also his *In I De anima*, lect. 1, para. 15: "The essential grounds of things are unknown to us."

50. Thomas Aquinas, *Summa Contra Gentiles*, 3, 19; trans. Anton C. Pegis, in *Introduction to St. Thomas Aquinas*, ed. Anton C. Pegis (New York: The Modern Library, 1948), 439 (hereafter *SCG*). The passage continues: "Now the perfection of an image consists in representing the original by a likeness to it, for this is why an image is made. Therefore all things exist for the purpose of acquiring a likeness to God, as to their last end."

51. Bernard Lonergan, *Insight: A Study of Human Understanding*, 5th ed, *Collected Works of Bernard Lonergan*, ed. Frederick E. Crowe and Robert M. Doran, vol. 3 (Toronto: University of Toronto Press, 1992), 714.

larger than the range of possible answers."⁵² The created intellect achieves its *telos* when it grasps its intellectual impoverishment. *Hoc est ultimum cognitionis humanae de Deo; quod sciat se Deum nescire,* Aquinas says, "This is the ultimate in human knowledge of God: to know that we do not know Him."⁵³ The subject is decentered by the negative theology of the Middle Ages. We are not in command of all we survey. "Calculative thinking" must be subordinated to *contemplatio,* reverential awe in the face of the mystery of existence. The Scholastics do not share the presumptions of the totalizing onto-theologies of modernity. The coherence of our intellectual life depends on an insight that is never our own. In relation to the divine archetype, the perfection of intelligibility achieved in human knowing is an asymptotic approximation, a finite advance on infinity. For the medieval mind, two orders of intelligibility, one finite, the other infinite, intersect in everything that can be experienced. One cannot more profoundly underscore the mysticism of everyday life.

52. Ibid., 662.
53. Thomas Aquinas, *Quaestiones disputata De potentia* q. 7, a. 5, ad 14 (hereafter *De potentia*).

CHAPTER SIX

LUTHER

*An original form of religiosity breaks forth in Luther, which
is not even seen in the mystics.*

HEIDEGGER

The year 1917 was a turning point for Heidegger. Prior to 1917, he never openly questioned the Roman Catholic/Scholastic appropriation of philosophical methods into theology. After 1917, Heidegger began to regard Scholasticism as the site of the hegemony of theoretical speculative-aesthetic concepts in Christianity and the consequent forgetting of factical Christian life. The catalyst in this reversal was Heidegger's discovery of Protestantism, Schleiermacher, Dilthey, and above all, Luther. We know Heidegger was reading Luther as early as 1909, although evidence of an intensive study of Luther only appears ten years later.[1] Heidegger came to believe that Luther had correctly identified Scholasticism as an illegitimate fusion of Christianity and Greek metaphysics. Luther's purge of Christian theology of Aristotelian-Scholastic concepts became Heidegger's paradigm for the phenomenological destruction of the ontological tradition. Luther reduced theology to primordial Christian faith; Heidegger would reduce ontology to historical life.[2]

In the 1919 letter to Krebs breaking with "the system of Catholicism,"

---

1. Otto Pöggeler reports that in a conversation, Heidegger told him that he studied Luther's lectures on Romans as a theology student, that is, between 1909 and 1911. Pöggeler, "Heidegger's Luther-Lektüre," 194.

2. As van Buren puts it, when Heidegger returned to full-time teaching in 1919, he understood himself to be a Luther of Western metaphysics. Van Buren, *Young Heidegger*, 167.

Heidegger had pledged not to sink to "the peevish and intemperate diatribes of an apostate," nor to forget the "values [that] are enshrined in medieval Catholicism" or the Catholic tradition, which he continued to hold in "high regard." He would prove his abiding esteem in his "phenomenology of religion," which would "draw heavily on the Middle Ages."[3] From the 1917–19 notes and the early Freiburg lectures, we see that this irenic tone was for Krebs's benefit alone. At the time he wrote the letter, Heidegger regarded mysticism as a proto-Reformation of isolated voices asserting the claims of "the genuine primordial Christian standpoint" against the overpowering system of Christendom. "The ancient Christian achievement was distorted and buried through the infiltration of classical science into Christianity. From time to time it reasserted itself in violent eruptions (as in Augustine, in Luther, in Kierkegaard). Only from here is medieval mysticism to be understood.... [T]he struggle between Aristotle and the new 'feeling for life' continued in medieval mysticism and eventually in Luther" (*GA*58 205). Primal Christianity broke with Greek cosmology, asserting the primacy of the concrete and historical over the ideal, universal, and formal. "The historical is somehow co-given in the essence of Christianity itself" (*GA*56/57 26). In the Middle Ages, Greek cosmology prevailed over Christian facticity. The Scholastic appropriation of Plato and Aristotle eclipsed the primordial Christian experience. "The inner experiences and the new attitude of life were pressed into forms of expression in ancient science" (*GA*58 61). Heidegger's early phenomenology of religion (1920–21) was an effort to rehabilitate and formalize the historical self disclosed in early Christian experience, in medieval mysticism, and in the Reformation. Philosophy shares with Luther the task of emancipating "inner experience" from ancient science (*GA*58 61).

The significance of Luther for the young Heidegger has long been a topic of discussion, even if we are only now, with the publication of the *Gesamtausgabe*, in a position to evaluate it.[4] The early Freiburg lectures are full of scattered references to Luther.[5] From 1919 to 1923, Heidegger

---

3. Heidegger, quoted in Ott, *Biographie*, 107/107.

4. See, for example, Schaeffler's 1978 examination of Lutheran themes in *Sein und Zeit*, Schaeffler, *Frömmigkeit des Denkens*, chap. 1.

5. References to Luther in Heidegger's early Freiburg lectures: *GA*56/57 18; *GA*58 62, 204–5; *GA*60 283; 308; 309; *GA*61 7, 182–83; *GA*63 5, 14, 27, 46, 106; in *SZ*: 10, 190 n. iv.

immersed himself in private research on Luther.[6] Jaspers remembers visiting Heidegger in April 1920. He "watched him at his Luther studies, and saw the intensity of his work."[7] Julius Ebbingaus tells of spending evenings with Heidegger in 1921 reading Luther.[8] Heidegger planned to publish a paper on Luther and the ontological foundations of late medieval anthropology—a work that never transpired.[9] Rudolph Bultmann regarded Heidegger as a Luther expert, inviting him to participate in his seminars on the New Testament and give occasional lectures on Luther.[10] Textual evidence supports tracing the following Heideggerian themes back to his Luther research: running ahead toward death *(Vorlaufen zum Tode); Destruktion;* fallenness; and conscience. However, Luther's most significant influence on the young Heidegger was the critique of Scholasticism as the *theologia gloriae,* the presumption of a natural and speculative access to God, which is no longer possible for us after the Fall. Through a progressive forgetting of the meaning of faith and a substitution of Aristotle for the Bible, medieval Christendom lost touch with the crucified God. *Theologia crucis* is the antidote: resolute cleaving to the *Deus absconditus,* the God cloaked in humility and shame, hidden in the suffering of Christ. Heidegger conceives the hermeneutics of facticity as an atheological complement to Luther's *theologia crucis,* a philosophy that stays with the Godforsakenness of human life and leaves to theology the thematization of the world of meaning disclosed in faith.[11]

---

6. Van Buren speculates that Heidegger began to read Luther seriously in 1918 after reading Paul Natorp's two-volume *Deutscher Weltberuf: Geschichtsphilosophische Richtlinien* (Jena: Eugen Diederichs, 1918). Natorp's book situates Luther as a transitional figure in the development of German philosophy, between Rhineland mysticism and nineteenth-century idealism. Husserl had recommended Natorp's book in a letter of September 10, 1918. See van Buren, *Young Heidegger,* 146. Certainly in the 1916 *Schlusskapitel,* Heidegger shows no signs of any interest in Luther. From the note "Das religiöse Apriori" (*GA60* 313), dated 1917 by Kisiel and Denker, however, we see Heidegger already taking up the Protestant critique of Catholicism. The first textual reference to Luther is the 1919 note, "Mystik (Direktiven)" (*GA60* 308).

7. Karl Jaspers, "On Heidegger," *Graduate Faculty Philosophy Journal* 7 (1978): 108–9.

8. Van Buren, *Young Heidegger,* 149.

9. Theodore Kisiel, "Why the First Draft of *Being and Time* Was Never Published," *Journal of the British Society for Phenomenology* 20 (1989): 5.

10. See Bultmann's letter to Hans von Soden of 23 December 1923, quoted in Ott, *Biographie,* 124/25.

11. See Jaromir Brejdak, *Philosophia crucis: Heideggers Beschäftigung mit dem Apostel Paulus* (Frankfurt am Main: Peter Lang, 1996), 180–82. Van Buren calls Heidegger's early work an *"ontolo-*

Theologia Gloriae—Theologia Crucis

In the early Heidegger's interpretations of the history of philosophy and theology, Luther's de-Hellenization of Christianity is singled out as a moment when facticity comes once again to the fore. Luther attacked Scholasticism as the *theologia gloriae,* the theology that substitutes metaphysics for authentic discipleship and presumes to "have" God by seeing the divine glory omnipresent in creation. He distinguishes it sharply from the *theologia crucis,* the theology that "speaks of the crucified and hidden God."[12] The *theologia gloriae* boasts of a sure metaphysical knowledge of God deduced from empirical evidence. In Luther's view, the speculative notion of an omnipotent and omniscient first cause is idolatry, the construction of a God of our own making, a God over whom we wield a rational mastery. "The condition of this life is not that of having God but of seeking God," Luther argues.[13] Faith is not motivated in the Scholastic *desiderium naturale,* the natural desire for God. It is not something that we do, but something that is done for us. Scholastic philosophical theology is a sinful effort to mitigate the terror of living under the judgment and mercy of the revealed God. The *theologia crucis* waits for God's Word and grace and does not presume to know anything about either by its own power.

The foundation of Luther's rejection of the *theologia gloriae* is his view of the extreme corruption of nature brought about by the Fall. Although we should be able to see "the invisible things of God" shining through creation, our reason is factically bound to a perverse will that cannot let God be God because it itself desires to be God. In the 1924 lecture in Bultmann's seminar, Heidegger gave an overview of Luther's understanding of sin and its ramifications for theology.[14] Heidegger notes that for

---

gia crucis," "the attempt to think being through the 'cross' of historicity and factical life." Van Buren, *Young Heidegger,* 167.

12. Martin Luther, "Explanations of the Ninety-Five Theses," trans. H. J. Grimm, in *Luther's Works,* ed. Jaroslav Pelikan (vols. 1–30) and Helmut T. Lehmann (vols. 31–55) (Philadelphia: Fortress Press, 1955–), vol. 31, 225 (hereafter *LW*vol.#).

13. *LW*25, *Lectures on Romans,* trans. by Walter G. Tillmanns and Jacob A. O. Preus (Saint Louis, Mo.: Concordia University Press, 1972), 225.

14. Martin Heidegger, "Das Problem der Sünde bei Luther," in *Sachgemässe Exegese: Die Protokolle aus Rudolf Bultmanns Neutetamentlichen Seminaren 1921–51,* ed. Bernd Jaspert (Marburg:

Luther it is impossible to exaggerate the effects of original sin. The logic of salvation implies a complete corruption of human nature through sin: the greater the Fall, the greater the redemptive act. The Redemption reveals infinite mercy. Hence the Fall is the most extreme corruption imaginable, a calamity greater than which none other can be conceived.[15] Sin is an ontological category in Luther (*Existenzbegriff*—Heidegger's term). It signifies the basic turning from God *(aversio Dei)* that disrupted and distorted human nature. Adam and Eve knowingly and willfully rejected God's dominion. As a result, the human race suffered a complete ontological corruption: *natura hominis est corrupta*. We once enjoyed the presence of God—Adam and Eve "heard Him walking in Paradise at the breeze of the day" (Gen 3:8). After the Fall, a direct knowledge of God is no longer possible: "Reason [is] entirely corrupt and altogether changed!" Luther proclaims.[16]

With Bultmann's students, Heidegger examines how Luther conceives the essence of sin as a resistance to the way things are, an inability to let God be God. In our fallen state, our spontaneous and "natural" desire is not to know God but to be God. According to Luther, "Man is by nature unable to want God to be God. Indeed, he himself wants to be God, and does not want God to be God *(velle se esse deum et deum non esse deum)*."[17] Because of this essential corruption of the will, we cannot achieve anything through works or moral effort. The human will twists everything with its perverse intention to make something of itself on its own and be free of God. "Just as reason is overwhelmed by many kinds of ignorance, so the will has not only been confused but has been turned away from God and is an enemy of God. It enjoys rushing to evil, when

---

N. G. Elwert, 1996), 28–33; English translation: "The Problem of Sin in Luther," trans. John van Buren, in Heidegger, *Supplements*, 105–110 (hereafter *PSL*). Heidegger's source texts are Luther's 1516 *Quaestio de viribus et voluntate hominis sine gratia disputata*, the 1517 *Disputatio contra scholasticam theologiam*, the 1518 *Disputatio Heidelbergae habita*, and the 1544 commentary on Genesis, *In primum librum Mose enarrationes*.

15. See *LW*1, *Lectures on Genesis 1–5*, trans. George V. Schick (Saint Louis, Mo.: Concordia Publishing House, 1958), 142: "This manifold corruption of our nature should not be minimized; it should rather be emphasized.... This should be emphasized, I say, for the reason that unless the severity of the disease is correctly recognized, the cure is also not known or desired. The more you minimize sin, the more will grace decline in value."

16. *LW*1 142.

17. Martin Luther, "Disputation Against Scholastic Theology," thesis 17, in *LW*31 10.

the opposite should have happened."[18] From human nature, nothing is to be expected.[19] In this disordered state, any philosophical knowledge of God we might attempt to achieve, any effort to conceptualize God in suspension of revelation, inevitably yields a pseudo-theology, a strategy for ignoring revelation and setting up a God of our own making, ultimately setting ourselves up as God.

Luther's soteriology of extreme corruption attacks the Scholastic principle, "grace does not destroy nature, but presupposes and perfects it" *(Gratia non tollit naturam sed eam supponit et perficit)*.[20] Scholasticism assumes a substantially intact nature. We do not need to be essentially transformed but only elevated by grace. The Scholastics rationalized this by positing that our original intimacy with God was not essential to our nature, but a supernatural gift, something added on, a *donum superadditum*. The Fall has brought about the loss of God's gift of presence, yet the loss of a supernatural gift is not a corruption of nature. What has been given can be lost without any violence to human nature. Therefore the Scholastics argue that the Fall has darkened our intellect and misdirected our will but left our nature intact. Constitutive of this nature is a relationship to God, a natural orientation of intellect and will to God. We are on the lookout for God before we hear revelation and are naturally disposed to recognize Him. Luther reverses this position in order to maximize the urgency of the Redemption: because Adam and Eve's intimacy with God was a natural state of being, their loss of the divine presence represents a total corruption of nature.[21] With obvious admiration for Luther's proto-phenomenological instinct, Heidegger points out that Luther takes issue with Scholastic soteriology on the basis of experience. Luther argues, "Let us rather follow experience, which shows that we are born from unclean seed and that from the very nature of the seed we acquire ignorance of God, smugness, unbelief, hatred against God, dis-

---

18. *LW*1 142.

19. Heidegger cites theses 29 and 30 of Luther's *Contra scholasticam:* "The best and infallible preparation for grace and the sole means of obtaining grace is the eternal election and predestination of God.... On the part of man, however, nothing precedes grace except ill will and even rebellion against grace." *PSL* 29–30. See *LW*31 11.

20. Aquinas, *ST* 1a, q. 1, a. 8, ad 2.

21. On this point, Heidegger quotes Luther's 1544 lectures on Genesis. *LW*1 164–66.

obedience, impatience, and similar grave faults."[22] According to Luther, Scholastic *scientia* is motivated by the desire to be God: the Scholastics grasp at the modicum of knowledge about God available to us in creation and inflate it into a metaphysical theology. The *theologia gloriae* is a theology of actuality, of overtness, of sure possession of knowledge. Luther writes, "He who speculates about God deals with God no differently than a cobbler judges his leather."[23]

Luther's distinction between *theologia gloriae* and *theologia crucis* is expressed in a few key theses from the *Disputatio Heidelbergae*:

That person is not rightly called a theologian who looks upon the invisible things of God as though they were clearly perceptible through things that have actually happened (Thesis 19). He deserves to be called a theologian, however, who understands the visible and manifest things of God seen through suffering and the Cross (Thesis 20). A theology of glory calls evil good and good evil. A theology of the Cross calls the thing what it actually is (Thesis 21). That wisdom which sees the invisible things of God in works as perceived by man is completely puffed up, blinded, and hardened (Thesis 22).[24]

Karl Barth interprets the *theologia gloriae* as the presumption of "open and direct access to the final mystery... the necessity and possibility of immediate knowledge of God."[25] According to Barth, the medieval mind

---

22. *LW*1 166. It would be incorrect, however, to maintain that Luther's soteriology of extreme corruption is based on experience alone. The premise of Luther's doctrine of salvation is the revelation of God's infinite love. Only in the light of the Christ-event can we recognize the depravity of human fallenness, moral impotence, and malice. Revelation shows Luther what could not otherwise be known, the infinite mercy of God; experience confirms what is revealed, the extent of our Fall.

23. *LW*25 167.

24. Ibid.

25. Karl Barth, *The Theology of John Calvin*, trans. Geoffrey W. Bromiley (Grand Rapids, Mich.: W. B. Eerdmans, 1995), 31. Barth's commentary on Luther's distinction is so vivid and to the point that it bears quoting at length. Ibid., 26–27: "[Medieval theology] attempts and achieves a knowledge of God in his glory, purity, and majesty. In the word of the Bible and the theology of the church it does not simply find denoted and described the mystery as such but signposts marking a dialectical path to the heart of the mystery, so that for those who take this path there is no longer any mystery. It recognizes no barrier, no command that it should stop at the object intended in the Bible or in dogma. In the difficulty and obscurity that first conceal the object it simply hears a challenge in some way, notwithstanding the problems, to lay hold of the object. It is venturesome in the way in which it sets goals and tries to reach them. It is youthfully fresh and healthy and robust and sparkling in all that it does. As readers we feel that we are in the hands of guides who with

is entranced by a childlike optimism that no mystery remains ultimately closed to it; it presumes that the speculative power of the human mind has no intrinsic limits. Scholasticism fuses Christian theology with Greek metaphysics on the assumption that the desire for knowledge is motivated in the *desiderium naturale*. For Luther, the desire for knowledge must be crucified if we are to be saved, for it is a covert desire to be God. Hence God reveals Godself in a wisdom that is foolishness to the human intellect, the revelation that starves our natural appetite for knowledge.

Heidegger discusses the three Heidelberg theses in his 1920/21 course "Augustinus und der Neuplatonismus" (*GA*60 282). The context is an interpretation of Augustine's onto-theology and its "proof" text, Romans 1:20: "For the invisible things of God ever since the creation of the world are clearly seen in the things that have been made." On the basis of this text, Augustine and the Scholastics assumed a basic knowledge of God manifest in creation, a natural revelation of a constantly present God whose divinity is accessible to the intellect independent of revelation. According to Heidegger, "Luther was the first to genuinely understand the passage [Rom 1:20]" (*GA*60 282). How did Luther read it? Some scholars hold that Luther rules out the possibility of metaphysical theology, others, only that Luther rules out the efficacy of metaphysical theology for building up wisdom and opening us to revelation.[26] Heidegger reads

---

absolute certainty and confidence know what they want.... [With later medieval theology,] access became extraordinarily difficult, but all the difficulties with which it [the mystery] was seen to be surrounded simply made it higher and more precious and caused it to be lauded more fervently. In a disturbing parallel the cathedral pillars became improbably more lofty and the naked eye had reason to fear that they might not ever meet. Yet with unerring certainty they converge in the Gothic arch, even if only in the semidarkness of the vault."

26. See Walther von Loewenich, *Luther's Theology of the Cross,* trans. Herbert J. A. Bouman (Belfast: Christian Journals, 1976), 174 n. 13. If we turn to Luther's commentary on Romans, we see that he does not deny that Paul affirms a natural knowledge of God. However, under the pressure of sin, we cannot but misinterpret the "natural revelation." Luther writes: "The fact that he [Paul] is speaking here of the natural knowledge of God is clear.... [T]hese things [of God] are recognized in a natural way by their effects, that is, from the beginning of the world it has always been true that the 'invisible things of God, etc.' He states this so no one should quibble and say that only in our time could God be known. He could be and can be known from the beginning of the world.... That to all people, and especially to idolaters, clear knowledge of God was available, as he says here, so that they are without excuse and it can be proved that they had known the invisible things of God, His divinity, likewise His eternal being and power, becomes apparent from the following: All those who set up idols and worship them and call them 'gods' or even 'God,' believing

Luther's *theologia crucis* as the theology of a factically Godforsaken creature, a creature that *de facto* knows nothing of God "by nature." In 1920, he appeared to endorse Luther's critique: "The determination of the object of theology cannot be accomplished by way of a metaphysical reflection on the world ... the way of theology swings off sharply from the way of metaphysics" (*GA*60 282). The only philosophical task left for Godforsaken humanity is the elaboration of being-without-God, that is, an atheological hermeneutics of facticity.

The Symbiosis of the Theologia Crucis and the Hermeneutics of Facticity

The *theologia gloriae* is symptomatic of Dasein's fall into the inauthentic preoccupation with the present-at-hand *(Vorhandensein)*. The *theologia crucis* turns away "from the intuition and contemplation of the present" toward "that which is not yet."[27] Heidegger holds that with this denial of a theology of presence, Luther retrieves the relational and enactment senses of primordial Christianity. Only the one who renounces the appetite for constant presence and embraces the day-to-day annihilation of not having God understands revelation.[28] The *theologia crucis* does not fly from the factic into Greek metaphysics. It is an intentional relation to a presence-in-absence. The *theologia crucis* makes the Christian trans-

---

that God is immortal, that is, eternal, powerful, and able to render help, clearly indicate that they have a knowledge of divinity in their hearts ... a knowledge or notion of divinity which undoubtedly came to them from God, as our text tells us. This was their error, that they did not worship this divinity untouched but changed and adjusted it to their desires and needs." *LW*25 156–58. Sin has destroyed our ability to interpret these traces of the divine properly. In his commentary to theses 19, 20, and 21 of the *Disputatio Heidelbergae*, Luther again recognizes Paul's claim that a modicum of knowledge of the divine is always available to people everywhere. To thesis 19, he comments: "The invisible things of God are virtue, godliness, wisdom, justice, goodness, and so forth. The recognition of all these things does not make one worthy or wise." *LW*31 52. The invisible things of God *are* perceptible in creation and conscience, yet the perception of them does not make us wise. We are constitutively incapable of correctly responding to the natural evidence for divinity, and in this sense, we can say that "metaphysics does not lead to a knowledge of the true God." The sin of the *theologia gloriae* is not *presuming* to see traces of God in creation, but rather becoming puffed up, blinded, and hardened by what *we can see* of God in creation. Cf. von Loewenich, *Luther's Theology of the Cross*, 27.

27. *LW*25 361–62.
28. See Brejdak, *Philosophia crucis*, 88.

parent to historical existence. Luther's hidden God has an affinity with the *via negativa* of medieval mysticism, as Luther himself acknowledged. However, faith for Luther is not a religious intuition, nor does it lead to mystical experience: it is fulfilled in nonintuitive enactment. We enact faith by living faithfully, not by enjoying mystical experiences.[29] In a 1919 note, Heidegger writes that on the one hand, Luther's doctrine of faith is built on the interiority developed in medieval mysticism; on the other hand, Luther breaks free of the aestheticism of the Middle Ages (*GA*60 310). In Luther's view, any elevation of interior experience or mystical intuition over the revealed Word is pride and presumption.[30] Like Paul who lives out of the radical temporality of expecting the new creation, the theologian of the Cross waits for the hidden God "in fear and trembling" (Phil 2:12), expecting "the day of the Lord," to burst upon us "like a thief in the night" (1 Thes 5:2). The waiting is a being-toward-the-future that recapitulates the past. Having no speculative object to lighten the burden of always becoming a Christian, the theologian of the Cross stays with the uncertainty and unresolvedness of time.[31]

29. Particularly attracted to Rhineland mysticism, Luther spoke on occasion the language of mysticism, writing on such time honored mystical themes as *Gottesgeburt* (*LW*31 73). In 1516, he edited an anonymous mystical treatise under the title *A Spiritually Noble Little Book* (later renamed *Theologia Deutsch*), holding that its simple experiential approach to the Christian life was truly evangelical, "a wisdom of experience," rather than "a wisdom of theology."

30. Von Loewenich comments: "Theology of the Cross is theology of revelation, while for mysticism the historical revelation is only a preliminary step to a direct, unbroken, and unmediated intercourse between God and the soul.... Since the God of the theology of the Cross is the God of historical revelation, he is always an acting God, he remains person, for he never becomes an 'abyss,' a 'nothing' in which the soul can be submerged.... Viewed from their center, mysticism and the theology of the Cross form the harshest kind of antithesis." Von Loewenich, *Luther's Theology of the Cross*, 155-56. See *LW*25 257 ff.

31. Van Buren draws out this implicit connection between the *theologia crucis* and the hermeneutics of facticity: "Since God is a mystery 'hidden in suffering,' in the cross, there is here nothing present before-the-hand that can be conceptually objectified, built up into the speculative dominion of a Christianity, Inc., and calculated in *theoria*, contemplation. There is no starting point in 'the humility and shame of the cross' for onto-theological speculation to move from the visible to knowledge of the invisible, because what is given here is not the eternal, power, glory, the kingdom, but the very opposite: time, weakness, suffering, exile, the death of the King on the cross. *Outos estin Jesous ho basileus*, this is Jesus the King (Mt 27:37). The cross is 'a scandal to the Jews and *moria*, foolishness, stupidity, absurdity to the Greeks' (1 Cor 1:23). What confronts human reason is 'the paradox' (Kierkegaard). The only theological access to this *Deus absconditus* and the 'glory' here is through an anxious and wakeful *theologia crucis* that believes in 'matters that we do not see.'" Van Buren, *Young Heidegger*, 160.

The faith of the *theologia crucis* is not a deficient mode of cognition, not belief because intuition is lacking, but resoluteness. In a 1917 note, Heidegger reflected upon the fundamental difference between Luther's notion of faith and the Scholastic-Catholic conception: "Believing and believing are foundationally different in Protestantism and Catholicism—noetically and noematically different experiences. The 'holding-for-true' of Catholic faith is founded in something totally other than the *fiducia* of the Reformers" (*GA*60 310). Holding for true has not only a different relational sense from trusting in a promise; it has a different content sense. In Heidegger's view, Lutheran faith is a future-oriented comportment that recapitulates the past, the promise of salvation, in a temporalizing being-toward-absence. It is essentially historical, fastening the believer to the life-world. Catholic faith, in Heidegger's view, is a theoretical comportment that intends objective knowledge. Intentionally the act is devoid of temporal reference; it is a static being-toward-intuitive-fulfilment.[32]

As a metaphysical concept denoting the radiant presence of that which never changes, the shining forth of timeless *essentia*, the *noema* of intuition, *gloria* is the antithesis of what is revealed in the Crucified.[33] Just as the theologian betrays revelation in seeking to grasp and possess the *gloria* of God, so does the philosopher betray the factic in presuming a certain and apodictic knowledge of being. In the 1935 *Einführung in die Metaphysik*, Heidegger traces *gloria* back through its Greek root, *doxa*, to the notion of radiant presence in the present. *Doxa* is derived from the Greek verb *dokeo*, to show oneself, to enter into the light (*GA*40 110–13/87–88). *Gloria/doxa* is constant presence, timeless actuality, being that is always intuitively available. The *theologia gloriae* mitigates the tempo-

32. Cf. Aquinas *ST* 2a 2ae, q. 1, a. 4; q. 1, a. 5.
33. Cf. van Buren, *Young Heidegger*, 161, 187: "It is precisely the quietistic, ocular-aesthetic relational sense of Greek and medieval metaphysics that Luther characterizes as *gloratio*, glorying. Whereas the ocularism of Greek metaphysics can be seen in its emphasis on *theoria* (a metaphorical term that signifies the spectator [*theoros*] at the festival of the being of beings, as it were), its aesthetic aspect in Kierkegaard's sense can be seen in the experience of this seeing as noetic desire (*orexis*) that is completely filled by the radiant presence-before-the-hand of being and is thus the highest stage of pleasure (*hedone*). This desire is in fact described by Plato as 'eating' at the 'feast of logos,' such that the being of beings appears here as a kind of cosmic banquet table of Ideas at which the reverent philosophical guest sits" (*Republic* 585–86; *Timaeus* 20C).

ralizing experience of faith with the consolation of a constantly present God, just as metaphysics covers over temporality with the contemplation of timeless essences. The hermeneutics of facticity swings off sharply from the way of metaphysics; Luther and Heidegger find themselves moving in the same direction. The suggestion of a symbiotic relationship between Luther and Heidegger in one way goes against the grain of both of them. Luther intends his theology as a nonphilosophical theology of the revealed world, a theology that has no need of philosophy and no intention of contributing to it. Heidegger intends his hermeneutics of facticity as atheological, receiving no essential impulses from theology and remaining silent on theological questions. Yet we find that Luther's and Heidegger's conceptions of human being overlap precisely at the point where they take issue with philosophy or theology. By divorcing philosophy from theology, both Luther and Heidegger have in fact brought them together on new terms. Luther has a modicum of respect for a philosophy that stays within its proper limits and articulates in a theologically neutral way the state of fallen humankind. Heidegger praises a theology that elaborates "a more original interpretation of human being's being toward God prescribed by the meaning of faith and remaining within it" (*SZ* 8/6). Each of them envisions the possibility of a philosophical or theological counterpart, a symbiotic other, which neither directly supports nor refutes his own project.

It is intriguing to note that Heidegger also shares with Luther his interest in a nontheological, factically oriented Aristotle, the Aristotle of the *Ethics* and the *Physics*. In scattered references to Aristotle, Luther reveals his fascination for a side of Aristotle that he believed the Scholastics did not understand, the Aristotle whose object is not God but life. "It is very doubtful whether the Latins comprehended the correct meaning of Aristotle," Luther writes.[34] Luther lectured on the *Nicomachean Ethics* in 1508 and 1509.[35] In 1517, he began to write a commentary on Aristot-

---

34. *LW*31 12. The Luther expert Gerhard Ebeling argues that Luther defends the true Aristotle against Scholastic distortions. See Gerhard Ebeling, *Luther,* trans. R. A. Wilson (Philadelphia: Fortress Press, 1970), 89.

35. See Martin Luther, "To the Christian Nobility of the German Nation Concerning the Reform of the Christian Estate," trans. Charles M. Jacobs and James Atkinson, in *LW*44, *The Christian in Society I*, ed. James Atkinson (Philadelphia: Fortress Press, 1966), 201 n. 212.

le's *Physics*.³⁶ The commentary, if it was ever written, did not survive, but the *Contra Scholasticam* is believed to have grown out of it.³⁷ He lectured on the *Physics* in 1519. "I know this book inside out, since I have already explained it privately twice to my fellow friars without using the commentaries," Luther said, boasting that he understood it "better than St. Thomas or Duns Scotus."³⁸ Yet Luther also writes that Aristotle's *Physics* contains "no real knowledge of the world of nature."³⁹ He recommends banishing all Aristotle from the university curriculum except for those works that could help students in their preaching, namely, *Logic, Rhetoric,* and *Poetics*. When Aristotle is properly understood, the incompatibility between theology and metaphysics becomes apparent. Of the *Contra Scholasticam*, Luther writes, "These theses were discussed and debated by me to show, first, that everywhere the Sophists of all the schools have deviated from Aristotle's opinion and have clearly introduced their dreams into the works of Aristotle whom they do not understand. Next, if we should hold to his meaning as strongly as possible (as I proposed here), nevertheless one gains no aid whatsoever from it, either for theology and sacred letters or even for natural philosophy. For what could be gained with respect to the understanding of material things if you could quibble and trifle with matter, form, motion, measure, and time—words taken over and copied from Aristotle?"⁴⁰ Nevertheless, Luther borrowed concepts from Aristotle's *Ethics* and *Physics* to explicate the theological anthropology of the New Testament.⁴¹ The human being, Luther argues, has a unique relationship to the privation *(steresis)* intrinsic to physical being. Human nature is not a potency for an actualization that can be ex-

---

36. "I wish nothing more fervently than to disclose to many the true face of that actor [Aristotle] who has fooled the church so tremendously with the Greek mask, and to show to them all his ignominy, had I only time! I am working on short notes on the *First Book of Physics*." Martin Luther to John Lang, February 8, 1517, in *LW* 48, *Letters*, ed. and trans. Gottfried G. Krodel (Philadelphia: Fortress Press, 1963), 38.

37. See Harold J. Grimm, introduction to "Disputation Against Scholastic Theology," in *LW* 31 6.

38. Martin Luther to George Spalatin, March 13, 1519, in *LW* 48 112; "To the German Nobility," *LW* 44 201.

39. Luther to Spalatin, March 13, 1519, in *LW* 48 112.

40. "A Statement Concerning the Heidelberg Disputation Made By Luther Apparently Soon After Its Conclusion," in *LW* 31 70.

41. See van Buren, *Young Heidegger*, 199.

pected in the natural order, being that has not yet arrived at its fullness; it is being that never arrives. The believer, Luther writes, "is always beginning, seeking, and renewing his quest ... And he who does not renew his quest loses what he has found, since one cannot stand still on the road of God."[42] A human being is not one being among others, but a mode of non-being:

> Through this new birth one moves from sin to righteousness, and thus from non-being, through becoming to being. And when this has happened one acts justly. But from this new being, which is really a non-being, a human being proceeds and passes to another new being through passion, that is, through becoming new, one proceeds to a better being, and from this again into something new. Thus it is most correct to say that human being is always in privation, always in becoming or in potentiality, in matter, and always in action. Aristotle philosophizes about such matters, and he does it well, but he is not understood in this sense. Human being is always non-being.[43]

Luther's analysis is theological anthropology. Aristotle does not philosophize about sin, justification, and righteousness, but he does philosophize about the mode of being of not-yet-being. Luther's work is *theology*, not philosophy. However, in elaborating the meaning of revelation, Luther simultaneously affirms certain ontological truths. He believes that these can also be philosophically verified, even if he does not argue for them philosophically. Creation is groaning and in travail under the pressure of non-being. It is in labor, giving birth to the new. Creatures are not finished essences, actually and fully present. Everything must be interpreted from the perspective of incompleteness. Luther writes: "You will be the best philosophers and the best explorers of the nature of things if you will learn from the apostle to consider the creation as it waits, groans, and travails, that is, as it turns away in disgust from what now is and desires that which is still in the future. For then the study of the nature of things, their accidents and their differences, will quickly grow worthless. . . . Look how we esteem the study of the essences and actions and inactions of things and the things themselves reject and groan over their own essences and actions and inactions! We praise and glorify the

42. *LW*25 225.
43. *LW*25 433–35.

knowledge of that very thing which is sad about itself and displeased with itself!"⁴⁴

It is not Aristotle who provides Luther with the most suitable language to speak about the travail of being but Paul. With his eschatological vision, Paul is driven to find a nonreifying and dynamic language with which to speak of a creation that leans toward the future. Luther describes Paul's thinking in this respect as "philosophizing":

> For the creation waits. The apostle [Paul] philosophizes and talks about things in a different way than the philosophers and metaphysicians do. For the philosophers so direct their gaze at the present state of things that they speculate only about what things are and what quality they have, but the apostle calls our attention away from a consideration of the present and from the essence and accidents of things and directs us to their future state. For he does not use the term "essence" or "activity" of the creature, or its "action," "inaction," and "motion," but in an entirely new and marvelous theological word he speaks of the "expectation of the creation," so that because his soul can hear the creation waiting, he no longer directs his attention to or inquires about the creation itself, but rather to what it is awaiting.⁴⁵

Paul "philosophizes" to make a theological point. The theologian is called to preach Christ crucified. However, the people best qualified to speak on philosophical matters are Christians because they alone understand God's plan for creation. Luther comments: "Just as a person does not use the evil of passion well unless he is married, so no person philosophizes well unless he is a fool, that is, a Christian."⁴⁶ Luther does not part company with Paul on this point, but he toys with the idea of a Christian philosophy, that is, a properly philosophical approach to philosophical subjects that is in some sense illuminated by revelation. His hesitation to rule out the possibility of metaphysics in the *Disputatio Heidelbergae* can be read as an openness to a philosophical theology developed in the light of the Cross.

In 1921, Heidegger argued that Luther's exposure of a decisive distortion of Christian theology by Aristotelian-Scholasticism opened up rad-

---

44. *LW*25 361–62.
45. *LW*25 361–62.
46. Luther, "Heidelberg Disputation," thesis 30, in *LW*31 41.

ically new possibilities for rethinking the basic concepts of philosophy (*GA*61 7). The 1922 *Natorpbericht* outlines a methodologically atheistic retrieval of Aristotle. Luther's disentanglement of Aristotle and Christian theology is presented as the theological prolegomena to the *Destruktion* of the ontological tradition. Heidegger plans to go beyond both modern Protestantism, which he felt betrayed Luther, and German idealism, which failed to grasp Luther's philosophical significance. He projects "a genuine explication of Luther's new basic religious position and its immanent possibilities" (*PIA* 252/125). The Aristotle book would complement Luther's theological project without explicitly contributing to theology; it would purge metaphysics of Christian concepts just as Luther had purged Christianity of metaphysical concepts.[47] A metaphysics free of theology would interpret things as they show themselves in themselves. As Luther had endeavored to retrieve the authentic sense of Christian existence as being-underway, so Heidegger would undertake a philosophical interpretation of temporal existence. The first stage would be a *Destruktion* of metaphysics and a reduction of its basic concepts to non-Christian sources. The *Destruktion* would begin with a recognition of the situation, the *Wirkungsgeschichte* of Scholasticism, which had made the authentic Aristotle so difficult to access (hence the subtitle to the text, "Indications of the Hermeneutical Situation"). With Luther, Heidegger would free Aristotle from his position in Scholastic metaphysics and "loosen up" the non-Scholastic Aristotle of the *Nicomachean Ethics*—not the theoretician of the unmoved mover, but the proto-phenomenologist of factual ethical life. The text begins with a preliminary interpretation of the concept of *phronesis*. The theoretical demonstrative knowing practiced in metaphysics, *episteme*, is not appropriate to ethical life. In ethics, we do not aesthetically speculate about timeless essences, but improvise historically. Concerned with the business of living, we apply provisional understanding in ever-changing situations.

In the *Natorp Bericht*, Heidegger argues that to understand the phil-

---

47. See van Buren, *Young Heidegger*, 165–66: "Heidegger wanted to use these possibilities to rethink not only theology, but also ontology. Neither Luther nor the theological and philosophical movements he inspired finished the deconstructive commentary on Aristotle and Aristotelian Scholasticism that the young Luther had started. My conjecture is that it was Heidegger who, as it were, finished it."

osophical significance of "Luther's new religious position," we must go to his sources: Paul, Augustine, and the late Scholasticism against which Luther pitted himself (Duns Scotus, Ockham, Gabriel Biel, Gregory of Rimini). Luther showed that the Scholastic doctrines of God, the Trinity, the Fall, Sin, and Grace were pervaded by Aristotelian metaphysics; they were "mediated interpretations of life." "Theological anthropology must be traced back to its basic philosophical experiences and motives" (*PIA* 250/125). Philosophy censures God-talk for it is this-worldly, "the grasp of factical life in its decisive possibilities for being" (*PIA* 246/121). Philosophy can "not presume that its foundational tendency directly accesses and determines God" (*GA*61 197). It stays with the most basic terms of life. Philosophy cannot "have" God as its theme because it is called to interpret "life."

> First of all, if philosophy is not a contrived preoccupation with just any "generalities" whatsoever, and with arbitrarily posited principles (a preoccupation which merely runs alongside life itself); but if it exists rather as a questioning knowledge, i.e., as research, simply as the genuine, explicit actualization of the tendency toward interpretation that belongs to life's own basic movements (movements within which life is concerned about itself and its own Being); and secondly, if philosophy intends to view and to grasp factical life in its decisive possibilities of Being; i.e., if philosophy has decided radically and clearly on its own (without regard for any bustling about with respect to world-views) to make factical life speak for itself on the basis of its very own factical possibilities; i.e., if philosophy is fundamentally atheistic and if it understands this about itself;—then it has decisively chosen factical life in its facticity and has made this an object for itself. (*PIA* 246)

A philosophy committed to "research," not to generalities and world-views, but to going along with life in its spontaneous self-interpretation, that is, a hermeneutics of facticity, cannot be theistic. To allow belief in a God or an afterlife to influence questioning is a betrayal of facticity. Heidegger presupposes that factical life experience is nontheistic, that we have no natural experience of God. As a questioning interpretation of life's "decisive" and "factical" possibilities, philosophy cannot believe because God is not one of our basic possibilities for being. Primordially we experience ourselves as beings for whom a relation to God is no longer even a possibility. Heidegger's methodological atheism is not intended as a substantive atheistic philosophy.

> [Philosophy is] "atheistic," but not in the sense of a theory such as materialism or something similar. Every philosophy which understands itself in what it is must— as the factical *how* of the interpretation of life—know (and it must know this precisely when it still has some "notion" of God) that life's retreat towards its own self (which philosophy achieves) is, in religious terms, a show of hands against God. But only then is philosophy honest, i.e., only then is philosophy in keeping with its possibility free from misleading concern which merely talks about religiosity. [One may well ask] whether the very idea of a philosophy of religion (especially if it makes no reference to the facticity of the human being) is pure nonsense. (*PIA* 246/193–94 n. 9)

Not only must faith be suspended in philosophy because it already has its answers; God cannot be addressed in philosophy. God is not given to philosophy to think. Facticity is godless. Hence philosophy must be nonreligious and atheological: "If fundamental definitions of human being which are dogmatically theological are to be excluded in radical philosophical reflection on human being (it is not just this but rather the positively ontological problematic which is hindered by this approach, insofar as it already has an answer), then we must refrain from an explicit and especially a hidden, inexplicit orientation to already defined ideas of human being" (*GA*63 29/24). The hermeneutics of facticity lets life interpret itself on its own terms. As such, it is a "show of hands against God."

Heidegger's hermeneutics of facticity is what a theologian of the Cross would expect to find in an authentic philosophy that had "suspended" the revelation: a rebellious humanism and a celebration of finitude. If in the Crucifixion, God has said "no" to the merely human, philosophy's "yes" to the meaning immanent in life is a "no" to God's "no." Heidegger has deliberately designed a philosophy symbiotic with Lutheran theology. A symbiotic organism does not exist on its own; its life is enabled by the life of another organism. Luther is the symbiotic other to Heidegger's hermeneutics of facticity, that is, Heidegger has implicitly assented to a Lutheran assumption. His hermeneutics of facticity can no longer be regarded as theologically neutral.

Lutheran Themes in Sein und Zeit

Apart from two brief unilluminating references, Luther does not appear to play a significant role in *Sein und Zeit*.[48] And yet, Heidegger's doctrines of *Destruktion*, fallenness, guilt, being-unto-death, and conscience, have clear Lutheran parallels. Heidegger's scattered theological disclaimers show that he was conscious of the theological overtones of the *Daseinanalytic*. After his intense involvement with Protestant theology in the '20s, he seems to have wished to downplay the relationship between the existential anthropology of *Sein und Zeit* and its theological sources, for the connection brings the alleged theological neutrality of his phenomenology into question. Yet a hidden theological agenda appears all the more likely the louder Heidegger denies it. Indeed, how can he deny some relationship to theology when he appropriates terms like fallenness, guilt, and conscience directly from the theological tradition?

Van Buren argues that the notion of *Destruktion*, the method of dismantling a corrupt tradition to return to its sources, is originally Lutheran. He points out that in the *Disputatio Heidelbergae*, Luther uses the word *destruere* (to destroy).[49] In Paul's First Letter to the Corinthians, 1:19, God's wisdom is revealed as the "destruction" of human wisdom. But the

---

48. See *SZ* 10/8: "Theology is slowly beginning to understand again Luther's insight that its system of dogma rests on a 'foundation' that does not stem from a questioning in which faith is primary and whose conceptual apparatus is not only insufficient for the range of problems in theology but rather covers them up and distorts them"; *SZ* 190 n. 1/404 n. 4: "It is no accident that the phenomena of anxiety and fear, which have never been distinguished in a thoroughgoing manner, have come within the purview of Christian theology ontically and even (though within very narrow limits) ontologically. This has happened whenever the anthropological problem of man's being towards God has won priority and when questions have been formulated under the guidance of phenomena like faith, sin, love, and repentance.... Luther has treated the problem of fear not only in the traditional context of an interpretation of *potentia* and *contritio*, but also in his commentary on the Book of *Genesis,* where, though his treatment is by no means highly conceptualized, it is all the more impressive as edification." Heidegger references *LW*1 170–76.

49. "'God destroys [*perdit*] the wisdom of the wise.'... So also in Jn 14:8 where Philip spoke according to the theology of glory: 'Show us the Father,' Christ immediately dragged back [*retraxit*] his flighty thought and led him back [*reduxit*] to himself... through the cross works are destroyed [*destruuntur*] and the old Adam... is crucified... [one must be] destroyed and reduced (*redactus*) to nothing through the cross and suffering...." *LW*31, *Career of the Reformer I*, trans. Harold J. Grimm (Philadelphia: Muhlenberg, 1957), 53–57, 44; see van Buren, "Martin Heidegger. Martin Luther," 167–72.

resonance is much deeper than linguistic: Luther destroys medieval theology in order to free up the concealed sources of the Christian tradition. In the light of the references to Luther in the 1922 *Natorpbericht*, where Heidegger first outlines the method of *Destruktion*, a connection is hard to deny. However, it remains purely methodological. Heidegger appropriates Luther's method into phenomenology—ostensibly something that he could do without any particular commitment to Luther's theology.

More problematic is the possible connection between Luther's notion of sin and the priority of the inauthentic to the authentic in Heidegger. For Heidegger, authenticity is a modification of our inauthentic and fallen state of being, not the other way around. For Luther, the human being is wholly distorted by sin. Both Luther and Heidegger locate what might otherwise be regarded as a *degeneration* from an original state of wholeness at the origin of human existence. After the Fall, sin is no longer experienced as a disfiguration of an original righteousness, but as our default mode of being. We are sinners first, and only with grace, saved. Thus the Lutheran Christian does not aim to preserve his human nature from further occasions of sin. Rather he understands himself and his fellow human being to be "originally" fallen. He seeks deliverance from himself, not merely a restoration of human nature. Inauthenticity in Heidegger is an analogous state of "original sin" into which we are thrown. The negative with which we have to do is not a negation of the positive, it is what is most original and in that sense positive. Truth and authenticity are derivations or modifications of our original fallenness. They are not simply given by nature; they must be laboriously achieved.[50]

A less speculative connection exists between Heidegger and Luther

50. Notice the intensity of Heidegger's denial of a theological connection between the ontological notion of fallenness and Christian theology: "Our existential, ontological interpretation thus does not make any ontic statement about the 'corruption of human nature,' not because the necessary evidence is lacking but because its problematic is *prior to* any statement about corruption or incorruption. Ontically, we have not decided whether human being is 'drowned in sin,' in the *status corruptionis*, or whether he walks in the *status integritatis* or finds himself in an interim stage, the *status gratiae*. But faith and 'worldview,' when they state such and such a thing and when they speak about Dasein as being-in-the-world, must come back to the existential structures set forth, provided that their statements at the same time claim to be *conceptually* comprehensible" (*SZ* 179–80/168). If we had not been suspecting a hidden theological agenda prior to this section of the book, this self-revealing claim certainly draws attention to the possibility. Cf. *GA*20 391/283: "It should be noted here that the explication of these structures of Dasein has nothing to do with any

concerning being-unto-death. Heidegger used the following passage from Luther's commentary on Genesis as a motto for his 1921/22 Aristotle course (*GA*61 182): "Right from our mother's womb we begin to die" (*Statim enim ab utero matris mori incipimus*).⁵¹ In a footnote in *Sein und Zeit*, Heidegger acknowledges that Christian theological anthropology "from Paul right up to Calvin's *meditatio futurae vitae*—has always kept death in view" (*SZ* 249 n. 1/408 n. 6). Being-unto-death is a central theme in Luther. "The summons of death comes to us all," Luther writes, "no one can die for another. Everyone must fight his own battle with death by himself, alone. We can shout into another's ears, but every one must himself be prepared for the time of death, for I will not be with you then, nor you with me."⁵² Luther does not merely repeat the Christian trope that we all must face our maker, Luther speaks of the solitary nature of dying. Death singles us out from the crowd. Heidegger will stress this point in his own language, arguing that death is our ownmost nonrelational possibility for being not to be bypassed.

The strongest resonance with Luther occurs in Heidegger's notion of conscience.⁵³ Luther's famous declaration at his heresy trial was an em-

---

doctrine of the corruption of human nature or any theory of original sin. What is involved here is a pure consideration of structures, which *precedes* all such considerations. Our consideration must be differentiated quite sharply from any theological consideration. It is possible, perhaps necessary, that all of these structures will recur in a theological anthropology. I am in no position to judge how, since I understand nothing of such things. I am of course familiar with theology, but it is still quite a way from that to an understanding. Since this analysis time and again incurs this misunderstanding, let me emphasize that it proposes no covert theology and in principle has nothing to do with theology. These structures can just as well determine the mode of being of a man or the idea of a humanity in the Kantian sense, whether one assumes with Luther that man is 'sodden with sin,' or that he is already in the *status gloriae*." See also *SZ* 306 n. 1/410 n. 2: "The being-guilty that belongs primordially to the constitution of being of Dasein is to be distinguished from the *status corruptionis* as it is understood by theology. Theology can find an ontological condition of its factical possibility in being-guilty as it is defined existentially. The guilty contained in the idea of this *status* is a factical indebtedness of a completely unique kind. It has its own attestation that remains fundamentally closed off to every philosophical experience. The existential analysis of being-guilty does not prove anything *for* or *against* the possibility of sin. Strictly speaking, one cannot even say that the ontology of Dasein leaves this possibility open at all *of its own accord* since, as philosophical questioning, it 'knows' nothing about sin in principle."

51. *LW*1 196.
52. Martin Luther, "Eight Sermons at Wittenberg, 1522," trans. John W. Doberstein, *LW*51 70.
53. On conscience, Heidegger references the Protestant theologian, M. Kähler's, *Das Gewissen* (1878) and his entry in the *Realenzyklopädie für protestansche Theologie und Kirche*. *SZ* 272 n. 1/409 n. 8.

phatic (if not entirely unprecedented) elevation of conscience above all secular and ecclesiastical authorities. When his examiners at the Diet of Worms asked Luther (on pain of excommunication and possibly worse), "Do you or do you not repudiate your books and the errors which they contain?" Luther replied "Unless I am convicted by Scripture and plain reason—I do not accept the authority of popes and councils, for they have contradicted each other—my conscience is captive to the Word of God, I cannot and I will not recant anything, for to go against conscience is neither right nor safe. God help me. Amen." When pressed further, he added: "The pope is no judge of matters pertaining to God's word and faith. But the Christian man must examine and judge for himself."[54] This is not a new notion of conscience. The Scholastics also spoke of how one must obey even an erring conscience. What is new here is the emphasis on the incommunicability or *Jemeinigkeit* of conscience. Luther's conscience is as alone before God as each one of us will be in our death. The call is not to become informed by listening to legitimate authorities. In the light of the corrupt nature of all earthly authority, conscience has no recourse and thrusts the believer back on himself. Luther's conscience submits only to "Scripture and plain reason." It must determine for itself the meaning of Scripture and its application to daily life. Conscience in Heidegger is our only possibility for awakening from our immersion in the They, the anonymous herd who have relieved Dasein of the burden of explicitly choosing its possibilities. Lost in inauthentic living, Dasein makes no choices and is carried along by the They. The transformation required for it to make a choice cannot come from 'outside,' for it is precisely an awakening to the inauthenticity of obeying external voices over one's own voice that is at issue. "When Dasein thus brings itself back from the 'they,' the they-self is modified in an existentiell manner so that it becomes *authentic* being-one's-self. This must be accomplished by *making up for not choosing*. But making up for not choosing signifies *choosing to make this choice*—deciding for a potentiality-of-being, and making this decision from one's own self. In choosing to make this choice, Dasein *makes possible*, first and foremost, its authentic potentiality-of-being. But because Dasein is lost in the

---

54. Luther, quoted in Roland H. Bainton, *The Reformation of the Sixteenth Century* (Boston: Beacon Press, 1952, 1956), 60–61.

'they,' it must first *find* itself. In order to find *itself* at all, it must be 'shown' to itself in its possible authenticity" (*SZ* 268/248). Similarly Luther's conscience does not allow him to transfer his responsibility before God onto an external authority.

Heidegger's Hidden Theological Agenda

Sein und Zeit is mired in the theological heritage it seeks to overcome. This critique is not new. In 1953 Heidegger's student, Karl Löwith argued that Heidegger's thinking of being in terms of time is based primarily on a "religious . . . and eschatological consciousness."[55] While emancipating itself from the *matter* of the Jewish and Christian theological traditions, it remains committed to the *form* of Jewish-Christian thinking. Heidegger retains the Jewish-Christian notion of time as being toward an *eschaton,* an irreversible end point, which makes every event at once singular and accidental, and infinitely significant. Tracing European nihilism to the vacuous anthropocentrism that results when the God of the Jewish-Christian heritage dies, but the conceptions of humanity and time which He inaugurated remain, Löwith criticizes Heidegger for remaining too Christian to understand the ontological orientation of the Greeks: "How distant is this eschatological-historical thinking, for which everything counts merely as seed-sowing and preparation for an arriving future, from the originary wisdom of the Greeks, for whom the history of time was philosophically insignificant because they directed their view toward eternal beings and beings-which-are-thus-and-not-different rather than toward what is in each case accidental, which could also be otherwise."[56]

But perhaps the earliest version of the critique of Heidegger's hidden theological agenda came from Max Scheler who suspected that something theological was moving beneath the surface of *Sein und Zeit* when he reviewed the copy of the book Heidegger had sent him in 1927.[57] Sche-

---

55. Karl Löwith, *Martin Heidegger and European Nihilism,* trans. Gary Steiner, ed. Richard Wolin (New York: Columbia University Press, 1995), 38–39.
56. Ibid., 39.
57. Max Scheler, "Reality and Resistance: On *Being and Time,* Section 43," trans. Thomas J. Sheehan, *Listening* 12 (1977): 61–73.

ler comments: "What is Dasein and 'being-in-the-world' supposed to mean? Here he introduces the word 'world' which is not only very ambiguous... but also pregnant with the whole theistic theology of the past, because world possesses a definite meaning only in opposition to 'God'.... Aren't these the gloomy old theologoumena of Calvinist origin (cf. also 'thrownness'), which are here translated into an apparently pure ontological language?"[58] Scheler wonders if some of the peculiar turns of Heidegger's phenomenology owe more to his religious disposition than to *die Sachen Selbst*:

Isn't dread—for example, the dread which gave birth to the myth of original sin—an historical product which I'd say can be demonstrated very precisely in its particular causes? For my part I am convinced that ever since Judaism and Christianity defined Western man, he has lived under a disproportionately greater burden of dread than any other type of man in the world, and that this weight of dread in great measure conditions his enormous world-activity, his hunger for power and his never-resting thirst for 'progress' and technological transformation of the world; and furthermore that this dread has emerged in a very peculiar and strong way in Protestantism.[59]

Hannah Arendt repeated the charge that *Sein und Zeit* is determined by hidden theological springs in a 1946 review of *Sein und Zeit*.[60] Heidegger makes the self into what the tradition called God, a being who needs no others in order to be itself. Heidegger thereby denigrates the being-together of human communal life. At the same time, by underscoring the finitude of human being, Heidegger has effectively removed any sense of divinity from philosophy. We are left with the isolation and incommunicability of the divine being and none of its world-saving transcendence.

Man as the identity of *Existenz* and essence appeared to give a new key to the question concerning Being in general. One need only recall that for traditional metaphysics God was the being in whom essence and existence coincided, in whom thought and activity were identical, and who was therefore interpreted as

58. Ibid., 63, 64.
59. Ibid., 72.
60. Hannah Arendt, "What is Existenz Philosophy?" first published in the *Partisan Review*, 1946, reprinted in *The Phenomenology Reader*, ed. Dermot Moran and Timothy Mooney (New York: Routledge, 2002), 345–61.

the otherworldly ground for all this world's Being,—in order to understand how seductive this scheme was. It was, in fact, the attempt to make man directly the 'Master of Being.'... After man was discovered as the being for whom he has so long taken God, it appears that such a being is also, in fact, powerless, and that there is no 'Master of Being.' The only things that remain are anarchical modes of Being.... Seen from the point of view of Nietzsche, who had always nobly tried to make man a real 'Master of Being,' Heidegger's philosophy is the first absolutely and uncompromisingly this-worldly philosophy.[61]

Arendt reads Heidegger as a demolisher of philosophical theology, a kind of antitheologian, who remains in spite of himself entangled in theology. The only theology compatible with *Being and Time* is one that rejects it as blasphemous, the inevitable presumption of fallen humanity, the systematic self description of the creature in the grips of an *aversio Dei*. *Being and Time* has no "ontological" foundations to offer theology; it has only a No to the theological way of life.[62]

The most recent thinker to add his voice to this chorus of critique is Jacques Derrida. Derrida points to Heidegger's ontic excursus as the weak point in *Sein und Zeit*. In order to elaborate Dasein's being-unto-an-end fully, Heidegger needs to foray into the ontic and examine a specific if unstated ideal of being-in-the-world. The move undermines the ontology by importing, and thereby prescribing, an ethical-religious ideal: resoluteness-unto-death. "Heidegger's chapter on being-toward-death culminates in a series of questions that threaten to bring down the whole edifice that Heidegger was constructing, by mandating the return of what had been so carefully excluded and thereby confirming that ul-

---

61. Ibid., 354–56.

62. Arendt's critique however is not theologically motivated. It is a political critique. Heidegger represents yet another subordination of the active to the contemplative life, therefore a denigration of the political and the social. This is nowhere more in evidence than in Heidegger's notion of Dasein as isolated self: "Heidegger arrives at this ideal of the Self as a consequence of his making Man what God was in the earlier ontology. Such a highest being is, in fact, possible only as a unique individual being who knows no equals. What consequently appears as 'Fall' in Heidegger, are all those modes of human existence which rest on the fact that Man lives together in the world with his fellows. To put it historically, Heidegger's Self is an ideal which has been working mischief in German philosophy and literature since Romanticism. In Heidegger this arrogant passion to will to be a Self has contradicted itself; for never before was it so clear as in his philosophy that this is probably the one being which Man cannot be.... The most essential characteristic of this Self is its absolute egoism, its radical separation from all its fellows." Ibid., 356–57.

timately the distinction between the ontological and the ontic cannot be sustained."[63] Derrida identifies the specific ontic importation operative in *Being and Time* as the Jewish-Christian-Islamic ideal of faithful existence: "Neither the language nor the process of this analysis of death is possible without the Christian experience, indeed, the Judaeo-Christian-Islamic experience of death to which the analysis testifies."[64]

Heidegger's hidden theological assumption—factical Godforsakenness—violates the rule of ontic noncommitment intrinsic to the methodology of formal indication. "In formal indication ... any uncritical lapse into a particular interpretation of existence—for example Kant's or Nietzsche's—ought to be avoided from the start, so that we can free up the possibility of pursuing a genuine science of the phenomenon of existence" (*GA9* 10–11/9). This edict forbidding ethical-religious commitment in ontology is repeated in *Sein und Zeit* as the stipulation that Dasein is not to be interpreted in terms of any particular mode of being-in-the-world but in terms of its "average everydayness." Yet in the analysis of being-unto-death, the neutral terrain of average everydayness is left behind, and one extreme ontic possibility for being-in-the-world is consulted for a clue as to how ontology can "grasp" Dasein "as whole." Heidegger is clearly aware of the danger of violating the neutrality of ontology with this move. Yet he insists that it is necessary and unavoidable. "But does not a definite ontic interpretation of authentic existence, a factical ideal of Dasein, underlie our ontological interpretation of the existence of Dasein? Indeed. But not only is this fact one that must not be denied and we are forced to grant; it must be understood in its *positive necessity*, in terms of the thematic object of our inquiry" (*SZ* 310/286). The ontological must be approached through the ontic. An existentiell possibility for being must be projected first if the existential analysis is to receive the necessary illumination. Heidegger assumes that the "definite ontic interpretation of authentic existence" confirms itself in its capacity to indicate the truth about Dasein formally. The resultant formal ontology ostensibly does not prescribe this existentiell possibility over others, but leaves all possibilities for being-in-the-world untouched, neither prescribed nor

63. Jacques Derrida, *Aporias: Dying—awaiting one another as the "limits of truth,"* trans. Thomas Dutoit (Stanford, Calif.: Stanford University Press, 1993), 80.
64. Ibid.

censured. Is it not the case that with resoluteness-unto-death, one existential possibility is *prescribed* as the way for Dasein to authenticate itself? Heidegger thinks that he has avoided this trap: "Nevertheless, how are we to find out what constitutes the 'authentic' existence of Dasein? Without existentiell understanding, all analysis of existentiality remains without foundation. Does not an ontic conception of existence underlie our interpretation of the authenticity and totality of Dasein, an ontic interpretation that might be possible, but need not be binding for everyone? Existential interpretation will never seek to take over a *fiat* as to those things that, from an existentiell point of view, are possible or binding. But must it not justify itself with regard to *those* existentiell possibilities that it uses to give the ontic base for the ontological interpretation?" (*SZ* 312/288). Such a justification would be necessary if the ontological interpretation proved to be content-determined, that is, if it failed to be formally indicative. Heidegger believes that his ontology remains purely formal in spite of the necessary excursion into the ontic; it prescribes nothing and hence leaves everything as it should be. "Our formal indication of the idea of existence was guided by the understanding of being in Dasein itself.... The idea of existence which we have posited gives us an outline of the formal structure of the understanding of Dasein in general, and does so in a way that is not binding from an existentiell point of view" (*SZ* 313/289–90). If this were in fact the case, why would one "existentiell possibility" be threatened, even extinguished, by Heidegger's purely formal ontology? Why would the Scholastic/Roman Catholic way of life, for example, where living is understood as being-held-in-being by a Creator God, whose glory shines through creation, and in whose image we exist, be censured by Heidegger's ontology? A formally indicative ontology would leave all religious and ethical debates as it finds them. It would practice a policy of strict noninterference. We would find no guidance in the ontology for settling, for example, Luther's debate with the Scholastics. We would not be able to decide whether Dasein is Godless, Godforsaken, or divinized on the basis of ontology. Insofar as Heidegger's ontology does in fact decide this theological issue, it fails to be formally indicative.

I believe that reading Heidegger, not as he read himself, as a facilitator of authentic theology, but rather as something of a theological terrorist, can greatly illuminate his ambiguous 1927 lecture "Phänomenologie und Theologie." The setting of the lecture, which was intended as a farewell to theology, was Marburg University. Here Heidegger had come into contact with contemporary Protestantism, Bultmann, but also the "neo-orthodoxy" or "dialectical theology" made famous by Karl Barth's 1919–22 *Der Römerbrief*, and represented at Marburg by Barth's friend and collaborator, Eduard Thurneysen. Heidegger supported and contributed to the Protestant effort to develop a nonmetaphysical theology. Yet Heidegger remained a philosopher and an ontologist, and in the end, he would not allow any diminishment of philosophy's claim to exclusive access to basic ontological concepts. The talk of faith as the mode of existence "occurring with the Crucified," and the sharp defense of the sovereignty of a theology that justifies itself on its own terms, is situated on solidly Protestant ground.[65] However, Heidegger's articulation of a role for philosophy as ontological corrective of theology (a residue of the Scholastic model of philosophy as a "handmaiden" to theology) threatens the independence of theology. Heidegger does not follow Barth into a nonnegotiable divorce of theology from philosophy. With the Scholastics, he establishes a communication between philosophy and theology on the basis of a shared ontological horizon. Philosophy serves as "a formally indicative ontological corrective of the ontic, and in particular, of the pre-Christian content of basic theological concepts" (*GA9* 65/52).

Theology's task is "to grasp the substantive content and the specific mode of being of the Christian occurrence, and to grasp it solely as it is testified to in faith and for faith" (*GA9* 51–54/40–47).[66] This is an echo of the reference in *Sein und Zeit* to the "new theology," which finally grasps the force of Luther's objection to metaphysically founded theology (*SZ* 8/6).[67] Philosophy, on the other hand, is primordial science; as such, it

---

65. *GA9* 54/45: "Faith is the believing-understanding mode of existing in the history revealed, i.e., occurring, with the Crucified."

66. Cf. *GA9* 9/6: "[Theology is] a thinking and questioning elaboration of the world of Christian experience, i.e., of faith."

67. Gadamer remembers Heidegger making a remark in Marburg in 1923, after a lecture by Thurneysen, that the true task of theology is "to find the word that is capable of calling one to faith and preserving one in faith." Hans-Georg Gadamer, "Die Religiöse Dimension," in *Gesammelte Werke*, vol. 3, 308–19, at 315; English: *Heidegger's Ways*, 167–80, at 175; idem, "Marburger Theologie," 197/29.

must be methodologically independent of all worldviews and value systems. Christianity is a value system. Therefore a Christian philosophy is an impossibility. In Heidegger's Nietzschean phase (the 1930s), the polemic became much stronger: philosophical questioning not only methodologically suspends faith, it is an existential stance that precludes faith. To believe is to exclude oneself from the philosophical life.[68] Philosophy aspires to give a true account of the "things themselves," irrespective of the worldview held by the philosopher, even if such an account always remains provisional and limited. Just as it makes no sense to speak of a "Protestant mathematics," genuine philosophy cannot be aligned with any particular religious commitment (*GA*24 27/20).[69]

Heidegger's objection to Christian philosophy does not assume that philosophers must lift themselves out of their concrete life situation and achieve a freedom from presuppositions. This would contradict the "as" structure of *Verstehen*. *Sein und Zeit* §31 defines the inescapable situatedness of understanding in historically determined horizons of interpretation. Yet the passage also calls for the transformation of prejudgments, purging understanding of arbitrary and capricious presuppositions acquired "by chance ideas and popular conceptions," in order "to guar-

---

68. Etienne Gilson articulated the most well known defense of the notion of Christian philosophy. A Christian philosophy is a rational and defensible philosophical position, directed, informed, and inspired by a nonphilosophical religious doctrine. Gilson sees no contradiction between holding a position on faith and simultaneously defending it philosophically, even needing faith to be able to think it through. The major advances of Scholastic over Greek philosophy, for example, the notion of God as *ens infinitum*, or the distinction between *essentia* and *existentia*, can be traced to a historical fact: the Scholastics (Christian, Jewish, and Muslim) were informed by the revelation of the name of God to Moses: "I am who am" *(Ego sum qui sum)* (Ex 3:14). Philosophy remains philosophy, whether a Christian or an atheist does it; however, the philosopher who thinks revelation cannot but philosophize differently. Revelation does not provide philosophical answers to philosophical problems, yet it gives the philosopher an indication of where to look for solutions, "a criterion, a norm of judgment, a principle of discernment and selection, allowing him to restore rational truth to itself by purging away the errors that encumber it." Etienne Gilson, *The Spirit of Mediaeval Philosophy*, trans. A. H. C. Downes (London: Sheed and Ward, 1936; reprint, Notre Dame: University of Notre Dame Press, 1991), 31–33.

69. That this was not always Heidegger's position is clear from letters and publications prior to 1919. See Heidegger's application of 20 August 1913 for a grant from "The Constantin and Olga von Schaezler Foundation in Honour of St. Thomas Aquinas": "The obedient undersigned intends to devote himself to the study of Christian philosophy." Heidegger, quoted in Ott, *Biographie*, 80/77. See also references to "the true worldview" of philosophy in the *Habilitationsschrift*, *GA*1 407–8/252.

antee the scientific theme by developing these in terms of the things themselves" (*SZ* 153/143). The task is not to free oneself of all presuppositions—an impossibility in a historical inquiry—but to enter into the hermeneutical circle in the right way. Christian philosophy is untenable to Heidegger because its faith-presuppositions are based, not on "the things themselves," but on an alleged revelation. By a movement away from theoretical formulations of the divine, methodologically atheistic philosophy stays with the divine absence. The theologian is free to take other directions and begin, not with the factic, but with the believed.[70] Philosophy, unlike theology, is not a worldview; it does not provide direction in life.[71] The foundations of every human belief system are in principle accessible to philosophical research.[72] A so-called Christian philosophy in Heidegger's view is not a formally neutral interpretation of being but a religiously motivated and determined interpretation. It does not uncover the variety of historical and religious contexts in which philosophers find themselves but commits itself to one of them.

The question of the relationship of philosophy to theology is not a question about worldviews but a question about the relationship between two sciences. On the one hand, theology, with its concept of revelation, is

70. In the 1924 *Begriff der Zeit,* Heidegger held that theology and philosophy must part company on the analysis of time because theology begins with a datum of faith, eternity, while philosophy must start with the factic. The theological starting point is not illegitimate; it is the proper way for theology to investigate the question of time: "In a theological sense—and you are at liberty to understand in this way—a consideration of time can only mean making the question of eternity more difficult, preparing it in the correct manner, and posing it properly" (*BZ* 2). Theology has its proper task, and when it remains within its methodological boundaries, resisting the temptation to turn itself into metaphysics or ontology, philosophy has no right to interfere with it.

71. A worldview is "not only a conception of the contexture of natural things but at the same time an interpretation of the sense and purpose of the human Dasein and hence of history" (*GA24* 4–5/5). As a modification of being-in-the-world, a worldview is an essential part of being human. "It is just because this positivity—that is, the relatedness to beings, to world that is, Dasein that is—belongs to the essence of the world-view, and thus in general to the formation of the world-view, that the formation of a world-view cannot be the task of philosophy.... Philosophy can and perhaps must show, among many other things, that something like a world-view belongs to the essential nature of the Dasein. Philosophy can and must define what in general constitutes the structure of a world-view. But it can never develop and posit some specific world-view qua just this or that particular one." *GA24* 12–13/10.

72. "There is entrusted to philosophy the primordial ontological conditions of the possibility of any world-view as something to be questioned; i.e., as something that becomes visible only in the rigor of research." *PIA* 246/121.

unlike any other science. On the other hand, as the thematization of a being that "in a certain manner is always already disclosed prior to scientific disclosure," theology has something in common with the other positive sciences; it presumes an unthematized preconcept of being (*GA9* 48/41). Drawing on Overbeck, Heidegger names the theme of theology "Christianness," the mode of existence revealed to Christian faith. Christianness is a way of being-in-the-world motivated by faith. Authentic Christian theology is not speculative knowledge of God, not "some coherent order of propositions about facts or occurrences which we simply agree to," but the scientific thematization of faithful being-in-the-world.[73]

Heidegger's articulation of the theological concepts of revelation and faith owes much to Luther. Revelation is a showing of the hiddenness of God. Heidegger cites Luther: "Faith is permitting ourselves to be seized by the things we do not see" (*GA9* 53/44). Giving myself over to the Crucified in faith, I part-take in the revelation. As the thematization of the mode of being disclosed in this partaking, theology cannot prop itself up with philosophical or historical arguments without ceasing to be what it is. Theology is "the science that faith of itself motivates and justifies" (*GA9* 55/46). It elaborates the meaning of faith for faith, but it does not thereby enable faith or make it easier. On the contrary, theology makes faith more difficult. It shows that faith is "not knowledge, but rebirth," not self-possession and certainty, but surrendering to "a possibility of existence as one which the Dasein concerned does not independently master, in which it becomes a slave, is brought before God, and is thus born *again*" (*GA9* 53/44).

But then Heidegger moves to the other side and says something with which Luther would certainly not agree. Heidegger argues that revelation does not give the theologian any insight into ontology: "The believer does not come to know anything about his specific existence, for instance, by

---

73. "The essence of faith can formally be sketched as a way of existence of human Dasein that according to its own testimony—itself belonging to this way of existence—arises *not from* Dasein or spontaneously *through* Dasein, but rather from that which is revealed in and with this way of existence, from what is believed. For the 'Christian' faith, that being which is primarily revealed to faith, and only to it, and which, as revelation, first gives rise to faith, is Christ, the crucified God.... The imparting of this revelation is not a conveyance of information about present, past, or immanent happenings; rather, this imparting lets one 'part-take' of this event that is revelation." *GA9* 52–53/44.

way of a theological confirmation of his inner experiences" (*GA9* 53/44). Ontology is strictly the domain of philosophy, "the free questioning of purely self-reliant Dasein." Because it lacks ontological grounding, theology surrenders its autonomy and is subordinated to philosophy, which, unique among the sciences, has "the task of directing all other non-theological, positive sciences with respect to their ontological foundation" (*GA9* 65/53). If theology does not address the most fundamental ground of thinking, then it has no claim to ultimacy. Kant's separation of the faculties of philosophy and theology ostensibly "made room for faith"; in fact, it philosophically neutered theology so that it could never again muddle in philosophy.[74] Heidegger is doing something similar, affirming at once theology's sovereignty over its own subject matter, while limiting its scope. Because a pre-Christian content inevitably enters into theology, philosophy's prerogative extends into theological terrain. Where philosophy retains the right to correct the ontological concepts presumed by theology, theology has no place critiquing the vision of existence coming forth in philosophy. Theology does not draw on philosophy to establish its data; its subject matter is revealed to it. But once it begins to thematize the revelation, it inevitably employs concepts that have their origins in non-Christian Dasein's pre-understanding. The ontological presupposition is sublated *(aufgehoben)* into theology, raised up, transformed yet essentially preserved in a theological mode.[75]

What does it mean that philosophy serves as "a formally indicative

---

74. Immanuel Kant, "The Conflict of the Faculties," trans. Mary J. Gregor and Robert Anchor, in Immanuel Kant, *Religion and Rational Theology*, ed. Allen W. Wood and George di Giovanni (New York: Cambridge University Press, 1996), 237–327.

75. "Though what is revealed in faith can never be founded by way of a rational knowing as exercised by autonomously functioning reason, nevertheless the sense of the Christian occurrence as rebirth is that Dasein's prefaithful, i.e., unbelieving existence is sublated *(aufgehoben)* therein. Sublated does not mean done away with, but raised up, kept, and preserved in the new creation. One's pre-Christian existence is indeed existentielly, ontically, overcome in faith. But this existentiell overcoming of one's pre-Christian existence (which belongs to faith as rebirth) means precisely that one's overcome pre-Christian Dasein is existentially, ontologically included within faithful existence. To overcome does not mean to dispose of, but to have at one's disposition in a new way. Hence we can say that precisely because all basic theological concepts, considered in their full regional context, include a content that is indeed existentielly powerless, i.e., *ontically* sublated, they are *ontologically* determined by a content that is pre-Christian and that can thus be grasped purely rationally. All theological concepts necessarily contain that understanding of being that is constitutive of human Dasein as such, insofar as it exists at all." *GA9* 63/51.

ontological corrective of the ontic, and in particular, of the pre-Christian content of basic theological concepts"? A *formally indicative corrective* would problematize the enactment sense of a phenomenon by suspending its relational and content senses. A formally indicative *ontological corrective* of an ontic content problematizes the enactment sense of a notion of being implicit in an ontic inquiry. Theology is subject to philosophical critique when it makes ontological claims.

Is theology, in its own self-understanding and its traditional formulations, Catholic or Protestant, ever merely an "ontic" science? Has it ever in any tradition allowed itself to be confined to the ontic, that is, has it ever *not* made ultimate claims about the basic presuppositions of knowledge and existence? Theology has an essential claim to ultimacy, and a philosophy that would "communicate" with theology must either reject its claim or accept it as a limit to its own purview. Heidegger says that the worldview constituted by faith in revelation is dialectically opposed to "the form of existence that is an essential part of philosophy." It would seem that philosophy is more than an ontically neutral ontology, for why else would theology take issue with it? Phenomenological ontology has some kind of implicit theological stance that makes it antagonistic to theology. Heidegger's characterization of theology as a "positive science," having more in common with chemistry and botany than with philosophy, would satisfy neither a Barthian nor a Scholastic. As a positive science, theology could not in any way represent a challenge to ontology. It is difficult to make this consistent with Heidegger's claim that philosophy and theology are "mortal enemies." Like old foes who are only truly communicating with each other when they recognize the other as their mortal enemy, philosophy and theology face each other as deadly opponents with mutually exclusive claims to ultimacy.[76] These strong state-

---

76. "This peculiar relationship does not exclude but rather includes the fact that *faith*, as a specific possibility of existence, is in its innermost core the mortal enemy of the *form of existence* that is an essential part of *philosophy* and that is factically ever-changing. Faith is so absolutely the mortal enemy that philosophy does not even begin to want in any way to do battle with it. This existentiell opposition between faithfulness and the free appropriation of one's whole Dasein is not first brought about by the sciences of theology and philosophy but is prior to them. Furthermore, it is precisely this opposition that must bear the possibility of a community of the sciences of theology and philosophy, if indeed they are to communicate in a genuine way, free from illusions and weak attempts at mediation." *GA*9 66/53.

ments, which show a diversity of irreconcilable influences—Duns Scotus, Luther, Kierkegaard, Overbeck—do not fuse into a single coherent view on the relationship of philosophy to theology. Heidegger is torn between his attraction to the revelational positivism of Barth and Thurneysen and his conviction that ontology remains foundational for the sciences, theology included. Ultimately Heidegger's tenuous proposal for maintaining communication between philosophy and theology cannot withstand these tensions and "Phänomenologie und Theologie" breaks apart at the seams.

We are now in a position to understand a problem that has received a great deal of inconclusive and confusing treatment in the literature: Heidegger's silence on the question of God in *Sein und Zeit*. Heidegger has deliberately designed a philosophy that can enable a radical (albeit ontologically neutered) theology of revelation. The serious problem is not Heidegger's critique of "onto-theology" but Heidegger's implicit assent to Lutheran Godforsakenness. The Godforsaken is not ignorant of God; he is rather abandoned by God. This is a theological position, as Luther would be the first to argue; it can only be justified theologically.

CHAPTER SEVEN

PRIMAL CHRISTIANITY

*Above all Martin Heidegger's existential analysis of
Dasein appears to be nothing more than a secular philosophical
presentation of the New Testament insight into human existence.*

RUDOLF BULTMANN

In the light of the early Freiburg lectures, it is hard to deny Rudolf Bultmann's claim that a direct relationship exists between the *Daseinanalytic* and early Christianity.[1] Heidegger and Bultmann, a specialist on the New Testament at Marburg University, worked closely together during Heidegger's Marburg years. Heidegger participated in Bultmann's seminars on New Testatment theology and gave lectures to Bultmann's students. In addition to the lecture "Das Problem der Sünde bei Luther," which Heidegger gave in Bultmann's seminar in 1924, the lecture *Der Begriff der Zeit* was delivered that same year to the Marburg Theologians Society. In this short piece, Heidegger's thinking on being-unto-an-end comes into sharp focus. The likelihood that this was a product of Bultmann's theological influence is strong. Bultmann in turn was deeply influenced by Heidegger's "existentialism," which served him as a conceptual frame within which to understanding the thinking of the first

---

1. Rather than complain that the New Testament is being interpreted [by Bultmann] with "categories drawn from Heidegger's philosophy of Existenz," Bultmann argues that we should be "shocked, that philosophy already sees on its own what the New Testament says." Rudolf Bultmann, "Neues Testament und Mythologie. Das Problem der Entmythologisierung der neutestamentlich Verkündigung," in *Kerygma und Mythos. Ein theologisches Gespräch*, ed. Hans Werner Bartsch (Hamburg-Volksdorf, 1951), 15 ff. See Pöggeler, "Heideggers Luther-Lektüre," 187.

Christian community. Heidegger and Bultmann shared an interest in retrieving the *ethos* of early Christianity. Bultmann wanted to free it from mythology; Heidegger, from Scholastic theology.

Heidegger was already well into his religion research by the time he met Bultmann. The two Freiburg courses, "Einleitung in die Phänomenologie der Religion" (1920) and "Augustinus und der Neuplatonismus" (1920–21) (both published in *GA*60), represent the apogee of his work in the phenomenology of religion. The method and content of these lectures reflect Heidegger's involvement with radical Protestantism, both professionally and personally. These are resolutely anti-Scholastic, formally atheistic interpretations of theological texts. Together with Heidegger's reading of Luther, and "Phänomenologie und Theologie," they show Heidegger's ambivalent position on the relationship of phenomenological ontology to Christian theology. Three apparently incompatible possibilities for understanding that relationship emerge from the texts: (1) Bultmann's contention: Heidegger secularizes Christian theology; (2) Heidegger's claim in "Phänomenologie und Theologie": phenomenology leaves theology untouched insofar as theology remains concentrated on its proper subject matter, Christian faith; (3) a third possibility: Heidegger obliterates theology by making it obsolete and ontologically insignificant. There are good reasons in support of each of these positions. They can only be made mutually compatible by distinguishing two kinds of theology, one which Heidegger leaves intact (radical Lutheranism), the other which he makes impossible (Scholastic, or more broadly, Roman Catholic). Heidegger "secularizes" in the sense that he "finds" ontological indications (not to be misconstrued as proofs) for the New Testament view of the human being as fallen and thrown. He leaves a Lutheran interpretation of fallenness intact while censoring any metaphysical (i.e., Scholastic) interpretation of fallenness. On the other hand, he obliterates Scholastic theology by denying its foundation: the analogical unity between uncreated and created being. Heidegger's polemical relationship to Scholastic theology is, then, the key to understanding his approach to the New Testament, to Augustine, and to Christian theology in general.

The Early Christian Breakthrough to the Historical Self

It is clear from unpublished notes and numerous references in the early lectures that Wilhelm Dilthey's effort to establish the conditions of historical knowledge had a profound influence on the young Heidegger, perhaps even determining the direction of his religion research.[2] In his *Einleitung in die Geisteswissenschaften*, Dilthey traces historical consciousness back through the Reformation to early Christianity.[3] The religious experience of the early Christian community precipitated a turn away from Greek metaphysics and made possible spontaneous expressions of the historical self. Heidegger's claim, "Christian religiosity lives temporality as such" sums up Dilthey's thesis (*GA*60 80). In a differentiation of consciousness that set them apart from the Greeks and Romans, the Christians understood time as a drama of unique and unrepeatable moments culminating in a definite end. Human life was a trial overshadowed by a final and irrevocable judgment, which looms over us and comes toward us from out of our collective past. Every moment of an individual life is, as Kierkegaard puts it, of decisive significance.[4] Dilthey traces this sense for history to Christian otherworldliness. Christianity repudiated the stability of the Greek approach to life. For the Christian, the world was not a spectacle to be enjoyed but a temporal trial through which the self comes into being or perishes. The first Christians were not aesthetes but ascetics, turned inward, where they had discovered a new order of being. Individuality and historicity were no longer regarded as accidental to the soul. The individual self, the self in its living attestation to itself, becomes the locus of truth. In historical life, the individual rises to God or falls into perdition. The minute and hidden events of the inner life, the incommunicable moment of conversion, personal experiences of fallenness and grace, constitute a concrete and temporal path

---

2. See *GA*9 13 f; *GA*61 7, 82, 117; *GA*63 42, 69, 108. Heidegger's references to Dilthey in the phenomenology of religion lectures are terse but telling. See *GA*60 37. See also the recently translated 1925 lecture, "Wilhelm Dilthey's Research and the Struggle for a Historical Worldview," in Heidegger, *Supplements*, 147–76. Kisiel has examined Heidegger's notes on Dilthey in his *Genesis of Being and Time*, 100–105.

3. Dilthey, *Einleitung in die Geisteswissenschaften*, 250–67/228–39.

4. Kierkegaard, *Philosophical Fragments*, 18.

to God. Socrates promoted a formal introspection, to "know thyself" as the Oracle at Delphi commanded, but the data of interest to him were not historically situated feeling, personal commitment, and relationship; rather, his interest was in the timeless essence of rational life, the intellect, *nous*, which lifts us above the particularities of individual existence to something more ideal, certain, and lasting. Where the self in Socratic self-knowledge participates in the universality, immutability, and immateriality of ideas, Christianity takes an opposite approach: an intensification of the ambiguities of facticity and historical life.

Crucial to understanding Heidegger's approach to Christianity and Scholasticism at the time of the religion lectures is Dilthey's opposition between Hellenistic and Christian spiritual life. Greek spiritual life is according to Dilthey extraverted, outwardly directed, toward the contemplation of the aesthetic perfection of the universe and political action. Christian spiritual life, on the other hand, is introverted, inwardly directed. "The [Christian] will goes beyond all this [politics] . . . and back into itself."[5] These alternative psychological orientations generate different approaches to knowledge. For the Greek, knowing is mirroring an object. For the Christian, knowing is interior experience, a "simple awareness of what is given in personality and in consciousness of the self."[6] The turn within is precipitated by a new conception of the divine. No longer identified with "the splendor, the power, and the happiness of life," the divine is now associated with "servitude and suffering." Consequently, the inner life of the individual, "the poorest human heart, restlessly agitated within narrow limits by the nature of its existence," is brought into sharp relief. This inner world, the site of "the consciousness of the inner freedom of man," is ignored by the Greeks with their ideals of immutability and immateriality. The doctrine of the Incarnation changes everything. "God's essence has entered whole and without remainder into the revelation in Christ. God's essence, instead of being grasped in the self-enclosed concept of substance of antiquity, was now caught up in historical vitality. And so *historical consciousness*, taking the expression in its highest sense, first came into being."[7] No longer a shadow realm, understood only in

---

5. Dilthey, *Introduction to the Human Sciences*, 228.
6. Ibid., 229.   7. Ibid., 230.

reference to eternal ideas, history is reconceived as the real world. The soul now communes with the divine in the heart. "In the inner recesses of one's will, one experiences God as will, person to person."[8] Dilthey places great emphasis on the Christian belief in an immediate presence of God in the soul. Prayer validates the inner life of the individual. "The deep secret of this religion lies in the relation between experience of one's own states and God's activity in the soul and in destiny; it is here that religious life has its own proper realm, removed from knowledge of the common sort, indeed from every kind of conceptualization."[9]

Dilthey's study is characterized by a polemic with Scholastic theology. He sets up an opposition between early Christian interiority and Greek aestheticism, a tension that is unhappily resolved in the Scholastic "counterpart to ancient metaphysics."[10] By fusing these mutually exclusive ways of thinking, Scholasticism betrayed the early Christian breakthrough to interiority and historicity. Dilthey writes, "It was the tragic destiny of Christianity to extract the holiest experiences of the human heart from the quiet of the individual's life and introduce them among the motive forces of world-historical mass movements, and to evoke mechanistic morality and hierarchical hypocrisy in the process."[11] The Scholastics did not build on Augustine the mystic who had plumbed the depths of the historical self, but on Augustine the metaphysician who had fused Christianity and neo-Platonism into an "objective system" of "theoretically and epistemologically grounded ... religious experience." Clearly under the influence of Schleiermacher, Dilthey understands Christianity as entirely a matter of feeling, a purely internal experience of the heart or "the will." In its struggle to articulate its unique mode of living, Christianity broke through to this inner world and developed a nonmetaphysical mode of self-interpretation ("understanding," rather than "explanation"). The medieval revival of ancient philosophy betrayed Christian subjectivity by subsuming it "into the conceptual framework of the external world, which governed it with respect to relations of space, time, substance and

---

8. Ibid., 232.   9. Ibid.
10. Ibid., 233.
11. Ibid. Heidegger cites this passage in his unpublished notes. See Kisiel, *Genesis of* Being and Time, 101.

causality."¹² Such a sublimation could only amount to a deterioration. "To develop this content in dogma was at the same time to alienate it."¹³ Rather than thematizing history, the Scholastics thematized eternity; rather than developing the notion of conscience, the Scholastics developed natural law; rather than engaging faith as a mode of historical existence, the Scholastics defined faith as a deficient mode of theoretical cognition.

A true follower of Schleiermacher, Dilthey does not regard these early Christian ideas as the exclusive property of Christianity. On the contrary, they are structures embedded in human consciousness and must be liberated from their doctrinal setting or universalized. To some degree, Heidegger takes up this task in his formalization of Pauline theology. In the 1919–20 lecture course "Grundprobleme der Phänomenologie," Heidegger describes the experience of Christian conversion as "the historical paradigm" for "the turn to the self-world." With its relentless attention to inner motivation, the "primal Christian consciousness of life" *(urchristliches Lebensbewußtsein)* becomes Heidegger's model for the hermeneutics of facticity.¹⁴

Formalizing Early Christian Eschatology

Heidegger's purely methodological interest in religion in the phenomenology of religion lectures frustrated his students to the point of protest. In the first half of the lecture course, Heidegger was forced to break off his discussion of formal indication after students complained to the dean that the *Privatdozent* was not teaching religion in his religion class.¹⁵ Only at this point does Heidegger begin to speak about a concrete religious phenomenon, conversion and discipleship in the letters of Paul.

---

12. Dilthey, *Introduction to the Human Sciences*, 233.
13. Ibid.
14. "The most profound historical paradigm for the noteworthy process of shifting the center of gravity of factic life and the life-world into the self-world and the world of inward experience is given for us in the emergence of Christianity. The self-world as such enters into life and becomes lived as such. What lies forth in the life of the primal Christian communities signifies a radical reversal of the directional tendency of life. It is usually thought of as a denial of the world and asceticism. Here lie the motives for the development of completely new contents of expression which life fashions—even up to that which we today call history" (GA58 61–62).
15. Kisiel, *Genesis of Being and Time*, 171.

His anger at having to change his approach is evident in the student transcripts. He openly mocks his students' impatience with the formalism of phenomenology. Infected by their age, they want concrete results instead of the labor of thinking. Under coercion, Heidegger embarks upon his Paul interpretation, certain that the students will misunderstand it entirely.[16] His students were understandably confused. Heidegger is not interested in God or the evidence for religious claims, but in the kinds of formal moves made by those who would speak about religious experience. His lectures are not intended to add in any way to the case for or against Christianity or theism. This creates an ambiguity that threatens to destroy the coherence of the interpretation. On the one hand, Heidegger's approach seems to presume that the meaning of Christian experience is transcendentally accessible to philosophy. On the other hand, the method of formal indication, central to this lecture, is designed to preserve the integrity of religious experience.

The formalistic approach to religious texts is not original. It determined the philosophies of religion of Kant, Hegel, Schopenhauer, and Feuerbach. Heidegger intends to avoid the naive rationalism of these approaches, the assumption that a criterion of rationality worked out in philosophy can act as a tribunal over religious phenomena.[17] He means to let religion to its own terms and give a "phenomenological understanding of primal Christian religiosity" (*GA60* 76). The criterion of such an understanding will not be imported from without; it will be immanent to the subject matter. "Authentic philosophy of religion does not emerge from pre-established concepts of philosophy and religion. Rather, the possibility of philosophical comprehension is given by a determinate religiosity,

---

16. "Philosophy, as I understand it, is in a difficulty. The listener in other lectures is assured, from the beginning on: in art history lectures he can see pictures; in others he gets his money's worth for his exams. In philosophy, it is otherwise, and I cannot change that, for I did not invent philosophy. I would, however, like to save myself from this calamity, and lecture to you, beginning in the next session, on history; and indeed I will, without further consideration for the starting-point and method, take a particular concrete phenomenon as the point of departure, however for me under the presupposition that you will misunderstand the entire study from beginning to end" (*GA60* 65).

17. "If one understands the task of the philosophy of religion in a totally naive way, one can say: religion should be conceptualized in a philosophical way. Religion is then projected into an understandable context. In this way the situation of the philosophical religious problem becomes dependent on the concept of philosophy" (*GA60* 75).

for us the Christian" (*GA*60 124). Yet Heidegger's aim is neither theological nor religious. He is not interested in either decrying or promoting Christianity. The task is to elaborate the sense for history emerging from Paul phenomenologically. He assumes that the enactment structure of these texts can be freed of special theological content and phenomenologically corroborated, without either violating the religious meaning of the text or committing philosophy to any particular religious view. The how of early Christian experience is to be thematized without denying that its enactment in a religious context exceeds the compass of phenomenology.

Heidegger's source texts are Galatians and First and Second Thessalonians. He is particularly interested in Paul's account of the Christian life as one of conversion and waiting. Others have remarked how eschatology, the principal teaching of the early Christian community, holds up a mirror to time, not the Greek/Middle Eastern eternal return of the same but the linear rush of unrepeatable moments, flying toward an irreversible end point.[18] Heidegger zeroes in on Paul's notion that the elect

---

18. The sense of time in early Christianity has since Bultmann became a central theme in the literature. See Rudolf Bultmann, *Primitive Christianity in Its Contemporary Setting* (Philadelphia: Fortress Press, 1975), 180–88: "It is clear that the early Christian doctrine of man is diametrically opposed to that which prevailed in the Greek tradition. Man is not regarded as an instance of universal human Being, which in its turn is seen to be an instance of cosmic Being in general. There is no attempt to escape from the questionableness of man's own individuality by concentrating on the universal law or the cosmic harmony. . . . The Stoic shuts the door to all encounters and lives in the timeless Logos. The Christian opens himself to these encounters, and lives from the future. The understanding of Christian existence [is] as a life in which God is always One who comes, and as a life which is always a future possibility. . . ." See also Rosemann, *Understanding Scholastic Thought*, 130: "The Christian view of time that can be gathered from the New Testament is not circular or cyclical, but linear. Possessed of a definite beginning and an end, Christian time 'progresses' in a sense in which Greek time cannot, it moves from creation through the Fall and the history of Israel to the Redemption of humanity through Christ and the coming of the Kingdom. Only such a linear history can be teleological, that is to say, oriented toward a goal. What is more, the idea of historical uniqueness obviously makes sense only if history does not repeat itself. Therefore, what seemed like 'foolishness' to the Greeks—namely the Christian belief in the salvation of humankind once and for all through an historical individual, Jesus Christ—becomes intelligible if placed in the context of the Christian linear understanding of time and history. In Christianity, every moment in history matters, because it constitutes an unrepeatable step toward the end." For a philosophical analysis of the Christian sense of time, which surpasses Heidegger's both in depth of insight and range of vision, see Michael Theunissen's superb "Der Gebetsglaube Jesu und die Zeitlichkeit des Christseins," in Michael Theunissen, *Negative Theologie*, 321–77.

are not distinguished by moral rectitude but by wakefulness; they are transparently temporal, grounded in the past event of having become a Christian, the transience of the present with its persecution and suffering, and the ineluctable reality of the future, when Christ will return. The first phenomenon Heidegger examines is the "being-of-having-become" *(Gewordensein)*. Paul pleads with the Thessalonians to "remember" who they have "become" in Christ. He calls them back to the historical moment of their birth into the Christian community. At a determinate moment in time, when they heard the word preached to them and believed, the Thessalonians became Christians. The becoming was not knowledge but conviction, not reflection but action. The repletion of the moment in the daily renewal of faith is an experience of certainty, but not the certainty of knowledge. It is the certainty of commitment, what Heidegger will call resoluteness *(Entschlossenheit)* in *Sein und Zeit*. The Thessalonians must continually repeat the moment in which they became Christians. Only thus will they find the courage to endure the persecution that must follow. They know who they are and what they must do with a conviction deeper than theoretical certainty.[19] In this intensification of the factic conditions of life, early Christianity enacts the *how* of being historically related to oneself *(das Wie des Sich-Verhaltens)*. "Having-become is not, in this life, [just] any incident you like. Rather, it is incessantly co-experienced, and indeed such that their Being now is their having-become [*Gewordensein*]. Their having-become is their Being now" (*GA60* 66).

The Thessalonians are not absolved from the ongoing task of continually accomplishing this becoming; finality is not something that the Christian enjoys. In this life, Christian discipleship is ceaseless becoming, living in the advent of the *eschaton*, the final resolution. Paul does not tell the Thessalonians when the end will happen. Nor does he say that it cannot be known. He condemns as unbelief the effort to calculate the when. The point of living in expectation of Christ is to acquire the proper relationship to the now. What is decisive is how the disciple relates faith in the once and future Christ to concrete living. When the Thessalonians ask Paul about when the Day of the Lord will come, Paul tells them that

19. Heidegger comments, "This knowledge is entirely different from any other knowledge and memory. It arises only out of the situational context of Christian life experience" (*GA60* 65).

they do not need to know the day or the hour. His response highlights the fundamental difference between waiting for an event and authentic temporal life. To expect the Christ is to live with urgency, to dwell in the crisis of always being underway. "The experience is an absolute distress which belongs to the life of the Christian himself. The acceptance is an entering-oneself-into anguish" (*GA*60 97). In this relentlessly intense futural existence, the disciple becomes Christian. Christ is the future, but a future that is now. By living toward the future, the disciple resists self-abstraction from the now and attains for the first time an authentic relationship to the present. The future is the God he already knows, the one who has already come. As the disciple races toward the finish line, he runs toward what has been. Heidegger comments: "The question concerning the when leads back ultimately to my conduct. The way in which the *parousia* fits into my life refers backwards to the enactment of this life itself.... The when is determined by the how of the conduct of life, and the latter for its part is determined by the enactment of the factic experience of life in each and every one of its aspects... What must count for the Christian is only the now in which the situation in which he actually stands becomes enacted, not the expectation of an event that is to take place at some fixed point in future time" (*GA*60 104–6, 114).

Early Christian eschatology is not simply the expectation of some event that has not yet occurred; it is the appropriation of an event that has already happened. But it is not only appropriation; it is also the expectation of that which is still to come. The one who is to come is the one who has already come. The common sense understanding of the future as that which is yet to come and hence has not happened, and the past as that which has happened and hence is not to come, is turned upside down. Christ is the already/not yet. Pauline eschatology is waiting for that which has already happened. This paradoxical inversion of common time brings a new meaning of the present into view. The point of the waiting and appropriating is to enact an authentic relationship to the *now*; to be converted; to live in Christ *now*. This enactment is simultaneously a running ahead and a recapitulation. And because it is both of these at once, it is the fullness of a moment that is not separate from what went before and what is yet to come, a *now* that is constitutively determined by the already/not yet, a present that is a relation to the future through the past.

To know that he is called is for the early Christian, not a possessed knowledge, but a commission. The knowledge is nothing without performance. It is not a concept but a *Vollziehen,* an accomplishment. What then could it offer philosophy? If the Christian's knowledge of life is intimately bound to Christian living, what has philosophy to learn from it? Heidegger is careful to avoid the mistakes of nineteenth-century *Religionsphilosophie,* which posited a transcendental access to the a priori essence of religion. The method of formal indication, so painstakingly developed here, is meant to avoid this fallacy. The religious meaning of these terms is putatively untouched by the philosophical elaboration. Relational-sense is suspended. The terms are lifted from their concrete context by the suspension and await a new application in a non-religious context, in the hermeneutics of facticity, where they must mean something different. Heidegger senses the hollowness of the formal interpretation: "Now we give a *formal schematic* of the phenomenon. Without preunderstanding the entire context one cannot extract a single reference. The formal schematic of the explication has meaning only in the formal articulation, [for] it does not emerge in the enactment of phenomenological understanding. In its formal elevation what is authentic is lacking" (*GA*60 95).

Two levels of meaning are operative here, one given with the lecture, the other, not given, lacking, outstanding. What is given is formal, and therefore empty, content-poor, indicative of a task that is yet to be performed; what is not-given is the authentic meaning of the phenomenon. The formal indication abnegates itself. By virtue of being given, conceptually available, it betrays the subject. When it is properly understood it is clear that nothing is clear; it is understood that nothing has been understood. Heidegger does not underestimate the gap that separates those who attend his lecture in phenomenology from the experience of the early Christians. On the contrary, the method of formal indication exacerbates distance and difficulty: "The understanding is made difficult in its enactment itself; this difficulty grows constantly the nearer it approaches the concrete phenomenon. It is the difficulty of putting-oneself-into-another's-place, which cannot be supplanted by a fantasizing-oneself-into or a 'vicarious understanding'; what is required is an authentic enactment" (GA60 100).

Is this difficulty unique to reading a religious text? Does the problem of enactment become especially acute when philosophy tries to put itself into the mode of being of a theologically determined existence? Or is this a more universal difficulty, the problem of thinking facticity that attends every phenomenological investigation? It seems that faith does not present any *special* difficulty to phenomenology. The problem of accessing the meaning of theological existence is the problem of accessing facticity. The factic acts as a transcendental structure through which all modes of living are to be interpreted. In his identification of the inaccessibility of the ontological relation-sense with the inaccessibility of the factic, Heidegger abrogates the uniqueness of theological existence. The Christian sense for life is not unique; it is a religious expression of human being-in-the-world.

"Einleitung in die Phänomenologie der Religion," which Heidegger did not want published in his lifetime and considered destroying, proves that the concept of time in *Sein und Zeit* is not Greek but biblical. This is not to deny that Heidegger found indications of temporality in Aristotle's ethics. But *kairos* in Aristotle is not being-unto-death. It is the grasp of the concrete situation in the context of applying a moral principle.[20] *Sein und Zeit* is not an ethics or a way of living (these remain on the level of the ontic and the existentiell) but a formal eschatology. Like the early Christian's anticipation of Christ's return, Dasein "temporalizes" being in its retention of itself, and its projection of itself into possibility. The temporalization is determined by directedness to the impossible possibility, death. The possible does not emerge from pure nothingness but from the past. The past is not gone but lives in the moment and makes it what it is.

---

20. I would question William McNeill's claim in his *Glance of the Eye*, 45 n. 29: "Heidegger does not simply read the early Christian sense of the *kairos* that he finds in St. Paul into Aristotle's *Nicomachean Ethics*. Rather, it is surely Aristotle (mediated by Luther, and, of course, in conjunction with Husserl) who first provides Heidegger with the phenomenological eye and conceptuality with which to analyze the temporality of the *kairos* in a manner attentive to 'the things themselves.'" I think that Aristotle's practical philosophy and early Christian eschatology are fused in *Sein und Zeit*—which accounts for its artificiality.

This structure of fused temporal horizons is lifted directly out of Pauline eschatology. The moment of Christian conversion, which is every moment of the Christian life, is horizoned by the *parousia*. The Christian awaits that which will fulfill his having become a Christian. The past and the future merge into one ecstatic horizonal moment of being a Christian. Exactly what this phenomenological repetition of Christian eschatology signifies—secularization, an implicit theological position, or a denial of theological eschatology—is disputable. What is clear, however, is that the repetition has significance for understanding the ontological status of theology. There is nothing theologically neutral about this phenomenology of religion.

Augustine

Heidegger's intermittent but intensive studies of Augustine are documented in a variety of sources, from scattered remarks in lectures and correspondence, to the 1921 lecture course, "Augustinus und der Neuplatonismus," and a still unpublished lecture on Augustine's treatise on time, delivered in 1930 to the monks at Beuron.[21] Like his reading of Paul, Heidegger's approach to Augustine in the 1921 lectures also has a Diltheyan root. According to Dilthey, Augustine carried Christian interiority further than any previous author. Yet Augustine failed to follow through with his breakthrough. Dominated by neo-Platonism and "the objective authorities of the Catholic Church," Augustine inaugurated 1000 years of revived Greek metaphysics. Dilthey balances his praise for Augustine's originality with sharp criticism: "Thus out of his self-reflection, chiefly

---

21. Martin Heidegger, "Des heiligen Augustinus Betrachtung über die Zeit. Confessiones Liber X," Bibliotheca Beuronensis, Erzabtei St. Martin, Beuron, Germany. To be published in *GA*80. On Augustine and Heidegger, see Kisiel, *Genesis of* Being and Time, 105–8; Craig J. N. de Paulo, "The Augustinian Constitution of Heidegger's Being and Time," *American Catholic Philosophical Quarterly* 77 (2003): 549–68; idem, *Being and Conversion* (Xlibris Corporation: 2002); idem, ed., *Augustine, Heidegger and Augustinian Phenomenology* (New York: Fordham University Press, 2005); Friedrich Wilhelm von Hermann, "Die 'Confessiones' des Heiligen Augustinus im Denken Heideggers," in Esposito and Porro, *Quaestio* 1:113–46; idem, *Augustinus und die phänomenologische Frage nach der Zeit* (Frankfurt am Main: Vittorio Klostermann, 1992); Costantino Esposito, "Heidegger und Augustinus," in *Annäherungen an Martin Heidegger*, ed. Hermann Schäfer (Frankfurt am Maim: Campus, 1997), 275–309.

through the Platonic concept of the *veritates aeternae*, metaphysics surfaced once again."[22] The Christian breakthrough to the most intimate sphere of personal existence was biblical, but the thematization of the experience, according to Dilthey, was Augustine's contribution. A new respect for the "matter" of an individual life distinguishes the *Confessions* from ancient autobiographies. For Augustine, Dilthey writes, "the whole external world is only of interest in so far as it means something for the life of his soul."[23] Heidegger was so impressed by Dilthey's analysis of Augustine that he cited long passages from it in his notes, including the following, where Dilthey remarks on Augustine's breakthrough to a new topic for philosophy: "life":

> Here at last [in Augustine] an enormous reality emerges in self-consciousness, and this knowledge swallows up all interest in studying the cosmos. Hence this self-examination is not merely a return to the epistemological ground of knowledge, and what derives from it is not merely theory of knowledge. In this awareness, the very essence of his self occurs to a human, and his conviction of the reality of the world is at last assigned its place; above all the essence of God is apprehended in that awareness, indeed it seems to half uncover even the mystery of the Trinity. This intimate awareness includes not just thinking but the totality of my person. Using an expression both profound and true, Augustine calls the object of self-certainty *life*.[24]

In "Augustinus und der Neuplatonismus," Heidegger offers an interpretation of *Confessions*, Book 10 (*GA*60 157–299). Heidegger's reading of Augustine's notion of care *(cura)* comes to fruition in *Sein und Zeit*, where it morphs into the doctrine of *Sorge*.[25] In the course of Augustine's self-analysis, it emerges that the *how* of being a self is care, modified as trouble *(molestia)*, trial *(tentatio)*, and restlessness *(cor inquietum)*. Heidegger notes that for Augustine *cura* takes one of two directions. It is either dispersed among the things of the world—in which case it is a tor-

---

22. Dilthey, *Introduction to the Human Sciences*, 235.
23. Ibid., 234.
24. Ibid.
25. Heidegger acknowledged his debt to Augustine in a 1925 dry run of the principle themes of *Sein und Zeit*: "It was seven years ago, while I was investigating these structures in conjunction with my attempts to arrive at the ontological foundations of Augustinian anthropology, that I first came across the phenomena of care" (*GA*20 418/302).

ment to itself—or recollected in a concentrated love for God. Heidegger repeats Dilthey's critique: Augustine's insight into the ontology of the human being, even at the moment of breakthrough, is obscured by his neo-Platonic theorizing. The factical ground of being human is forgotten and a neo-Platonic *telos,* eternal-truth *(veritas aeternae),* is substituted in its place. Augustine ostensibly smothers the historical self with neo-Platonic theology: being in its primary sense becomes the being of the worldless, eternal, uncaused cause. The unique attributes of human being disengaged in the *Confessions,* restlessness, care, the being of the past in memory, and being toward the future, are denigrated to shadows, half-real, participated being—not positive phenomena, but privations of the fullness of being that God alone enjoys. The move is of decisive significance in Heidegger's new post-Lutheran interpretation of Scholasticism. Augustine's existential thrust went underground in the Middle Ages, living on the fringes of the theological tradition, in medieval mysticism, while his revived and Christianized Greek metaphysics took central stage.

Augustine's self-experience is not Descartes's reflective grasp of a worldless ego, but the knowledge and love constitutive of an emphatically en-worlded existence. Heidegger notes this difference between Augustine's polemic with ancient skepticism and Descartes's *cogito ergo sum.* In a passage from *The City of God,* Augustine says that he cannot doubt that he *lives* because he is in fact living: "We exist; we know that we exist, and we are glad of this existence and knowledge. . . . In respect of those truths I have no fear of the arguments of the Academics. They say, 'Suppose you are mistaken?' I reply, 'If I am mistaken, I exist.' A non-existent being cannot be mistaken; therefore I must exist, if I am mistaken."[26] Augustine cannot doubt that he lives because he is immersed in life—his thinking is an expression of life. Heidegger comments: "Self-certainty can only be interpreted from out of factical being, it is only possible in faith" (*GA*60 299).

The self is disclosed in the state of being troubled over oneself *(oneri mea sum).*[27] "In your eyes," Augustine prays, "I have become a problem to

---

26. Augustine, *City of God,* trans, Henry Bettenson (New York: Penguin Books, 1972), bk. 11, chap. 26, p. 459. Dilthey comments on the same text. Cf. Dilthey, *Introduction to the Human Sciences,* 234 ff.

27. Augustine, *Confessions,* bk. 10, chap. 28, p. 202.

myself, and that is my sickness" *(in cuius oculis mihi quaestio factus sum, et ipse est languor meus).*[28] To problematize the self in this way is not the enactment of a reflective relationship. The self only comes to know itself in trial and temptation; it is fundamentally opaque to itself and only grasps itself obliquely. As Heidegger puts it, *molestia* is "the *how* of factical experiencing" (GA60 231). The self is tormented by the dissipation of its desires. Yet it remains hidden from itself, and so a deliberate, reflective reordering is not even possible. Augustine writes: "I have great fear of my secrets which your eyes know but mine do not" *(multum timeo occulta mea, quae norunt oculi tui, mei autem non).*[29] The process of recollecting and properly directing *cura* must be surrendered in "fear and trembling" to the grace of the God who alone sees into our hearts.

Heidegger examines how Augustine's notion of the happy life is formally indicated in the relational-sense of distress over one's life. The task is to remember God, and on the strength of the memory, to love God with one's whole heart: "Late have I loved you, beauty so old and so new" *(Sero te amavi, pulchritudo tam antiqua et tam nova).*[30] Augustine searches the caverns of memory for traces of the God who cannot be found among the things of nature. Yet his memory does not contain an image of God. How can he look for God if God is not remembered? How can we look for that which we have never known? We may not know God, but we know our hunger for Him. The desire itself becomes a clue, the *how* takes precedence over the *what*. To seek God is not to seek that which we once had and have since lost. It is rather to be directed toward an end that makes our present state of existence intolerable. To seek the *vita beata*, Augustine says, is to seek God. The search is not guided by a memory, but by a present concern. Kisiel puts it well: "*How* the happy life in the search for it is alive in us will expose *what* is thereby intended. And so Augustine does not get around to defining the *vita beata* content-wise, as he had originally intended. Instead, the question abruptly changes and he confronts the problem of *how he can come to* the happy life."[31] Because the happy life is negatively intended, it can be present to the soul in absence (GA60 196). Heidegger fixates on this content-poor yet for-

---

28. Ibid., bk. 10, chap. 33, p. 208.
29. Ibid., bk. 10, chap. 37, pp. 214–15.
30. Ibid., bk. 10, chap. 27, p. 201.
31. Kisiel, *Genesis of Being and Time*, 198.

mally over-determined desire for God as a phenomenologically charged structure. As primarily a relational-sense, the happy life is "only genuinely there in a context of enactment. It must be existentially manifest . . . in a determinate articulated factical historical context of enactment" (*GA*60 198).

Heidegger's 1921 critique of Augustine contains an original version of the critique of onto-theology. Augustine's faith does not grasp a *what*. God is not available to Augustine for detached theoretical inspection. God is only present in absence. The divine shows itself by *not showing* itself. To substitute an objective concept for the God formally indicated in our desire for happiness is to destroy the primary referent of religious language: not a thing but a possibility for being, a particular form of life. According to Heidegger, the substitution of an ontic intention, an object, for a purely factical structure is precisely what happens when the disclosures of historicity in Augustine are subsumed into neo-Platonic metaphysics. The restlessness of human existence resolves itself in the *tranquillitas* of the *visio beatifica*. Augustine writes "What else is it to live happily and blessedly but to possess an eternal object through knowing it?"[32] The happy life is objectified, transferred to a realm beyond history. Enjoyment of that which does not change, a fundamentally aesthetic and non-temporal comportment, becomes the basic orientation of life. This is "neo-Platonic axiologization," the imposition of a hierarchy of values onto the factic. "Thus was the turn to metaphysics brought about: the eternal truths are the ideas in the absolute consciousness of God. A parallel analysis is applied to the experience of will. Knowledge takes on the character of the essence of substance. The human soul is changeable, yet it extends to an unchangeable ground, the inner experience of the existence of God" (*GA*60 164).[33] With reference to Luther's *theologia crucis*, Heidegger describes this decisive interjection of Greek metaphysics into Augustine's thinking as the root that blossoms into Scholastic philosophical theology. *Contemplatio* is substituted for the *expectatio* of Christian faith. "The fundamental aesthetic meaning of enjoying *(frui)*: that which

---

32. Augustine, *Eighty-Three Different Questions*, trans. David L. Mosher, in *The Fathers of the Church*, vol. 70 (Washington, D.C.: Catholic University of America Press, 1982), 49–52.

33. Cf. Dilthey, *Introduction to the Human Sciences*, 233–37.

is enjoyed *(fruendum)* is tripartite, intelligible and beautiful things ... incorruptible and ineffable beauty—God. *Frui* is the fundamental characteristic of the basic Augustinian comportment to life. Its correlative term is beauty; it contains an aesthetical moment, as does the *summum bonum.*—Therewith a basic dimension of the medieval object of theology (and of spiritual history in general) is determined: it is the specifically Greek concept. The enjoyment of God *(fruitio Dei)* is a decisive concept in medieval theology; it is the main motive that leads to the development of medieval mysticism" (*GA*60 272).

Nonetheless, Augustine remains exceptionally sensitive to the factic. This ontological instinct shows itself in his treatise on time (*Confessions*, Book 11). Heidegger acknowledged the importance of Augustine's theory of time in several places.[34] However, it was in the Beuron lecture that he stressed the radicality and primordiality of Augustine's understanding of time. Heidegger situates Augustine's treatise on time alongside Aristotle's fourth book of the *Physics* and Kant's "Transcendental Aesthetic" of the *Kritik der reinen Vernunft* as one of the three pioneering treatments of time in the history of Western philosophy. He argues that the *Confessions* is misinterpreted as an autobiography. Rather, it is a three-part interpretation of the historical self, part one consisting of the account of Augustine's life (Books 1–9), part two, the analysis of memory (Book 10), and part three, the analysis of time, creation, and the Trinity (Books 11, 12, and 13). Augustine's repetition of his life story discloses the self as essentially constituted by development, change, and conversion, that is, by time. Augustine makes an advance over Aristotle by uncovering the intimate relationship between time and the soul. Aristotle raised the question of the being of time, asking if time, which consists in the counting of moments, has some relation to the soul: "But if nothing other than the soul or the soul's mind were naturally equipped for numbering, then if there were no soul, time would be impossible."[35] Augustine shows that time does not exist without the soul. Because neither the past nor the future have being in themselves, they can only subsist in the soul: the being of the past is its presence in memory *(memoria)*, the being of the future

34. *BZ* 5–6; *GA*24 325–26/229–30; *SZ* 427/391.
35. Aristotle, *Physics*, 4.14.223a, 25. See *SZ* 427.

is its presence in anticipating *(expectatio),* and the being of the present is its continuing presence in perception *(contuitus).* By remembering, I give the past being; by expecting, I give the future being. I stretch myself backward and forward and open up the temporal horizon. In a striking foreshadowing of *Sein und Zeit,* time, Augustine concludes, is an extension of the soul *(distentio animi).*

The Significance of Heidegger's Religious Sources

Augustine's breakthrough to the self was concomitant with his discovery of his need for God—a fact Heidegger conveniently overlooks. In his flight from God, the years of rebellion prior to his conversion, Augustine's self was a fragmented and chaotic swirl of passions, lacking unity and direction. Faith illuminated the precariousness of his existence, unified the unrelated events of his life, and synthesized the otherwise conflicting passions of his heart. Why is it that Augustine's self shows itself in the God-relation? The question can also be directed to Heidegger's interpretation of Paul. Why is it that temporality comes into sharpest focus in the context of a religiously intensified existence?

Augustine understands the human being as a stretching toward absolute presence, a divinity that is not comprehended but anticipated. Within the horizon of this anticipation, the finitude of every being becomes visible, as though profiled against light. Dasein, by contrast, stretches toward nothingness. From out of the opening created by the stretch, all creative possibilities for understanding and being emerge. Heidegger assumes Augustinian restlessness is separable from its theological context. However, Augustinian restlessness is not theologically indifferent. Without the thought of God, Augustine would not have been driven to think about the self as he did. Far from mitigating the disclosure of the self, Augustine's idea of God lights up the self from within. Augustine is able to give an account of *who he is* because he at last understands *where he is going.* "God" does not name a content for Augustine but a life tendency, a possibility for being-in-the-world in a different way. The "axiologization" is his effort to work out the details of how the God-relation is to be enacted.

Augustine would passionately condemn Heidegger's contention that the hermeneutics of the self could be in principle atheistic. Without the obscure experience of God in prayer, Augustine would have no sense of himself. Existence becomes an issue for Augustine only in the context of his longing for God. "Because I am not full of you [God], I am a burden to myself" *(quoniam tui plenus non sum, oneri mihi sum).*[36] Heidegger's formalized restlessness, his "theologically neutral" portrait of the troubled self without that which troubles it, succeeds no more than his formalized eschatology. *Angst* is primarily religious and cannot be properly thematized without a religious referent. We may formally indicate the referent with the term "death." But to speak of Dasein's experience of death without addressing the religious questions and symbols that have always accompanied it (Heidegger's strategy) is not formalization but distortion.

Heidegger turned abruptly from theological sources to Aristotle in 1921. Was this turn motivated by a desire to distance himself from the theological tradition in which the first part of his career was enmeshed, perhaps to correct Dilthey and show that the experience of the historical self is not, as it appears, bound up with Christian theology?[37] Heidegger could not have found his being-unto-death in Aristotle's ethics, for the simple fact that it is not there. *Eudaimonism* lacks the stark contrast between the fullness of the *eschaton* and the transience of the moment, which Dilthey held to be crucial to the disclosure of history.[38] Aristotelian happiness is emphatically this-worldly, the practice of moderation in a life lacking nothing. To measure the instant against a moral principle is indeed to profile the present against the future. But to anticipate your whole life as a being-before-God—this is a projection on a different scale, so much more intense that it is in fact different in kind.

36. Augustine, *Confessions,* bk. 10, chap. 28, p. 202.

37. Caputo remarks that Heidegger's drawing on both Aristotle and early Christianity in the hermeneutics of facticity stands in marked contrast to the later "myth of the single origin" of thinking in pre-Socratic philosophy. See John D. Caputo, *Demythologizing Heidegger* (Bloomington: Indiana University Press, 1993).

38. William McNeill argues that Heidegger finds a figure for ecstatic temporality in Aristotle's practical syllogism. In applying an ethical principle, we return to the moment in the light of our projected end. The exercise of virtue summons forth our character. To this degree, it is an enactment of our past in light of what we deem to constitute happiness, our future. McNeill writes: "Practical vision is ultimately *eschatological* in that it discloses, and thus itself comprises, in its very operation, an *eschaton* that marks the limit of *logos.*" McNeill, *Glance of the Eye,* 44. To call this an eschatological moment, however, seems farfetched.

If we believe Heidegger in "Phänomenologie und Theologie," authentic Christian theology is released to its own possibilities by ontology. But an inauthentic theology, which dilutes the faith with ontological concerns, and presumes to have something to say about matters philosophical or ontological, is silenced. What is in fact going on here is philosophy setting the proper boundaries to theology. Heidegger has promoted a certain version of Christianity by so structuring his ontology as to disallow others. A Catholic ontologically anchored theology, and a liberal Protestant theology, both of which would argue for a mutual exchange between philosophy and theology (although for different reasons and to different ends), are ontologically precluded by the analysis of Dasein as a Godless, irredeemably temporal, being-unto-death. A radical Protestant theology of revelation, which seeks no fusion with philosophy and regards revelation as a No to philosophy, remains the only possibility for theology.

In the 1936 Schelling lectures, Heidegger answers the charge of secularization with the accusation that Christian theology is itself bound up with an inauthentic appropriation of philosophical themes. "Christian theology is a Christianization of non-Christian philosophy and only for this reason can Christian theology be secularized. All theology of faith is only possible on the ground of philosophy, even when it regards philosophy as the devil's work" (*GA42* 87).[39] On this view, it would seem that the secularization of Christian themes in *Sein und Zeit* is philosophy reclaiming from Christianity what is rightfully its own. Certainly Heidegger has no historical ground to stand on here. It is a historical fact that the notions authenticity, guilt, conscience, and being-unto-an-end, which Heidegger appropriates in *Sein und Zeit* (and significantly alters to be sure), only enter into the Western conversation with the emergence of Christianity. But Heidegger's point runs deeper than this. One must distinguish a historical event from its ontological ground. The question is: what are

39. Cited in Phillip Capelle, "'Katholizismus,' 'Protestantismus,' 'Christentum' und 'Religion,'" 366. Capelle argues that too few commentators have recognized the pluralism in Heidegger's theological positions and the unresolved tensions behind this plurality. Capelle is particularly sensitive to the two sides of Heidegger's theological views: on the one hand, his sympathy for radical Protestantism and his attack on Catholicism from this perspective; on the other hand, the basically anti-Christian thrust of his thinking. Capelle does not presume to have an answer for how these two positions fit together. He does, however, point out that the old adage that Heidegger has secularized Christian theology fails to do justice to this ambiguity in Heidegger's thinking.

the sources of the Christian notions of authenticity, guilt, conscience, and being-unto-an-end? Heidegger is suggesting that these are not rooted in a supernatural revelation but in the ontology of the human being. In this light, a re-reading of Heidegger's scattered footnotes in *Sein und Zeit* discussing certain theological parallels to phenomenological ontology is called for.[40] Heidegger repeatedly claims that, contrary to appearances, his phenomenology does not draw on theological sources. This is highly doubtful in the light of Heidegger's early work on the phenomenology of religion. In fact, it seems almost absurd given the plethora of theological references in *Sein und Zeit* (not to mention all the theological works Heidegger studied but does not reference).[41]

Not only has Heidegger drawn from religious sources in order to develop an understanding of history, both Kierkegaard and Dilthey before him made their specific breakthrough to historical consciousness and *Existenz* in the context of theological research. Why have Christian theological texts repeatedly inspired philosophy in this way? What is there in the Christian story that drives us to rethink human life in such a way that factical dimensions of it hitherto hidden from view emerge into the light? For both Paul and Augustine, God is clearly and unequivocally Creator, the source and ground of all that is. Could it be an accident that

---

40. See div. 1, chap. 6, n. 4; sec. 45, n. 6; div. 2, chap. 1, n. 6. Note especially div. 2, chap. 3, n. 2: "The being guilty that belongs primordially to the constitution of being of Dasein is to be distinguished from the *status corruptionis* as it is understood by theology. Theology can find an ontological condition of its factical possibility in being guilty as it is defined existentially. The guilty contained in the idea of this status is a factical indebtedness of a completely unique kind. It has its own attestation that remains fundamentally closed off to every philosophical experience. The existential analysis of being-guilty does not prove anything *for* or *against* the possibility of sin. Strictly speaking, one cannot even say that the ontology of Dasein leaves this possibility open at all *of its own accord* since, as philosophical questioning, it 'knows' nothing about sin in principle" (SZ 306 n. 1 / 410–11). See also the disclaimer in sec. 38: "Our existential ontological interpretation thus does not make any ontic statement about the 'corruption of human nature,' not because the necessary evidence is lacking but because its problematic is *prior to* any statement about corruption or incorruption. Falling prey is an ontological concept of motion. Ontically, we have not decided whether human being is 'drowned in sin,' in the *status corruptionis*, or whether he walks in the *status integritatis* or finds himself in an interim stage, the *status gratiae*. But faith and 'worldview,' when they state such and such a thing and when they speak about Dasein as being-in-the-world, must come back to the existential structures set forth, provided that their statements at the same time claim to be *conceptually* comprehensible" (SZ 180/168).

41. Kisiel has compiled a bibliography of Heidegger's reading list on the phenomenology of religion during the years 1917–19. See Kisiel, *Genesis of Being and Time*, 525–26.

the thought of the Creator appears simultaneously in the tradition with the breakthrough to history and the discovery of the self? Or is there an essential relationship between these things? If there is—and it appears more than likely—we would have to say, in sharp contradiction to Heidegger and the critics of "onto-theology," that it is only in thinking ourselves created that we come to know what it means to be a self.

CHAPTER EIGHT

THE EFFORT TO OVERCOME SCHOLASTICISM

O Lord our God, when Moses asked of Thee as a most true Doctor, by what name he should name Thee to the people of Israel . . . Thou didst reply: Ego sum qui sum; wherefore art Thou true Being, total Being.

DUNS SCOTUS

Heidegger's later critique of onto-theology is rooted in his earliest efforts to de-Christianize metaphysics. It is no longer disputable that he was directly inspired by Luther's de-Hellenization of Christianity. Luther attempted to purify Christian theology of Greek metaphysics by dismantling the Aristotelian-Scholastic superstructure that had grown up over it; Heidegger undertook a complementary purification of metaphysics from Christian theology through a *Destruktion* of ontology down to its original Greek sources. I have argued that Heidegger's appropriation of a Lutheran paradigm for the *Destruktion* of the history of ontology is not theologically neutral; on the contrary, it is theologically motivated. Heidegger's Christian faith took a radical turn between 1916 and 1919, when he became Luther's silent partner, if not openly advocating Godforsakenness, at least constructing a phenomenology that reflects such a theological state. Heidegger's assumption that the horizon of being is time was intended to serve both philosophy and Lutheran theology. By uprooting the notion of *ens infinitum* and rendering it philosophically impossible, Heidegger hoped to free up both the factic sources of ontology and the biblical sources of theology.

Heidegger's effort to overcome Scholasticism, which culminated in the critique of onto-theology, began in his earliest lectures on phenomenology. In scattered theological disclaimers, he revealed his agenda: the deliberate disengagement of philosophy from the theistic horizon of medieval and early modern thinking. Initially, the effort appeared as the argument that facticity and God cannot be brought into relation with one another. The hermeneutics of facticity must resist the temptation to interpret facticity in non-factical terms. The notion of God as infinite or eternal being must be suspended. In the 1921 Aristotle lecture course, Heidegger claimed that philosophy betrays primordially given life when it speculates about infinite being. When philosophy loses itself in theology, it becomes a symptom of life's own inability to remain true to itself; in the language of *Sein und Zeit*, philosophical theology is an expression of inauthenticity. "With this infinity, life blinds itself, annuls itself. Incarcerating itself, life lets itself go. It falls short. Factical life lets itself go precisely by expressly and positively fending off itself" (*GA61* 108). By the end of the '20s, the argument developed into a more radical break with metaphysics and its theological support, the Scholastic notion of God as First Cause. The tension between facticity and infinity was recast in terms of temporality and constant presence. Philosophy's difficulty in thinking the factic becomes the challenge of thematizing temporality, a challenge repeatedly avoided in the metaphysical tradition. Metaphysics reduces being to an a-temporal mode of presence: to be is to be constantly present. Scholasticism is the chief culprit here with its twin notions of *essentia* and *existentia*, which are delivered over to modernity as categories exhaustive of ontology. To be is to be constantly present as a what (essence) or a that (existence). In the '30s, '40s, and '50s, Heidegger's effort to overcome Scholasticism hardened into the critique of creation metaphysics, onto-theology, and calculative reason. Facticity, temporality, and finitude are forgotten in systems of philosophy that posit an apodictic grasp of the cause of beings, the *prima causa*, the *summum bonum*, or the *causa sui*. In his later writing, Heidegger argued that metaphysics is essentially onto-theological. Onto-theology is at work in any philosophy of religion where "philosophy, of its own accord, and by its own nature, requires and determines how the deity enters into it" (*ID* 123/56). Metaphysics is inherently idolatrous.

The Destruktion *of Medieval Ontology*

The 1923/24 lecture course *Einführung in die phänomenologische Forschung* (GA17) is Heidegger's first full scale *Destruktion* of the ontological tradition. Heidegger shows how Husserl's original impulse "to the things themselves" becomes diverted by the search for certainty or "known knowledge." As a result, Husserl remains caught up in the Cartesian project. But lurking behind Descartes is the true root of the modern will to certainty, Scholasticism. Under the title "Rückgang auf die scholastische Ontologie. Das verum esse bei Thomas von Aquin" [The Deterioration in Scholastic Ontology. The Being of Truth in Thomas Aquinas] (*GA17* 162–94), Heidegger examines how Aquinas, by defining truth in relation to judgment, prepares the ground for modernity.[1] The Cartesian *res cogitans/res extensa* dichotomy is ostensibly grounded in the Thomistic interpretation of truth as correspondence between intellect and thing *(adaequatio rei et intellectus)*. According to Heidegger, truth is denied its own mode of being in Aquinas; truth *is* only to the degree that it stands in relation to an intellect that judges correctly. A proto-Cartesian figure is operative in Aquinas's interpretation of Aristotle's *De anima*. The knowing soul, the being that is in a manner all things, is identical in form to what is known. The true is a being *for* intellect, essence given a specific mode of existence in intellect: "Insofar as every being is graspable through the soul, the soul is in certain manner everything, it is the being-uncovering and being-possessing, the having of all beings" (*GA17* 169). The reduction of truth to a relation to intellect denies the ontological ground proper to truth itself; *verum* is merely another way of saying that something is grasped by the intellect. Truth no longer refers to the self-showing of things but to the adequacy of an intellectual act.

Heidegger looks at how Aquinas's notion of transcendental truth *(verum transcendens)* applies the *adaequatio* model to characterize God's relation to essences. By thinking essences, God invests them with the transcendental relation that makes them possible. Where in Descartes, the certainty of perception is anchored in the transparency of the *cogito,* in Aquinas, the certainty of judgment is ultimately anchored in the abso-

---

1. Heidegger's source texts are Aquinas's *De ver.*, q. 1, aa. 1, 2, 3, 4, 8, 9, and *ST* 1a, q. 2, a. 3.

lute *intentio* of the divine intellect. *Verum transcendens*, the truth of being and the condition of the possibility of judgmental truth, is the relation of created beings to the eternal intellect, the original being-known of all beings by the divine intellect.[2] When *adaequatio* is divinized in *verum transcendens*, it becomes impossible to think truth without reference to judgment. In Heidegger's reading, it is a small step from this Scholastic apotheosis of judgment to modern subjectivism. Descartes's *res cogitans/ res extensa* simplifies the *adaequatio* paradigm but preserves its essential structure. Truth is being for intellect. Being for intellect can be mathematized, calculated, and controlled. Thus does the way to technology open in the thirteenth century.

Heidegger closes the analysis with a look at Aquinas's five ways. He endeavors to show that implicit in each of the proofs for God's existence is an understanding of world, which will prove foundational for Descartes's notion of reality as extended thing *(res extensa)*. In the first way, the proof from movement, world is understood as a thing in movement, that is, as an act-potency composite. The second way, the proof from efficient causality, presupposes an interpretation of world as effect, something worked, and brought about through an act. The third way, the proof from necessity, presupposes world as that which can be other than it is, world as contingent thing. The fourth way, the proof from degrees of perfection, presupposes world as graded thing, that which exists in varying degrees. The fifth way, the proof from design, presupposes world as product, that which is determined to a certain end. World is conceived as moveable, effect, contingent thing, graded, and directed to a certain end, as that which is in various ways caused and therefore, as that which can be calculated, measured, and predicated.

An equally dismissive approach mars Heidegger's 1927 *Destruktion* of the distinction between *essentia* and *existentia* in Aquinas, Scotus, and Suárez (*GA*24 144–69/102–20). According to Heidegger, medieval ontology is exhausted in these two ontic categories, ostensibly "derived from Aristotle." "The medieval period shows no new approaches," Heidegger writes. "We cannot keep to the medieval terms, because they are not original but translations of ancient concepts. It is only by turning to the

2. See Aquinas, *De ver.*, q. 1, a. 4; a. 8.

latter that we shall be able to make visible their true origin" (*GA24* 144, 148/102, 105). Heidegger argues (unconvincingly) that the distinction was known to the Greeks, if only in an undeveloped form. It had "been well known since Aristotle and taken for granted as something self-evident" (*GA24* 110/78). Without proof, we are told that the distinction occurs in Plotinus, Proclus, Iamblichus, and is baptized by Dionysius the Pseudo-Areopagite. Through Scholasticism, the distinction becomes bound up with the metaphysics of creation. As a means for distinguishing uncreated from created being, the distinction eclipses the factic: if essence and existence, whatness and thatness, are presumed to exhaust the ontological field, Dasein must remain unexplored. Dasein is never a *what* or a *that*, but always only a *who*. The Greek paradigm for the distinction, the difference between *eidos* and *ousia*, has its roots in facticity (as do all genuine philosophical notions), but their factical origins are concealed in the Latin terms. The factical ground of the distinction can only be accessed through a *Destruktion* of the Latin terms back to their Greek roots.

It is not at all clear that *existentia* is derived from a Greek term. Etienne Gilson and Joseph Owens, for example, hold *existentia* to be a distinction lacking to Greek ontology.[3] After an examination of certain proto-phenomenological features of medieval ontology, Heidegger offers a forgettable analysis of the distinction between *essentia* and *existentia* in Aquinas, Scotus, and Suárez. Aquinas's *distinctio realis* is misread through Giles of Rome, who infamously argued that essence and existence are two things that are joined in creation (a position that Gilson has proven is not faithful to Aquinas).[4] Scotus's *distinctio formalis* is bare-

---

3. See especially Owens, *Doctrine of Being*.

4. See Gilson, *Being and Some Philosophers*, 172: "The very common mistake about this fundamental thesis of Thomism is always due to the same overlooking of the reciprocal character of efficient causality and formal causality. 'To be' is not a thing distinct in itself from 'essence' as from another thing. It is not, for the simple reason that taken in themselves, 'to be' and essence are not 'things.' Their composition alone is what makes up a thing, but they both become, so to speak, 'real' because 'to be' then is to be a 'being,' just as 'to be such' is to be 'such a being.' Actual existence, then, is the efficient cause by which essence in its turn is the formal cause which makes an actual existence to be 'such an existence.' Since they represent irreducibly distinct modes of causality, essence and existence are irreducibly distinct, but the reality of their distinction presupposes their composition, that is, it presupposes the actual reality of the thing. Existence is not distinct from essence as one being from another being; yet, in any given being, that whereby a being both is and actually subsists is 'really' other than that whereby it is definable as such a being in the order of substantiality."

ly mentioned. The focus of Heidegger's attention is Suárez, who seems to fascinate him because he alone did not bind the distinction to the doctrine of creation but rather, maintained that it was grounded in things themselves. Here, Heidegger notes, "the actual given being is taken as the primary court of appeal" (GA24 139/99). Nevertheless, like the Scholastics who preceded him, Suárez remains on the level of the ontic.

In the substantive section of the lecture, Heidegger endeavors to show how the ostensible Greek prototypes of *essentia* and *existentia*, *eidos* and *ousia* are derived from "a productive comportment of Dasein" (GA24 147/105). The distinction between *essentia* and *existentia*, Heidegger argues, translates ancient concepts that were originally employed to describe the making of artifacts. They were appropriated by medieval theologians to explain the theological dogma of creation, but they need no theology to be understood. All production proceeds by way of an image that acts as the producer's model, the form or *eidos* in Aristotle's metaphysics, "that which a thing already was" *(quod quid erat esse)*. When a thing is produced, the *eidos* is actualized and given existence. The product is released into a state of independence from its producer and becomes a real thing. For Scholastic theology, all beings are actualizations of possibilities, essences to which existence is added. God is distinguished from all that He produces in so far as He alone does not need to be produced. Things have a preexistence in God—they are essences without existence—as the form of an artifact has a preexistence in the mind of the artisan.

The prephilosophical notion, *eidos*, as the model or image by which a being is crafted or made, becomes in Plato the concept of eternal form. The model that precedes the production is understood to be free of imperfections—the idea in the mind of the craftsman is a vision of a flawless product. Consequently, *eidos* is interpreted as timeless being. Production externalizes *eidos* and releases the product into independent existence. This is the genesis of the modern notion of being as object of intuition: that which shows itself as existing, independent of the perceiver. The prephilosophical meaning of *ousia* is property, that which is present-at-hand in a household, that which, at any given moment is available for use and over which I have the right of disposal. *Ousia* comes to mean *Vorhandensein*, the objective presence corresponding to *eidos*.

In Heidegger's view, the *essentia/existentia* distinction not only fails to contribute anything new to the tradition, it succeeds in covering up these primordial Greek concepts, which are vital indications of Dasein. Heidegger notes that the Scholastic substitutes for *eidos* and *ousia* lack the Greek reference to a human producer. Scholasticism obscures an important indication of Dasein operative in the Greek. A producer is not a product; thus, the everyday understanding of production implies a difference between producer and produced. When Christianity appropriates Greek ontology in a theology of creation, all being becomes product in relation to the Creator. The producer, God, is a nonfactical being, a being outside of time. The nonproduct character of Dasein is forgotten.

Heidegger concludes by observing that being cannot be exhausted by terms drawn from production; not every being is constituted by whatness and thatness. "The basic concept of *essentia*, whatness, first becomes really problematic in the face of the being we call Dasein. The inadequate founding of the thesis as a universally ontological one becomes evident. If it is to have an ontological significance at all, then it is in need of a restriction and modification" (*GA*24 170/120). Dasein is never at hand like an object; it cannot be accessed in terms of *essentia* and *existentia*. *Existenz*, unique to Dasein, is fundamentally different from "having existence" *(existentia).* "Dasein, cannot at all be interrogated as such by the question what is this? We gain access to this being only if we ask: who is it? Dasein is not constituted by whatness but—if we may coin the expression—by *whoness*. The answer does not give a thing but an I, you, we" (*GA*24 169/119–20).

Heidegger returned to *essentia* and *existentia* in the section of the 1941 Nietzsche lectures entitled "Die Metaphysik als Geschichte des Seins."[5] The Scholastics are assigned their ignominious place in "the history of being" as the chief perpetrators of the forgetfulness of being in the modern age. The distinction between *essentia* and *existentia* is no longer interpreted as merely a Latinization of Greek ontology and an occasion for the forgetting of Dasein; it is now the epoch-making moment that makes metaphysics possible. "The division into whatness and thatness does not

---

5. *GA*6.2 363–416; English translation: "Metaphysics as the History of Being," in Martin Heidegger, *The End of Philosophy,* trans. Joan Stambaugh (New York: Harper & Row, 1973), 1–54.

just contain a doctrine of metaphysical thinking. It points to an event in the history of being" (*GA*6.2 366/4). *Essentia* and *existentia* configure being as effected thing, work, or present-at-hand entity, that which can be caused, made, calculated, and manipulated. Heidegger traces *existentia* to *actualitas*, which is derived from *agere*, "to act." To exist is to have an *essentia* that is given *actualitas* through efficient causality, to be brought into actual being from a prior state of possible being. Within the horizon of *actualitas*, being is reduced to the spatio-temporal nexus of causes thematized by natural science. Only that *is* which acts or is capable of causally acting on another.

Actualitas is a Latinization of *energeia*, the Greek term for a thing's coming to stand in its outward appearance. For Aristotle, *energeia* is the process by which a being is brought to presence, gathering into itself all the movements that converge upon its moment of appearance. *Actualitas*, on the other hand has an inescapable causal reference. Through the translation of *energeia* into *actualitas*, thinking loses touch with *physis*, the spontaneous upsurge of being from nothingness. In Heidegger's reading of Aristotle, *energeia* means "presencing as work." This is not a causal act by which a thing is effectively brought to stand over and against us, but "the presencing, standing there in unconcealment, of what is set up" (*GA*6.2 368/5). The primordial notion of work has a temporal reference that is absent from the Scholastic notion of *actualitas*. The work does not timelessly exist but gathers into itself all that has gone into bringing it about. The work rests in its being completed. A sense for the spontaneous emergence and withdrawal of beings, still alive in Aristotle's notion of *energeia*, is lost in the Scholastic translation.

The Scholastic reduction of being to a causal nexus is complete in the apotheosis of cause, the creator God.[6] The notion of the First Cause who

---

6. "The causal character of being as reality shows itself in all purity in that being which fulfills the essence of being in the highest sense, since it is that being which can never not be. Thought 'theologically,' this being is called 'God.' It doesn't know the state of possibility because in that state it would not yet be something. In every not-yet there lies a lack of being, in that being is distinguished by permanence. The highest being is pure actuality always fulfilled, *actus purus*. Effecting is here the persisting presencing of itself of what persists of itself. This being *(ens)* is not only what it is *(sua essentia)*, but in what it is, it is always also the persistence of what it is *(est suum esse non participans alio)*" (*GA*6.2 378–79/15).

is being itself *(ipsum esse)* represents the definitive supplanting of unconcealment with constant presence; it is as such the metaphysical concept *par* excellence. It eclipses *physis;* no being spontaneously emerges when all is caused. "Because the whole of being is the effected and effecting product of a first producer, an appropriate structure enters the whole of beings which determines itself as the co-responding of the actual produced being to producer as the highest being" (GA6.2 382/18). The "appropriate structure" of being, the paradigm for the relation to beings, becomes correspondence, *adaequatio.* As in 1924, Heidegger draws a close connection between Scholastic theology and modern ontology. For the Scholastics, judgment is the authentic way of relating oneself to beings that have been created through an act of divine judgment. Certainty becomes the way of securing *actualitas* within thinking. Where God is the bearer of truth in the Middle Ages (the one who establishes being as *verum transcendens*), the human is the bearer of the truth in modernity, establishing being as clear and distinct cognition *(clare et distincte percipio).* "Certainty decides about the adequate relation to what is real" (GA6.2 388/24).

Heidegger's twenty-year polemic with Scholasticism can be summed up in the following three theses: (1) Scholasticism makes certainty (apodictic judgment/*scientia*) the proper mode of access to beings. This epistemological relation is theologically established in the Scholastic interpretation of divine creation as an act of judgment; (2) Scholasticism always considers being in ontic terms, as whatness, objective presence, or *actualitas* and thus fails to acknowledge the ontological difference; (3) Scholasticism sets up world as product and delivers to modernity the conceptual paradigm it needs to get technology off the ground. That each of these accusations applies to most forms of philosophical theism should not be overlooked. Heidegger's polemic with Scholasticism is rooted in a more basic opposition to the notion of divine creation.

Onto-theology and Thomism

The question of the degree to which the onto-theology critique implicates Aquinas is a recurrent theme in the Thomistic reception of Heidegger. Many authors argue that Heidegger's critique is aimed at totalizing a priori systems, not Aquinas's creationism. Aquinas, unlike Hegel, for example, explicitly recognizes the finitude of human thinking. Others hold that the onto-theology critique implicates all ontologies that invoke a Creator. I am of the latter opinion. Heidegger's life project is to think the finitude of being without referencing the infinite. The difficulty in deciding the question is that Heidegger's onto-theology critique has a thick and a thin version, and Heidegger is not always clear on the distinction between the two. The thick version is directed at any ontology that references God as an explanation of why beings are. It has its seeds in the early Heidegger's Luther-inspired theological silence, and comes to its most acute expression in the '20s and early '30s. In the 1928 lecture course *Metaphysische Anfangsgründe der Logik im Ausgang von Leibniz*, Heidegger argues that philosophy has no resources to articulate a notion of God. The theistic interpretation of transcendence as that which exceeds and finitizes human experience is philosophically unclarified. Its ground is not a putative experience of that which exceeds Dasein but rather, the over-passing essential to Dasein's being. Dasein is always transcending, "crossing-over," not only in so-called religious experience, but in the everyday experience of care. As such, transcendence does not indicate divinity but finitude. In a characteristic aside, Heidegger adds that the philosopher who forswears all easy theological talk in the interest of remaining faithful to facticity is the genuinely religious thinker; the others, those who presume to speak of God in philosophy, are chatterers and idolaters.[7]

---

7. See *GA26* 211 n. 3/165 n. 9: "The problem of transcendence must be drawn back into the inquiry about temporality and freedom, and only from there can it be shown to what extent the understanding of being qua superior power, qua holiness, belongs to transcendence itself as essentially ontologically different. The point is not to prove the divine ontically, in its 'existence,' but to clarify the origin of this understanding-of-being by means of the transcendence of Dasein, i.e., to clarify how this idea of being belongs to the understanding-of-being as such.... The idea of being as a superior power can only be understood out of the essence of 'being' and transcendence, only in and from the full dispersal belonging to the essence of transcendence ... and not by an interpretation referring to an absolute You, nor to the *bonum* as value or as the Eternal.... The above is purposely not dealt with in the lectures, because precisely here and now, with the enormously phony religiosity, the dialectical illusion is especially great. It is preferable to put up with the cheap accusation of atheism, which if it is intended ontically, is in fact completely correct. But might not the presumably ontic faith in God be at bottom godlessness? And might the genuine metaphysician be more religious than the usual faithful, than the members of a 'church' or even than the 'theologians' of every confession?" Cf. *PIA* 246/193–94 n. 9.

In the 1935 lecture course *Einführung in die Metaphysik,* Heidegger argues that theists cannot genuinely ask ontological questions because they erroneously believe that they already have their answer. The basic question of metaphysics, why is there something rather than nothing, is assumed to be answered in the God-hypothesis: things are because God created them. But this is not a philosophical answer to the question. It may function as a theological "answer" for the purpose of faith. But, in fact, such an answer does not respond to the question at all because it cannot ask it. Theology forecloses the question. The point of the question is not simply to find an answer but to incite in the questioner that state of wonder that is open enough to grasp beings in their sheer upsurge from nothingness. The theist has no eyes to see this.[8]

The thick onto-theology critique is deeply bound up with Heidegger's Lutheran sympathies, as I have argued. Philosophy in its Godforsaken state has no tongue to speak of God. The notions of transcendence, infinity, and eternity are projections of Dasein's own experience of freedom and temporality. We have no experience of God as such.

The thin onto-theology critique belongs to the later Heidegger. It is not a moratorium on God-talk as such but a critique of the God of metaphysics, the *causa sui,* who is posited as a solution to the problem of epistemological foundations. Knowledge of this principle allows the human being to arrogate to itself a divine overview. This construct is at work in all metaphysics insofar as metaphysics is a search for explanations. It comes to its sharpest expression, not in Scholasticism, but in modern rationalism and German idealism. The modern system builders elevate human understanding by inscribing within it an a priori grasp of the ground from which everything causally emerges. The critique came to the fore in Heidegger's posthumously published 1936 manuscript *Beiträge zur Philosophie (Vom Ereignis),*[9] the 1946 *Humanismusbrief,*[10] and the 1957 lecture "Die onto-theo-logische Verfassung der Metaphysik."[11] In these texts, Heidegger breaks his earlier theological silence and speaks of how the divine might enter into philosophy without philosophy falling into ontotheology. For example, in the *Beiträge,* Heidegger writes: "Considered ac-

---

8. *GA*40 8–10/7–9.
10. *GA*9 352 ff./267 ff.
9. *GA*65 409–17, 437–39/288–93, 308–10.
11. *SZ* 35–73/42–76.

cording to *metaphysics*, god must be represented as the most-being, as the first ground and cause of beings, as the un-conditioned, in-finite, absolute. None of these determinations arises from the divine-character of god but rather, from what is ownmost to a being as such, insofar as this is thought as what is constantly present, as what is objective and simply in itself and is this, in representing, explaining, attributed as what is most clear to god as ob-ject" (GA65 438/308). What is striking about this passage is that Heidegger no longer regards the divine as the topic of a nonphilosophical discourse (theology). Thinking is now approaching a position of saying something on this subject. Philosophy has, in Heidegger, overcome metaphysics. It no longer needs a God to explain beings. It turns to the divine to understand the divine on divine terms.

In the *Humanismusbrief*, Heidegger speaks of philosophy clearing a space for the thinking of the divine. "The human being is the shepherd of being ... called by being itself into the preservation of being's truth" (GA9 342/260). This being that both summons us and depends upon us is not God, or a ground of things. But this is not atheism: ontology can no more be atheistic than it can be theistic. It must acknowledge the boundaries which thinking sets for itself (GA9 352/267). The task for philosophy is to illuminate being in itself and to experience it in its truth. Does this thinking of being have any religious significance? Ontology does not lead upward into eternal act but downward into finitude and the all-consuming vortex of time. Nevertheless, insofar as it truthfully articulates the human situation, thinking (somehow) clears a space for the appearance of an unanticipated and unknowable divinity *(Wesensraum der Gottheit)* (GA9 352/267). Here the critique of onto-theology is not a moratorium on God-talk but a rejection of totalizing discourses that use a concept of God as a foundation for an a priori system. Heidegger's target is not the divine (singular or plural, philosophy cannot decide) but the postulate of an eternal cause of being, which could give rationality a calculative hold on beings.[12]

---

12. Merold Westphal has summarized the thin critique of onto-theology as follows: "The 'onto-theological constitution of metaphysics,' as he [Heidegger] understands it, means that God enters into philosophy, but only on philosophy's terms. God must be the unity of the universal and the highest in order to be *das Erste* and *das Letzte* as *ratio* and as *logos*. In other words, God must not merely be an all-encompassing principle in and for Godself, but in and for the totalizing project

Clearly, Descartes, Spinoza, Leibniz, and Hegel are guilty of using a concept of God as a foundation for a rational a priori system. Is Aquinas also guilty of onto-theology in this sense? The retrieval of the negative element in Aquinas is key to answering this question. Aquinas cannot use a concept of God as a foundation for a totalizing discourse because he does not have one. Aquinas affirms *that* God is, but he does not know *what* God is.[13] Lacking a concept of God, he never tries to be totalizing in his thinking. He does not build a system, but systematically thinks about that modicum of being which is given us to think. At its edges, his thinking unravels into mystery. As Josef Pieper points out, the negative element in Aquinas does not simply concern theology, it also concerns ontology.[14] Because God/being is unknown to us, an abyss lies at the heart of every created thing.[15] Where Descartes founds science on his indubitable possession of clear and distinct ideas, Aquinas says, "We do not know substantial forms as they are in themselves" *(formae substantiales per se ipsas sunt ignota)*.[16] To comprehend the thing would be to comprehend the mind of God, for created things are a likeness of the Creator. Hence Pieper speaks of an essential knowability paradoxically conjoined with an essential unknowability in every created thing. "Not only God Himself but also things have an 'eternal name' that man is unable to utter."[17]

---

of human thought. God must be the Alpha and the Omega in order that the human thinker can stand at the beginning and end of all things, including all in a comprehensive gaze. Thus the problem with causal talk about God is not that it reduces God to a kind of cosmic billiard ball; for, especially in the ex nihilo tradition, metaphysics has by no means forgotten the difference between infinite, creative causality and finite, efficient causality. The problem is rather that God is conceived as *causa prima* and *causa sui* in order to satisfy demands of a particular, human intellectual project, one that culminates, anything but innocently, in modern technology." Westphal, *Overcoming Ontotheology*, 231–32.

13. This is Aquinas's reason for rejecting Anselm's ontological argument. See Aquinas, *ST* 1a, q. 2, a. 1.

14. Josef Pieper, *The Silence of St. Thomas* (South Bend, Ind.: St. Augustine's Press, 1999), 47–71.

15. See chapter 5, note 49.

16. Aquinas, *Quaestio disputata De spiritualibus creaturis*, a. 11, ad 3.

17. Pieper, *The Silence of St. Thomas*, 65. See also ibid., 59–60: "This relation on which the truth of things is fundamentally based—the relation between natural reality and the archetypal creative thought of God—cannot, I insist, be known formally by us. We can of course know things; we cannot formally know their truth. We know the copy, but not the relation of the copy to the archetype, the correspondence between what has been designed and its first design. To repeat, we have no power of perceiving this correspondence by which the formal truth of things is consti-

Heidegger blurs this important difference between Scholastic theology and modern onto-theology.

Authors such as Merold Westphal have successfully interpreted the thin onto-theology critique as fully consistent with theism, a condemnation of a certain kind of idolatry in metaphysics. Westphal argues that the thin onto-theology critique is not in principle opposed to a theological position that does not presume absolute knowledge:

> The believer might [legitimately] speak as follows: "In affirming God as Creator I am affirming that there is an explanation of the whole of being and I am pointing in the direction of that explanation; but I am not giving it, for I do not possess it. To do that I would have to know just *who* God is, and just *how* and *why* God brings beings into being out of nothing. But both God's being and God's creative action remain deeply mysterious to me.... My affirmation of God as Creator is not onto-theological because it is not in the service of the philosophical project of rendering the whole of being intelligible to human understanding, a project I have ample religious reasons to repudiate."[18]

The Heideggerian purists are less inclined to leave room for Westphal's minimal philosophical theism. In a recent article, Paolo-Ludovika Coriando offers a summary of the current Heideggerian view of Aquinas, informed by Heidegger's *Beiträge* and its doctrine of "the last god."[19] Coriando charges Aquinas with (1) identifying God and being; (2) making God into the highest being; (3) using this presupposition of a highest being to erect a hierarchy of being, which then, in a circular fashion grounds the five proofs for the existence of this highest being; and (4) presupposing being as "objective presence" *(Vorhandenheit)* and allowing this presupposition to determine his philosophy and theology. Heidegger alone frees "the divine" *(das Göttlichen)* from these constructs. Coriando does not explain how (1) and (2) are even compatible. If God is being itself, how could He be the highest being? Surely the highest being would

---

tuted. Here we can notice how truth and unknowability belong together.... It is part of the very nature of things that their knowability cannot be wholly exhausted by any finite intellect, because these things are creatures, which means that the very element which makes them capable of being known must necessarily be at the same time the reason why things are unfathomable."

18. Westphal, *Overcoming Onto-Theology*, 7.

19. Paolo-Ludovika Coriando, "Das thomanische 'summum ens' in ereignisphänomenologischer Sicht," in Esposito and Porro, *Quaestio*, 1:235–43.

participate in being (alongside all lesser beings) and could not therefore be being itself. Coriando shows no sensitivity to the care with which Aquinas and his more serious readers distinguish the being in which all things participate *(ens commune* or *esse non-subsistens)* from the being of God *(ipsum esse subsistens)*.

Coriando tells us that Heidegger distinguishes himself as a genuine servant of the divine by offering at last an alternative to onto-theology and separating the divinity of the gods from the being of beings. These are, apparently, infinitely distant and incommensurable structures. They are not hierarchically related but stand wholly outside one another such that we can say that the gods are being-less and being is godless. Coriando quotes Heidegger: "The denial of being of 'the gods' means proximally only that being is not 'above' the gods, but neither are these above being" (*GA65* 438/308–9). Coriando comments:

> The denial shows the impossibility of traditional "metaphysical" determination of the divine. The denial of being of the "divine" signifies a freeing of the divine from every expression of being and essence, a renunciation of every conceptual determination, which would force the divinity of God into the sphere of objectifiability. Insofar as it is said that the divine *is not*, insofar as "being is denied of the gods in advance" (*GA65* 437), the sphere of the divine is freed from the grounding chains of ontotheologically interpreted being, and brought forward into an undecidability, in which the gods transcend the apparent obviousness of the talk of being and non-being. The possibility of a traditional theistic or atheistic standpoint is foreclosed by thinking.[20]

This is the now-familiar theme of Heidegger as negative theologian, one who affirms the divine but denies the *analogia entis*. There is no continuity between being and the divine and therefore no way of moving from the discussion of one to the other. "In the thinking of the *Beiträge* the divine is, in contradistinction to the metaphysical question about God, the being-less, the no-longer-a-being, the non-representable and inexpressible."[21] The language with which we articulate being, not only the language of metaphysics, but also the language of phenomenological ontology, has no application to the divine. Lacking a language with

---

20. Coriando, "Das thomanische 'summum ens,'" 240.
21. Ibid., 241.

which to speak of the divine, Heidegger gestures to "the last god," whose appearance can paradoxically neither be expected nor not-expected. Thus is the human being's "factical thrownness in the face of the enduring secret" brought to the fore.[22]

The later Heidegger's agnosticism-as-radical-piety has become popular among "postmodern" philosophers of religion (see Caputo, et al.). What is not, however, widely recognized is that an agnostic piety (or a revelational positivism) has dangerous repercussions for human culture, namely theocracy, Biblical fundamentalism, and irrationality. The revelation of a God who is wholly discontinuous with ontology is, as Barth never tires of telling us, a No to human knowledge and culture. Aquinas's *analogia entis* is intended to avoid this one-sided position by affirming a basic if ineffable continuity between the being of creation and the being of the Creator. At the same time, the analogy maintains the infinite difference between the created and the uncreated, and thus it also avoids the pitfalls of the opposite extreme, the rationalism that makes God continuous with created ontology and transparent to human reason and its consequence, the elevation of the human to the place of the divine. Neither the thick nor the thin version of the onto-theology critique preserves the delicate balance between identity and difference of Aquinas's *analogia entis*.

Aquinas's middle way between the extremes of agnosticism and rationalism has proven exceptionally difficult to negotiate. Early Reformation theology seizes on the agnostic extreme, underscoring the gratuity of revelation, and collapsing the *analogia* into separation. Modern onto-theology, developing the rationalist extreme under the influence of seventeenth-century humanism, collapses the *analogia* into identity. Luther exaggerates the similarity between God and being posited by the defenders of the *analogia entis*. Without difference, it would not be an *analogia*. On the other hand, modern attackers of Lutheran "one-sidedness" are often too quick to forget that in the *analogia* the unlikeness infinitely *exceeds* the likeness. Finite things image God, but we do not know exactly how and will not know until we see the essence of God in the *visio beatifica*. This does not mean, however, that things are unintelligible or that

22. Ibid., 242.

human intelligence is of no use; on the contrary, it means that things are infinitely intelligible. Finite intelligence has before it an infinite task.

Crucial to understanding the *analogia entis* is Aquinas's denial of a concept of absolute being.[23] As Siewerth points out, there is no concept of being in Aquinas (no *conceptus entis*), only a thinking of being *(conceptio entis)*. Hence Aquinas holds that our knowledge of God is limited to *nominal* definitions, provisional descriptions of God, which lack full explanatory power. Aquinas's term for God, "subsistent being itself" *(ipsum esse subsistens)*, expresses insight into the correct use of God-language, not insight into the essence of God.[24] Nominal definitions point away from themselves and invite their own surpassing. Aquinas's objection to Anselm's ontological argument is at root an objection to Anselm's implicit idolatry. Essential knowledge of God is impossible for a finite intellect. God is the *primum analogatum*, affirmed to exist, but never adequately conceptualized or grasped as a content. We can know *that* God is; we cannot know *what* God is. God is an inconceivable, infinite positivity, the fullness of the act of existence, *esse*, which even on a finite level, is never a concept.[25] Judgment is ordinarily consequent upon the grasp of an essence; yet God's existence is judged without a disclosure of essence. God is affirmed in the judgment that the ground of all judging cannot be

---

23. As Brian Shanley puts it, "To us *(quoad nos)*, the identity in God of essence and existence remains opaque.... The assertion that essence and existence are identical in God is really a negative claim rather than one based upon knowledge of the divine essence." Brian J. Shanley, *The Thomist Tradition* (Dordrecht: Kluwer, 2002), 180. See also Etienne Gilson, *Elements of Christian Philosophy* (New York: Mentor Omega, 1960), 119: "The negative theology of Thomas Aquinas is an energetic and eminently positive effort of the mind against the self-deception that it knows the essence of the highest object."

24. See Lonergan, *Insight*, 35–36: "Both nominal and explanatory definitions suppose insights. But nominal definitions suppose no more than an insight into the proper use of language. An explanatory definition, on the other hand, supposes a further insight into the objects to which language refers. The name 'circle' is defined as a perfectly round plane curve, as the name 'straight line' is defined as a line lying evenly between its extremes. But when one goes on to affirm that all radii in a circle are equal or that all right angles are equal, one is no longer talking of names. One is making assertions about the objects which names denote."

25. See Armand Maurer, introduction to Aquinas, *On Being and Essence* (De ente et essentia), trans. Armand Maurer (Toronto: Pontifical Institute of Mediaeval Studies, 1968), 18: "The mystery of being *(esse)* is identical with the mystery of God; if we know what *esse* is, we would know the essence of God, for only in him is *esse* an essence or nature. In creatures *esse* does not have the status of an essence; they have essences which are other than *esse* and which exist by participating in the divine *esse*."

accessed by a judgment. Each of Aquinas's five ways ends in a negation: God is not a motion in any finite sense of the term, God is not a cause in the series of efficient causes, and so on. The five proofs set up binaries binding on all that can be thought: act/potency, cause/effect, necessity/contingency, only to deny the binary of that which grounds it. Aquinas endeavors to think both similarity and dissimilarity, the positive *(kataphatic)* way and the negative *(apophatic)* way. He holds that God is in one sense "being," in another sense distinct from "being." What he never argues, *pace* Coriando, is that God is the highest instance of the genus being. In distinction from this delicate balancing act, Luther's path is relatively simple: for the paradoxical and inexpressible similar/dissimilar of the *analogia*, he substitutes dissociation. God and what appears to us as being are incommensurable. At some very early point in his career, Heidegger took Luther's path, and as Coriando helps us see, he never second-guessed his choice.

Heidegger shows no signs of ever having truly understood the radical break with Greek ontology in Aquinas's notion of being. "In the mind of Thomas Aquinas, the notion of being underwent a remarkable transformation," Gilson writes. Being no longer meant form *(eidos)* as it did for Plato, or substance *(ousia)* as it did for Aristotle; it meant *esse*, the act signified by the verb "to be."[26] Aquinas dissociates act from form in the notion of *esse*, and makes it possible to conceive infinity as perfection—a break with Greek "circular thinking."[27] When form or *eidos* is no longer identified with being, the ideal, the concept, becomes potency to a more fundamental act. *Essentia* is a limitation of *esse*, a contraction of the act of being to determinate structure. *Substantia* is a further contraction of *esse* to a particular *this*. In itself, *esse* is act without determination or limit. Containing within itself all formal differences, "in a more excellent way than other things," *esse* is participated in by everything that exists yet remains free of all generic, specific, and individual determinations.[28] In its concretization and finitization in the thing, *esse* is released from God and channeled into determinate thinghood.[29] Hence *esse* shows itself in

26. Gilson, *History of Christian Philosophy*, 368; cf. idem, *Spirit of Mediaeval Philosophy*, 74–76.
27. Gilson, *Being and Some Philosophers*, 174.
28. Aquinas, *On Being and Essence*, trans. Maurer, 62.
29. See W. Norris Clarke, *The One and the Many: A Contemporary Thomist Metaphysics* (Notre

everything without being reducible to anything. It is "the most formal of all things" *(maximum formale omnium)*.³⁰

Created *esse* (Siewerth's *ipsum esse non-subsistens*) is time-horizoned. It is the most temporalized of acts, the coming into presence of that which could be, that which, for the moment is, but need not be. *Esse* is not found apart from things; it is not itself a thing but something that a thing "does." It is not static, but the pure energy of *be-ing* (the participle understood here as a verb), the dynamic act of a thing's *being posited* outside the merely possible.³¹ Aquinas says that *esse* is to *essentia* as light is to the illuminated.³² The light metaphor shows that *esse* must be traced back to something other than *essentia*. In creation, God releases the energy of His infinite *esse* into a limited mode. The release is not a mechanical production of one thing from another—Heidegger also misrepresents this point. Creation is not a production at all. It is an act of self-limitation by which the being who has no other allows for another. The creature has a nature proper to itself and so we speak of *essentia* as the thing's formal cause, that to which the thing owes its determinate structure. Yet without God's efficient causality, neither the thing nor the thing's essence would have *esse*.³³ *Esse* is not a thing that can be separated from another thing, not a thing that comes together with a second thing *(essentia)* to compose a third thing, the existing substance.³⁴ The interpretation of the *distinctio realis* as a distinction between two things *(res)* originated two years after

---

Dame, Ind.: University of Notre Dame Press, 2001), 151: "The essence is like the restrictive channel along which flows and expresses itself the encapsulated energy of the act of existence."

30. Aquinas, *ST* 1a, q. 7, a. 1.

31. See Gerald B. Phelan, *The Existentialism of St. Thomas*, ed. Arthur G. Kirn (Toronto: Pontifical Institute of Mediaeval Studies, 1967), 77: "Things which 'have being' are not 'just there' (Dasein) like lumps of static essence, inert, immovable, unprogressive and unchanging. The act of existence *(esse)* is not a state, it is an act, the act of all acts, and, therefore, must be understood as act and not as any static and definable object of conception. *Esse* is dynamic impulse, energy, act,—the first, the most persistent and enduring of all dynamisms, all energies, all acts. In all things on earth the act of being *(esse)* is the consubstantial urge of a nature, a restless, striving force, carrying each being *(ens)* onward, from within the depths of its own reality to its full achievement, i.e., fully to be what by its nature it is apt to become."

32. See Aquinas, *In III Sent.*, d. 6, q. 2, a. 2, resp: "Being is always to be found in a thing, and is the act of a being, just as light is the act of the illuminated."

33. See Etienne Gilson, *The Christian Philosophy of St. Thomas Aquinas*, trans. L. K. Shook (New York: Random House, 1956), 448 n. 30.

34. Gilson, *Being and Some Philosophers*, 172.

the death of Aquinas with the writings of Giles of Rome.[35] According to Joseph Owens, Aquinas seldom uses the term *realis* to characterize the distinction between *esse* and *essentia*. Generally he avoids the term because of its connotation of a distinction between two things.[36] Things all have essences; *esse* has no essence. It is not a *what,* not a form, but an act that is in itself free of all determinate form.

What might Heidegger reply to this defense of Aquinas? He would have to concede that Aquinas does not identify being and substance. However, he would probably point out that, by identifying being with act, Aquinas nonetheless de-temporalizes being. *Esse* is "something fixed and at rest in being" *(aliquid fixum et quietum in ente).*[37] To be means to be the being of that which subsists and persists through time. Being is the *actus essendi,* the act of an essence, that is, the act of subsisting. God, *ipsum esse subsistens,* is not an exception to this de-temporalization but its primary instance. The point of the distinction between the being of God and the being of every created thing is to emphasize that *subsistence* is most perfectly found in God and only secondarily found in creatures. God cannot be called a substance in the same way that all other beings are called substances because God is *absolutely* subsistent, that is, absolutely present. God imparts something of this ontological stability to every created thing. That which is perfectly fixed and at rest (God) is most properly called being; that which is relatively fixed and at rest (substance) has being in a secondary sense; that which is not fixed and at rest in any way, but requires another being in order to exist (accident) has being in a qualified and derivative sense. The hierarchy of being is established in terms of changelessness, fixity, freedom from time.[38] A form can be de-

---

35. See Giles of Rome, *Theoremata de esse et essentia,* 19, ed. Edgar Hocedez (Louvain, 1930), 134, 11–13: "And just as matter and quantity are two things, so essence and being are really different things." Cajetan also understood the distinction in terms of a distinction between things. See his *In de ente et essentia,* chap. 5, ed. M. H. Laurent (Turin, 1934), 161, no. 102. Bañez was even more explicit. See his *In Primam partem summae theologiae,* I, 3, 4, ed. L. Urbano (Madrid and Valencia, 1934), I, 147a: "Being is really distinct from essence as thing from thing *(tanquam res a re).*"

36. See Aquinas, *In I Sent.,* d. 19, q. 2, a. 2; *De ver.,* q. 27, a. 1, ad 8. See Joseph Owens, *An Elementary Christian Metaphysics* (Milwaukee, Wis.: Bruce Publishing Company, 1963), 104n.

37. Aquinas, *SCG* I, 20.

38. The following passage shows that Aquinas differentiates the nominal and verbal sense of being and is, therefore, not guilty of substantializing it. Nonetheless, he identifies being with constant presence. This, for Heidegger, is enough to prove that Aquinas is forgetful of being: "For [is]

stroyed by God, but it cannot be "corrupted." It has no potency for non-being. Being is *actualitas,* presence in the present, capacity to abide all change and stand alone. Time is the theater of actualizations, the drama of a "now" that has no past and no future because it is in itself eternal. The now abandons the past to non-existence and enters a future that before its arrival has no being.[39] Such thinking is, according to Heidegger, metaphysical/onto-theological: it conceals temporality by absolutizing a particular mode of time: the present.

In his own defense, Aquinas would reject Heidegger's privileging of absence over presence, possibility over actuality, as irrational and atheistic. Heidegger's Lutheran assumption of Godforsakenness, which reappears in his later thinking as the separation of divinity from ontology, puts him in direct opposition to the creationism of Thomas Aquinas. No agreement is possible here: Heidegger and Aquinas speak out of diametrically opposed horizons.

Reading Aquinas after Heidegger

Thomists have a love/hate relationship with Heidegger. On the one hand, they are delighted that, after centuries of epistemology and positivism, a twentieth-century thinker has almost single-handedly revived ontology. Heidegger draws attention to problems central to Aquinas, for example, the difference between being and a being, or the inconceivability of being. On the other hand, Thomists must reject Heidegger's systematic effort to remove the notion of a Creator from ontology. In any case, they have found Heidegger unignorable. The challenge of understanding Heidegger's objections to metaphysics/onto-theology has been the occasion for a fertile rethinking of Aquinas.

---

means that which is understood after the manner of absolute actuality [*in intellectu per modum actualitas absolutae*]. For *is,* when it is expressed without qualification, means to be in act [*in actu esse*], and therefore it has its meaning after the manner of a verb. But the actuality, which is the principal meaning of the verb *is,* is indifferently the actuality of every form, either substantial or accidental act. Hence it is that when we wish to signify that any form or act actually inheres in any subject, we signify it by this verb *is,* either simply or according to some qualification—simply in the present tense; according to some qualification, in the other tenses." Aquinas, *In I Peryermenias,* lect. 5, no. 22. Translated in Gilson, *Being and Some Philosophers,* 220.

39. Gilson, *Being and Some Philosophers,* 160, 168. Cf. Owens, *Christian Metaphysics,* 52.

While the Europeans have been busy rereading Aquinas in the light of Heidegger for seventy years, the English-speaking world has suffered from a lack of translations of seminal post-Heideggerian Thomistic studies.[40] For many years, John Caputo's *Heidegger and Aquinas* was the only English monograph on the topic. Caputo's exposition of the unresolvable tension between Heideggerian ontology and Thomistic metaphysics contains some bibliographical information on the German and French literature. In the end, Caputo rejects these attempts at mediation. Aquinas interprets being causally, as *actualitas*, the effect of God's causal actualization of *essentia*. Heidegger rethinks being in the kinetic-temporal doubles of emergence/withdrawal, unconcealment/concealment, presence/absence. According to Caputo, one either takes a stand with Aquinas and Aristotelian-Scholasticism against Heidegger, or vice versa, but one cannot, *pace* Siewerth and Rahner, be a Thomistic Heideggerian.[41] Heidegger's *Sein* is not a cause; it is that which shows itself in and through the process in which beings come to be. Being is not a being, a what or a that, but the open horizon or "clearing" *(Lichtung)* that makes beings possible. For Aquinas by contrast, being is the act by which a thing becomes real, not the unconcealing that makes present, but the cause that produces.

Caputo is sympathetic to Max Müller who endeavors to free Aquinas from substance metaphysics by developing Aquinas's neo-Platonic metaphysics of participation.[42] "To be" for Aquinas is to participate in the coming into presence of infinite *esse*. The divine ground, *ipsum esse*, transcends form and remains unthought in every metaphysical investigation. This is the mystical heart of Aquinas's metaphysics, the unnameable mystery against which all rational constructs suffer shipwreck. For Caputo, however, Aquinas's notion of participation does not represent the heart of Aquinas's metaphysics but its undoing. As in Aquinas's career, which ended with the famous mystical experience that convinced him that all he had written was "straw," and after which he wrote no more,[43]

---

40. See the bibliography in Esposito and Porro, *Quaestio*, 1:463–77.

41. Ibid., 61–99.

42. Max Müller, *Existenzphilosophie im geistigen Leben der Gegenwart*, 3rd ed., rev. and enl. (Heidelberg: F. H. Kerle, 1964), 145.

43. James A. Weisheipl, *Friar Thomas d'Aquino: His Life, Thoughts, and Works* (Garden City, N.Y.: Doubleday, 1974), 321.

Caputo holds that the notion of *ipsum esse* leads to an "overcoming" of metaphysics, silence in the presence of the unconceptualizable source of all that is. Aquinas's successor, Meister Eckhart, perfected Aquinas's negative theology by explicitly identifying God with the nameless ground.[44]

In his earlier work, *The Mystical Element in Heidegger's Thought*, Caputo contrasts Scholasticism with medieval mysticism, holding that Heidegger's abolition of the former leaves the latter to some degree intact. He sketches a series of analogies between Heidegger's notion of being and Eckhart's *Gottheit*, without equating the two.[45] For both Eckhart and Heidegger, the experience of being is not an accomplishment but an occurrence; we can at best prepare for it by cultivating the openness that Eckhart calls in Middle High German *Gelâzenheit*, inadequately translated as "releasement." In the recovery of a relationship to being, both Eckhart and Heidegger see a return to truth from an everyday state of falsehood. Heidegger's distinction between the inauthentic self, lost in the anonymity of "the they" *(das Man)*, and the authentic self is a phenomenological figure of Eckhart's distinction between "the outer" and the "inner man." The former is dispersed among the multiplicity of sense experiences and worldly desires; the latter is unified and inviolably alone *(abgeschieden)* in its standing before God.[46]

However much the convergence of language, Eckhart remains a Christian theist and Heidegger a post-Christian thinker. Caputo points out that this foundational difference manifests itself in Heidegger and Eckhart's conflicting views on the meaning of being. For Heidegger, being is finite because it cannot be thought apart from the nothing: it reveals itself only in the transcendence of Dasein, "being-held-out-into-the-nothing" (GA9 115/91). For Eckhart, being is infinite, the unlimited *esse* in which

---

44. Caputo, *Heidegger and Aquinas*, 246–87.

45. Caputo, *Mystical Element*, 140–217. Cf. Sikka, *Forms of Transcendence*, 109–86. Also working with the problematic dichotomy of "metaphysical" Scholasticism and "non-metaphysical" mysticism, Sikka extends the examination beyond the more traditional Eckhart-Heidegger comparison to parallels between Heidegger and Bonaventure, Johannes Tauler, and Jan van Ruusbroec. Heidegger's relationship to Eckhart is a well-researched topic. In the German literature, see Helting Holger, *Heidegger und Meister Eckhart. Vorbereitende Überlegungen zu ihrem Gottesdenken* (Berlin: Duncker & Humblot, 1997); Bernhard Welte, *Meister Eckhart. Gedanken zu seinen Gedanken* (Freiburg: Herder, 1979). In the preface, Welte acknowledges that the work was born of a conversation about Eckhart he had with Heidegger in 1976.

46. Caputo, *Mystical Element*, 140–270.

everything participates. Eckhart and Heidegger's notions of being are at best analogous: Eckhart's *esse* does for creation what Heidegger's *Sein* does for beings.[47] Heidegger parts company with Eckhart at precisely the place where he parts company with every Scholastic: on the question of the relation of being to God. Eckhart thinks *esse* in relation to infinite being, which excludes all potency and therefore, temporality; Heidegger thinks *Sein* in relation to the being which we ourselves are, that is, within the radically finite horizon of time.

Gustav Siewerth studied under Heidegger at the University of Freiburg in the late 1920s and early 1930s. Untroubled by his teacher's growing antipathy for Scholasticism, and at considerable personal expense to himself in Nazi Germany, which had little patience or tolerance for "Christian philosophers," Siewerth interpreted Aquinas through Hegel and Heidegger in his 1930–31 doctoral dissertation, *Die Metaphysik der Erkenntnis nach Thomas von Aquin* [*The Metaphysics of Knowledge in Thomas Aquinas*] and his 1937 *Habilitationsschrift*, *Die transzendentale intellektuelle Anschauung bei Thomas von Aquin. Der Grund der Möglichkeit der Gotteserkenntnis* [*Transcendental Intellectual Intuition in Thomas Aquinas: The Condition of the Possibility of Knowledge of God*]. All but banished from the academy by the Nazis, he continued his Thomistic research without an academic post, producing several major works that rethink Aquinas's metaphysics in the light of nineteenth- and twentieth-century German speculation.[48] The originality and depth of his work greatly exceed his reputation in the English-speaking world, where he is scarcely known. Hans Urs von Balthasar regarded Siewerth as the greatest philosopher of the twentieth century.[49] In 1963, William Richardson described Siewerth's

47. Ibid., 183–84.
48. See *Gustav Siewerth. Gesammelte Werke*, vols. 1–4, ed. Wolfgang Behler and Alma von Stockhausen (Düsseldorf: Patmos, 1971–87). Andrzej Wierciński has recently published the first English monograph on Siewerth. See his *Inspired Metaphysics? Gustav Siewerth's Hermeneutic Reading of the Onto-Theological Tradition* (Toronto: Hermeneutic Press, 2003). See also idem, *Über die Differenz im Sein. Metaphysische Überlegungen zu Gustav Siewerths Werk* (Frankfurt am Main: Peter Lang, 1989); idem, *Die scholastischen Vorbedingungen der Metaphysik Gustav Siewerths* (Frankfurt am Main: Peter Lang, 1991); Emmannuel Tourpe, *Siewerth 'après' Siewerth. Le lien idéal de l'amour dans le Thomisme spéculatif de Gustav Siewerth et la visée d'un réalisme transcendantal*, Bibliothèque Philosophique de Louvain, vol. 49 (Louvain: Peeters, 1998); Manuel Cabada Castro, *Sein und Gott bei Gustav Siewerth* (Düsseldorf: Patmos, 1971).
49. Hans Urs von Balthasar, "Abschied von Gustav Siewerth," *Hochland* 56 (1963/64): 182–84.

work as "the most ambitious attempt thus far to let Heidegger's experience shed light on another type of thought.... [It] offers the most edifying spectacle of one of Europe's most powerful minds exuberantly engaged in his task."[50]

According to Siewerth, Heidegger's critique of *Seinsvergessenheit* indicts most of the history of philosophy with the exception of Aquinas, the last thinker of the difference between being and beings until Heidegger. For Siewerth, the question of ontological difference is the beginning of every genuine metaphysical inquiry. Metaphysics inevitably takes one of two directions: a monism in which the ontological difference is reduced to appearance (Platonism, Scotism, conceptualism, essentialism), or a pluralism, in which the difference is held to be irreducible (Aquinas, Heidegger).[51] Only in the latter is the difference problematized to the point where it becomes a creative spur that drives philosophy out of its perennial temptation to remain in the abstract. Medieval *Seinsvergessenheit* begins with Scotus, for whom being is exhausted in *essentia*. The Scotist denial of the real distinction of *essentia* and *existentia* and the related notion of *univocatio entis* (the denial of the inconceivability of God) set the stage for the subjectivism of German idealism.

Against this trend, Siewerth unfurls a set of Thomistic concepts reinterpreted in the light of Hegel and Heidegger. With other "existential Thomists," Siewerth distinguishes being *(esse)* from beings *(entia)* on the grounds that the latter possess *essentia*, whatness, which can be abstracted and conceptualized; the former is pure non-essential act. However, an "existentialist" formulation of the *distinctio realis* is not enough to meet Heidegger's critique of *Seinsvergessenheit*, for both whatness *(essentia)* and thatness *(existentia)* belong to the being of substances. Siewerth goes further than Gilson and distinguishes act and subsistence: the former is the pure, nonsubstantive, dynamic energy of coming into presence; the latter is the stasis of that which has come to be. Act finds subsistence in a being while remaining distinct from it. Every substance is in act, but not every act is subsistent.

The distinction between act and subsistence underscores the often

---

50. Richardson, *Through Phenomenology to Thought*, 687.
51. Wiercinski, *Metaphysik Siewerths*, 19–20.

overlooked Thomistic distinction between God and being. God "intimately" indwells every being as the act which is closest to it, for nothing is closer to a being than the act by which it is.[52] Yet God is not the being of things *(ens commune)*. If there were no difference between the *esse* of things and the *esse* of God, everything would be God. The being of a being is a *non-subsistent* act *(ipsum esse non-subsistens)*, the power that effects the sheer upsurge of beings from nothingness. Neither a being nor God, created being only comes to realization in a being and depends upon the subsistent being of God as much as beings depend upon it.[53] The being of God, on the other hand, is subsistent act *(ipsum esse subsistens)*, that which resides in itself, infinite, eternal, self-sufficient, excluding all potency, and requiring nothing else in order for it to be. As that which effects the emergence into presence of a being, created being is horizoned by the nothingness of primordial potency. "It [*Das Sein*] is so insignificant in itself that it is nothing but a pure 'indication' of the origin."[54] Nevertheless, as the first creation, created being is the image of God. Just as the triune God is a mediation through otherness (the Father is Father by virtue of the relation to the Son, etc.), the being of a being is an identity-in-difference, an identity that realizes itself through its other. Being, the "realizing reality" *(wirklichende Wirklichkeit)*, is the first created expression of God's kenotic nature. Siewerth describes it as "diminished" being, paradoxically "complete and simple but not subsistent." It is neither identical with beings nor with God. Siewerth writes: "In so far as Being does not subsist and exist in itself, a frailty prevails in it that is grounded in emanation or realization as such, whereby Being differs essentially from the simple inwardness of God."[55] "It is present *(da)*, it operates and appears in each individual thing, in each genus, each species, and each individual, provided they are actually found in reality—but at the same time, by withdrawing into its unlimited, unadulterated simplicity and indetermination as into an impenetrable mystery, it is never encompassed by a being."[56]

52. Aquinas, *ST* 1a, q. 8, a. 1.
53. Wiercinski, *Differenz im Sein*, 63.
54. Siewerth, *Thomismus*, 342–43, quoted in Wiercinski, *Inspired Metaphysics*, 169.
55. Siewerth, "Das Sein als Gleichnis Gottes," 677, quoted in Wiercinski, *Inspired Metaphysics*, 163.
56. Gustav Siewerth, "Das Sein als Gleichnis Gottes," in *Siewerth. Werke*, vol. 1: *Sein und Wah-*

The mystery of the being of things indicates the deeper mystery of the being of God without coinciding with it. The image of God, the pure act of being, is "poured" into the being of things, without ever allowing itself to be defined by that relationship.[57] God's first act is to let "something" be other than Himself through the self-negating differentiation of *esse non-subsistens*. The act repeats a more primordial moment of difference, the original procession of persons within the Godhead. The *not* is always with God inasmuch as the Son, He who is *not* the Father, has eternally proceeded from Him as begotten. This original negation within the divine is the archetype for all difference. Made possible by God's original self-negation, being is the irruption of difference out of identity. The self-emptying Trinity images itself in that which only exists insofar as it empties itself into being.

Siewerth believes that this nonsubstantive notion of being can accommodate Heidegger's kinetic-temporal *physis*, while preserving the Scholastic principle of the subsistence, eternity, and infinity of God. As sheer possibility of determination, created being is the condition of the possibility of there being anything other than God. It is the principle of difference, potency, movement, time. Heidegger describes temporality as pure outsidedness, "the outside itself itself" (*GA*24 377, 267). Properly understood, temporality images being, the self-emptying principle, which in turn images God, the original self-differentiating identity. The original "ecstaticon," the primordial "outside itself," is, in Siewerth's ontology, not time but divine kenosis, the act by which the Father begets the Son.

Siewerth's contemporary, Karl Rahner, a Jesuit who studied under Heidegger in the mid-1930s, takes a transcendental approach to his post-

---

rheit, ed. Wolfgang Behler and Alma von Stockhausen (Düsseldorf: Patmos, 1975); English: *Philosophizing with Gustav Siewerth: A Translation of Das Sein als Gleichnis Gottes*, trans. Andrzej Wiercinski (Toronto: Hermeneutic Press, forthcoming).

57. Siewerth's point is firmly grounded in many texts of Aquinas. In *De ente et essentia*, Aquinas writes: "If we say that God is pure being, we need not fall into the mistake of those who held that God is that universal being by which everything exists. The being that is God is such that no addition can be made to it. Because of its purity, therefore, it is being distinct from all other being." Aquinas, *On Being and Essence*, trans. Maurer, 60–61; See also Aquinas, *De potentia*, q. 7, a. 2, ad. 4: "God's being which is his essence is not universal being *(ens commune)* but being distinct from all other being: so that by his very being God is distinct from every other being"; English: Aquinas, *On the Power of God*, trans. English Dominican Fathers (Westminster, Md.: Newman Press, 1952).

Heideggerian reading of Aquinas. He argues that what is needed is not a new Thomist metaphysics but a new Thomist theory of knowledge.[58] Drawing on Joseph Maréchal's answer to Kant, Rahner retrieves Aquinas's notion of *excessus*, the Pseudo-Dionysian methodological principle that the attributes of God can only be approximately known through exponentially intensifying the positive qualities of sensible things.[59] Rahner sees a natural dynamism for infinite being in the human intellect's insatiable hunger for knowledge, an a priori directedness to the absolute in all our acts of questioning and willing. The operation of the agent intellect presupposes a "transcendental experience" of the infinite, a prethematic, nonobjective fore-grasp of the unlimited expanse of all possible reality.[60] Rahner understands *excessus* as the fore-grasp *(Vorgriff)* of totality that makes possible, not only knowledge of God, but knowledge itself.

In *Geist in Welt*, Rahner looks at Aquinas's answer to the question, How is knowledge of a sensible singular possible? How exactly do we apply universal concepts to our sense intuitions of individuals (what Aquinas calls the *conversio ad phantasmata*)?[61] The apprehended form of a

58. Rahner's early philosophical works are crucial for understanding his relationship to Heidegger. See his Ph.D. dissertation, *Geist in Welt: zur Metaphysik der endlichen Erkenntnis bei Thomas von Aquin* (Munich: Kösel, 1957); English: *Spirit in the World*, trans. William Dych (New York: Continuum, 1968); idem, *Hörer des Wortes. Zur Grundlegung einer Religionsphilosophie* (Munich: Kösel-Pustet, 1941); English: *Hearer of the Word*, trans. Joseph Donceel (New York: Continuum, 1994). See also idem, "Heidegger and Theology," *Theological Studies* 26 (1965): 86–100. Rahner's student Emerich Coreth developed Rahner's metaphysics in even more Heideggerian directions, while remaining faithful to Rahner's Thomistic principles. See Emerich Coreth, *Metaphysik. Eine methodisch-systematische Grundlegung* (Innsbruck: Tyrolia, 1964); English: *Metaphysics*, trans. Joseph Donceel, with a critique by Bernard Lonergan (New York: Herder and Herder, 1968). No less influential than Heidegger on Rahner is the work of the Belgian Thomist Joseph Maréchal. See his *Le Point du départ de la métaphysique: Leçons sur le développement historique et théorique du problème de la connaissance*, 5 vols. (Brussels: L'Edition Universelle, 1944–49). For a selection translated into English, see *A Maréchal Reader*, trans. and ed. Joseph Donceel (New York: Herder and Herder, 1970). For an interpretation of Maréchal's position, see Michael Vertin, "La finalité intellectuelle: Maréchal et Lonergan," in *Au point de départ: Joseph Maréchal entre la critique kantienne et l'ontologie thomiste* (Brussels: L'Edition Lessius, 2000), 447–65; idem, "Maréchal, Lonergan, and the Phenomenology of Knowing," in *Creativity and Method*, ed. Matthew Lamb (Milwaukee, Wis.: Marquette University Press, 1981), 411–22.

59. Rahner, *Geist in Welt*, 156–218/146–236.

60. Ibid., 146–56/136–45.

61. Rahner's source text is Aquinas, *ST* 1a, q. 84, a. 7: "Whether the Intellect Can Actually Understand through the Intelligible Species of Which It Is Possessed Without Turning to the Phantasm?" Aquinas's answer is no. The answer elaborates the process through which the intellect,

concrete thing is *profiled* against the possible. It is grasped as limited to the matter in which it is first encountered, yet embracing further possibilities of instantiation beyond the particular instance. This horizon of universality is itself profiled against the whole of being.[62] The whole intended in *excessus* is not an object, but the horizon of all objects whose infinite range exceeds every objectification. The horizonal disclosure of the finite profiled against the infinite is Rahner's version of the ontological difference. The being of beings is the infinite horizon of possibility cogiven with every finite actuality. This infinite possibility is in turn grounded in the infinite actuality of absolute being.

Rahner's strongest resonance with Heidegger is his grasp of the foretheoretical nature of the experience of being. The *excessus* is nonconceptual; it is never adequately objectified. As the horizon of our average everyday existence, it is experienced but never defined, indicated through words that point to it, but never properly articulated in language. The *excessus* is not primarily a principle of knowledge; it is the horizon of our being-in-the-world, our average and everyday fore-theoretical being-with-self, being-with-others, and being-among-things. Rahner corrects Heidegger's agnostic being-in-the-world by disengaging this average and everyday experience of God as one of Dasein's existentials. The basic concepts of metaphysics, causality, the principles of identity and noncontradiction, the proofs for the existence of God, are derived from a more fundamental, precategorial experience, a "knowledge of God" that "is always present unthematically and without name."[63]

It is no surprise that Rahner's philosophical theology does not satisfy the Heideggerians. In his careful study of Rahner and Heidegger, Thomas Sheehan writes: "Rahner's transcendental grounding of metaphysics in human cognition continues to move within the parameters of the metaphysics which Heidegger adjudges to be 'forgetful of being.'"[64]

---

enriched by the abstracted universal, returns to the sensible singular and understands it as a concrete instantiation of an essence.

62. Rahner, *Geist in Welt*, 156/145.

63. Karl Rahner, *Foundations of Christian Faith*, trans. William Dych (New York: Crossroad, 1978), 20.

64. Thomas Sheehan, *Karl Rahner: The Philosophical Foundations* (Athens: Ohio University Press, 1987), 4.

Rahner's divergence from Heidegger revolves around the interpretation of transcendence. For Heidegger, transcendence is at root an experience of nothingness; for Rahner, transcendence is an experience of God. Heidegger's boredom and anxiety, the sinking of the whole of beings into insignificance, disclose the finitude of being, for in the nothing, being itself is disclosed as dependent upon the transcendence or the nothingness of Dasein. For Rahner, the reverse is true. The experience of nothingness is only possible on the ground of an a priori affirmation of the absolute fullness of being. "The real issue in transcendental method," Sheehan comments, "is the *content* of the transcendence which that method discloses, that is, the scope of man's movement. Does human transcendence consciously, even if only unthematically, reach the very being of God? Or does it land in a cloud of unknowing?"[65] According to Aquinas, human transcendence is *directed* toward the being of God. It does not "reach" it this side of death. This directedness does lead into a cloud of unknowing, for we know that we are directed to God, but we do not know what God is.

Both Siewerth and Rahner seek resources in Aquinas's ontology that would allow for a modification of Heidegger's phenomenology of finite being. Jean Luc Marion, the most important voice in the debate about the possibility of philosophical theology after Heidegger, has moved in a different direction. Influenced by Emmanuel Levinas's critique of Heidegger, Marion abandons the language of being and with it, to some degree, Aquinas. His early work *God Without Being* is an exploration of the possibilities left to theology when it no longer seeks to anchor knowledge of God in ontology. Naming the moment as a postmodern opportunity to return to a foundational maxim of Christianity—a principle of Christian grammar as old as Augustine—that anything we say about the infinite God is said in language bound to the finite, and is to that degree a falsification, Marion retrieves a neo-Platonic Franciscan version of the *via negativa*. The collapse of metaphysical theology is not necessarily the victory of atheism.

Marion is wise to the "double idolatry" manifesting itself in Heidegger's putatively neutral ontology. Heidegger's contention—that only

---

65. Ibid., 118.

on the basis of the understanding of being determined by ontology can theology begin to understand what the name God is to signify—is exposed as yet another agenda for subsuming God under human logic.[66] The ontology that forbids us to speak of God tears down the idol of the "highest being," only to set up another idol: ontological difference. Heidegger intends to clarify a priori the ontological terms of a possible divine disclosure. By making ontology anterior to theology, Heidegger's ontology is yet another confinement of God to the measure of our thinking. "By definition and decision, God if he must be thought, can meet no theoretical space [cut] to his measure, because his measure exerts itself in our eyes as an excessiveness. Ontological difference itself, and hence also Being, becomes too limited (even if they are universal, or better: because they make us a universe, because in them the world 'worlds') to pretend to offer the dimension, still less the 'divine abode' where God would become thinkable."[67]

Marion makes a trenchant case for respecting the primacy of revelation over being, even within philosophy. Idolatry in philosophy can be avoided only by displacing being as the proper name for God:

At issue here is not the possibility of God's attaining Being, but quite the opposite, the possibility of Being's attaining to God. With respect to God, is it self-evident that the first question comes down to asking, before anything else, whether he is? Does Being define the first and the highest of the divine names? When God offers himself to be contemplated and gives himself to be prayed to, is he concerned primarily with Being? When he appears as and in Jesus Christ, who dies and rises from the dead, is he concerned primarily with Being?[68]

Marion correctly situates onto-theology in early modern philosophy. In their search for a principle that could ground an exhaustive system, Descartes, Spinoza, and Leibniz made the *causa sui* the axiom of a rigorously deductive ontology. This domestication of God leads to His less-than-sudden death in the nineteenth century. He was long dead by the time Nietzsche got to Him because He had long since ceased to be that "greater than which none other can be conceived" *(maius cogitari nesquit)* and had become the most clear and distinct idea, the a priori

---

66. *GA*9 352/267.
67. Marion, *God Without Being*, 44–45.
68. Ibid., xx.

ground of all other clear and distinct ideas. "The 'death of God' exclusively concerns the failure of the metaphysical concepts of 'God': in taking its distance from all metaphysics, it therefore allows the emergence of a God who is free from onto-theology."[69] Marion endorses Pseudo-Dionysius's contention that the proper name of God is not being, but *agathon,* the good. God is the good beyond being, the absolute gift that gives only itself. To call God "the good" is to name Him, not by reference to beings and their attributes, but by reference to His most characteristic act, self-donation.[70]

Aquinas rejects the pseudo-Dionysian position on the divine names because he believes that "the good" inscribes form into the divine. We know *that* God is, we do not know *what* God is—no essence, not even goodness, is absolutely applicable. The divine name, Aquinas writes, "does not signify form, but simply being itself. Hence since the being of God is his essence itself, which can be said of no other . . . , it is clear that among other names this one *(ipsum esse)* specially nominates God."[71] Marion disagrees: goodness does not predicate form of God; on the contrary, it is the remotion of all form from the divine. God is that to which we have absolutely no conceptual access. The breakdown of predication frees up alternative modes of discourse, for example, praise.[72] This for Marion is a philosophical theology free of idolatry: "The first praise, the name of goodness, therefore does *not* offer any most proper name and decidedly abolishes every conceptual idol of 'God' in favor of the luminous darkness where G—d manifests (and not masks) himself, in short, where he gives himself to be envisaged by us."[73]

A Thomist might argue that Marion elevates the name goodness over being because of what it *means:* self-diffusion. God is the gift that gives

---

69. Ibid., xxi.

70. See ibid., 81: "As, by definition and intention, every doctrine of divine names strives to 'destruct' (in the Heideggerian sense) the idolatrous primacy of a human point of view supposed to be unavoidable in the principle of the nomination of G—d, as in addition the primacy of *ens* over the possible divine names rests on the primacy of human conception, Saint Thomas attempted—consciously or not, it matters little—to abstract the *ens* from the doctrine of the *Divine Names.* From the point of view of the understanding apprehending an object, the *ens* becomes first. From the point of view of the Requisite that gives itself without limit, goodness remains first."

71. Aquinas, *ST* 1a, q. 13, a. 11.   72. Marion, *God Without Being,* 76.
73. Ibid.

only itself. So Marion names Him the good. Yet the *whatness* of every name other than being is precisely why Aquinas subordinates them all to *ipsum esse*. As signifying a *whatness*, a content, a meaning, *bonum* limits the infinite. *Esse* alone is free of *whatness*. It is pure *thatness*.[74] Marion's answer to this objection: the good is chosen as the name of God, not because of some philosophical insight into God's essence, but because of what God does. God gives Himself. That means God is a revealer. Marion seems to be deliberately, perhaps even enthusiastically, blurring the distinction between philosophy and revealed theology. The question about the divine names is traditionally a philosophical question: what can we know about God without recourse to special texts and religious revelations? Aquinas said we can know *that* He is, and that His essence is to exist; hence Being is his proper name. Clearly the dying and rising of Christ reveals something other than being, but how can philosophy appropriate this while remaining itself? Philosophy is the questioning search for a reasonable account of everything. It may discover that such an account is not entirely possible without revelation, but that is something other than arguing from revelation. Marion takes the demise of metaphysics within philosophy as an opportunity to reiterate his own version of revelational positivism:

> Can the conceptual thought of God (conceptual or rational, and not intuitive or mystical in the vulgar sense) be developed outside the doctrine of Being (in the metaphysical sense, or even in the non-metaphysical sense)? Does God give himself to be known according to the horizon of Being or according to a more radical horizon? *God Without Being* barely sketches an answer, but does sketch it: God gives himself to be known insofar as he gives himself—according to the horizon of the gift itself. The gift constitutes at once the mode and the body of

---

74. After debating with Thomists on the issue, Marion conceded the point that Aquinas's identification of God with being does not subsume God under a human measure. The *analogia entis* preserves the distance between infinite and finite being. See his preface to the English edition of *God Without Being*, p. xxiii: "Even when he thinks God as *esse*, Saint Thomas nevertheless does not chain God either to Being or to metaphysics. He does not chain God to Being because the divine *esse* immeasurably surpasses (and hardly maintains an *analogia* with) the *ens commune* of creatures, which are characterized by the real distinction between *esse* and their essence, whereas God, and He alone, absolutely merges essence with *esse*: God is expressed as *esse*, but this *esse* is expressed only of God, not of the beings of metaphysics. In *this* sense, Being does not erect an idol before God, but saves his distance."

revelation. In the end the gift gives only itself, but in this way it gives absolutely everything.[75]

Marion's more recent work has introduced nuances in his earlier position. He no longer references "the body of revelation" but rather, speaks of revelation as a philosophical possibility. Directly attacking Heidegger's effort to keep the notion of revelation out of philosophy, he raises the question of whether or not phenomenology must think it as a possibility since it is methodologically committed to a strict inclusivism. A thing is given to the degree that it is thinkable and thereby meets the minimum criteria necessary for philosophical consideration. A phenomenology that has not lost its way in a transcendental analysis of subjectivity but is truly *Sache* oriented, following the phenomenological reduction all the way, not only back to the given, but back to *givenness,* should in fact investigate the limit case of an absolute givenness. Under the rubric of "the saturated phenomena," Marion explores modes of givenness that overwhelm their correlative intentions. In the most extreme case this would be a givenness that gives itself absolutely, with no possible intentional correlate. A genuinely divine revelation, the self-disclosure of a transcendent God, would be such an absolute gift. Phenomenology, by a strict obedience to its own methodology, engages that which has traditionally been regarded as the domain of theology. "Is it necessary to confine the possibility of the appearing of God to the uninterrogated and supposedly untouchable limits of one or the other figure of philosophy and phenomenology, or should we broaden phenomenological possibility to the measure of the possibility of manifestation demanded by the question of God?"[76]

Marion's postmodern *via negativa* has been hugely influential. Laurence Hemming, for example, building on Marion, argues that Heidegger's silence is not the atheism that denies the possibility of responsible, thoughtful faith. "Does Heidegger therefore refuse the Christian God?" Hemming writes. "Or rather, does he refuse the way the Christian God has been woven into human thinking? Is his atheism not precisely *this* refusal?"[77] Heidegger has apparently made metaphysical theol-

---

75. Ibid., xxiv.
76. Marion, *Being Given*, 242.
77. Hemming, *Heidegger's Atheism*, 18.

ogy impossible. Now the ground is cleared for genuinely thinking God. It seems to me, however, that Heidegger refuses a theological voice precisely by taking one. A philosophy that theologizes is refused; a theology that denies the possibility of philosophical theology by proclaiming the one-sidedness of revelation is enabled. Luther would be delighted. But is this a genuinely *philosophical* refusal of a theological voice? Or is it, as it appears to be, mere assertion? Why should philosophy renounce its own inner *telos* to attempt to speak of that which surpasses speech, to push the boundaries of explanation as far as they can go?

After decades of Heideggerian purges, repeated attempts to purify philosophy of religion, or religion of philosophy; after the death of God, reenacted with morbid solemnity every few years as yet another thinker discovers that "being is finite," I have the temerity to suggest that metaphysics did not come to an end in the first half of the twentieth century. The future of philosophical theology depends upon a much more careful articulation of the distinction between being as it is disclosed phenomenologically—pure contingency, permeated by nothingness, as fragile and insubstantial as every moment of time (Aquinas's *esse non-subsistens*)—and divine being, the exclusion of all contingency, nothingness, and temporality, the negation of every negation. This distinction could be the ground of an unapologetic philosophical theology, a philosophical theology which is not embarrassed by the traditional proofs for God's existence, nor so beguiled by them that it cannot see the force of the objections of Kierkegaard, Nietzsche, and Heidegger; a philosophical theology that asks the question about the relationship of being to God because it must ask it if it is to be faithful to itself.

Luther had theological reasons for silencing philosophy. The Crucifixion of the Son appeared to him as proof that we are no longer naturally drawn to God, quite the reverse. In such a situation, philosophical theology could only be a careful fiction strategically constructed to avoid facing the truth. Whether or not this is a correct interpretation of the significance of the Crucifixion is not for philosophy to decide. Philosophy spontaneously speaks about God because it tolerates no arbitrary censure of any dimension of human experience.

CHAPTER NINE

BEING-BEFORE-GOD IN THE MIDDLE AGES

*The human being is directed to God as to a certain end that
exceeds the comprehension of reason.*

THOMAS AQUINAS

Scholasticism did not leave the Jewish-Christian sense of history as it found it nor did it annul it. It sublated the early Christian understanding of time, fusing it with Hellenistic theoretical structures into a distinctively new way of being Christian. Greco-Roman "circular thinking" (the emphasis on the eternity of form) and Jewish-Christian historical thinking (the emphasis on the singularity of event), which initially tended to conflict with one another, achieved a precarious balance in Scholasticism. The Jewish-Christian historical sense was initially antagonistic to cultural and scientific life. There was no sense in building up culture when the Last Day was imminent. Greco-Roman circular thinking, on the other hand, lacked a sense of *haecceitas*. If every moment was an eternal repetition of what has been, nothing was genuinely singular. The Scholastic task was to raise up these two extremes into a synthesis that would preserve what is true in each.[1]

---

1. Rosemann, *Understanding Scholastic Thought*, 185: "The conflict between Greek wisdom and the 'foolishness of the Cross' can thus, from another coin of vantage, be viewed as a conflict between Greek circularity and Christian linearity. I submit that, when the heritage of Greek thought became fully accessible to the Latin West in the thirteenth century, the tension between the 'circle' and the 'line' was the basic structure underlying the Schoolmen's attempts to reconcile the newly discovered sources with the Christian tradition."

The question of the legitimacy of the fusion of the horizons of Paul and Aristotle was hotly debated by the Scholastics. As the condemnations of 1277 show, even after Aquinas, Christendom was not perfectly comfortable with the theological appropriation of Aristotelian science. But Christianity is not a thing that could be preserved in the purity of its original manifestation. It has itself the mode of being of Dasein. Its essence only emerges through its history, its *Wirkungsgeschichte.* Thus it had to change and grow to remain itself. As Christianity developed into Scholasticism, it absorbed impulses from Greco-Roman culture that exceeded the theological horizon of the early Christian community. The early Christians lacked the temporal distance necessary to make a definitive judgment about pagan culture. Augustine was reaching for a synthesis that was yet to come. Aquinas and Scotus, emboldened by twelfth-century Christian humanism, assumed that something good and true had come forward in the ancients, which it was the duty of the Christian thinker to take up once again.

Certainly the religiosity of the Middle Ages was different from that of early Christianity. The apocalyptic edge was in one sense gone. In another sense, it was internalized. Thus it could be compatible with the pursuit of culture and science. Apocalypse no longer meant expecting the end of the world; it meant transparently living one's being-toward-the-end. Medieval religiosity was both messianic and mystical. It lived in the already/not yet, perhaps even more emphatically than the early Christian community itself.

This delicate balance is evident in much medieval art. A late medieval wood-carved crucifix, life-sized, from the Rhineland, shows the Man of Sorrows dead on the Cross, his thorn-crowned head bowed on his chest. Blood runs down his face and his tortured body. But his hands are no longer fastened to the wood; they are folded upon his chest in a gesture of peace. The symbols of the four Evangelists are painted on each of the four ends of the cross: a bull, a lion, an eagle, and an angel. This crucifix is a paradox: it says two seemingly opposed things at the same time. On the one hand, it speaks of the suffering servant (Is 53:3–5), a favorite theme of late medieval art: the innocent man, who has taken on himself punishment for sin, so disfigured by pain that we cannot bear to look at him. On the other hand, it speaks of the glorious kingly Christ of John's Gospel, the one who has conquered death. He does not cry out in God-forsakenness (Mk 15:34). With the composure of a seated Buddha, he looks heavenward and says: "It is accomplished" (Jn 19:30). The hands are free from the cross, folded across his chest in a gesture commonly seen in medieval depictions of the Annunciation. Like the Virgin singled out from among all women, this Christ is humbled by the glory bestowed upon him. His gesture is one of thanksgiving, of simultaneous submission and ennoblement. This is the Crucified as the form of beauty itself. The signs of the Evangelists on the four ends of the cross transform the instrument of torture into a mandala, a symbol of wholeness. On this cross, the world does not end, it begins.

Here is the fullness of medieval religiousness with all of its tensions intact: childlike delight in creation and world-weariness, exuberant sensuality and grim penance, boundless gratitude for the goodness of the earth and otherworldly asceticism. The medieval mind delighted in the world, as a child delights in a meadow on a summer day, and simultaneously despaired of the world, longing for release from suffering. The earth was an undeniable good. The human being was created in the divine image and in Mary, singled out to be *capax Dei*, capable of bearing God. In its ennoblement of the earthly, the medieval affirmation of life exceeded the greatest excesses of pagan nature-worship. Medieval Christendom's intense devotion to Mary was related to its equally intense devotion to the Eucharist and the places associated with the earthly life of Christ. Mary was the human being perfected, free of sin, as she was intended to be. Although she lacked the omniscience of her divine son, her fully human will was entirely surrendered to the divine will. In the Eucharist, the medieval believer worshiped a similar nearing of the transcendent, what Eliade describes as the coincidence of the sacred and the profane: bread, the matter we eat to sustain our bodies, transformed into divinity. In the Eucharist as in Mary, matter was revealed to be capable of bearing divinity. The attachment to the places associated with the earthly life of Christ (the inspiration for the Crusades), like the cult of relics and the practice of pilgrimage, expressed the same medieval sensitivity. Places and physical things, like history itself, could be eternally validated. The three icons of medieval religion, the Virgin Mary, the Eucharist, and the Holy Land, each touch upon what Carl Gustav Jung calls "the fourth," the material correlate of grace.[2] Medieval religion did not revere an intrinsic holiness in matter, but a bestowed holiness. Nature could not claim it for itself by right. The essence of medieval religion consisted in this insight, which distinguished medieval mysticism from ancient paganism. Nature was not divine but divinizable.

Thomas Aquinas's notion of *potentia obedientialis* articulates this medieval insight into the intrinsic goodness of matter in the language of Aristotelian theology.[3] This innovation on Aristotle's distinction between active and passive potency (without which, Aquinas could not say that "grace perfects nature")[4] defines nature's ontological orientation to the divine, while maintaining the transcendence of God. If nature were oriented to the divine in such a way that divinization were achievable through its own act—if it had an active potency for divinity—the transcendence of God would be violated. God would not transcend nature; on the contrary, he would be enclosed within it. He would be the *telos* of nature. According to Aquinas, nature has a passive potency for divinity; it is open to receiving an act of God directly. The act, should it come, would be gift. It would not be predictable or inscribed into our ontology. Nor would it be imposed on us. It would be given freely and could only be received freely. The human being is potentially obedient, that means, potentially *capax Dei*, a potency which is actualized in the grace which descends upon Mary and gives her the power to say *fiat*, be it done to me according to your will (Lk 1:38).

Yet the redeemed human being is still fallen. The earth is also a veil of tears. Sickness and death are the proximate future of every one of us. Renounce the world, hide in a wilderness, a cloister, a hermitage, and do penance for sin (rupture from God), for the Last Day is certain, if not imminent. The Christ will return and the wicked will be cast out from the presence into Gehenna, "where the worm does not die and the fire is not quenched" (Mk 9:48). The blessed will be ushered into the gar-

---

2. See Carl Gustav Jung, *Memories, Dreams, Reflections,* trans. Richard and Clara Winston (New York: Random House, 1965), 202n, 332–39, 397.

3. Thomas Aquinas, *Quaestiones disputatae De virtutibus in communi,* q. 1, a. 10, ad 13.

4. Aquinas, *ST* 1a, q. 1, a. 8, ad 2.

den of the Lamb. The medieval genius consisted in the ability to think both these thoughts at once—not in words, for such paradoxes escape language, but in images. Medieval imagery shows us a religiosity that delighted in life, irrepressibly curious about everything under the sun, exuberantly creative, building churches whose gargoyle-besieged pinnacles still soar into the sky. And it shows us a religiosity that longed for release from life, looking beyond this world to a more perfect world. Medieval religion lived the already/not yet. It refused to collapse either side of the paradox into a one-sided secular rationalism or a one-sided theological irrationalism. Philosophy and science were to be pursued with all of the intensity and optimism with which they were pursued in the ancient world. But they were to recognize their limit in the revelation that surpasses anything deducible or definable by human reason. The *theologia crucis* and the *theologia gloriae* were both necessary interpretations of the one infinitely meaningful event. God was partially revealed in the glory that shines through creation, but He was only fully revealed in the hidden glory of the Crucified.

Luther, like most of his modern successors in science and philosophy, was not able to think in paradoxes. He learned from late medieval nominalism the power of reductionism: isolate one side of a complex reality, define it, and declare it the whole truth. The monk who hated reason was one of the first rationalists. Luther's objections to Scholastic theology may be traced back to his basic theological objection to the Scholastic thesis of the natural directedness of the human being to God. For Luther, the notion of a natural desire for God, the *desiderium naturale,* fails to recognize the disfiguration wrought by Original Sin, and so undermines our need for Redemption. Note that this is a theological, not a philosophical objection. Aquinas defends the *desiderium naturale* with matchless precision: "The human being is directed to God as to a certain end which exceeds the comprehension of reason," *(homo ordinatur ad Deum, sicut ad quemdam finem, qui comprehensionem rationis excedit)*.[5] This directedness is not faith, but a predisposition for faith. I call it *religiousness*. By this I mean an ontological not an ontic category, a structural and formal feature of human being-in-the-world. In the modern age, it has been variously de-

---

5. Aquinas, *ST* 1a, q. 1, a. 1.

scribed as the "taste and feeling for the infinite,"[6] "the feeling of absolute dependence," "the feeling of ultimate concern,"[7] the *"mysterium tremendum et fascinans,"*[8] the experience of "the wholly other,"[9] or the unthematic pre-understanding of God.[10] Religiousness can be expressed in negative terms as an absence of something that we feel ought to be there, "an all-encompassing lack of presencing presence."[11] Or it can be expressed in more positive terms as the *excessus* against which every grasp of a finite being is profiled.[12] It is the infinity, which is paradoxically *not yet*, glimpses of which are continually breaking through the finite. Only because of this continual overwhelming of limits, do we know the finite as

---

6. Schleiermacher, *On Religion*, 35.

7. Friedrich Schleiermacher, *The Christian Faith*, trans. H. R. Mackintosh and J. S. Stewart (Edinburgh: T & T Clark Publishers, 1999), 12 ff. See Paul Tillich, *Systematic Theology* (Chicago: University of Chicago Press, 1951), vol. 1, 11–12: "The religious concern is ultimate; it excludes all other concerns from ultimate significance; it makes them preliminary. The ultimate concern is unconditional, independent of any conditions of character, desire, or circumstance. The unconditional concern is total: no part of ourselves or our world is excluded from it; there is no 'place' to flee from it. The total concern is infinite: no moment of relaxation and rest is possible in the face of a religious concern which is ultimate, unconditional, total, and infinite. The word 'concern' points to the 'existential' character of religious experience. We cannot speak adequately of the 'object of religion' without simultaneously removing its character as an object. That which is ultimate gives itself only to the attitude of ultimate concern. It is the correlate of an unconditional concern, but not a 'highest thing' called 'the absolute' or 'the unconditioned,' about which we could argue in detached objectivity. It is the object of total surrender, demanding also the surrender of our subjectivity while we look at it. It is a matter of infinite passion and interest (Kierkegaard), making us its object whenever we try to make it our object." See also p. 211: "'God' is the answer to the question implied in man's finitude; he is the name for that which concerns man ultimately. This does not mean that first there is a being called God and then the demand that man should be ultimately concerned about him. It means that whatever concerns a man ultimately becomes God for him, and conversely, it means that a man can be concerned ultimately only about that which is God for him."

8. See Rudolf Otto, *Das Heilige*.

9. Gerardus van der Leeuw, *Phänomenologie der Religion* (Tübingen: J. C. Mohr, 1977), 3.

10. See Rahner, *Christian Faith*, 53: "This unthematic and ever-present experience, this knowledge of God which we always have even when we are thinking of and concerned with anything but God, is the permanent ground from out of which the thematic knowledge of God emerges which we have in explicit religious activity and in philosophical reflection. It is not in these later that we discover God just as we discovered a particular object of our experience within the world. Rather, both in this explicitly religious activity directed to God in prayer and in metaphysical reflection we are only making explicit for ourselves what we already know about ourselves in the depths of our personal self realization."

11. Enders, "Ist 'Religion' wirklich undefinierbar?" 86.

12. Rahner, *Geist in Welt*, 156/145.

such. Heidegger's pre-understanding of temporality would not be possible without a pre-understanding of eternity.

The best-known atheist of the twentieth century, John Paul Sartre, also recognizes religiousness as an essential structure of human being. What I call religiousness, he calls the "useless passion" of being human, the desire for simultaneous possession of "being-for-itself" (subjectivity) and "being-in-itself" (thinghood). The human being longs for a resolution of the incompleteness of freedom, longs to become something definite and in-itself, while at the same time remaining free, forever detached from all particular ways of being. Sartre understands God as the oxymoron of a subjectivity that is both "for-itself" and "in-itself," both free and absolutely realized. That the "in-itself-for-itself" is an absurdity for Sartre by no means diminishes the phenomenological reality of the religious impulse he is here describing. Everything the human being does is to be interpreted as an expression of this primordial desire for divinity.[13] Sartre's argument highlights the "average and everydayness" of religiousness. Religiousness is not only rapture, ecstasy, and revelation. It is also the inexplicable dissatisfaction with everything, the inconsolable longing for *more being*, which overtakes us in our moments of joy and boredom.

Markus Enders calls for a distinction between *religio* as the virtue of "giving God his due," and the ontological condition of its possibility.[14] The latter—religiousness—everyone experiences; it is in this sense, natural or ontological. The former—*religio,* the virtue of *pietas*—is the *habitus* of some. Enders wishes to retrieve something of the counter-cultural and heroic nature of *religio* in a culture as resolutely irreligious as ours. Piety or impiety may indeed be an "ontic" affair in the sense of concern-

13. See Jean-Paul Sartre, "The Desire to be God," in idem, *The Philosophy of Existentialism*, ed. Wade Baskin (New York: Philosophical Library, 1965), 70–71: "The best way to conceive of the fundamental project of human reality is to say that man is the being whose project is to be God. Whatever may be the myths and rites of the religion considered, God is first 'sensible in the heart' of man as the one who identifies and defines him [man] in his ultimate and fundamental project. If man possesses a pre-ontological comprehension of the being of God, it is not the great wonders of nature nor the power of society which have conferred it upon him. God, value and supreme end of transcendence, represents the permanent limit in terms of which man makes known to himself what he is. To be man means to reach toward being God. Or if you prefer, man fundamentally is the desire to be God."

14. Aquinas regards the gift of religiosity *(pietas)* as a supernatural perfection of the virtue of justice. *ST* 1a 2ae, q. 68, a. 4, ad 2.

ing, not *the* form of our being-in-the-world, but *a* form of being-in-the-world. In the same way, the virtue of prudence is not necessary to a phenomenological description of the human being. The human being is not essentially prudent; neither is it essentially pious. Schleiermacher made the mistake of confusing *religio* with the condition of its possibility, with the consequence that piety became for him as natural as breathing. How are we to understand holiness as the unique quality of a religiously lived life if all are by nature pious? Schleiermacher's version of Protestantism, which diminishes the distinction between saintliness and everydayness, had the undesired effects of emptying churches and collapsing Christianity into bourgeois European culture. But to follow Luther, Barth, and the early Heidegger to the other extreme, to deny religiousness for the sake of preserving the absolute otherness of God, is to do violence to human experience.

Religiousness is not the measure of God; it is, rather, *potentia obedientialis,* openness to the possibility of receiving the divine. According to Aquinas, we are not directed to something the terms of which are known a priori. God need not confirm our categories and expectations. We are directed to "a certain end that exceeds the comprehension of reason." The *excedit* indicates an anticipation of One who will exceed and reconfigure expectations. Religiousness is openness to divine interference, the expectation of infinite surprise. God is an excess, which continually overwhelms our "natural" horizon. We are the most inexplicable of creatures, a finite being with an infinite end. Our perfection is in a strange way not natural to us, which means it is not *our* perfection. We are directed, not to the perfection of ourselves as we now exist, but to transformation. Aquinas is, on this point, close to Nietzsche's Zarathustra: "man" is something that must be overcome.[15] We are othered in our very identity. We are called to a self-emptying, kenotic ecstasy of unity with the self-emptying divinity whose perfection is manifest in the Crucified. Religiousness is agitation with our present state of being, the overwhelming feeling of a possible fullness that is not now and not ours, but yet *could be.* Without religiousness, there would be no religion. If we felt no longing for more,

---

15. Friedrich Nietzsche, *Thus Spoke Zarathustra: A Book for None and All,* trans. R. J. Hollingdale (New York: Penguin, 1978), prologue.

we would be satisfied with a life in which all of our biological needs were fulfilled. Religiousness shows itself in the secular wherever we see infinite dissatisfaction with the present: the lassitude of intelligent teenagers who find the goals offered to them by their elders "boring"; the disproportionate and doomed energy we put into our love affairs, our careers, our pursuit of social, or increasingly, environmental justice; the transient ecstatic expectation of newness which accompanies the beginning of a trip. Heidegger speaks of angst and guilt, but he has not properly named the emptiness at the heart of the human being. For this emptiness is not simply empty. It is first of all the glimmer of a fullness that overwhelms our anticipations of what fullness and wholeness could mean.

To do justice to ontological religiousness, we need a phenomenology of religion that is both mystical and messianic. The fullness of being is already here—we have always already understood it—and not yet. I suggest, therefore, that we speak, not of a being-toward-God, but a *being-before-God*. I mean hereby to inscribe into the phenomenology of religion an unresolvable ambiguity. Being-before-God is to be both temporally and spatially understood. The temporal meaning of the term: we are the being that must suffer the absence of God, the being for whom God is future. The spatial meaning: we are the being that is always already summoned before God, the being that stands before the Face. For the most part, our religious life is a being-before-God in the temporal sense, a life of longing and unsatisfiable seeking. But in rare and ecstatic moments it becomes a being-before-God in the spatial sense. God lifts the veil from our eyes, summons us out of our "world" into His world and we feel surrounded, upheld and held in the gaze of an undeniable Reality. *Pace* Derrida and the deconstructivist theologians, we cannot give an absolute priority to the messianic (the *via negativa* is not first theology), without doing violence to the structure of religiousness. Negative theology is a crucial moment in religious thinking. Pseudo-Dionysius, *The Cloud of Unknowing*, Meister Eckhart, Jacob Boehme, and John of the Cross saved Christian theology from congealing into a pseudo-science of the divine. But the *via negativa* presumes a *via positiva*. Both poles must be held in a dynamic tension, which Luther tore asunder (thereby achieving a one-sided stasis): the *theologia gloriae*, being-before-God (spatial sense), and *the theologia crucis*, being-before-God (temporal sense). These no more cancel each other out than resolutely facing the future cancels out living in the present. In the fullness of the religious life, they are coactive. The mystics who experience the presence of God never presume to possess this in its fullness. They do not prematurely regard themselves as having arrived at something that can only be theirs in the *visio beatifica*. The presence is always gift—it is never earned or deserved. As gift, it is contingent upon the granting that gives it. Religious life, then, is lived between these two senses of being-before-God, a dynamic interplay between absence (anticipating) and presence (enjoying).

Religiousness is actualized in historically differentiated forms of religiosity. It is a potency that comes to act in concrete expressions of faith. These can in turn be elaborated by thematizing their relational-senses, their intentional or *how*-structures. The intentional structure of medieval Christianity, the *how* of medieval faith, is being-toward-accountability. This formal structure need not be moralistically interpreted. That the medieval believer felt called to give an account of himself does not mean that he believed he could only be justified by performing certain actions. It meant, rather, that salvation would involve the whole of his temporal existence. All times would be recapitulated in the account; no moment, however insignificant, would be forgotten. The anticipation of a return of all moments led to a uniquely powerful sense of individual responsibility.

Here is the root of Heidegger's notion of authenticity. Others have traced the Western concept of individual responsibility to the notion of divine judgment. Kierkegaard points out that living in fear of judgment drives the individual into appropriating existence and intensifies the incommunicability of subjectivity: "It follows from the fact that the concept 'judgement' is not made *en masse*. People can be put to death *en masse*, can be sprayed *en masse*, can be flattened *en masse*—in short in many ways they can be treated as cattle, but they cannot be judged as cattle, for cattle cannot come under judgement. No matter how many are judged, if the judging is to have any earnestness and truth, then each individual is judged."[16] Jan Patočka also grounds moral responsibility in the

---

16. Sløren Kierkegaard, *The Sickness unto Death: A Christian Psychological Exposition for Upbuilding and Awakening*, trans. Howard V. Hong and Edna H. Hong (Princeton, N.J.: Princeton University Press, 1983), 123.

singularity of divine judgment. The individual faces judgment; the judgment singularizes it, removes it from any genus in which it could conceal itself and demands that it stand alone. The singularization of death is intensified in the relation to a personal God, for it is no longer simply death which confronts us, it is infinite love, before which we are always guilty. "The responsible man as such is a *self*, an individual that doesn't coincide with any role that he might happen to assume—something Plato expresses through the myth of the choice of destiny; he is a responsible self because, in confronting death and in dealing with nothingness, he takes upon himself what only each one of us can realize in ourselves, that which makes each of us irreplaceable. Now, however, individuality has been related to infinite love and man is an individual because he is guilty, *always* guilty with respect to that love. Each is determined as individual by the uniqueness of what situates him in the generality of sin."[17] Derrida comments: "The person can become what it is only in being paralyzed, in its very singularity, by the gaze of God. Then it sees itself seen by the gaze of another, 'a supreme, absolute and inaccessible being who holds us in his hand not by exterior but by interior force.'"[18] Only in being beheld by another, not just anyone, but the other who is wholly other, do I come to myself. Only thus am I accountable. The divine gaze does not paralyze (Derrida's rhetoric goes astray here); rather, it frees. Thus beheld am I capable of beholding myself and hence acting freely and responsibly. Responsibility, Patočka says, is not a Greek concept; it is Jewish.

Responsibility is maximized in faith. The believer comes face to face with the nullity of temporal life. He sees that finitude means the possibility of not-being and, what amounts to the same, of never-having-been. Because he is never fully present in his life—every instant disappears into the abyss from which it came—he is faced with the possibility that *none of this matters*. He can hide from this disturbing possibility by preoccupying himself with things at hand. Indeed, unbelief must repress this thought, for the possibility that *none of this matters* is incompatible with earning a living, or building a home. But the possibility remains and sur-

---

17. Jan Patočka, *Heretical Essays on the Philosophy of History*, trans. Erazim Kohak (Peru, Ill.: Open Court Publishing, 1996), 116, quoted in Derrida, *The Gift of Death*, 52.

18. Derrida, *The Gift of Death*, 6.

faces in moments of despair. Faith returns to this possibility only to annul it. In resolutely choosing being-toward-accountability, that is, in the act of faith, the believer faces the possibility that nothing matters by negating it, and affirming, not theoretically, but in every thought and action, that, on the contrary, *everything matters*. The possibility of the not-mattering is annulled in the most extreme possibility for being: not death, but eternal life. The not-mattering of temporal existence is annulled in resoluteness toward one's ownmost possibility for being-forever. But faith is not a mitigation of distress over the possibility of nothing mattering. It is not the pie-in-the-sky that makes life bearable. On the contrary, it is the most honest and transparent encounter with this possibility, a dialogue with despair, which annuls the possibility, not by distraction or repression, but by allowing oneself to be grounded transparently in God.[19] Faith actualizes the possibility that possibility itself will become necessity. Faith believes that eternal life will bring it back to every lost moment, every unguarded gesture, every spontaneous expression of generosity or selfishness. The believer will be called to give an account.

Much of what Heidegger has to say concerning resoluteness unto death applies here, but it must be qualified by the discovery that our "ownmost non-relational possibility not to be bypassed" is not the possibility of death but the possibility of life. Eternal life is not a possibility in the sense of a natural capacity, or the fact that the soul is created immortal. Eternal life is a possibility in the sense that it may be given us by the power which creates and preserves us. The reformers argued that Christianity teaches death and resurrection, not immortality. However, even in a doctrine of natural immortality such as Aquinas's, the soul remains radically contingent on the divine will. The doctrine of divine preservation stipulates that for the soul *to be* it must be held in being by God. Augustine holds that the soul has the possibility of immortality through grace. But it has also therefore the possibility of death. Only the angels possess immortality by nature. It was not impossible for Adam to die, but it was possible for him not to die *(non imposse mori sed posse non mori)*.[20] Should we be graced with immortal life, we would find that this eternity

---

19. Kierkegaard, *Sickness*, 14.
20. Augustine, *De Genesi ad Litteram*, bk. I, 25, n. 35.

is indeed our ownmost possibility, for nothing could be more authentically our own than our whole life come back to us.[21]

The believer is gripped by a concern for himself *before* God, where the "before" is understood both temporally and spatially. Thrown toward recapitulation, faith anticipates being brought back to what had been. Thrown toward restoration, faith anticipates the enactment of what ought to have been. Thrown toward resurrection, faith anticipates the absolute transformation that neither recapitulates and restores nor destroys, but raises up into the new. This historically saturated faith is alive in the Middle Ages, not only in mysticism, but also in Scholasticism. The God whose name is *ipsum esse* is not here and now, except in graced moments of illumination. He is the One who is anticipated in the desire and fear of recapitulation, restoration, and resurrection. The soul has the burden and privilege of experiencing the insubstantiality of finite being *(esse non-subsistens)* from within. Faith seeks understanding; nature seeks God; time seeks eternity.

The seed of historical consciousness is discovered in ancient Jewish and early Christianity eschatology and incubated in Scholasticism until it emerges into its own in modern thinking. As the most nuanced analysis of historical consciousness extant, *Sein und Zeit* belongs to the history of Jewish-Christian literature, unwittingly and under protest.

---

21. It is interesting to note in this respect that Aquinas, unlike Scotus, argues for an eternal return of earthly images in the *visio beatifica*. Holding fast to his doctrine of abstraction, whereby nothing can be known unless it is mediated through a sense phantasm, Aquinas holds that the media by which we see God in the next life are the sense images stored in our memory from this life. This means, of course, that *everything* comes back in eternity. Aquinas, *ST* 1a, q. 89, a. 5.

SELECTED BIBLIOGRAPHY

Full references of works consulted are given with the first citation in the text. Below is a list of primary texts and the most significant secondary sources. Translations are given after the original reference. Significant separate volumes of collected translated writings are listed on their own.

Heidegger's Collected Works *(Gesamtausgabe, GA)*

Vol. 1, *Frühe Schriften*. 1912–16. Ed. Friedrich-Wilhelm von Herrmann. Frankfurt am Main: Vittorio Klostermann, 1978.

Vol. 5, *Holzwege*. 1935–46. Ed. Friedrich-Wilhelm von Herrmann. Frankfurt am Main: Vittorio Klostermann, 1977.

Vol. 6.2, *Nietzsche II*. 1939–46. Ed. Brigette Schillbach. Frankfurt am Main: Vittorio Klostermann, 1997. English: *Nietzsche. Vol. II. The Eternal Return of the Same*. Trans. David Farrell Krell. New York: Harper & Row, 1984.

Vol. 9, *Wegmarken*. 1919–58. Ed. Friedrich-Wilhelm von Herrmann. Frankfurt am Main: Vittorio Klostermann, 1996. English: *Pathmarks*. Ed. William McNeill. Cambridge: Cambridge University Press, 1998.

Vol. 10, *Der Satz vom Grund*. 1955–56. Ed. Peter Jaeger. Frankfurt am Main: Vittorio Klostermann, 1997. English: *The Principle of Reason*. Trans. Reginald Lilly. Bloomington: Indiana University Press, 1991.

Vol. 12, *Unterwegs zur Sprache*. 1950–59. Ed. Friedrich-Wilhelm von Herrmann. Frankfurt am Main: Vittorio Klostermann, 1985. English: *On the Way to Language*. Trans. Peter D. Herz. New York: Harper & Row, 1971.

Vol. 13, *Aus der Erfahrung des Denkens*. 1910–76. Ed. Hermann Heidegger. Frankfurt am Main: Vittorio Klostermann, 1985.

Vol. 15, *Seminare*. 1951–73. Ed. Curd Ochwadt. Vittorio Klostermann: Frankfurt am Main, 1986. English: *Four Seminars*. Trans. Andrew Mitchell and François Raffoul. Bloomington: Indiana University Press, 2003.

Vol. 16, *Reden und andere Zeugnisse eines Lebensweges*. 1910–76. Ed. Friedrich-Wilhelm von Herrmann. Frankfurt am Main: Vittorio Klostermann, 2000.

Vol. 17, *Einführung in die phänomenologische Forschung*. 1923–24. Ed. Friedrich-Wilhelm von Herrmann. Frankfurt am Main: Vittorio Klostermann, 1994.

Vol. 19, *Platon: Sophistes*. 1924/25. Ed. Ingeborg Schüßler. Frankfurt am Main: Vittorio Klostermann, 1992. English: *Plato's Sophist*. Trans. Richard Rojcewicz. Bloomington: Indiana University Press, 1997.

Vol. 20, *Prolegomena zur Geschichte des Zeitbegriffs*. 1925. Ed. Peter Jaeger. Frankfurt am Main: Vittorio Klostermann, 1994. English: *History of the Concept of Time:*

Prolegomena. Trans. Theodore Kisiel. Bloomington: Indiana University Press, 1992.

Vol. 24, *Die Grundprobleme der Phänomenologie.* 1927. Ed. Friedrich-Wilhelm von Herrmann. Frankfurt am Main: Vittorio Klostermann, 1997. English: *Basic Problems of Phenomenology.* Trans. Albert Hofstadter. Bloomington: Indiana University Press, 1982.

Vol. 26, *Metaphysische Anfangsgründe der Logik im Ausgang von Leibniz.* 1928. Ed. Klaus Held. Frankfurt am Main: Vittorio Klostermann, 1978, 1990. English: *The Metaphysical Foundations of Logic.* Trans. Michael Heim. Bloomington: Indiana University Press, 1984.

Vol. 40, *Einführung in die Metaphysik.* 1935. Ed. Petra Jaeger. Frankfurt am Main: Vittorio Klostermann, 1983. English: *An Introduction to Metaphysics.* Trans. Ralph Manheim. Garden City, N.Y.: Doubleday, 1961.

Vol. 56/57, *Zur Bestimmung der Philosophie.* 1919. Ed. Bernd Heimbüchel. Frankfurt am Main: Vittorio Klostermann, 1999. English: *Towards the Definition of Philosophy.* Trans. Ted Sadler. New York, London: Continuum, 2000.

Vol. 58, *Grundprobleme der Phänomenologie.* 1919–20. Ed. Hans-Helmuth Gander. Frankfurt am Main: Vittorio Klostermann, 1992.

Vol. 60, *Phänomenologie des religiösen Lebens.* 1917–21. Ed. Claudius Strube. Frankfurt am Main: Vittorio Klostermann, 1995. English: *The Phenomenology of Religious Life.* Trans. Matthias Fritsche and Jennifer Anna Gosetti. Bloomington: Indiana University Press, 2004.

Vol. 61, *Phänomenologische Interpretationen zu Aristoteles. Einführung in die phänomenologische Forschung.* 1921–22. Ed. Walter Bröcker and Käte Bröcker-Oltmanns. Frankfurt am Main: Vittorio Klostermann, 1994. English: *Phenomenological Interpretations of Aristotle: Initiation into Phenomenological Research.* Trans. Richard Rojcewicz. Bloomington: Indiana University Press, 2001.

Vol. 63, *Ontologie. Hermeneutik der Faktizität.* 1923. Ed. Käte Bröcker-Oltmanns. Frankfurt am Main: Vittorio Klostermann, 1995. English: *Ontology and the Hermeneutics of Facticity.* Trans. John van Buren. Bloomington: Indiana University Press, 1999.

Vol. 65, *Beiträge zur Philosophie (Vom Ereignis).* 1936–38. Ed. Friedrich-Wilhelm von Herrmann. Frankfurt am Main: Vittorio Klostermann, 1989, 1994. English: *Contributions to Philosophy (From Enowning).* Trans. Parvis Emad and Kenneth Maly. Bloomington: Indiana University Press, 1999.

Vol. 77, *Feldweg-Gespräche.* 1944–45. Ed. Ingrid Schüßler. Frankfurt am Main: Vittorio Klostermann, 1995.

Separate Works by Heidegger, Correspondence, and Collected Translations

Basic Writings. Ed. David Farrell Krell. New York: HarperCollins, 1993.

The Concept of Time. Begriff der Zeit (BZ). 1924. German-English edition. Trans. William McNeill. Oxford: Blackwell, 1989.

"Contributions to *Der Akademiker,* 1910–1913." *Graduate Faculty Philosophy Journal* 14–15 (1991): 486–519.

"Drei Briefe Martin Heideggers an Karl Löwith." In *Zur philosophischen Aktualität Heidegers*, ed. Dietrich Papenfuss and Otto Pöggeler, vol. 2, 27–39. Frankfurt am Main: Vittorio Klostermann, 1990.

The End of Philosophy. Trans. Joan Stambaugh. New York: Harper & Row, 1973 (Contains a translation of "Die Metaphysik als Geschichte des Seins," *GA*6.2, 363–416).

Gelassenheit. Pfullingen: Günther Neske, 1959. English: *Discourse on Thinking*. Trans. John M. Anderson and E. Hans Freund. New York: Harper & Row, 1966.

"Des heiligen Augustinus Betrachtung über die Zeit. Confessiones Liber X." 1930. Bibliotheca Beuronensis, Erzabtei St. Martin, Beuron.

Identität und Differenz (ID). Pfullingen: Günther Neske, 1957. English: *Identity and Difference*. Trans. Joan Stambaugh. New York: Harper & Row, 1969.

Die Kategorien und Bedeutungslehre des Duns Scotus. Tübingen: Mohr, 1916. Reprinted in *GA*1. English: *Duns Scotus' Theory of the Categories and of Meaning*. Trans. Harold Robbins. Ph.D. diss., De Paul University, 1978.

Martin Heidegger und Elisabeth Blochmann. Briefwechsel 1918–69. Ed. Joachim W. Storck. Marbacher Schrifften. Marbach am Neckar: Deutsche Schillergesellschaft, 1989.

Martin Heidegger/Heinrich Rickert. Briefe 1912 bis 1933. Ed. Alfred Denker. Frankfurt am Main: Vittorio Klostermann, 2002.

"Mein Weg in die Phänomenologie." 1963. *Hermann Niemezer zum 80. Geburtstag*. Tübingen, 1963. Reprinted in *Zur Sache des Denkens*. Tübingen: Niemeyer, 1969. English: "My Way in Phenomenology." In *On Time and Being*, trans. Joan Stambaugh. New York: Harper & Row, 1972.

"Phänomenologische Interpretationen zu Aristoteles. Anzeige der hermeneutischen Situation" *(PIA)*. 1922. *Dilthey Jahrbuch für Philosophie und Geschichte der Geisteswissenschaften* 6 (1989): 228–69. English: "Phenomenological Interpretations in Connection with Aristotle. An Indication of the Hermeneutical Situation." Trans. John van Buren. In *Supplements. From the Earliest Essays to* Being and Time *and Beyond*, ed. John van Buren, 111–45. Albany: State University of New York Press, 2002.

Preface to *Heidegger: Through Phenomenology to Thought*, by William J. Richardson. The Hague: Nijhoff, 1963.

"Das Problem der Sünde bei Luther" *(PSL)*. In *Sachgemässe Exegese: Die Protokolle aus Rudolf Bultmanns Neutestamentlichen Seminaren 1921–51* (14 and 21 February 1924), ed. Bernd Jaspert, 28–33. Marburg: N. G. Elwert, 1996. English: *Supplements*. Trans. John van Buren.

Sein und Zeit (SZ). 1927. 17th ed. Tübingen: Max Niemeyer, 1993. English: *Being and Time*. Trans. Joan Stambaugh. Albany: State University of New York Press, 1996.

Supplements. From the Earliest Essays to Being and Time *and Beyond*. Ed. John van Buren. Albany: State University of New York Press, 2002.

Vorträge und Aufsätze (VA). 1954. Pfullingen: Günther Neske, 1978.

Other Works

Aquinas, Thomas. *On Being and Essence.* Trans. Armand Maurer. Toronto: Pontifical Institute of Medieval Studies, 1968.

———. *Opera Omnia.* Leonis XIII P.M. ed. Romae: Ex typographia polyglotta S.C. de Propaganda fide, 1888.

———. *Summa Theologica.* Trans. Fathers of the English Dominican Province. New York: Benzinger Brothers, 1948.

Augustine. *Confessions.* Trans. Henry Chadwick. Oxford: Oxford University Press, 1991.

———. *On the Holy Trinity.* Trans. Arthur West Haddan. Grand Rapids, Mich.: W. M. B. Eerdmans, 1956.

Barash, Jeffrey Andrew. *Martin Heidegger and the Problem of Historical Meaning.* With a preface by Paul Ricoeur. 2nd rev. ed. New York: Fordham University Press, 2003.

Bernasconi, Robert. "On Heidegger's Other Sins of Omission: His Exclusion of Asian Thought from the Origins of Occidental Metaphysics and His Denial of the Possibility of Christian Philosophy." *American Catholic Philosophical Quarterly* 69, no. 2 (1995): 333–49.

———. "Repetition and Tradition: Heidegger's Destructuring of the Distinction Between Essence and Existence in *Basic Problems of Phenomenology.*" In Kisiel and van Buren, eds., *Reading Heidegger from the Start,* 123–56.

Bonaventure. *The Mind's Road to God.* Trans. George Boas. Library of the Liberal Arts. Indianapolis: Bobbs-Merrill, 1953.

Braig, Carl. *Vom Sein. Abriß der Ontologie.* Freiburg: Herder, 1896.

Brejdak, Jaromir. *Philosophia crucis: Heideggers Beschäftigung mit dem Apostel Paulus.* Frankfurt am Main: Peter Lang, 1996.

Buren, John van. "The Ethics of *Formale Anzeige* in Heidegger." *American Catholic Philosophical Quarterly* 69, no. 2 (1995): 157–70.

———. "Martin Heidegger. Martin Luther." In Kisiel and van Buren, eds., *Reading Heidegger from the Start,* 159–74.

———. *The Young Heidegger: Rumor of the Hidden King.* Bloomington: Indiana University Press, 1994.

Capelle, Philippe. "'Katholizismus,' 'Protestantismus,' 'Christentum' und 'Religion' im Denken Martin Heideggers. Tragweite und Abgrenzungen." In Denker, Gander, and Zaborowski, eds., *Heidegger Jahrbuch,* 1:346–70.

———. *Philosophie et théologie dans la pensée de Martin Heidegger.* Paris: Cerf, 1998.

Caputo, John D. *Heidegger and Aquinas: An Essay on Overcoming Metaphysics.* New York: Fordham University Press, 1982.

———. "Heidegger and Theology." In *The Cambridge Companion to Heidegger,* ed. Charles B. Guignon, 270–88. Cambridge: Cambridge University Press, 1993.

———. *The Mystical Element in Heidegger's Thought.* Athens: Ohio University Press, 1978.

Casper, Bernhard. "Das theologisch-scholastische Umfeld." In Esposito and Porro, eds., *Quaestio* 1:11–22.

Clarke, W. Norris. *The One and the Many: A Contemporary Thomist Metaphysics.* Notre Dame, Ind.: University of Notre Dame Press, 2001.

Copleston, Frederick. *A History of Philosophy.* Vol. 2. *Medieval Philosophy.* New York: Image Books, 1962.
Coreth, Emerich, Walter M. Neidl, Georg Pfligersdorffer, et al., eds. *Christliche Philosophie im Katholischen Denken des 19. und 20. Jahrhunderts.* Graz: Styria, 1987.
Coriando, Paola-Ludovica. "Das thomanische 'summum ens' in ereignisphänomenologischer Sicht." In Esposito and Porro, eds., *Quaestio* 1:235–43.
Courtine, Jean-François, ed. *Heidegger 1919–1929. De l'herméneutique de la facticité à la métaphysique du "Dasein."* Paris: J. Vrin, 1996.
Crowell, Steven Galt. *Husserl, Heidegger, and the Space of Meaning: Paths Toward Trancendental Phenomenology.* Evanston, Ill.: Northwestern University Press, 2001.
Dahlstrom, Daniel O. *Heidegger's Concept of Truth.* Cambridge: Cambridge University Press, 2000.
———. "Scheler's Critique of Heidegger's Fundamental Ontology." In *Max Scheler's Acting Persons: New Perspectives,* ed. Stephen Schneck, 67–92. Amsterdam: Rodopi, 2002.
Deely, John. *The Tradition via Heidegger: An Essay on the Meaning of Being in the Philosophy of Martin Heidegger.* The Hague: Nijhoff, 1971.
Denker, Alfred. *Historical Dictionary of Heidegger's Philosophy.* Lanham, Md., and London: Scarecrow Press, 2000.
———. ed. *Heidegger/Rickert Briefe.* See Martin Heidegger, *Martin Heidegger/Heinrich Rickert. Briefe.*
———. ed. (with Hans-Helmuth Gander and Holger Zaborowski). *Heidegger-Jahrbuch.* Vol. 1. *Heidegger und die Anfänge seines Denkens.* Freiburg im Breisgau and Munich: Karl Alber, 2004.
Derrida, Jacques. *The Gift of Death.* Trans. David Wills. Chicago and London: University of Chicago Press, 1995.
Dilthey, Wilhelm. *Einleitung in die Geisteswissenschaften. Gesammelte Schriften.* Vol. 1. Stuttgart: Teubner, 1973. English: *Introduction to the Human Sciences.* Trans. Ramon J. Betanzos. Detroit: Wayne State University Press, 1988.
Dreyfus, Hubert L., and Mark A. Wrathall, eds. *A Companion to Heidegger.* Malden, Mass.: Blackwell, 2005.
Eckhart, Meister. *Deutsche Predigten und Traktate.* Ed. Josef Quint. Munich: Carl Hanser, 1965.
———. *Meister Eckhart: The Essential Sermons, Commentaries, Treatises, and Defense.* Trans. Edmund Celledge and Bernard McGinn. New York: Paulist Press, 1981.
———. *Meister Eckhart: A Modern Translation.* Trans. Raymond B. Blakney. New York: Harper & Row, 1941.
———. *Meister Eckhart: Teacher and Preacher.* Trans. Bernard McGinn. New York: Paulist Press, 1986.
Enders, Markus. "Ist der Mensch von Natur aus religiös? Zur Aktualität und Wiederkehr der Relgion." In *Bildung. Identität. Religion. Fragen zum Wesen des Menschen,* ed. Hans Poser and Bruno B. Reuer, 221–39. Berlin: Weidler Buchverlag, 2004.
———. "Ist 'Religion' wirklich undefinierbar? Überlegungen zu einem interreligiös

verwendbaren Religionsbegriff." In Enders and Zaborowski, eds., *Phänomenologie der Religion*, 49–87.
———, ed. (with Holger Zaborowski). *Phänomenologie der Religion. Zugänge und Grundfragen.* Freiburg and Munich: Verlag Karl Alber, 2004.
Erfurt, Thomas of. *Grammatica speculativa.* Trans. G. L. Bursill-Hall. London: Longman, 1972.
Esposito, Costantino. "Heidegger und Augustinus." In *Annäherungen an Martin Heidegger,* ed. Hermann Schäfer, 275–309. Frankfurt am Main: Campus, 1997.
———, ed. (with Pasquale Porro). *Quaestio. Annuario di storia della metafisica.* Vol. 1. *Heidegger e i medievali. Atti del Colloquio Internazionale Cassino 10/13 maggio 2000.* Turnhout, Belgium: Brepols, 2001.
Fehér, István M. "Heidegger's Understanding of the Atheism of Philosophy: Philosophy, Theology, and Religion in His Early Lecture Courses up to *Being and Time.*" *American Catholic Philosophical Quarterly* 69, no. 2 (1995): 189–228.
Fox, Matthew. *Original Blessing: A Primer in Creation Spirituality.* Sante Fe, N.Mex.: Bear & Company, 1983.
Gadamer, Hans-Georg. "Heideggers 'theologische' Jugendschrift." *Dilthey Jahrbuch für Philosophie und Geschichte der Geisteswissenschaften* 6 (1989): 228–34.
———. *Heidegger's Ways.* Trans. John W. Stanley. Albany: State University of New York Press, 1994.
———. "Sein Geist Gott." In Hans-Georg Gadamer, *Gesammelte Werke.* Vol. 3. *Neure Philosophie I,* 320–32. Tübingen: Mohr, 1987. English: "Being Spirit God." In *Heidegger's Ways,* trans. John W. Stanley, 181–95. Albany: State University of New York Press, 1994.
Gander, Hans-Helmuth. *Selbstverständnis und Lebenswelt: Grundzüge einer phänomenologischen Hermeneutik im Ausgang von Husserl und Heidegger.* Frankfurt am Main: Vittorio Klostermann, 2001.
Gilson, Etienne. *Being and Some Philosophers.* Toronto: Pontifical Institute of Mediaeval Studies, 1952.
———. *History of Christian Philosophy in the Middle Ages.* New York: Random House, 1955.
———. *The Spirit of Mediaeval Philosophy.* Trans. A. H. C. Downes. London: Sheed and Ward, 1936.
Grabmann, Martin. "Die Entwicklung der mittelalterlichen Sprachlogik." In *Mittelalterliches Geistesleben. Abhandlung zur Geschichte der Scholastik und Mystic,* ed. Ludwig Ott, vol. 1, 104–46. Munich: Max Heuber, 1926.
Greisch, Jean. *L'Arbre de vie et l'arbre du savoir: le chemin phénoménologique de l'herméneutique heideggérienne.* Paris: Cerf, 2000.
Gudopp, Wolf-Dieter. *Der Junge Heidegger : Realität und Wahrheit in der Vorgeschichte von "Sein und Zeit."* Frankfurt am Main: Marxistische Blätter, 1983.
Guignon, Charles B., ed. *The Cambridge Companion to Heidegger.* Cambridge: Cambridge University Press, 1993.
Hemming, Laurence P. *Heidegger's Atheism: The Refusal of a Theological Voice.* Notre Dame: Indiana University Press, 2003.
Herrmann, Friedrich-Wilhelm von. *Augustinus und die phänomenologische Frage nach der Zeit.* Frankfurt am Main: Vittorio Klostermann, 1992.

Hurd, Robert, L. "Heidegger and Aquinas: A Rahnerian Bridge." *Philosophy Today* (Summer 1984): 105–37.
Husserl, Edmund. *Ideen zu einer reinen Phänomenologie und phänomenologischen Philosophie*. Vol. 1. *Allgemeine Einführung in die reine Phänomenologie*. Ed. Walter Biemel. *Husserliana*. Vol. 3. The Hague: Nijhoff, 1950, 1976. English: *Ideas Pertaining to a Pure Phenomenology and to a Phenomenological Philosophy*. Vol. 1. *General Introduction to a Pure Phenomenology*. Trans. F. Kersten. The Hague: Nijhoff, 1982.

———. *Ideen zu einer reinen Phänomenologie und phänomenologischen Philosophie*. Vol. 2. *Phänomenologische Untersuchungen zur Konstitution*. Ed. Marly Biemel. *Husserliana*. Vol. 7. The Hague: Nijhoff, 1956. English: *Ideas Pertaining to a Pure Phenomenology and to a Phenomenological Philosophy*. Vol. 1. *General Introduction to a Pure Phenomenology*. Trans. F. Kersten. The Hague: Nijhoff, 1982.

———. *Logische Untersuchungen*. Vol. 1. *Prolegomena Zur Reinen Logik*. Ed. Elmar Holenstein. *Husserliana*. Vol. 18. The Hague: Nijhoff, 1975, 1984. English: *Logical Investigations*. 1900–1901. 2nd ed. Trans. J. N. Findlay. New York: Humanities, 1970.

———. *Logische Untersuchungen*. Vol. 2. *Untersuchungen zur Phänomenologie und Theorie der Erkenntnis*. Ed. U. Panzer. *Husserliana*. Vols. 19 and 20. The Hague: Nijhoff, 1984. English: *Logical Investigations*. 1900–1901. 2nd ed. Trans. J. N. Findlay. New York: Humanities, 1970.

Kierkegaard, Søren. *The Concept of Anxiety*. Trans. R. Thomte and A. B. Anderson. Princeton, N.J.: Princeton University Press, 1980.

———. *Concluding Unscientific Postscript to Philosophical Fragments*. Trans. Howard V. Hong and Edna H. Hong. Princeton, N.J.: Princeton University Press, 1992.

———. *Practice in Christianity*. Trans. Howard V. Hong and Edna H. Hong. Princeton, N.J.: Princeton University Press, 1991.

———. *Philosophical Fragments. Johannes Climacus*. Trans. Howard V. Hong and Edna H. Hong. Princeton, N.J.: Princeton University Press, 1985.

———. *The Sickness unto Death: A Christian Psychological Exposition for Upbuilding and Awakening*. Trans. Howard V. Hong and Edna H. Hong. Princeton, N.J.: Princeton University Press, 1983.

Kisiel, Theodore. *Heidegger's Way of Thought*. Ed. Alfred Denker and Marion Heinz. New York: Continuum, 2002.

———. *The Genesis of Heidegger's* Being and Time. Berkeley: University of California Press, 1993.

———, ed. (with John van Buren). *Reading Heidegger from the Start: Essays in His Earliest Thought*. Albany: State University of New York Press, 1994.

Lask, Emil. *Die Logik der Philosophie und die Kategorienlehre*. Vol. 2 of *Gesammelte Schriften*, ed. Eugen Herrigel. Tübingen: J. C. B. Mohr, 1923.

Leidlmair, Karl. "Carl Braig (1853–1923)." In Coreth et al., eds., *Christliche Philosophie*, vol. 1, *Neue Ansätze im 19. Jahrhundert*, 409–19.

Loewenich, Walther von. *Luther's Theology of the Cross*. Trans. Herbert J. A. Bouman. Belfast: Christian Journals, 1976.

Lotz, Johannes Baptist. *Martin Heidegger und Thomas von Aquin. Mensch—Zeit—Sein*. Pfullingen: Günther Neske, 1975.

Luther, Martin D. *Martin Luthers Werke*. Weimar: Hermann Böhlaus, 1883. English: *Luther's Works*. Ed. Jaroslav Pelikan and Helmut T. Lehmann. Philadelphia: Fortress Press, 1955–.

Marion, Jean-Luc. *Being Given: Toward a Phenomenology of Givenness*. Trans. Jeffrey L. Kosky. Stanford, Calif.: Stanford University Press, 2002.

———. *God Without Being. Hors-Texte*. Trans. Thomas A. Carlson. Chicago: University of Chicago Press, 1991.

Maritain, Jacques. *Distinguer pour unir ou les degrés du savoir*. 7th ed. Paris: Desclée de Brouwer, 1963. English: *The Degrees of Knowledge*. Trans. Gerald B. Phelan, from the 4th ed. New York: Charles Scribner's Sons, 1959.

———. *Existence and the Existent*. Trans. Lewis Galantiere and Gerald B. Phelan. New York: Pantheon, 1948.

Maurer, Armand. *The Philosophy of William of Ockham in the Light of Its Principles*. Toronto: Pontifical Institute of Mediaeval Studies, 1999.

McGrath, Sean J. "The Facticity of Being Godforsaken: The Young Heidegger's Accommodation of Luther's Theology of the Cross." *American Catholic Philosophical Quarterly* 79, no. 2 (Spring 2005): 273–90.

———. "The Forgetting of *Haecceitas*: Heidegger's 1915–1916 *Habilitationsschrift*." In *Between the Human and The Divine: Philosophical and Theological Hermeneutics*, ed. Andrzej Wiercinski, 355–77. Toronto: Hermeneutic Press, 2002.

———. "Heidegger and Duns Scotus on Truth and Language." *Review of Metaphysics* 57, no. 2 (December 2003): 323–43.

———. "Die scotistische Phänomenologie des jungen Heidegger." In Denker, Gander and Zaborowski, eds., *Heidegger-Jahrbuch*, 1:243–58.

McNeill, William. *The Glance of the Eye: Heidegger, Aristotle, and the Ends of Theory*. Albany: State University of New York Press, 1999.

Ott, Hugo. *Martin Heidegger: Unterwegs zu seiner Biographie*. Frankfurt am Main: Campus, 1988. English: *Martin Heidegger: A Political Life*. Trans. Allan Blunden. London: HarperCollins Publishers, 1993.

———. "Zu den katholischen Wurzeln im Denken Martin Heideggers. Der theologische Philosoph." In *Martin Heidegger. Kunst—Politik—Technik*, ed. Christoph Jamme and Karsten Harries, 225–39. Munich: Wilhelm Fink, 1992. English: "Martin Heidegger's Catholic Origins." *American Catholic Philosophical Quarterly* 69, no. 2 (1995): 137–56.

Overbeck, Franz. *Über die Christlichkeit unserer heutigen Theologie*. Darmstadt: Wissenschaftliche Buchgesellschaft, 1989.

Owens, Joseph. *The Doctrine of Being in the Aristotelian Metaphysics: A Study in the Greek Background of Mediaeval Thought*. With a preface by Etienne Gilson. 3rd rev. ed. Toronto: Pontifical Institute of Mediaeval Studies, 1978.

———. *An Elementary Christian Metaphysics*. Milwaukee, Wis.: The Bruce Publishing Company, 1963.

Pöggeler, Otto. "Heidegger's Luther-Lektüre im Freiburg Theologenkonvikt." In Denker, Gander, and Zaborowski, eds., *Heidegger-Jahrbuch*, 1:185–96.

Rahner, Karl. *Foundations of Christian Faith*. Trans. William Dych. New York: Crossroad, 1978.

———. *Geist in Welt. Zur Metaphysik der endlichen Erkenntnis bei Thomas von*

Aquin. Munich: Kösel, 1957. English: *Spirit in the World*. Trans. William Dych. New York: Continuum, 1968.

———. *Hearer of the Word*. Trans. Joseph Donceel. New York: Continuum, 1994.

Richardson, William. *Heidegger: Through Phenomenology to Thought*. The Hague: Nijhoff, 1962.

Rosemann, Philipp W. *Understanding Scholastic Thought with Foucault*. New York: St. Martin's Press, 1999.

Safranski, Rüdiger. *Ein Meister aus Deutschland. Heidegger und seine Zeit*. Munich: Carl Hanser, 1994. English: *Heidegger: Between Good and Evil*. Trans. Ewald Osers. Cambridge: Harvard University Press, 1998.

Schaeffler, Richard. *Frömmigkeit des Denkens. Martin Heidegger und die katholische Theologie*. Darmstadt: Wissenschaftliche Buchgesellschaft, 1978.

Scheler, Max. *Gesammelte Werke*. Vol. 9. *Späte Schriften*. Ed. Manfred Frings. Bern: Francke, 1976.

———. "Reality and Reistance: On *Being and Time*, Section 43." Trans. Thomas J. Sheehan. *Listening* 12 (1977): 61–73.

Schleiermacher, Friedrich. *The Christian Faith*. Trans. H. R. Mackintosh and J. S. Stewart. 2nd ed. Edinburgh: T & T Clark, 1989.

———. *Über die Religion: Reden an die Gebildeten unter ihren Verächtern*. 3rd and 4th ed. *Kritische Gesamtausgabe*. Vol. 12.1. Ed. Günter Meckenstock. Berlin: Walter de Gruyter, 1995. English: *On Religion: Speeches to its Cultured Despisers*. 3d ed. Trans. John Oman. London: Routledge & Kegan Paul, 1958.

Scotus, Johannes Duns. *Opera Omnia*. Ed. Giovanni Lauriola. Alberobello: AGA, 1998–.

Sheehan, Thomas J. "Heidegger's Early Years: Fragments for a Philosophical Biography." *Listening* 12 (1977): 3–20.

———. "Heidegger's Introduction to the Phenomenology of Religion." In *A Companion to Martin Heidegger's Being and Time*, ed. Joseph J. Kockelmans, 208–26. Washington, D.C.: Center for Advanced Research in Phenomenology and University Press of America, 1986.

———. "Heidegger's Lehrjahre." In *The Collegium Phaenomenologicum: The First Ten Years*, ed. Giuseppina Moneta, John Sallis, and Jacques Taminiaux, 77–137. Dordrecht: Kluwer, 1988.

———. *Karl Rahner: The Philosophical Foundations*. Athens: Ohio University Press, 1987.

———. "Notes on a 'Lovers' Quarrel': Heidegger and Aquinas." *Listening* 9 (1974): 137–43.

Siewerth, Gustav. "Martin Heidegger und die Frage nach Gott." *Gesammelte Werke*. Vol. 3. *Gott in der Geschichte. Zur Gottesfrage bei Hegel und Heidegger*. Ed. Alma von Stockhausen. Düsseldorf: Patmos, 1971. 245–59.

———. *Das Schicksal der Metaphysik von Thomas zu Heidegger. Gesammelte Werke*. Vol. 4. Ed. Wolfgang Behler and Alma von Stockhausen. Düsseldorf: Patmos, 1987.

———. "Das Sein als Gleichnis Gottes." *Gesammelte Werke*. Vol. 1. *Sein und Wahrheit*. Ed. Wolfgang Behler and Alma von Stockhausen. Düsseldorf: Patmos, 1975.

———. *Der Thomismus als Identitätssystem. Gesammelte Werke*. Vol. 2. Ed. Wolfgang Behler and Alma von Stockhausen. Düsseldorf: Patmos, 1979.

Sikka, Sonya. *Forms of Transcendence: Heidegger and Medieval Mystical Theology.* Albany: State University of New York Press, 1997.
Stewart, Roderick M. "Signification and Radical Subjectivity in Heidegger's *Habilitationsschrift.*" *Man and World* 12 (1979): 360–86.
Streeter, Ryan. "Heidegger's Formal Indication: A Question of Method in *Being and Time.*" *Man and World* 30 (1997): 413–30.
Theunissen, Michael. *Negative Theologie der Zeit.* Frankfurt am Main: Suhrkamp Verlag, 1991.
Vetter, Helmuth, ed. *Heidegger und das Mittelalter.* Frankfurt am Main: Peter Lang, 1999.
Volpi, Franco. *Heidegger e Brentano. L'aristotelismo e il problema dell'univocità dell'essere nella formazione filosofica del giovane Martin Heidegger.* Padua: Cedam, 1976.
Welte, Bernhard. *Zwischen Zeit und Ewigkeit.* Freiburg im Breisgau: Herder, 1982.
Westphal, Merold. *Overcoming Onto-Theology: Toward a Postmodern Christian Faith.* New York: Fordham University Press, 2001.
Wiercinski, Andrzej. *Inspired Metaphysics? Gustav Siewerth's Hermenteutic Reading of the Onto-theological Tradition.* Toronto: The Hermeneutic Press, 2003.
———. *Die scholastischen Vorbedingungen der Metaphysik Gustav Siewerths.* Frankfurt am Main: Peter Lang, 1991.
———. *Über die Differenz im Sein. Metaphysische Überlegungen zu Gustav Siewerths Werk.* Frankfurt am Main: Peter Lang, 1989.
Wolter, Allan, B. *The Philosophical Theology of John Duns Scotus.* Ed. Marilyn McCord Adams. Ithaca, N.Y.: Cornell University Press, 1990.
Wucherer-Huldenfeld, Augustinus Karl. "Zu Heideggers Verständnis des Seins bei Johannes Duns Scotus und im Skotismus sowie im Thomismus und bei Thomas von Aquin." In Vetter, ed., *Heidegger und das Mittelalter,* 41–59.

INDEX

Anselm, 149, 224
Aquinas, x, 4, 13–14, 18, 20, 31–32, 63, 65, 83, 149–50, 210–11, 216–17, 220–22, 223–30, 231–32, 234, 235, 237, 239–40, 244, 246, 247, 250, 255
Arendt, Hannah, 40, 174–75
Aristotle, 16, 27–29, 65–68, 74, 76–81, 152–53, 162–65, 166, 196, 202, 204, 213, 215, 244, 246
Augustine, xx, 9, 31–32, 60–61, 158, 189, 197–203, 203–4, 206, 244, 254

Bacon, Roger, 92
Barth, Karl, 3, 157, 178, 183–84, 223, 250
Bernard of Clairvaux, 85, 143–44, 147
Bernasconi, Robert, 3
Bonaventure, 14, 26, 32–33, 85, 148
Braig, Carl, 13, 29–34, 44
Brentano, Franz, 27–29, 63–64
Buhr, Heinrich, 55
Bultmann, Rudolph, 47, 185–86, 192

Capelle, Philppe, xiii, 43–44, 148, 205
Caputo, John, 35, 121, 141, 146, 204, 229–30
Casper, Bernhard, 19–20, 38–39,
Clark, W. Norris, 225
Coriando, Paolo-Ludovika, 221–25

Dahlstrom, Daniel, 4, 70
Derrida, Jacques, 19, 21–22, 175–76, 251, 253
Deely, John, 62, 66–67
Descartes, 4, 7, 39, 64, 199, 210–11, 220, 238
Dilthey, Wilhelm, 9, 46, 53, 146, 187–90, 197–99, 204, 206
Duns Scotus, John, 31, 35, 42, 74, 83, 88–119, 132, 232, 244

Eckhart, Meister, 120–21, 128–29, 131–33, 135–42, 144–48, 230–31, 251
Enders, Markus, 248, 249–50
Esposito, Costantino, 197

Gadamer, Hans-Georg, 56, 58–59, 178
Giles of Rome, 212, 227
Gilson, Etienne, 88–89, 99, 179, 212, 224, 225
Greisch, Jean, 11
Grabmann, Martin, 42, 89, 90
Gröber, Konrad, 27

Hegel, Georg Wilhelm Friedrich, 4, 7, 23, 44, 51, 53, 126–27, 133, 217, 220
Heidegger, Elfride, 46
Heidegger, Fritz, xv, xix
Hemming, Laurence Paul, 241
Honecker, Martin, 56
Hölderlin, Johan Christian Friedrich, xvi, 59
Husserl, Edmund, 6, 29, 39, 42, 63–64, 68–73, 77, 94, 97, 104, 110, 118–19, 139, 210

Jaspers, Karl, xix, 44, 53, 153
Jung, Carl, 246

Kant, Immanuel, 14–15, 30–31, 35, 39, 41, 92–96, 99, 118, 125, 182, 191
Kierkegaard, Søren, 51–53, 160–61, 187, 206, 248, 252
Kisiel, Theodore, xiv, 43, 45, 46, 70–71, 82, 96–97, 117, 130, 135, 148, 200
Krebs, Engelbert, 10, 14, 45–46, 49, 151–52

Lask, Emil, 93–97, 101, 110, 113, 139–40
Leibniz, 121, 220, 238
Levinas, Emmanuel, 19, 237
Lonergan, Bernard, 14, 111, 224, 149
Löwith, Karl, xii, 46, 173
Lotz, Johannes Baptist, 56, 113
Lotze, Hermann, 113
Luther, Martin, xiii, 2–3, 5–6, 9–10, 12, 17, 22, 48, 151–84, 186, 208, 223, 225, 242, 247, 250–51

Macquarrie, John, 3
Maréchal, Joseph, 235

Marion, Jean-Luc, ix–x, 237–41
Maritain, Jacques, 62–63
Maurer, Armand, 112, 224
McNeill, William, 196, 204
Müller, Max, 56, 229

Natorp, Paul, 43, 153
Nicholson, Graeme, xx
Nietzsche, Friedrich, ix, 59, 175, 179, 238, 250

Ockham, William, 5
Ott, Hugo, xiv, 33, 40, 42–43, 45, 46
Otto, Rudolf, 123
Overbeck, Franz, 47–48, 181
Owens, Joseph, 212

Patočka, Jan, 253
Paul, 3, 76, 158–9, 160, 165, 169, 171, 190–94, 197, 203, 206, 244
Phelan, Gerald, 226
Pieper, Josef, 220
Pius X, 13, 45
Plato, 15, 53–54, 44, 51, 76, 78, 146, 152, 161, 197–99, 201, 213, 253
Pöggeler, Otto, 48, 125
Pseudo-Dionysius, ix–x, 212

Rahner, Karl, 14, 234–37
Richardson, William, 27, 231–32
Rickert, Heinrich, 39, 41, 92–94, 109
Rosemann, Philipp, 4–5, 243

Safranski, Rüdiger, xvii
Sartre, Jean-Paul, 249

Scheler, Max, xii, 3–4, 173–74
Schelling, Friedrich Wilhelm Joseph, 30, 205
Schlegel, 124, 127–28
Schleiermacher, Friedrich, 49–51, 127, 139–40, 142–43, 250
Shanley, Brian, 224
Sheehan, Thomas, 15–16, 236
Siewerth, Gustav, 56, 88–89, 224, 229, 231–34, 237
Sikka, Sonya, 33
Suárez, Francisco, 212, 213

Tillich, Paul, 248
Theresa of Avila, 85, 147
Theunissen, Michael, 52, 192
Thomas of Erfurt, 42, 89–92, 95, 97–98, 105–9, 117
Thurneysen, Eduard, 178, 184
Tugendhat, Ernst, 82

van Buren, John, xiv, 48, 122–23, 134, 139, 151, 153, 160, 161, 166, 169
van der Leeuw, Gerardus, 248
Volpi, Franco, 28
von Balthasar, Hans Urs, 231
von Loewenich, Walther, 158, 160

Welte, Bernhard, 19, 53, 59, 230
Westphal, Merold, x, 6–7, 219–20, 221
Wiercinski, Andrzej, xx, 18, 231
Wittgenstein, ix, 57
Wolter, Allan, 110

The Early Heidegger and Medieval Philosophy: Phenomenology for the Godforsaken was designed and typeset in Minion by Kachergis Book Design of Pittsboro, North Carolina. It was printed on 60-pound Natures Natural and bound by Thomson-Shore of Dexter, Michigan.

www.ingramcontent.com/pod-product-compliance
Lightning Source LLC
Chambersburg PA
CBHW032030290426
44110CB00012B/737